Lecture Notes of the Institute for Computer Sciences, Social Informatics and Telecommunications Engineering   58

Andreas Timm-Giel   John Strassner
Ramón Agüero   Susana Sargento
Kostas Pentikousis (Eds.)

Mobile Networks and Management

4th International Conference
MONAMI 2012
Hamburg, Germany, September 24-26, 2012
Revised Selected Papers

 Springer

Volume Editors

Andreas Timm-Giel
Hamburg University of Technology, 21073 Hamburg, Germany
E-mail: timm-giel@tu-hamburg.de

John Strassner
Huawei Technologies, Santa Clara, CA 95050, USA
E-mail: john.sc.strassner@huawei.com

Ramón Agüero
Universidad de Cantabria, 39005 Santander, Spain
E-mail: ramon@tlmat.unican.es

Susana Sargento
University of Aveiro, 3810-193 Aveiro, Portugal
E-mail: susana@ua.pt

Kostas Pentikousis
Huawei Technologies, 10587 Berlin, Germany
E-mail: k.pentikousis@huawei.com

ISSN 1867-8211   e-ISSN 1867-822X
ISBN 978-3-642-37934-5   e-ISBN 978-3-642-37935-2
DOI 10.1007/978-3-642-37935-2
Springer Heidelberg Dordrecht London New York

Library of Congress Control Number: 2013935550

CR Subject Classification (1998): C.2, H.4, D.2, H.5.1

Typesetting: Camera-ready by author, data conversion by Scientific Publishing Services, Chennai, India

Printed on acid-free paper

Springer is part of Springer Science+Business Media (www.springer.com)

Preface

This volume is the result of the 4th International ICST Conference on Mobile Networks and Management (MONAMI), which was held in Hamburg, Germany during September 23–26, 2012, hosted by the Institute of Communication Networks (ComNets) at Hamburg University of Technology.

The MONAMI conference series aims at closing the gap between hitherto considered separate and isolated research areas, namely, multi-access and resource management, mobility and network management, and network virtualization. Although these have emerged as core aspects in the design, deployment, and operation of current and future networks, there is still little to no interaction between the experts in these fields. MONAMI enables cross-pollination between these areas by bringing together top researchers, academics, and practitioners specializing in the area of mobile network and service management.

This year, after a thorough peer review process, 15 papers were selected for inclusion in the main track of the technical program. In addition, MONAMI 2012 hosted two well-received workshops: the Second MONAMI Workshop on Smart Objects and the First Open Connectivity Services Workshop, organized in cooperation with the EU FP7 SAIL project. All in all, 25 papers were orally presented at the conference. Thirty-four Technical Program Committee (TPC) members made sure that each submitted paper was reviewed by at least three researchers with relevant expertise, including at least one TPC member.

The conference opened with a half-day tutorial on "Operating Heterogeneous Wireless Networks with SON (Self-Organizing Networks)," a key and emerging topic in modern mobile communications, presented by Henning Sanneck and Andreas Lobinger of Nokia Siemens Networks. John Strassner, CTO Software R&D Laboratory of Huawei, USA, opened the second day with a special tutorial on "Semantic Middleware for Orchestrating Behavior." This year's conference featured three keynotes: Sven van der Meer (Ericsson) gave his view on heterogeneous networks and big data during his talk entitled "HetNets, Big Data, Cloud, SDN...All Problems Solved and Your Lunch Served, Right?" Joel J. Fleck II (HP Labs) talked about cloud computing in his keynote "Slipping the Surly Bonds of Earth – Challenges of Dynamic Cloud Computing." Finally, Sajal K. Das (University of Texas at Arlington) complemented the Smart Objects workshop with his talk "Models for Service Discovery and Resource Management in Smart Environments." Last but not least, this year's conference featured a whiteboarding session (chaired by John Strassner) on "New Ideas in Computing." For full details on this year's program, visit www.mon-ami.org.

This volume includes the revised versions of all papers presented at MONAMI 2012 in a single-track format, organized thematically in five parts as follows; Mobile Networks in Part I; Heterogeneous Networks (HetNets) aspects are discussed in Part II; Part III presents new approaches related to Wireless

Communications; Part IV addresses Smart Objects and IoT Applications; and, Part V includes papers presenting forward-thinking solutions for Future Networks, embracing virtualization, security, and coding techniques.

Attendance increased in MONAMI 2012. The newcomers expressed their liking of the collegial atmosphere that characterizes the conference. This makes it an excellent venue for presenting novel research work as well as for fostering stimulating discussions between the attendees. The success of MONAMI 2012 reinforces its importance as a key annual conference in the calendar of researchers in this area. We are happy announce that the fifth edition of MONAMI will be hosted by Cork Institute of Technology in September 2013.

We close this preface by acknowledging the vital role that the TPC members and additional referees played during the review process. Their efforts ensured that all submitted papers received a proper evaluation. We thank EAI and ICST for assisting with organization matters, CREATE-NET and IEEE ComSoc Germany Section for technically co-sponsoring the event, and Hamburg University of Technology for hosting MONAMI 2012. The team that put together this year's event is large and required the sincere commitment of many folks. Although too many to recognize here by name, their effort should be highlighted. We particularly thank Elisa Mendini for her administrative support on behalf of EAI, and Imrich Chlamtac of CREATE-NET for his continuous support of the conference. Finally, we thank all delegates for attending MONAMI 2012 and making it such a vibrant conference!

December 2012

Andreas Timm-Giel
John Strassner
Ramón Agüero
Susana Sargento
Kostas Pentikousis

Organization

Organizing Committee

General Chairs

Andreas Timm-Giel Hamburg University of Technology, Germany
John Strassner Huawei, USA

Technical Program Committee Co-Chairs

Ramón Agüero University of Cantabria, Spain
Susana Sargento University of Aveiro, Portugal

Conference Manager

Elisa Mendini European Alliance for Innovation

Keynotes Chair

Rui Aguiar University of Aveiro, Portugal

Tutorials Chair

Oliver Blume Alcatel-Lucent Bell Labs, Germany

Publications Chair

Kostas Pentikousis Huawei Technologies, Germany

Web Chair

Jarno Pinola VTT Technical Research Centre of Finland, Finland

Steering Committee

Imrich Chlamtac, Chair CREATE-NET, Italy
Kostas Pentikousis,
   Co-chair Huawei Technologies, Germany
Symeon Papavassiliou National Technical University of Athens, Greece
Rui Aguiar University of Aveiro, Portugal

MONAMI 2012 Technical Program Committee

Ramón Agüero	University of Cantabria, Spain
Rui Aguiar	University of Aveiro, Portugal
Pedro Aranda	Telefonica, Spain
Hussein Badr	Stony Brook, USA
Javier Baliosian	Universidad de la Republica, Argentina
Oliver Blume	Alcatel-Lucent Bell Labs, Germany
Prosper Chemouil	Orange Labs FT, France
Hans Einsiedler	DT-Labs, Germany
Christian Esteve Rothenberg	University of Campinas, Brazil
Theo G. Kanter	Mid-Sweden University, Sweden
Alex Galis	University College London, UK
Marta García-Arranz	University of Cantabria, Spain
Jyrki Huusko	VTT, Finland
Martin Johnsson	Waterford Institute of Technology, Ireland
Symeon Papavassiliou	National Technical University of Athens, Greece
Kostas Pentikousis	Huawei
Anand R. Prasad	NEC Corporation, Japan
Rui Rocha	Instituto Superior Tecnico, Portugal
Javier Rubio-Loyola	CINESTAV, Mexico
Susana Sargento	University of Aveiro, Portugal
Peter Schoo	Fraunhofer-SIT, Germany
Joan Serrat	Universidad Politécnica de Catalunya, Spain
Fikret Sivrikaya	TU Berlin, Germany
Lucian Suciu	Orange Labs FT
Haitao Tang	NSN, Finland
Andreas Timm-Giel	Technical University of Hamburg-Harburg, Germany
Kurt Tutschku	University of Vienna, Austria
Dirk Stähle	Docomo, Germany
Koojana Kuladinithi	University of Bremen, Germany
Maciej Mühleisen	Technical University of Hamburg-Harburg, Germany
James Gross	RWTH Aachen, Germany
Timo Hämäläinen	University of Jyväskylä, Finland
Eduardo da Silva	University of Parana, Brazil
Philippe Bertin	Orange Labs FT, France

MONAMI 2012 Reviewers

Ramón Agüero	University of Cantabria, Spain
Chunlei An	Technical University of Hamburg-Harburg, Germany
Georgios Androulidakis	National Technical University of Athens, Greece
Pedro-Andrés Aranda	Telefónica I+D, Spain
Hussein Badr	Stony Brook University, USA
Javier Baliosian	Universidad de la República, Uruguay
Juliano-João Bazzo	State University of Campinas, Brazil
Philippe Bertin	Orange Labs, France
Oliver Blume	Alcatel-Lucent, Germany
Carsten Bormann	University of Bremen, Germany
Prosper Chemouil	Orange Labs, France
Johnny Choque	University of Cantabria, Spain
Hans-Joachim Einsiedler	Deutsche Telekom AG, Germany
Lucio-Studer Ferreira	IST, Portugal
José-Antonio Galache	University of Cantabria, Spain
Alex Galis	University College London, UK
Marta García-Arranz	University of Cantabria, Spain
David Gómez	University of Cantabria, Spain
James Gross	Aachen University, Germany
Jyrki Huusko	VTT, Finland
Martin Johnsson	TSSG, Ireland
Theo Kanter	Stockholm University, Sweden
Vassileios Karyotis	National Technical University of Athens, Greece
Koojana Kuladinithi	University of Bremen, Germany
Aris Leivadeas	National Technical University of Athens, Greece
Carmen López	University of Cantabria, Spain
Mikko Majanen	VTT, Finland
Florian Metzger	University of Vienna, Austria
Maciej Muehleisen	Technical University of Hamburg-Harburg, Germany
Thomas Poetsch	University of Bremen, Germany
Vassiliki Pouli	National Technical University of Athens, Greece
Matias Richart	Universidad de la República, Uruguay
Rui Rocha	University of Coimbra, Portugal
Christian-Esteve Rothenberg	State University of Campinas, Brazil
Javier Rubio	CINVESTAV, Mexico
Susana Sargento	University of Aveiro, Portugal
Peter Schoo	Fraunhofer Fokus, Germany

Table of Contents

Wireless Communications

Smart Objects and IoT Applications

Future Networks

Design and Implementation of the Open Connectivity Services Framework

Luis Diez[1], Olivier Mehani[2], Lucian Suciu[3], and Ramón Agüero[1]

[1] Universidad de Cantabria, Santander, Spain
{ldiez,ramon}@tlmat.unican.es
[2] NICTA, Sydney, Australia
olivier.mehani@nicta.com.au
[3] Orange Labs, Rennes, France
lucian.suciu@orange-ftgroup.com

Abstract. The Open Connectivity Services (OConS) framework is currently being defined within the framework of the SAIL project. Its main objective is to offer adaptive connectivity services to seamlessly address user and service requirements while complying with operator policies and dealing with the heterogeneous and changing network conditions of the future Internet. This paper describes a realization of this framework. It supports flexible integration of both legacy and novel mechanisms and protocols by mapping them to three abstract functional entities: information, decision and execution elements. Organization of these entities is done through an orchestration process to combine and integrate the various mechanisms into a full service for the user. We introduce the OConS protocol used for communication between the presented entities as well as the role played by the orchestration process. We then present the concrete example of a testbed based on this implementation, which shows the feasibility and effectiveness of the proposed approach.

Keywords: Future Internet, Connectivity Services, Access Selection, Implementation, Demonstration.

1 Introduction

Within the most promising research forums on Future Internet is an ongoing debate on the appropriateness of clean-slate approaches. Such approaches allow to sever the ties with the limitations of the currently deployed technologies, and support novel solutions better tailored to current needs. Conversely, following a less radical evolutionary path would allow for easier incremental deployment while avoiding the need for an altogether impossible *flag day*. So far, no clear direction has been agreed upon. A key element in working towards such an answer, however, is rooted in experimental initiatives aimed at testing the feasibility of one or the other approach.

The Scalable and Adaptive Internet Solutions (SAIL) project is one research initiative in the Future Internet realm [1], with a strong emphasis on integration

A. Timm-Giel et al. (Eds.): MONAMI 2012, LNICST 58, pp. 1–12, 2013.

and prototyping. It focuses on three core concepts: the use of information-centric networking (NetInf), the possibilities which appear with the advent of cloud networking concepts extending virtualization techniques to the network itself (CloNe) and the provision of seamless integration of legacy and future technologies into open connectivity services (OConS). The present paper focuses on the latter. Indeed, due to their rigidity and lack of large-scale dynamic reconfiguration capabilities, legacy connectivity services have increasing problems coping with the rapid evolution of communication requirements and patterns. New solutions are needed, which are dynamic, flexible and open, so as to be able to adapt to both the requirements of the different users and services as well as the ever-changing conditions of nowadays' heterogeneous networks. Within connectivity services, it has become specially relevant the design of multi-access systems which are extensively studied in the literature [2–7]. Some of them are focused on the integration of different technologies, for example, 3G and WLAN [8,9].

Resources to be controlled and the connectivity issues which this raises are numerous and varied, each of them with their particular characteristics, procedures, algorithms and protocols. A monolithic design would therefore not fare well in dealing with such issues. The approach proposed within OConS is that of a highly modular architecture flexible enough to cope with these conditions [10]. A preliminary version of this framework was presented in [11]. The services are structured into to three complementary phases (information gathering, decision making and execution enforcement), and the associated entities performing these tasks. Lately the focus has been put on the elements needed to organize and control these entities as well as the various procedures required to achieve this orchestration.

As already mentioned, one of the key aspects in this line of research is the assessment, over real platforms, of the proposed architectures, procedures and protocols. This is the main focus of this paper; it presents the activities towards an implementation of the OConS framework as well as the use of this implementation into a real testbed, and uses it as an evaluation of the feasibility of the proposed open connectivity concepts. The implementation of the OConS architectural entities is detailed, as well as the protocol supporting signalling and communication between them. A scenario where a wireless station needs to select its access network is then introduced to illustrate the use of the framework. It is then extended to show how the orchestration process is used to support on-the-fly integration of other mechanisms such as a dynamic mobility management scheme which uses tunnels to handle mobility at the network level.

This paper is structured as follows. Section 2 introduces the OConS architecture and presents implementation details of the entities and protocol. Section 3 presents the testbed setup, identifying the OConS components and their interactions. Proof-of-concept experimental results with this setup are reported in Section 4, while the paper is concluded in Section 5, which also covers directions for future work.

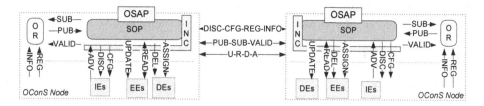

Fig. 1. Interactions between OConS elements. All communication goes through the INC, except for service requests through the OSAP, and the tighter SOP–OR link.

2 OConS Architecture

In this section, an overview of the OConS design and architecture is first presented, reminding the reader to its basic functional components and those orchestration elements which allow their coordination. We then detail their implementation and the needed communication protocol, which together form the basis of a common library to ease the integration of existing mechanisms within the OConS framework.

2.1 Architecture and Design

All conceptual elements in the OConS framework, as well as their interactions, is shown in Fig. 1 and described thereafter.

Basic Entities. The goal of OConS is to provide an open framework to support any type of connectivity service. This requires a rather high level of abstraction in defining its constituent components. In order to manage this intrinsic openness, three elementary and generic entities have been defined [10, 11].

Information Entities (IE) take care of gathering the relevant information, and provide it to interested parties following the generic data model defined in [12].

Decision Entities (DE) take data from the IEs and run a decision algorithm in order to determine which actions need be taken in light of this information.

Execution Entities (EE) enforce the decisions made by the DE and optionally report the status details of the execution of the task.

Levels of Orchestration. To support dynamic configuration, combination and instantiation of mechanisms and services, the instances of these three basic components need to be coordinated. This is the role of the *orchestration function*. For the sake of flexibility, it must cover the entire communication scope, thus bringing about three main orchestration levels [12].

Link Connectivity Services do not span further than one hop and are closely related to the physical and data-link layers and their operational parameters.

Network Connectivity Services affect the network and transport layers and are independent of end user applications. They usually involve two or more nodes.

Flow Connectivity Services are also related to the network and transport layers, but show a tighter link with the applications and services they support.

Orchestration Functionalities. The orchestration function is a key enabler for the applications, or OConS users, to request specific services from the framework. They respond to these requests by appropriately configuring the relevant OConS components.

The Service Orchestration Process (SOP) is in charge of coordinating and overseeing all the orchestrations tasks. It keeps track of the OConS mechanisms which are available and what they can offer. These mechanisms are defined as a combination of entities (*i.e.*, IEs and EEs) which a particular DE requires in order to inform and enforce a decision.

The Orchestration Service Access Point (OSAP) is the external interface of OConS to its users. It is the point of entry for user requests (*i.e.*, connectivity requirements), and that through which OConS can report back about the available capabilities or status.

The Orchestration Registry (OR) acts as a repository of all the entities within a node, as well as those discovered on other nodes. These entities can be combined to instantiate various mechanisms, which are also kept track of within the OR.

The Orchestration Monitor (OM) retains the statuses of the OConS components and mechanisms launched within different OConS-enabled nodes.

OConS Messaging. The previously introduced OConS entities and functionalities interact with each other by exchanging *OConS messages*. Dealing with a distributed set of components for which connectivity might not be fully established and vary widely, it is important to offer a communication facility which properly decouples messaging from the underlying communication technology. This is done through an inter-node communication hub (INC) which is in charge of relaying the messages to its destination, either locally or remotely, over whichever *transport method* (*e.g.*, local IPC, TCP/IP or Ethernet) is available to reach it. This is depicted in Fig. 1.

While messages to node-local entities (identified by their locally-attributed *entity ID*) can be passed directly, those to remote destinations are encapsulated in *OConS packets* which are wrapped into the relevant headers for the selected medium. The INC maintains a unique *node ID* which is mapped to the appropriate locator for the selected transport method. To ensure global uniqueness, these node IDs must be assigned following a random algorithm with good uniqueness properties. An example of such is that proposed for Unique Local IPv6 Addresses [13].

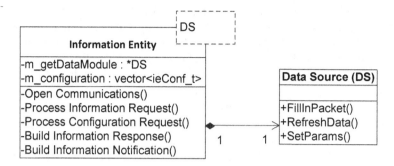

Fig. 2. Structure of the generic IE object provided by the OConS protocol library

2.2 Framework Implementation

We now introduce our implementation of these functional blocks and the corresponding orchestration logic. The communication model is based on *Request/Response–Notification* messages. For this purpose, an *OConS protocol library* has been implemented in C/C++ to provide low-level functionalities allowing the use of the OConS protocol and interfaces. The detailed description of interfaces, messaging and protocols is given in [12], but we summarize it here.

OConS Protocol Library. The library implements the common OConS communication facilities to enable both inter-entity and inter-node communications. It manages direct communication with the local INC and provides helper functions for message manipulation. These helpers are in charge of the encapsulation within the OConS headers based on which forwarding to the relevant entity or node through the INC. Message content manipulation is similarly abstracted from the on-wire TLV (Type, Length, Value)-based data representation from the entity implementation. Additionaly, the library provides high-level procedures to support the OConS orchestration functionalities, such as mechanism identification, entities registration or bootstrap management.

This library aims at offering a common background allowing the developer to implement the entities needed for a new connectivity mechanism, as well as to setup appropriate orchestration between those entities. From a system point of view, each entity, as well as the INC, appears as a separate process. The INC waits for connections of the local entities using IPC mechanisms, and listens on the various supported remote transport methods for OConS messages. At start-up, the entities connect to this local IPC and, after an initialisation phase where its entity ID is determined and its existence is recorded in the local OR, it can exchange OConS messages with both local and remote entities through the INC.

Generic Information Element Template. As they follow a rather regular pattern, the behaviour of IEs is easily generalised. The library therefore provides a C++ template for such a generic IE, which we provide as an example of how it can be used. Fig. 2 shows the structure of this object. It assumes that each IE is usable and configurable by one or more DEs requiring the exposed information. The generic IE is able to act both reactively, upon request from a DE, or proactively, sending it update notifications periodically.

The generic IE includes a reference to an object responsible for providing the particular information for a given instance. This exemplifies the modularity of the design, where the OConS layer is shared between all entities, but the actual operation, such as data collection in the case of an IE, is specific to the mechanism being provided. In this case, the outer class implements the *Information Entity* interface, while the *Data Source* (DS) class collects the data from actual sources such as hardware drivers or software systems. It is worth noting that the DS should be aware of the relevant parts of the OConS data model and properly represent the collected information according to this model. It is the role of the `FillInPacket()` method to do so.

3   Integration Tesbed

We recall that the main goal of this work is the empirical assessment of the feasibility of the OConS architecture, so as to fill the gap between architectural descriptions and specifications, and its implementation in real platforms. As the proposed framework is intended to cope with a wide range of different connectivity technologies and protocols with varied features, it is crucial to confirm that is it open enough to be effective. We present our experimental testbed work towards this in this section.

While one driving goal of the OConS framework is its openness, this is not necessarily the case of the underlying technologies. This limits the choices when developing such an experimental testbed to those pieces of hardware which drivers offer the possibility to access and manipulate low-level parameters. Moreover, it is desirable to focus on hardware available off the shelf as this is representative of the vast majority of already deployed equipments which OConS is intended to work atop. Considering these intrinsic limitations, the platform we developed is based on the IEEE 802.11 technology. The presence of heterogeneous networks is emulated by deploying multiple access points, configured to operate on orthogonal channels.

This approach, which undoubtedly presents some limitations, however also has clear advantages. Wi-Fi hardware drivers such as MadWifi[1] provide ample access to information and control interfaces, while `hostapd(8)`[2] makes it possible to use regular computers to deploy access points, therefore easing the deployment of modifications on the network side.

The proposed testbed implements parts of the overall OConS reference scenario [10], presented in Fig. 3. It comprises two access points and an end-user terminal. All three implement the OConS framework through the protocol library introduced in Section 2. The connectivity services available in this testbed

---

[1] `http://madwifi.org`
[2] `http://hostap.epitest.fi/hostapd/`

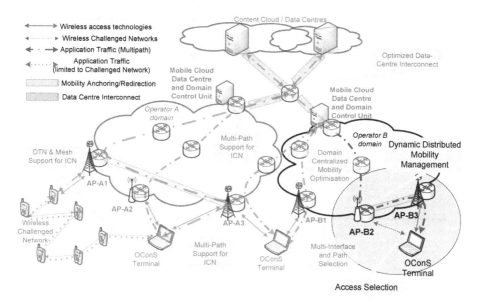

Fig. 3. The OConS overall scenario [10]. It includes mechanisms for end-user mobility such as access selection and distributed mobility management (bottom right).

include procedures for access selection and support for dynamic mobility management. Though often crudely merged in the literature, both mechanisms are clearly different: access selection takes place at the mobile node and usually relies on signal quality information from the access elements to decide which to use, while mobility management leverages in network anchor points to provide support for session continuity throughout access changes through the use of IPv6 tunnels [14]. Under the orchestration of the OConS framework these two mechanisms are able to collaborate, resulting in an improved and more flexible service.

The presented scenario supports a dynamic activation of mobility anchors at the access routers, so that a mobile node (MN) can use direct IP routing for sessions initiated while using the current access router, whilst forwarding traffic from the previous access routers, acting as temporary mobility anchors. The OConS approach, unifying these mechanisms into a common framework, enables them to interact—for example by allowing some triggering events (*e.g.*, layer-2 hand-offs) to enrich the decisions or by considering other pieces of information describing the connectivity context—to provide a finer-grained and more accurately controlled support of session continuity while providing network access through the current best access element.

Following the architectural description from Section 2, each of the nodes implements orchestration functionalities which coordinate the operation of their functional elements. One OConS mechanisms has been developed which links both connectivity procedures. It is embodied as one DE located at the MN, one EE similarly located and takes care of the layer-2 handover (it also triggers the

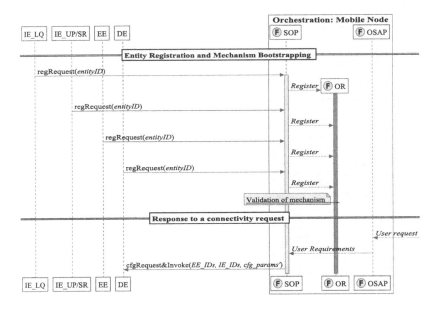

Fig. 4. Basic OConS Orchestration. Entities register to the SOP and OR via the INC. When all entities composing a mechanism are ready, the DE gets a notification.

subsequent layer-3 handover) and various IEs, providing contextual information so as to enrich the decision making process. The specific IEs and the information they provide is described below.

Radio channel quality (IE_{LQ}) is implemented as a scanning module which informs any subscriber entity about the current quality (SNR or RSSI) of each access point from a list of available and usable networks. This entity is located on the MN.

User profile (IE_{UP}) stores information about the type of user requesting a connectivity service. This is used so the DE can distinguish the privileges of a subscriber and maintain accounting tasks. This entity is also placed at the MN.

Service requirement (IE_{SR}) , also located in the AN, tags each type of data service to allow their particular management according to their specific requirements (*e.g.*, video streaming or file transfer).

Traffic load (IE_{TL}) stores information about the current traffic load at the access router, where it is located, so as to support load balancing.

Once all the entities have started up, the first orchestration steps take place. They comprise registration (Fig. 4), search and configuration (both in Fig. 5 in section 4). During this first discovery procedure, all entities register to the SOP by means of a *regRequest* primitive together with their information. This comprises both the entity type and entity ID as indicated in Fig. 4 (in which the circled F's indicates functionalities which have been implemented jointly with the INC), which are afterwards stored within the OR. Anytime a new entity registers, the SOP checks whether some new mechanisms have become available (that is, all the entities composing the mechanism are registered). If a new mechanism can be executed, the SOP informs the appropriate DEs about how to reach the rest of entities. At the bootstrapping the only entity configured is the DE by setting the IE/EEs which it has to use to perform the mechanism. The latter configurations (DE–IE) are discussed on the next section.

In a similar way, any OConS node can also carry out remote discovery provided there exists a common underlying transport method. In this case, the SOP starts this remote discovery if some mechanisms required depend on remote entities. It is interesting to highlight the fact that the current implementation incorporates this degree of flexibility and thus allows a mechanism to be defined by entities spanning different nodes.

4   Proof of Concept

This section presents some of the tests carried out on the testbed presented in section 3. The objective of these tests was the assessment of the correctness of the implementation. The points which have been verified to work at the time of this writing are presented below. Our focus was on the correctness of the OConS protocol implementation, and its usability to compose a distributed mobility management service from the available basic elements. Fig. 5 shows a sequence of OConS messages exchanged during one of the tests. It is based on the output of a monitoring and configuration GUI application which has been developed to ease the process of tracking the message exchanges.

The following verifications have been performed.

Entity registration with INC. This point has been previously discussed in Section 3. When started, each entity contacts the locally running INC to make it aware of their existence. This was previously illustrated in the top part of Fig. 4.

Mechanism dependency check. Upon receiving a registration request, the SOP checks the availability of a mechanism. If all entities to compose it are available, the INC informs the DE about the entity types and location, as the bottom part of Fig. 4.

Inter-entity communication for mechanism composition. The DE is able to correctly configure the appropriate IEs, requesting information or subscribing so as to be periodically notified. The EE properly responds to execution requests from the DE, providing information about the current execution (this was checked by removing networking privileges from the EE process and ensuring that it reports a connection failure).

Remote discovery. After the connection the INC starts the remote discovery service, which allows the DE to become aware of the remote entities which might extend and enhance the service, in particular with the possibility of using the $IE_T L$ mentioned in Section 3.

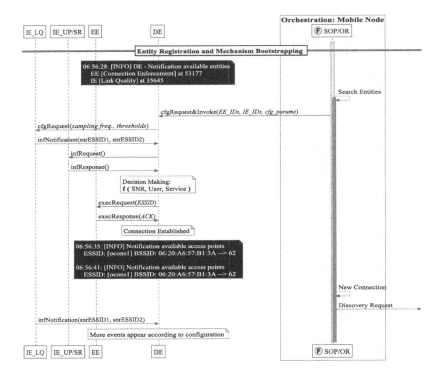

Fig. 5. Example sequence of OConS messages showing the search and registration of compliant IEs, their use by a DE, and the execution of the decision by the EE

Algorithms adaptability to context changes. Once the remote discovery has been carried out, the DE is able to adapt its operation. The selection algorithm can take into account new information which can be gathered from the remote entities, and react accordingly.

With this testbed setup, we have demonstrated that OConS allows for the integration of a very flexible platform. It enables easy extension and configuration, as well as the integration of new functionality, in the form of new entities which conforms to the framework. Moreover, a GUI allowing to monitor the information exchange and offering possibility of parsing their contents has been developed. This therefore complements the OConS protocol library with an invaluable debugging tool.

5   Conclusions

In spite of the relevance that the research on the Future Internet realm has recently gained, there is a clear need to foster the assessment of the corresponding architectures, protocols, techniques and algorithms over real testbeds. This is a crucial point to facilitate their forthcoming rollout. It is one of the leitmotifs of the SAIL project, which is supporting implementation-related activities. The Open Connectivity Services framework, which is one of the main components of the SAIL solution, is also pursuing this goal. This paper has presented an implementation of the OConS framework and its deployment over a real testbed. It described the OConS architectural entities and introduced the role played by the orchestration process, as a means to enable the integration of various mechanisms by the composition of various functional elements.

As an illustrative example we have shown the integration of an enhanced access selection process with a dynamic mobility management procedure, using the possibilities which are brought about by the OConS framework. Due to the intrinsic limitations of available technologies (especially considering the need to develop functionalities on the network side), we have used a Wi-Fi based testbed, although the implementation is generic enough so as to be used on top of any other technology.

Based on this preliminary demonstration, several lines of action have been opened. First of all we aim at introducing additional mechanisms (for instance, flow management and multi-path), orchestrating them to offer a better service to the OConS user. Besides, the current testbed will be extended so as to integrate different mobility management solutions. We will also foster the integration with the other SAIL components (NetInf and CloNe). Furthermore, we intend to release the OConS protocol library described here to let the community take advantage of the service composition flexibility afforded by the OConS framework.

Acknowledgments. This work is being carried within the SAIL Project under Grant Agreement Number 257448 of the Seventh Framework Programme of the European Union.

References

1. SAIL project, Description of project wide scenarios and use cases. EC Information Society Technologies Programme, Deliverable FP7-ICT-2009-5-257448-SAIL/D2.1(D-A.1) (April 2011),
   http://www.sail-project.eu/wp-content/
   uploads/2011/09/SAIL_DA1_v1_2_final.pdf
2. Pentikousis, K., Agüero, R., Gerbert, J., Galache, J.A., Blume, O., Pääkkönen, P.: The ambient networks heterogeneus access selection architecture. In: M2NM 2007: First Ambient Networks Workshop on Mobility Multiaccess, and Network Management (2007)
3. Perez-Romero, J., Sallent, O., Agusti, R., Karlsson, P., Barbaresi, A., Wang, L., Casadevall, F., Dohler, M., Gonzalez, H., Cabral-Pinto, F.: Common radio resource management: functional models and implementation requirements. In: IEEE 16th International Symposium on Personal, Indoor and Mobile Radio Communications, PIMRC 2005, vol. 3, pp. 2067–2071 (September 2005)
4. Perez-Romero, J., Salient, O., Agusti, R.: A novel algorithm for radio access technology, selection in heterogeneous b3g networks. In: IEEE 63rd Vehicular Technology Conference, VTC 2006-Spring, vol. 1, pp. 471–475 (May 2006)

5. Perez-Romero, J., Salient, O., Agusti, R.: A generalized framework for multi-rat scenarios characterisation. In: IEEE 65th Vehicular Technology Conference, VTC 2007-Spring, pp. 980–984 (April 2007)

6. Tolli, A., Hakalin, P., Holma, H.: Performance evaluation of common radio resource management (crrm). In: IEEE International Conference on Communications, ICC 2002, vol. 5, pp. 3429–3433 (2002)

7. Giupponi, L., Agusti, R., Perez-Romero, J., Sallent, O.: Joint radio resource management algorithm for multi-rat networks. In: IEEE Global Telecommunications Conference, GLOBECOM 2005, vol. 6, p. 3855 (December 2005)

8. Salkintzis, A.: Interworking techniques and architectures for wlan/3g integration toward 4g mobile data networks. IEEE Wireless Communications 11(3), 50–61 (2004)

9. Shenoy, N., Montalvo, R.: A framework for seamless roaming across cellular and wireless local area networks. IEEE Wireless Communications 12(3), 50–57 (2005)

10. SAIL project, Architectural concepts of connectivity services. EC Information Society Technologies Programme, Deliverable FP7-ICT-2009-5-257448-SAIL/D-4.1(D-C.1) (July 2011),
http://www.sail-project.eu/wp-content/uploads/
2011/08/SAIL_D.C.1_v1.0_Final_PUBLIC.pdf

11. Agüero, R., Caeiro, L., Correia, L.M., Ferreira, L.S., García-Arranz, M., Suciu, L., Timm-Giel, A.: OConS: Towards open connectivity services in the future Internet. In: Pentikousis, K., Aguiar, R., Sargento, S., Agüero, R. (eds.) MONAMI 2011. LNICST, vol. 97, pp. 90–104. Springer, Heidelberg (2012)

12. SAIL project, Architecture and mechanisms for connectivity services. Work in Progress, EC Information Society Technologies Programme, Deliverable FP7-ICT-2009-5-257448-SAIL/D4.2(D-C.2) (July 2012)

13. Hinden, R.M., Haberman, B.: Unique local IPv6 unicast addresses. Internet Requests for Comments, RFC Editor, Fremont, CA, USA, RFC 4193 (October 2005),
http://www.rfc-editor.org/rfc/rfc4193.txt

14. Johnson, D.B., Perkins, C.E., Arkko, J.: Mobility support in IPv6. Internet Requests for Comment, RFC Editor, Fremont, CA, USA, RFC 6275 (July 2011),
http://www.rfc-editor.org/rfc/rfc6275.txt

Centralized GW Control and IP Address Management for 3GPP Networks

Wolfgang Hahn and Henning Sanneck

Nokia Siemens Networks Research
St. Martin-Straße 76, 81541 Munich, Germany
{wolfgang.hahn,henning.sanneck}@nsn.com

Abstract. This paper discusses a shift of functionality in the 3GPP Evolved Packet Core (EPC) from distributed data plane gateways (GW) to centralized control nodes. In particular in deployments with largely distributed GWs cost savings for management of the network can be expected. As a special use case that takes advantage of the proposed architecture a GW relocation scheme is introduced that allows smooth migration of users from one GW to another.

Keywords: 3GPP, Evolved Packet Core, Gateway, Internet, IP address change.

1 Introduction

Today in packet data networks and in particular in mobile networks an exponential data traffic growth can be observed. This is a challenge for network operators. New technologies might help to cope with this traffic increase especially to manage the anticipated traffic demands in a cost efficient way.

1.1 Different Contrasting Technology Trends

Different technology trends are currently visible in industry and research:

- **Distribution** of "Internet GWs" and user plane processing in the network
  Benefits claimed for this distribution are more direct/optimal routing, decrease of the traffic latency and saving transport cost, in particular for local traffic (caches, CDN (Content Delivery Network), mobile to mobile traffic). Further advantages might be better fault tolerance compared to centralized approaches. In the 3GPP EPC network architecture this distribution could be applied to the GWs S/PGW or GGSN. This distribution introduces challenges as well such as increased need for GW relocations. Proposals to optimize the 3GPP procedures for this purpose have been given in [1] and [2].
- **Centralization** of management and control plane functions
  From an operational point of view it is beneficial to concentrate complex network management tasks to a limited number of sites. This helps reducing both operational cost and capital expenditure of the overall system: A shift of

A. Timm-Giel et al. (Eds.): MONAMI 2012, LNICST 58, pp. 13–27, 2013.

functions from the distributed network elements to centralized nodes could allow to more easily operate computing and storage tasks in cloud computing environments. The distributed network nodes could become less expensive as they can be reduced to a more simple standardized functionality.

In the transport network domain the paradigm of Software Defined Networking (SDN) has resulted in the OpenFlow specification that also leads to centralization of functions [3]. OpenFlow enables a centralized control plane and keeps the actual packet forwarding in the distributed switches. OpenFlow can be used to program the flow table in different switches and routers and a standardized interface exists between the OpenFlow controller and the distributed switches.

In general the centralized control can provide advantages due to the available overall network view.

The 3GPP EPC Rel.8 architecture has already acknowledged these trends by the split of control plane and user plane into the separated dedicated nodes MME (Mobility Management Entity) and S/PGW (Serving GW= SGW, PGW= PDN GW, PDN = Packet Data Network "connection").

Here it should be investigated if further centralization can be beneficial especially if the number of other network functions/nodes like the user plane (UP) GWs is increasing. Impacts to the function split between GWs and controllers are discussed compared to the current EPC architecture.

1.2   GW Functions Which Can Potentially Be Centralized

It is obvious that processing of the user plane has to be kept in the GWs as the user plane traffic should not be centralized. This applies for basic routing and switching tasks, but also more complex UP processing like Deep Packet Inspection (DPI), traffic tagging etc. Accounting and charging functionality can be seen as a borderline case: reporting of packet counts has to be provided by the GW, but managing prepaid budgets or formatting charging records for post processing can be done in the central controller.

2   IP Address Assignment in a Centralized Scheme

The increased number of GWs makes it more complicated to manage the network: Each GW needs to be configured and needs to maintain interfaces to different servers e.g. for operations, management or policy control. Also the backend servers may need some configuration per GW e.g. for security associations. A reduced number of interfaces would thus result in a reduced number of objects which need to be managed.

This is the case in particular for the IP address allocation for the user equipment. Figure 1 gives an example of operator backend servers that need to be connected to distributed GWs for this purpose. (The depicted GWs consist of SGW and PGW functionality in 3GPP terms.)

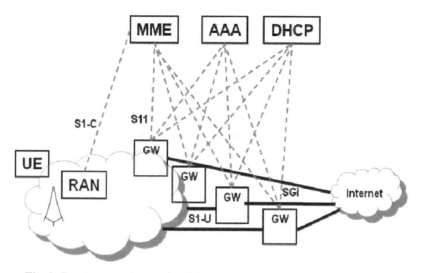

Fig. 1. Current network scenario with servers involved in IP address allocation

In this section it is considered how the distributed GWs' / (Access-) routers' functionality of assigning IP addresses to connected devices can be centralized into a central controller.

It can be expected that IPv6 will dominate in future networks. For IPv6 3GPP has defined an allocation method "in tunnel" that is quite similar to the fixed network to allow similar IP stack operation for fixed and mobile hosts. In case of IPv4 the "in tunnel" method is applicable for the so called "deferred IP address allocation" which also uses the already established user plane (UP) tunnel between the UE (User Equipment, mobile device) and the GW to run IP address assignment with DHCP (Dynamic Host Configuration Protocol). A DHCPv6 solution for IPv6 has been defined as well.

For the centralization of control functions that formerly have resided in the S/PGW a new central control entity is introduced called "Central Controller", see figure 2.

The proposed central controller/GW allocates IP addresses to devices/UE on behalf of distributed routers/GWs.

This central controller element combined with a group of distributed GW elements can be seen as one logical gateway entity. For the MME, the controller element represents distributed GW elements so that from MME point of view there is only one S/PGW element and the controller takes care of which distributed GW is used in which case. The MME connects to the GW control in figure 2 with the standardized S11 interface which is used to create and release sessions and contexts in the S/PGW that are needed to establish connections between the UE and the Internet.

The interface between the central controller and the distributed GWs will provide a subset of this functionality and may support also some modifications and additions depending on the solution. Therefore it is called S11+ interface in this paper. GTP-C (GPRS tunneling Protocol-Control) is a candidate protocol for S11+ interface.

The basic proposed architecture is depicted in Figure 2.

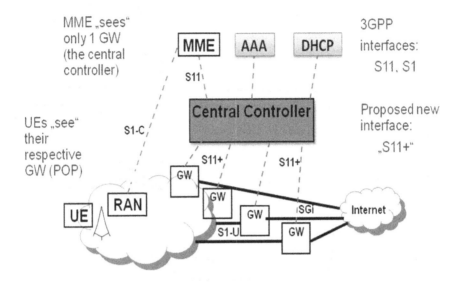

Fig. 2. Centralization of GW functions in a central controller

The physically distributed GWs in both figure 1 and 2 are the point of presence (POP) for the end devices/UEs in the Internet or other private networks where packets destined for the UE are routed to. Their location in the routing topology of the global Internet or other networks requires to assign particular IP addresses to the devices they serve. That is the reason why this functionality is usually located in each of the distributed GWs. The separation and centralization of that functionality to a site remote from the POP will not change the routing but allows for different types of optimization regarding the GW/POP selection and network management.

The proposed solution, shown in figure 3, contains the following building blocks:

- A central controller handles the IP address assignment including the IP layer signalling for the local link for hosts/ mobile UEs on behalf of distributed access routers or distributed GWs.
- A (GTP) tunnel is established from the BS (Base Station, evolved Node B in 3GPP for Rel. 8 (LTE) and higher) to the distributed GW as usual.
- A second UE-specific tunnel is established from the distributed GW to the central controller. The distributed GW includes a packet inspection and separation function that relays "IP layer control messages" (that have to be exchanged between the UE and the PGW) between the UP tunnel from the BS and the second user specific UP tunnel to the central controller. For other packets the (GTP) tunnel is terminated at the distributed GW and user packets are routed to and from the external network/Internet.
- The solution requires that the distributed GW inspects the UP traffic for "IP layer control messages" which refers especially to signalling needed to attain IP addresses like neighbour discovery messages (e.g. Routing Solicitation) or DHCP messages.

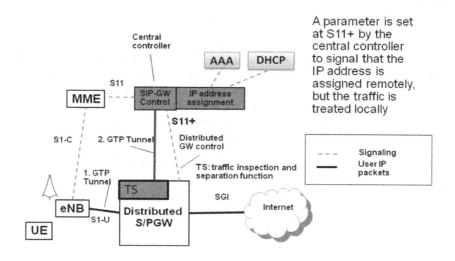

Fig. 3. User specific GTP tunnels at S1-U and S11+ interfaces

In the *tunnel establishment* a second tunnel (established from the distributed GW to the central controller) is needed to handle IP address allocation remotely from the distributed GW. Preferably it will be established at the time of session establishment when also the first tunnel between the BS and the distributed GW is created. To do so, the 3GPP standard procedures of [4] can be used with only minor modifications. During the attach procedure, the GTP tunnels are setup with session management messages. The central controller can use an S5 interface setup type of procedure for the second tunnel. A new parameter is set by the central controller to signal and enable the new functionalities that the address is assigned remotely, but the traffic is treated locally: "Remote IP address assignment and local SGi breakout interface (local PGW)".

The distributed GW still functions as PGW on the user plane and provides the packet routing to external networks/the Internet.

For the *IP address assignment* the standard 3GPP signalling messages between MME and SGW (S11 interface) are terminated in the centralized controller. For IPv6 bearers the central controller allocates a unique Interface ID for the UE as standardized in Rel.8 ([4] TS 23.401, section 5.3.1.2.2) and sends it during the attach procedure via S11, S1 interfaces and NAS session management signaling (signalling between MME and UE) to the UE.

After the selection of the distributed GW/POP, the central controller assigns the UE IP address (in IPv6 a Prefix) from the Prefix/address ranges of the selected POP (according to routing needs). For this purpose it can use internal data bases and/or functions typically provided by AAA (Authentication Authorization and Accounting) and DHCP servers, see figure 3.

The central controller triggers the context establishment in the selected distributed GW on the S11+ interface by the "create session" messages (see S11 interface procedures [4]). The mentioned new parameter indicates the application of the remote IP address assignment. The context establishment in the distributed GW activates then the traffic inspection and separation function in the distributed GW and the tunnel between distributed GW and central controller. It enables that the S1 GTP tunnel terminated in the distributed GW is inspected for IP control messages sent by the UE (those messages are usually exchanged between a host and the first hop router). These messages are then tunneled further to the central controller.

After establishment of the PDN connection (including radio bearer and S1 GTP tunnel) the UE may send Router Solicitation (RS) messages (for IPv6) to the network according to [5] [6] as usual to get an IPv6 address or DHCP messages for "deferred address allocation", see [4] (TS 23.401). The central controller is in the role of the first hop router and finalizes the address allocation: e.g. sends RA (Router Advertisement message) or works as DHCP relay for DHCP based address allocation and sends responses in the second tunnel to the distributed GW and back to the UE.

If IPv4 is used for the PDN connection the proposed IP L3 control message forwarding is only needed for "deferred IPv4 address allocation" with DHCPv4. Otherwise the mobile-specific ("out of band") signalling (S11, S1, NAS) has already provided the IP address to the UE.

As previously mentioned a motivation for the further centralization of control functions is the introduction of SDN technologies. In the figure below OpenFlow controlled switches collocated with GW functions are shown. The OpenFlow controller will then have an interface and cooperate with the central control functions described in this section.

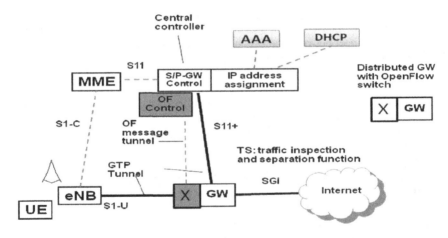

Fig. 4. Combination of GW and OpenFLow switch

3   Use Case GW Relocation with Central IP Address Assignment

3.1   Background of the Proposal

A centralized IP address assignment offers new improved ways to implement network functions in addition to replicating the existing functionality. Approaches like this can be also observed with the introduction of centralized control based on OpenFlow in networks: In addition to the more flexible handling of routing tables totally new mobility schemas can be introduces, e.g. see [7] on handling host mobility in wireless mesh networks.

In mobile networks the deployment of topologically distributed GWs requires more flexibility in GW relocation as with UE movement a locally chosen PGW may become non-optimal. But there might be also other reasons that require relocating UE/hosts to other GWs like the removal of hosts from selected GWs for energy saving, GW maintenance or load balancing. (Hence by the term "GW relocation" the relocation of a UE from one GW to another is considered.)

In 3GPP, the SGW can be changed due to UE mobility but the PGW is kept as a fixed anchor. To address the need for a PGW relocation 3GPP standards provide the 3GPP Rel.10 SIPTO (Selective IP Traffic Offload) feature: a GW change can be achieved by forcing the UE to release the current PDN connection and establish a new one. For this new connection an optimal PGW (and SGW) can be selected. Any change of a PGW results in a change of the UE IP address that is necessary to route packets to the new PGW (many applications are able to tolerate this IP address change e.g. by re-connecting or re-registering with the new IP address).

This solution has two drawbacks: firstly, there is a considerable interruption time of IP connectivity due to the needed tear down of the old connectivity and setup of the new PDN connection before packets can be transferred. Secondly, the re-establishment of a PDN connection is a complex procedure (as complex as a first connection establishment) and thus generates much signaling traffic for the control plane (MME). If the UE has only one PDN connection this results in a complete detach and attach procedure (see also 3.4 below).

In today's networks, first the host/UE is attached to a (new) GW or mobility anchor and then a new IP address is allocated as this is the function/task of the new GW. The new central IP address assignment concept proposed here allows to allocate first a new IP address to the UE/host and then, in a second step, perform a GW relocation.

The current 3GPP Release 10 SIPTO solution and its drawbacks have been shortly described above.

Research is also ongoing in IETF to distribute GWs/Routers together with distribution or centralization of mobility management based on Mobile IP or PMIP, see [8].The idea is to use the IP address (prefix) valid lifetime setting related to the IP address assignment of DHCP (Stateful Address Configuration RFC 2131 [9], RFC 3315 for DHCPv6 [10]) and of stateless IPv6 auto-configuration [5], [6]. [5] (RFC 4862, IPv6 Stateless Address Autoconfiguration) describes the usage of the timers and [6] (RFC 4861, Neighbour Discovery in IPv6) describes the message formats. The application of the "two timer" method (preferred lifetime and valid lifetime) was originally intended for host renumbering in a network and is reused here (renumbering is a case when for example a private network changes its Internet Service Provider (ISP) which results in new address assignments for the hosts of the private network). The method works as follows: A valid IP address can go from a valid state after expiration of a preferred lifetime to a deprecated state where the use is not forbidden but a new address may get higher priority. Later after the valid lifetime expires the old deprecated address disappears.

This behavior can be used advantageously in the process of GW relocation in a make-before-break way for minimized data path interruption: The central controller decides on the GW relocation, it selects a new GW, assigns a new IP address for the UE and pre-establishes the context in the new GW and the needed UP tunnels. The IP address change in the UEs/hosts is based on available IP layer functions. Two alternatives of this solution are described in more detail in the next two sections. There is no need to perform heavy-weight mobile-specific UE NAS session and mobility management signaling.

Different alternatives for IP address signaling are depending on the applied method:

- For DHCP with dynamic IP address assignment ("stateful address/prefix assignment") the central controller rejects UE refreshing requests for the old IP addresses (the UE has to renew the IP address after the lease time expires). The lease time may be selected according to operator policy and other criteria like user history (e.g. recognized mobility patterns) to have trigger points to check for GW relocation. There is also an option for forced renewal of the address triggered by the DHCP server [12].
- For IPv6 "stateless address configuration" the Central controller advertises the new IP address (RA) and at the same time may reduce the lifetime of the old address and force it to go to a deprecated state.
- The central controller may also use methods that might be standardized in future in IETF to make assigned IP addresses invalid.

A comparable method was also presented in [11] for life time management of local IP addresses assigned by local mobile access gateways (MAG). In this concept the assignment of the local IP addresses is still distributed among the MAG so that proxy mobile IP (PMIP) enhancements are needed to handle the IP address validity after hosts have performed a handover from one MAG to another.

3.2   Procedure and Architecture for GW Relocation

Two alternatives are presented here: in Alternative Alt-1 there is a "hard" switch between the old and new IP address and old and new GW, this method is described with DHCP based address allocation. Alternative Alt-2 contains an intermediate phase where old and new IP address are used in parallel and the old and new GW as well. This method is described for IPv6 stateless address auto-configuration.

As an optional function, especially for the alternative 1 described below, the old distributed GW may support the triggering of the path switch by checking when the UE takes a new IP address into use (checking the change of UE uplink (UL) packets source address). In case of using the new address it informs the central controller and triggers this way the GW change procedure (GW switch, handover).

The central controller switches the traffic path after information received from the old GW or after a timer expires. It releases old resources especially in the old GW. A new procedure/message is introduced to update the BS about the changed core network path / new GW (UL tunnel parameter, step 5 in figure 5).

Figure 5 shows a generalized procedure for the GW relocation and the involved nodes for each step:

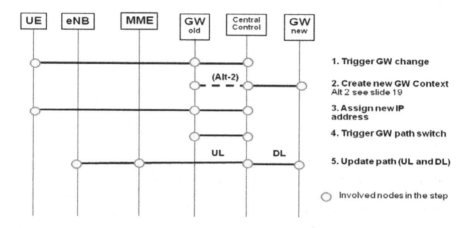

Fig. 5. Generalized GW relocation procedure

The following figures 6 and 7 show the traffic path before and after the GW change.

(Note: in these pictures the GTP tunnel to exchange IP layer control messages between distributed GWs and central controller is not depicted as UP tunnel but seen as part of the S11+ control interface information.)

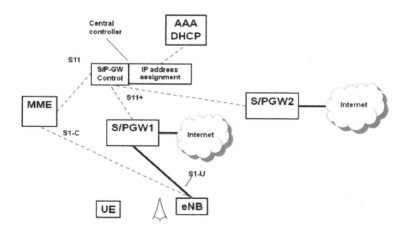

Fig. 6. Traffic path before GW relocation

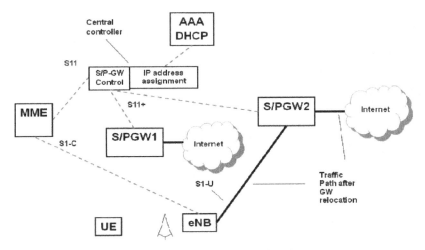

Fig. 7. Traffic path after GW relocation

In alternative 2 an *intermediate state* connecting the new and old distributed GW is introduced. The old GW combines then the downlink traffic with old and new UE destination address and forwards it to the S1-U interface/UE. This allows the UE/host to use deprecated and preferred new address in parallel for a smooth change of the IP addresses and a graceful degradation of the usage of the old address over a particular period in time. How long this time is can be controlled by the central controller by setting the timers appropriately. Figure 8 shows how the UE can receive downlink packets with both the old IP address (in old GW1) and the new IP address (in new GW2, routed over the old GW1) assuming all traffic is coming from the Internet.

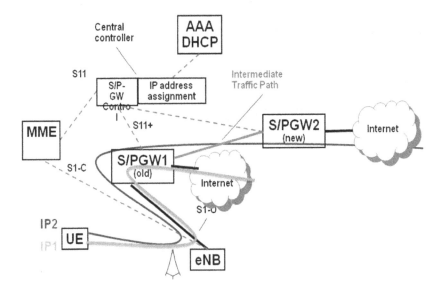

Fig. 8. Alternative solution with intermediate traffic path during GW relocation

3.3   Details of the GW Relocation Procedure

Trigger for GW Change

For candidate UEs for a GW relocation a trigger to start the procedure has one reason why to take into account the opportunity to run IP layer procedures to assign a new IP address. As there is today no means to remove the assigned IP addresses immediately from hosts, it means that the central controller has to keep track of the UE IP address valid timer and /or has to wait for a DHCP Request (Alt-1). Or it can start (based on internal conditions and status information) to run a forced renewal of the IP address using the DHCP reconfigure extension [12] or send routing advertisements (Alt-2).

Create a New GW Context

Before allocating a new UE IP address the central controller selects for the UE a new distributed GW. The procedures in this step can to large extend reuse existing session management procedures of [4] TS23.401 (Create session, Modify bearer...). Differences in parameter settings or new parameters are described below.

Alt 1

The central controller triggers the context establishment in the selected distributed GW on the S11+ interface by sending a "create session" messages to the new GW, providing the downlink tunnel endpoint parameters of the eNB (S1). The distributed GW provides its UL GTP parameters for the S1 tunnel back to the central controller. Together with this context establishment in the new distributed GW also the traffic separation function in the new distributed GW is activated and the tunnel between distributed GW and central controller for IP address handling is setup.

In the "Create session" request parameters, the PDN Address Allocation (PAA) parameter contains the new IP address (as in the static IP allocation schema when UE has a subscribed fixed address) selected by the central controller.

Alt 2

In this solution an intermediate path new GW - old GW – eNB is implemented:

The new GW context can be established with a create session message sent to the old GW (the old GW is addressed like a SGW). The create session message includes a new linkage parameter that informs the old GW that the traffic from the new tunnel of the new GW has to be combined with the existing traffic of the same UE in the S1 tunnel. This allows the old GW to forward downlink (DL) data from the new GW to the existing tunnel of the UE from the old GW to the eNB. With the traffic inspection and separation function the old GW learns if the UE has allocated a new IP address and forwards the UL IP packets (with the new IP address source address) to the tunnel to the new GW.

Assignment of the New IP Address

The central controller provides the functionality of the first hop router in the network and assigns the new UE IP address (in IPv6 a Prefix) from the Prefix/address ranges of the selected GW as described in section 2. The signaling of different protocol options are described in the following.

In the figures below the terms client and server are used with respect to the IP layer protocols DHCP and Neighbor discovery. In this context the client is a function of the host/UE and the server a function of the central controller. The central controller in this case combines the functions of the GW control (S11+ interface handling etc.) and the functions of the DHCP or AAA server.

Alt-1- Stateful DHCPv4/v6 based address allocation with central controller waiting for UE to renew the IP address due to lease timer:

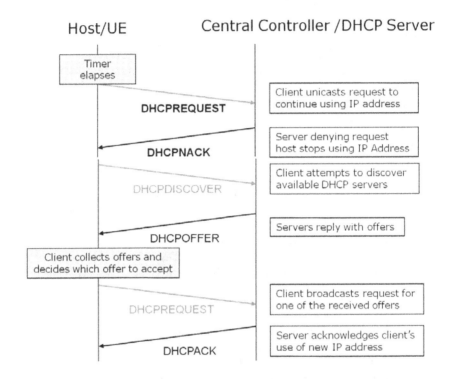

Fig. 9. DHCP based IP address change, Alt-1

Alt-2 - IP Address Assignment with IPv6 Stateless Address Auto-Configuration:
This method makes use of the timers in the Prefix Information option of the Router Advertisement. It allows to time out addresses and in this way, a graceful degradation of the functions/applications using the "old" address. This is the case when an address becomes "deprecated" and the use is discouraged but not forbidden. The higher protocol layers in the host get an indication to change to a new "preferred" address when starting a new communication or leave the source address selection to the IP layer.

The timer values can be set by operators in the central controller. The central controller could also keep track of the life time values assigned for different prefixes (this would make the IP address assignment no longer "stateless").

In figure 10 the controller supervises the lifetime of the assigned IP addresses and starts advertising a new Prefix when the old one gets deprecated. Another option for the controller would be to enforce that the old address goes to deprecated state by sending a RA message with the preferred lifetime set to zero or a short value. The valid lifetime may be reduced as well

(Note: The flow description includes also information of other steps of the procedure according to figure 5).

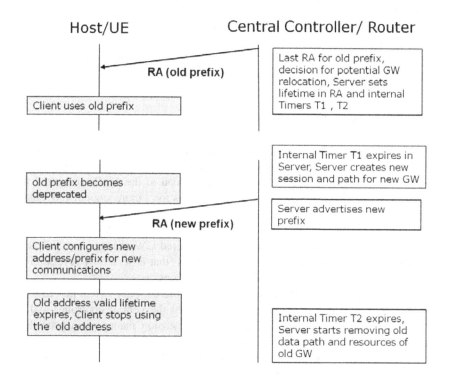

Fig. 10. RA based IP address change Alt-2

3.4   Evaluation of the Proposed GW Relocation Procedure

A comparison of the proposed GW relocation procedure with a 3GPP standard based GW relocation (based on SIPTO - Selective IP Traffic Offload) functionality is provided to highlight the advantages of the new method.

In SIPTO - if the UE moves away from the original local GW - the network breaks the connection and request the UE to re-establish the data connection. (This is processed in the NW usually when the UE reports its presence in a new location area.)

To illustrate the heavy signalling processing needed a message number count is given for all sent and received messages per UE:

- PDN disconnection indicating "reactivation requested"   4
- PDN connection request   8

All together for SIPTO the MME has to process 12 messages.

In contrast for the new proposed method the MME has only to proxy the new UL path tunnel parameters to the eNB (4 messages without any internal processing). This is the result from the fact that the new IP Address can be used by the UE in the same existing PDN connection as the old IP Address before. No mobile specific session or mobility management signaling is needed.

Only a small update is needed in the MME (to support the UL path switch procedure).

For the new controller session management procedures between the central controller and the distributed GW can re-use to large extent existing session management procedures implemented in SGW and PGW today.

4   Final Assessment and Conclusions

The proposed solution allows to concentrate the control functionality needed for IP address assignment and to implement a new mobility scheme. As a result, an increased number of GW relocations will not add additional load to the MME compared to a SIPTO like GW relocation procedure. It further allows for a more smooth GW change since the host/UE can adopt the new IP address over a period of time.

In addition to mobility related handing over of UEs from one GW to another, the method is well suited for network management-triggered GW changes, e.g. in case of an overload situation at some Internet exchange point (that is served by several GWs) or in case of switching off GWs for energy saving reasons.

Only a small update in the MME (e.g., to support the UL path switch procedure) is needed and session management procedures between the central controller and the distributed GW can re-use to large extent existing session management procedures implemented in SGW and PGW already today.

As the concept can be kept to large extent invisible for existing network elements (MME, eNB) a partial deployment in dedicated regions including distributed GWs with the novel functionality is possible. This allows for a smooth network migration.

On the other hand the provided solution introduces a new control element that needs to be instantiated, maintained and managed by the operator (but this would be anyway needed for the implementation of SDN concepts with centralized network control).

A central controller may also introduce a single point of failure (may be subject to attacks). Concepts to ensure reliability and security are part of ongoing research for the SDN/OF framework.

The future deployment of the presented concepts may depend on the adoption of SDN principles in communication networks (centralization of control and combination of transport and service network control) and may provide potential for future standardization for mobile networks (3GPP).

Acknowledgments. This research has been part of the CELTIC MEVICO project, funded in Germany by the BMBF (German Federal Ministry of Education and Research).

References

1. Hahn, W.: 3GPP Evolved Packet Core support for distributed mobility anchors - Control enhancements for GW relocation. In: Proceedings of 11th International Conference on Telecommunications for Intelligent Transport Systems, ITST 2011 (2011)
2. Hahn, W.: Flat 3GPP Evolved Packet Core - Improvement for multiple network connections. In: International Workshop on Mobility Management for Flat Networks, WPMC 2011, Brest, France (2011)
3. McKeown, N., Anderson, T., Balakrishnan, H., Parulkar, G., Peterson, L., Rexford, J., Shenker, S., Turner, J.: OpenFlow: Enabling Innovation in Campus Networks. ACM SIGCOMM Computer Communication Review 38(2), 69 (2008)
4. 3GPP TS 23.401-a40: GPRS Enhancements for E-UTRAN Access (2011)
5. Thomson, S., Narten, T., Jinmei, T.: IPv6 Stateless Address Autoconfiguration, RFC 4862 (September 2007)
6. Narten, T., Nordmark, E., Simpson, W., Soliman, H.: Neighbor Discovery for IP version 6 (IPv6), RFC 4861 (September 2007)
7. Dely, P., Kassler, A., Bayer, N.: OpenFlow for Wireless Mesh Networks. In: Proceedings of 20th International Conference on Computer Communications and Networks, ICCCN (2011)
8. Kuntz, R., Sudhakar, D., Wakikawa, R., Zhang, L.: A Summary of Distributed Mobility Management, draft-kuntz-dmm-summary-01 (2011)
9. Droms, R.: Dynamic Host Configuration Protocol, RFC2131 (March 1997)
10. Droms, R., Bound, J., Volz, B., Lemon,T., Perkins, C., Carney, M.: Dynamic Host Configuration Protocol for IPv6 (DHCPv6), RFC3315 (2003)
11. Korhonen, J., Savolainen, T.: Local Prefix Lifetime Management for Proxy Mobile IPv6, draft-korhonen-dmm-local-prefix-00.txt, Internet-Draft (March 4, 2012)
12. T'Joens, J., Hublet, C., De Schrijver, P.: DHCP reconfigure extension, RFC3203 (2001)

Denser Networks for the Future Internet, the CROWD Approach

Antonio de la Oliva[1], Arianna Morelli[2], Vincenzo Mancuso[3], Martin Draexler[4], Tim Hentschel[5], Telemaco Melia[6], Pierrick Seite[7], and Claudio Cicconetti[2]

[1] University Carlos III of Madrid, Spain
aoliva@it.uc3m.es
[2] INTECS Informatica e tecnologia del software, Italy
[3] Institute IMDEA Networks, Spain
[4] University of Paderborn, Germany
[5] Signalion GMBH, Germany
[6] Alcatel-Lucent Bell Labs, France
[7] France Telecom, France

Abstract. This paper presents the key ideas behind the ICT CROWD[1] (Connectivity management for eneRgy Optimised Wireless Dense networks) project, funded by the European Commission. The project moves from the observation that wireless traffic demand is currently growing exponentially. This growing demand can only be satisfied by increasing the density of points of access and combining different wireless technologies. Mobile network operators have already started to push for denser, heterogeneous deployments; however, current technology needs to steer towards efficiency, to avoid unsustainable energy consumption and network performance implosion due to interference. In this context, CROWD promotes a paradigm shift in the future wireless Internet architecture, towards global network cooperation, dynamic network functionality configuration and fine, on demand, capacity tuning. CROWD pursues four key goals: (*i*) bringing density-proportional capacity where it is needed, (*ii*) optimising MAC mechanisms operating in very dense deployments by explicitly accounting for density as a resource rather than as an impediment, (*iii*) enabling traffic-proportional energy consumption, and (*iv*) guaranteeing mobile user's quality of experience by designing smarter connectivity management solutions.

1 Introduction

Wireless data communication is a constituent part of everyday life for hundreds of millions of people. The number of wireless users is rapidly increasing, the offered load doubling every year, thus yielding a 1000x growth in the next ten years. Additionally, expecting high-quality services and high data rates is becoming normal rather than exceptional. Therefore, considering a density population of 5000 people/Km^2, which is typical of large European cities like London, Madrid, or Paris, and accounting for 20% of the population being mobile data

---

[1] The CROWD project is an accepted project under FP7 and will start on 01/01/2013.

A. Timm-Giel et al. (Eds.): MONAMI 2012, LNICST 58, pp. 28–41, 2013.
© Institute for Computer Sciences, Social Informatics and Telecommunications Engineering 2013

users, each demanding 1 Mbps, would lead to a demand of 1 Gbps/Km^2, which can be hardly provided by current wireless infrastructures. The figure grows further if we consider that the per-user demand is expected to increase ten-fold in the next 5 years.[2]

The solution to cope with this growing traffic demand necessarily entails using more points of access, by increasing their density (dense network deployments) and/or by using different wireless technologies (heterogeneous deployments).[3] Following this trend, operators have already started to push for denser deployments,[4] building micro-, pico- and femto-cells, and installing Wi-Fi hotspots in public areas to inject capacity where the data traffic demand is particularly high.

These efforts notwithstanding, we argue that increasing the number of points of access alone would not remove capacity and performance bottlenecks. In fact, dense deployments are not necessarily synonymous with higher capacity. The case of smart meters is a key example. It has been recently noticed that the diffusion of meters for gas and electricity, endowed with wireless transmitters using the 2.4 GHz ISM band, is generating erratic behaviour in Wi-Fi home devices in USA.[5] Furthermore, having a large number of deployed access points also influences the energy cost, especially for the network operator. In particular, today's access points and base stations running at zero-load consume almost as much energy as when running at full capacity. As a result, wireless dense networking can potentially lead to wireless chaos and huge energy waste.

Currently available solutions for optimising the operation of mobile and wireless networks, including recent advances in PHY-layer techniques like interference cancellation, are not sufficient for heterogeneous and dense deployments like the ones existing or under deployment. Indeed, while PHY approaches have been widely investigated to deal with very dense networks, they take a restricted PHY perspective; they do not consider that higher-layer mechanisms are required to globally optimise per-flow performance by orchestrating mechanisms at different layers and subsystems. Furthermore PHY-based optimisations do not scale with network density and cannot be easily extended to the case of heterogeneous wireless technologies. In fact, the complexity required to optimise multiple nodes in real time becomes prohibitively high when nodes use heterogeneous PHYs.

---

[2] Cisco Visual Networking Index: Global Mobile Data Traffic Forecast Update, 2010-2015.

[3] Noticeably, while PHY-layer improvements have produced only a 5x performance improvement over the past decades, and spectrum management has introduced a 25x gain, network capacity has been increased by a factor 1600 by reducing per-cell coverage as explained by Cooper's Law (see Martin Cooper at Arraycomm, http://www.arraycomm.com/technology/coopers-law)

[4] WLAN Scalability Test Report, Joint Universities Computer Centre, Sponsored by ARUBA Networks.
http://www.arubanetworks.com/pdf/technology/
whitepapers/wp_HiEd_JUCC_Rpt.pdf

[5] Smart meters blamed for Wi-Fi router traffic jam, CNET News.
http://news.cnet.com/8301-11128_3-57328603-54/
smart-meters-blamed-for-wi-fi-router-traffic-jam/

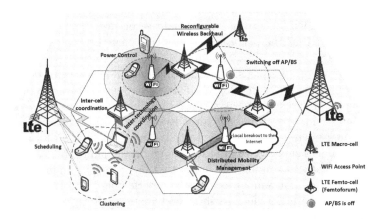

Fig. 1. Crowd Framework

In the above context, we aim at developing a novel networking framework that can satisfy future traffic demands by leveraging density and heterogeneity. Fig. 1 presents CROWD's vision of what are the required key technologies to support a very dense and heterogeneous wireless deployment. The depicted framework comprises small and large LTE cells, overlapping with each other and with Wi-Fi hotspots. As such, the framework accounts for managed (LTE-like) and unmanaged (Wi-Fi-like) deployments in the same geographical areas. Altogether, cells and hotspots form the CROWD access network. The other key component of the CROWD framework depicted in the figure is the wireless backhaul; with a very high density, it is unlikely that all the points of access can be reached with wired connections, due to installation costs and practical limitations, and hence some of them will have to rely on a wireless backhaul connection.

In a nutshell, the CROWD project aims at building high-capacity energy and resource-efficient wireless dense networks. To do so, the project will devise novel mechanisms for connectivity management, energy-efficient operation, scheduling and random access MAC enhancements, and dynamic backhaul optimisation. These mechanisms will be mutually integrated with each other and span across cell boundaries, technology boundaries, and access/backhaul network boundaries, jointly optimising the performance metrics of these subsystems.

The rest of the paper is structured as follows; Section 2 presents the key challenges to be addressed in order to take advantage of the increasing density on the RAN. Section 3 shows the current state of research regarding very dense deployments. The approach taken by the CROWD project in order to address the challenges identified in Section 2 is presented in Section 4. We conclude with Section 5.

2   Key Challenges

We next describe the key challenges that have been identified to realise a truly and effective very dense RAN. To do this, we provide in the following a general description of the challenges and then we identify for each one the different algorithms that contribute to its development.

2.1   Density-Proportional Capacity

In an ideal setting, the capacity increase would be proportional to the increase in the density of points of access. Therefore, a key challenge is to approach this ideal setting as much as possible by providing a capacity increase approximately proportional to the density increase. With small cells, enhancing LTE and WLAN MAC protocols can increase per-cell capacity to a few tens of Gbps. However, uncoordinated neighbour cells cannot simultaneously operate at full capacity due to interference in the limited available radio spectrum. In order to overcome these impairments and achieve a network throughput approximately proportional to the density of the deployed points of access, we propose to smartly manage interference in the radio spectrum via load-driven network selection and offloading schemes, distributed power control, opportunistic scheduling, and by properly supporting cooperative multipoint techniques (CoMP) in the backhaul. Similarly, fostering the formation of clusters of users and coordinating their access activity can yield coordinated resource utilisation, which would turn into higher throughputs.

2.2   Traffic-Proportional Energy Consumption

It is a key challenge to obtain wireless network energy consumption proportional to the volume of handled traffic. The energy consumed by today's network wireless nodes is barely sensitive to the traffic flows over the wireless links. Therefore, in order to save energy, we aim at modulating the long-term activity cycle of each device, in both access and backhaul, based on traffic conditions, i.e., by using smart algorithms to switch on/off base stations and access points. Furthermore, the use of distributed management mobility (DMM) solutions, jointly with the location planning of mobility anchors throughout the backhaul, will enable routing optimisation aiming at reducing load and energy costs in the backhaul. On a short-term operation timescale, we target energy saving through energy-driven opportunistic transmissions, thus using the channel at its best conditions, thereby requiring less transmission power and reducing retransmissions due to channel errors. Ideally, energy costs can be made proportional to the traffic by reducing to zero the energy overhead to run the equipment. Therefore, we will compare the energy consumption of the nodes, in Joules per transmitted bit, to the energy consumed over the radio interface. Considering that wireless devices are commonly utilised at 20-30% of the nominal capacity, traffic-proportional mechanisms are then expected to reduce the power consumption by up to 70%. This figure can be further improved by optimising the routing for minimal energy consumption in the backhaul.

2.3 Mobile User's QoE

Another key challenge is to obtain a mobility management system that guarantees Quality of Experience to users moving through dense, small cells where connectivity management is particularly challenging for mobile users. We target session continuity with stable QoE of mobile users by means of inter-cell and inter-technology management mechanisms. To this aim, we will consider the exploitation of the 802.21-like handover paradigms, the use of reconfigurable backhauls, and the development of DMM solutions. This objective is measurable in terms of handover blocking probability and variation of average bandwidth and end-to-end delay experienced by mobile users. Additionally, we will measure the backhaul load reduction due to dynamic reconfiguration solutions and DMM, and count the number of realizable scenarios and customers that can be accommodated in the network with QoE guarantees, as compared to the case of static backhaul solutions.

3 State of the Art

In this section we review the state of the art on the main concepts relevant to very dense networking concepts. Specifically, we discuss relevant solutions and proposals for connectivity management, energy efficient operation, MAC optimisation for IEEE 802.11 and 3GPP LTE, and backhaul optimisation mechanisms. For each of such topics, we also enlighten control/re-configurability issues known from literature, and identify the main innovations brought by the CROWD project.

3.1 Connectivity Management

The mobility scenario depicted in this work is based on the latest Evolved Packet System (EPS) architecture specified by the 3GPP (release 11), being its key advantage its ability to integrate heterogeneous access networks within the same operator core. Despite of these improvements, mobile operators are facing problems dealing with the sharp traffic increase. One of the causes of these problems is the actual design of the mobility protocols themselves, which are centralised (GTP [1], PMIPv6 [2], and DSMIPv6 [3]) and require all traffic being routed through some entity in the operator core that anchors the IP addresses used by the mobile node. This central anchor point is in charge of tracking the location of the mobile and redirecting traffic towards its current location. This way of addressing mobility management has several limitations that have been identified in [4]:

- Sub-optimal routing. Since the traffic of the mobile node is anchored at the central entity, the packets must cross the operator network to reach the central anchor point before arriving at the terminal.

– Per-terminal mobility management. Current solutions are not able to discern traffic with mobility requirements from other traffic. Therefore, mobility management services are provided with no differentiation to all traffic flows.

Due to these limitations, which are common to most of the connectivity management protocols being currently deployed, the IETF is looking at new protocols with distributed nature. In particular, there is a working group about to be chartered, called Distributed Mobility Management (DMM), addressing distributed connectivity management issues for mobiles. In parallel, the issues above mentioned have triggered a similar response within the 3GPP that has started looking at connectivity management protocols in order to provide new traffic offload capabilities and perform local breakout (traffic is forwarded directly to Internet without going through the mobile operator network core) as close as possible to the user, hence reducing the load in the operator core. The most promising technologies developed by 3GPP are Selected IP Traffic Offload (SIPTO) and Local IP Access (LIPA) [5].

The key difference between these 3GPP approaches and IETF DMM is that 3GPP solutions are focused on providing localised mobility support, enabling the users to move while anchored to the same GW but they do not provide global mobility, requiring the PDN connections to be deactivated and re-activated when not moving locally. Conversely, thanks to its distributed nature, DMM provides global mobility management. Summarising, CROWD will specify novel DMM protocols providing mobility at flow level, that account for access and backhaul using heterogeneous wireless technologies.

3.2 Network Energy Saving Mechanisms

Energy optimisation is nowadays drawing significant attention from the research community. Although much of the research in this area is focused on optimising the MAC and the physical layer of specific technologies (e.g., [6]), there is also significant work focused on reducing the overall energy footprint of complete networks. These ideas are built on top of the seminal work of Restrepo et al. [7], which introduced the idea of energy profile and the dependence of the energy consumption on the traffic load of a particular network component. Based on this work, in [8] some simple measurements about power consumption of networking devices are first presented; the authors then consider a network topology and evaluate the total network consumption given the power requirement of each element. Algorithms for selectively turning off base stations have been further proposed in the literature. Works as [9] and [10] investigated the possibility of switching off base stations in periods of under-utilisation. In [11] the authors propose to switch off nodes in areas with high density of routers. Results of such previous work show that the energy consumption can be reduced between 25-50%, at various times of the day, by using on-off techniques, although the association of users to the cell/AP must be controlled and new protocols must be designed to convey all the required information. Finally, Fehske et al. [12] investigate the possibility of lowering the energy consumption of cellular networks by deployment of small, low-power base stations, alongside the conventional sites. Their results show that the deployment of micro sites does not directly lead to a reduction in power consumption by relaxing the coverage requirements; however, it provides significant gains in spectral efficiency in high load scenarios.

The application of the existing algorithms mentioned above to very dense deployments of micro or femto cells alongside current macro cell deployments is not immediately obvious. In fact, on the one hand, dense deployments, along with agile algorithms to control the set of active base stations and wireless backhaul nodes, should improve efficiency. On the other hand, the denser and the more heterogeneous the deployment, the more difficult it becomes to compute optimisation solutions, and to supply input data for these optimisation algorithms.

3.3   MAC Enhancements for IEEE 802.11

The beahvior of IEEE 802.11 in dense deployments has been only partially addressed in the literature. Here we focus on the four technology aspects that are most relevant to CROWD: (*i*) MAC enhancements, (*ii*) multi-tier mechanisms, (*iii*) coordination techniques, and (*iv*) opportunistic medium access.

Regarding MAC enhancements, most of the work available in the literature addresses the problem of finding an optimal channel allocation. For instance, in [25] and [26] each AP chooses the best channel to operate based on the load of its neighbouring APs. The work in [27] and [31] focuses on heuristics for channel assignment in chaotic and dense wireless networks, referring with this term to the residential or urban areas where users deploy their networks without either taking too much care of AP configuration or considering the neighbouring APs configuration. Furthermore, authors of [28] propose a new 802.11-like MAC protocol (namely SRE MAC) in which the transmission priority of wireless stations adapts to the number of interfering stations, by tuning the contention window and the backoff parameters in either a centralised or distributed way.

A few multi-tier mechanisms using novel technologies such as Wi-Fi-Direct [29] have recently emerged, for instance [32] This mechanism takes advantage of the direct links temporarily established between wireless devices using Wi-Fi-Direct and inter-BSS Direct Link Setup (iDLS, [30]). The authors of [32] also report on prototypal implementation and experimental results. However, the application of such multi-tier mechanisms is not driven by network-wide optimisation objectives, and, in contrast to CROWD's vision, it does not account for inter-technology interoperation within the same transport session.

Within the category of coordination techniques, we found two kinds of works. First, there are analytical proposals focusing on the use of WLAN as a complementary tool for 3G networks [33]. Second, there are some studies and standardisation groups trying to coordinate different IEEE 802.11 APs to reduce interference and optimise channel allocation [34]. Again, existing work accounts for neither very high dense deployments nor for the presence of different wireless technologies, thereby requiring significant modifications to be adopted in the envisioned CROWD's framework.

Finally, opportunistic 802.11 networking is addressed in [35], which presents a mechanism that relies on open APs and spontaneous mobile devices working as APs. Furthermore, a few proposals on 802.11 modifications for distributed opportunistic scheduling have recently appeared. The authors of [36] and [37] take the first steps to study such mechanisms in which stations probe the channel and decide to transmit only if their channel quality is above a threshold, whereas the authors of [38] use control theory to analyse adaptive distributed opportunistic scheduling mechanisms. The available work focuses on MAC throughput optimisation. However, there is no solution available which aims at exploiting density as a resource.

3.4 3GPP LTE MAC Optimisation

At radio access level, LTE exhibits increased peak rates and spectral efficiency, and reduced latency, with respect to its previous generations, i.e., UMTS, HSPA, and HSPA+ due to a combination of physical and MAC layer enhancements, including the use of OFDMA, MIMO, high-order modulations and efficient coding rates. However, a huge potential exists in LTE, which is not fully exploited yet in current deployments and has many research challenges associated: self-optimisation and Inter-Cell Interference Coordination (ICIC). Self-optimisation, constitutes, together with self-configuration and self-healing, the Self Organising Network (SON) vision of the 3GPP introduced in the Release 8 of LTE and supported at European level by the FP7-ICT project SOCRATES. A promising research direction of self-optimisation is optimised handover [13] [14]. Self-optimisation concepts are part of the main objectives of CROWD, which will study them from the perspective of a highly dense network, in the case of homogeneous technology, and will investigate opportunistic use of multiple technologies available for a given user. The problem of inter-cell interference has been long studied (e.g., [15] [16] [17]), but the main problem was the lack of standardised inter-cell signalling. LTE solved this problem, since the X2 interface has been defined for direct communication between eNBs. However, while the X2 opens the door to practical optimisations for dynamic interference management, new research challenges are also created since the abstract optimisation models developed are hardly applicable under the physical and protocol constraints of the X2. The issue is further complicated in the case of heterogeneous networks, e.g., overlapping macro-, pico-, and femto-cells in the same area, which is reference scenario for CROWD. While some efforts exist in this context, e.g., [18] [19] [20] [21], the research is still in its infancy, and all the studies so far only use analysis or simulations as a means for validation. In CROWD we will advance the state of the art by delving into the details of the technology and providing an assessment based on test-bed experiments to bridge the gap between mathematical modelling and optimisation and realistic application. Finally, another area that is especially relevant to the subject of highly dense networks is that of Machine-to-Machine (M2M) communications. It is expected that there will be an explosion of smart things that will become connected wirelessly to the future Internet in the next years. While 3GPP recognised that optimal network for Machine Type Communications may not be the same as the optimal network for human to human communications [22], the issue is not expected to be addressed before 3GPP Release 12. In CROWD the issue of scalability will be specifically addressed, and this will have indirect impact on the use of LTE for M2M applications, which will be reinforced by liaising with the technical committee in ETSI that is dedicated to M2M.

3.5   Backhaul Optimisation Mechanisms

So far backhaul requirements for cooperation techniques and the influence of a constrained backhauls have been researched extensively for current (i.e., sparse) network topologies and densities [23]. Furthermore, the implementation of dynamic backhaul reconfiguration has been studied for wired, optical or wireless point-to-point backhaul networks [24]. This research, shows that dynamic backhaul reconfiguration can enable complex coordination schemes, as well as improve the efficient usage of the backhaul network in terms of energy consumption and quality of user experience. Those current approaches are the first ones to exploit backhaul reconfiguration as a means to enhance cooperation techniques, but the usable degrees of freedom for backhaul reconfiguration are limited because of fixed topologies (often tree-like) and deployed technologies. With the high density of the analyzed scenario, a wireless backhaul with more flexible topology options is more likely and we expect to exploit the benefits of dynamic backhaul reconfiguration beyond the current approaches. With these approaches the backhaul capacity will be near-proportional to the traffic and capacity demands requested by the new coordination schemes

4   The CROWD Approach

In the following we describe how the CROWD project approaches the key challenges specified in Section 2. These mechanisms and their interactions are illustrated in Fig. 2.

4.1   Connectivity Management Mechanisms

While dense networks offer new degrees of freedom that can be exploited by connectivity management schemes, they also pose some challenges to mobility. One of the key mechanisms of CROWD will be a connectivity management scheme that specifically targets session continuity (e.g., IP flow handover) in dense heterogeneous networks, network selection, and inter-technology coordination of LTE and 802.11. This will include: (i) investigating handover management at flow granularity, accounting for rapid variations of network conditions in dense environments; (ii) proposing network access schemes in presence of multiple candidate base stations, hotspot access points, and, possibly, ad-hoc relay nodes; (iii) developing clustering schemes for mobile users, in which groups of mobile users jointly request access to a base station through a few "opportunistically selected"

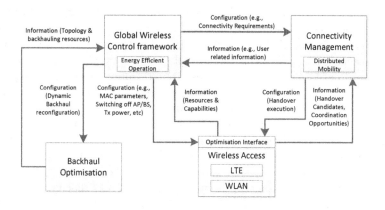

Fig. 2. Mechanisms tackled in CROWD and their relationship

nodes in the cluster, while the traffic is routed within the cluster by means of 802.11 (e.g., Wi-Fi direct); (iv) proposing distributed anchoring schemes for flows requiring mobility support, aiming at offloading the operator's network core from the huge traffic generated by user's demands. Overall, this connectivity management class of mechanisms aims at enhancing the Quality of Experience (QoE) of mobile users, and will therefore be evaluated in terms of outage probability, handover performance and bandwidth that can be guaranteed to mobile users in challenging mobility scenarios.

4.2   Energy Efficient Operation Mechanisms

In traditional WLAN and cellular systems, energy does not scale with transmission distance or with volume of exchanged data. In fact, the power consumption of access points and base stations is rather constant or only slightly affected by the effective traffic load of the device (10% variation). In this scenario, the CROWD project will tackle network-wide energy efficiency by targeting traffic-proportional wireless operations, e.g., by designing solutions for dynamically reconfiguring the topology of the wireless network. This will be done by exploiting an integrated operation/management of multiple heterogeneous access technologies, such as activating and deactivating cells and hotspots in a coordinated way while maintaining enough coverage to meet user's demands. The energy efficient operation mechanisms will be tightly synchronised with the connectivity management mechanisms described above, to ensure connectivity to all users.

4.3   MAC Optimisation Mechanisms for 802.11

The IEEE 802.11 MAC parameters such as the backoff counter and inter-frame spacing, as well as MAC mechanisms such as rate adaptation, were not designed for dense and interference-prone deployments. Hence, we will analyse MAC mis-behaviours and non-optimal MAC operations in presence of multiple interfering cells. We will also study the importance and limits of 802.11 MAC parameters and mechanisms when very small cells come into play, including power control, coordinated sleep cycles and distributed opportunistic medium-access techniques. Due to their inherent ability to optimise resource utilisation and minimise interference, these techniques aim at enhancing 802.11 MAC flexibility, thus yielding better configurability in interference-prone and dense scenarios. Considering the drawbacks of using unmanaged 802.11 wireless deployments with multiple access points operating on same or adjacent channels, typically driving to deep spatial performance bias, or even starvation, we expect that (distributed) coordination will bring dramatic improvements in terms of capacity, fairness, and predictability of performance. The techniques designed will rely on a number of parameters that will be configured by a global control framework to optimise the overall performance.

4.4   MAC Optimisation Mechanisms for LTE

In LTE, the most important optimisations are executed in the MAC, at Radio Resource Control (RRC) level, hosted by the base station. Among other mechanisms, scheduling, link adaptation and power control have a critical impact on optimisation, which is exacerbated further in highly dense networks. Noticeably, even though an interface for direct communication between base stations for handover related information, is defined by the standard, namely X2, that interface is not used for optimisations (i.e., in practice most of today's optimisations happen with local/cell-based scope). In contrast, CROWD will consider scheduling, link adaptation and power control for a leapfrogging technology advance based on inter-cell coordination, e.g., via X2. As for the metrics to evaluate the efficiency of the proposed mechanisms, we will not only use the aggregate network throughput, but also the available spatial and frequency reuse factors, which measure the ability of our schemes to reduce unnecessary interference by coordinating adjacent cells. Furthermore, ideal cell coordination would allow for performance to scale with the cell density, hence we aim at approximating such a scaling behaviour, and thus we will use distance between the proposed mechanisms and the ideal case as a metric of our success.

4.5   Backhaul Optimisation Mechanisms

As the wireless backhaul may potentially become the bottleneck for performance, we need to dynamically configure it for optimal performance. To this end, we will extend existing techniques for backhaul configuration to a wider range of back-haul technologies (wireless or wired) and make these backhauls reconfigurable to adapt them to the concrete traffic needs. Specifically, the project targets back-haul flexibility in terms of (i) traffic-proportional reconfiguration strategies, e.g., temporary pruning underutilised and unneeded backhaul nodes, (ii) on-demand capacity-injection strategies, e.g., reconfiguring the backhaul topology to sustain currently high-loaded areas and using cooperative multipoint techniques. With respect to current static backhauls, we expect to achieve traffic-proportional energy costs, and a considerably higher number of realizable scenarios (i.e., scenarios where all the demands can be satisfied).

4.6   Global Control Framework

In order to ensure that we bring the network to global optimal performance, all the previous mechanisms need to be configured by a global control framework. For instance, if connectivity management and backhaul optimisation are configured separately, performance will be suboptimal as compared to the case when they are jointly optimised. The same holds for the energy-efficient operation and the MAC optimisation mechanisms. In order to address this, CROWD will rely on a global control framework that interfaces with all the mechanisms and configures them for global optimal operation.As many of the control functions have stringent data rate or delay requirements towards multiple base stations or access points, one of the key issues that will be investigated in CROWD is the optimal location of such global decision points. For instance, some of the MAC layer techniques described above—like coordinated inactivity cycles and scheduling across cells—need to locate control decisions somewhere in the network where such processing functions can be executed with stringent delay requirements.

5   Conclusions

We foresee in the near future an explosion of new services that will require an increase in the bandwidth available to the end-user. There are several potential mechanisms to provide such an increased bandwidth, such as making available more spectrum, optimizing or developing new technologies and decreasing the size of the cell range. Historically, the approach more successful in terms of the increase of bandwidth consequence of its use, has been the decrease on the cell range. This is the approach followed by the CROWD project, providing higher capacity to the end-user by densifying the access network. This paper has presented the key challenges and concepts behind the CROWD initiative.

References

1. 3GPP, Evolved General Packet Radio Service (GPRS) Tunneling Protocol for Control plane (GTPv2-C), TS 29.274 (2011),
   http://www.3gpp.org/ftp/Specs/html-info/29274.htm
2. Gundavelli, S., Leung, K., Devarapalli, V., Chowdhury, K., Patil, B.: Proxy Mobile IPv6, RFC 5213 (Proposed Standard), Internet Engineering Task Force (2008),
   http://www.ietf.org/rfc/rfc5213.txt
3. Soliman, H.: Mobile IPv6 Support for Dual Stack Hosts and Routers, RFC 5555 (Proposed Standard), Internet Engineering Task Force (2009),
   http://www.ietf.org/rfc/rfc5555.txt

4. Chan, H.: Problem statement for distributed and dynamic mobility management, Internet-Draft (work in progress) (2011)
5. 3GPP, Architecture enhancements for non-3GPP accesses, 3rd Generation Partnership Project (3GPP), TS 23.402 (2011), http://www.3gpp.org/ftp/Specs/html-info/23402.htm
6. Jones, C., Sivalingam, K., Agrawal, P., Chen, J.: A survey of energy efficient network protocols for wireless networks. Wireless Networks (2001)
7. Restrepo, J.C.C., Gruber, C.G., Machuca, C.M.: Energy profile aware routing. In: IEEE International Conference on Communications Workshops (ICC Workshops 2009), p. 15 (2009)
8. Barford, P., Chabarek, J., Estan, C., Sommers, J., Tsiang, D., Wright, S.: Power Awareness in Network Design and Routing. In: IEEE INFOCOM, Phoenix, USA (2008)
9. Louhi, J.T.: Energy efficiency of modern cellular base stations. In: 29th International Telecommunications Energy Conference 2007, pp. 475–476 (2007)
10. Marsan, M.A., Chiaraviglio, L., Ciullo, D., Meo, M.: Optimal energy savings in cellular access networks. In: IEEE International Conference on Communications Workshops, p. 15 (2009)
11. Chen, B., Jamieson, K., Balakrishnan, H., Morris, R., Span: An energy-efficient coordination algorithm for topology maintenance in ad hoc wireless networks. Wireless Networks (2002)
12. Fehske, J., Richter, F., Fettweis, G.: Energy efficiency improvements through micro sites in cellular mobile radio networks. In: Proceedings of the IEEE Global Communications Conference (2009)
13. Lobinger, A., Stefanski, S., Jansen, T., Balan, I.: Load Balancing in Downlink LTE Self-Optimizing Networks. In: 2010 IEEE 71st Vehicular Technology Conference (VTC 2010-Spring), May 16-19, pp. 1–5 (2010)
14. Jansen, T., Balan, I., Turk, J., Moerman, I., Krner, T.: Handover Parameter Optimisation in LTE Self- Organizing Networks. In: 2010 IEEE 72nd Vehicular Technology Conference Fall (VTC 2010-Fall), September 6-9, pp. 1–5 (2010)
15. Rahman, M., Yanikomeroglu, H.: Interference avoidance through dynamic downlink OFDMA subchannel allocation using intercell coordination. In: Proc. IEEE VTC Spring 2008, pp. 1630–1635 (May 2008)
16. Rahman, M., Yanikomeroglu, H.: Enhancing cell-edge performance: a downlink dynamic interference avoidance scheme with inter-cell coordination. IEEE Transactions on Wireless Communications 9(4), 1414–1425 (2010)
17. Venturino, L., Prasad, N., Wang, X.: Coordinated Scheduling and Power Allocation in Downlink Multicell OFDMA Networks. IEEE Transactions on Vehicular Technology 58(6), 2835–2848 (2009)
18. Hong, Y.-J., Namyoon, L., Clerck, B.: System level performance evaluation of intercell interference coordination schemes for heterogeneous networks in LTE-A system. In: 2010 IEEE GLOBECOM Workshops (GC Wkshps), December 6-10, pp. 690–694 (2010)
19. Rahman, M., Yanikomeroglu, H., Wong, W.: Interference Avoidance with Dynamic Inter-Cell Coordination for Downlink LTE System. In: Wireless Communications and Networking Conference (2009)
20. Wang, J., Liu, J., Wang, D., Pang, J., Shen, G.: Optimised Fairness Cell Selection for 3GPP LTE-A Macro-Pico HetNets. In: 2011 IEEE Vehicular Technology Conference (VTC Fall), September 5-8, pp. 1–5 (2011)

21. Lopez-Perez, D., Guvenc, I., de la Roche, G., Kountouris, M., Quek, T.Q.S., Zhang, J.: Enhanced intercell interference coordination challenges in heterogeneous networks. IEEE Wireless Communications 18(3), 22–30 (2011)
22. 3GPP, Study on enhancements for Machine-Type Communications, TR 22.888
23. Samardzija, Huang, H.: Determining Backhaul Bandwidth Requirements for Network MIMO. In: EUSIPCO (2009)
24. Dräxler, M., Biermann, T., Karl, H., Kellerer, W.: Cooperating Base Station Set Selection and Network Reconfiguration in Limited Backhaul Networks. In: IEEE 23nd International Symposium on Personal, Indoor and Mobile Radio Communications, PIMRC 2012, Sydney, Australia, September 09-12 (2012)
25. Luo, H., Shankaranarayanan, N.: A distributed dynamic channel allocation technique for throughput improvement in a dense WLAN environment. In: Acoustics, Speech, and Signal Processing Proceedings, vol. 5, p. V 3458 (2004)
26. Drieberg, M., Zheng, F.-C., Ahmad, R., Olafsson, S.: An asynchronous distributed dynamic channel assignment scheme for dense WLANs. In: IEEE International Conference on Communications, ICC 2008., pp. 2507–2511 (2008)
27. Ihmig, M., Steenkistie, P.: Distributed dynamic channel selection in chaotic wireless networks (2007)
28. Ryoo, S., Bahk, S.: Spatial reuse enhanced MAC for wireless dense networks. In: Ubiquitous and Future Networks, ICUFN 2009, pp. 225–229 (2009)
29. Wi-Fi Alliance Specification, "Wi-Fi Peer-to-Peer (P2P) Specification v1.1 (2011)
30. Yoon, H., Kim, J.W., Hsieh, R.: iDLS: Inter-BSS direct link setup in IEEE 802.11 WLANs. In: International Symposium on Communications and Information Technologies, ISCIT 2007, October 17-19, pp. 1015–1020 (2007)
31. Manitpornsut, S., Landfeldt, B., Boukerche, A.: Efficient channel assignment algorithms for infrastructure WLANs under dense deployment. In: MSWiM 2009, p. 329337. ACM, New York (2009)
32. Yoon, H., Kim, J.: Collaborative streaming-based media content sharing in WiFi-enabled home networks. IEEE Transactions on Consumer Electronics 56(4), 2193–2200 (2010)
33. Doufexi, Tameh, E., Nix, A., Armour, S., Molina, A.: Hotspot wireless LANs to enhance the performance of 3G and beyond cellular networks. IEEE Communications Magazine 41(7), 58–65 (2003)
34. IEEE P802.11aa/D8.00, Draft Standard for Information Technology-Telecommunications and information exchange between systems-Local and metropolitan area networks-Specific requirements -Part 11: Wireless LAN Medium Access Control (MAC) and Physical Layer (PHY) Specifications - Amendment 3: MAC Enhancements for Robust Audio Video Streaming
35. Trifunovic, S., Distl, B., Schatzmann, D., Legendre, F.: WiFi-Opp: ad-hoc-less opportunistic networking. In: CHANTS, p. 3742. ACM, New York (2011)
36. Zheng, D., Ge, W., Zhang, J.: Distributed opportunistic scheduling for ad hoc networks with random access: An optimal stopping approach. IEEE Transactions on Information Theory 55(1), 205–222 (2009)
37. Tan, S.-S., Zheng, D., Zhang, J., Zeidler, J.: Distributed opportunistic scheduling for ad-hoc communications under delay constraints. In: Proceedings of IEEE INFOCOM (2010)
38. Garcia-Saavedra, A., Banchs, A., Serrano, P., Widmer, J.: The impact of imperfect scheduling on cross-layer rate control in wireless networks. In: Proceedings of INFOCOM (2012)

User-Centric Mobility Management Architecture for Vehicular Networks

Rodolfo I. Meneguette, Luiz F. Bittencourt, and Edmundo R.M. Madeira

Institute of Computing (IC) - University of Campinas (UNICAMP),
Av. Albert Einstein, 1251 - Campinas - São Paulo - Brazil
{ripolito,bit,edmundo}@ic.unicamp.br

Abstract. Vehicular Ad Hoc Network (VANET) is a subclass of Mobile Ad Hoc Networks that provides wireless communication among vehicles as well as between vehicles and roadside devices. Providing safety and user comfort for drivers and passengers is a promising goal of these networks. Some user applications need a connection to internet through gateways which are in the road side. This connection could generate an overhead of control messages and also the handover time among gateways can affect the performance of these applications. This paper proposes an architecture for intra- and inter-system management for virtual environments in vehicular networks, supporting user-driven applications. More specifically, we consider applications that depend on virtual environments which must be constantly updated, such as online gaming. To efficiently support these applications, the proposed architecture includes an extension of the 802.21 protocol to cope with the virtual environment updates. NS3 simulations were performed to evaluate the proposal over the proxy MIPv6 considering VANET and LTE networks as base stations. We observed that the proposed mechanism that extends the 802.21 protocol had a shorter handover time and lower packet loss when acting with the presented architecture.

Keywords: mobility communication, 802.21, vehicular network.

1 Introduction

Vehicular Ad Hoc Network (VANET) is a subclass of Mobile Ad Hoc Networks that provides wireless communication among vehicles as well as between vehicles and roadside devices. These networks have been of particular interest to the communication research area for several years. The benefits from researching in this area are twofold: (i) communication and automatic cooperation between vehicles offer great potential in reducing the number and impact of road accidents; (ii) user-driven applications can improve comfort for car, bus, and train passengers, as well as assist drivers to transit efficiently on the roads. For these reasons, Intelligent Transportation Systems (ITSs) that aim to streamline the operation of vehicles, manage vehicle traffic, assist drivers with safety and other information, along with provisioning of convenience applications for passengers, are no longer confined to laboratories and test facilities of companies [1].

A. Timm-Giel et al. (Eds.): MONAMI 2012, LNICST 58, pp. 42–56, 2013.

One way to classify vehicular network applications is to split them into two main categories [2] : safety and user (non-safety). Safety applications comprise public safety, traffic management, traffic coordination, and driver assistance. User applications include traveler information support and comfort. Comfort class involves applications that target the entertainment of the passengers, which include games, multimedia information exchange, among others.

In this paper we focus on user-driven applications, more specifically in applications that depend on virtual environments which must be constantly updated, such as online gaming. These applications are characterized by five interrelated requirements: interactivity, consistency, fairness, scalability, and continuity [3]. To achieve these requirements, related applications require a certain level of QoS. In gaming, the most important QoS metrics are end-to-end delay, throughput, and packet loss [4].

The way that virtual environment participants are connected directly affects levels of delay, packet losses, and throughput. For example, participants can be connected through the Internet. In vehicular networks, internet access needs a gateway that could use wireless technologies. This access can be done through Dedicated Short-Range Communications (DSRC) or Long Term Evolution (LTE) gateways placed along the road. A vehicle willing to access the Internet first propagates a query looking for gateways. Gateways receiving the query can respond to the requesting vehicle, which chooses one responder based on pre-defined criteria and starts to interact with it. This exchange of messages between the gateway and the vehicle may cause a high overhead that can impact on the virtual environment. Besides the overhead, the time of exchange from an access point to another can also affect the levels of delay, packet losses, and throughput.

This paper presents and evaluates a multi-access wireless network architecture focused on vehicular networks with support for collaborative virtual environments. The proposed architecture provides connection for applications, such that requirements of interactivity, consistency, scalability, and continuity in the virtual environment do not suffer significant impact due to handovers during mobility. The architecture considers the current state of active networks involving the mobile node to perform the selection of the network that best fits the application requirements. Our goal is to decrease the amount of control messages in the network thereby increasing the flow of useful packets and decreasing the amount of lost packets. To achieve this, we extended the 802.21 protocol by adding a new field to it so that each node also knows which applications are running, their users, and who is using the same applications in other nodes.

This paper is organized as follows. Section 2 describes concepts and technologies involved in vehicular networks (VANETs). Then, mobility management strategies and how to implement them in a heterogeneous environment, as well as the IEEE 802.21 standard, are presented. Section 3 discusses related work. Section 4 presents the proposed architecture for mobility management for vehicular networks, while Section 5 presents an analysis of the results, followed by the conclusion in Section 6.

2   Background

This section presents some basic concepts involved in this paper, introducing VANETs and mobility management.

2.1   VANET

Vehicular Ad Hoc Networks (VANETs) are aimed at communication between vehicles and / or between vehicles and roadside infrastructure [5]. They can use cell phone towers or even an outside access bridge for such communication. In 1999, the Federal ommunications Commission (FCC) allocated a frequency spectrum for inter-vehicle communication and between vehicles and roadside infrastructure, establishing rules and licensing services for the Dedicated Short Range Communications (DSRC) at the 5.9GHz band [6]. This protocol is an extension of IEEE 802.11, the 802.11p, being a technology for the vehicle environment at high speed. The physical layer (PHY) is adapted from the IEEE 802.11a PHY, and the multiple access control (MAC) layer is very similar to the IEEE 802.11 MAC [7].

Applications on the focus of this work, such as games, require quite modest data rates when compared to the DSRC data rate offer (6 Mb/s), with the majority of games generating under 100 Kb/s per player [8]. In [9] the authors set up a worst-case network load scenario based on the formula provided in [10], where the throughput $k(n)$ obtainable by each node n capable of transmitting W bits per second. If a game generates 100 Kb/s per player with 25 players in a game ($n = 25$, $W = 6$ Mb/s), the formula gives the achievable per-node throughput of 1 Mb/s, which is an order of magnitude higher than game requirements.

Devices suffer frequent disconnections and access point changes on their route due to: (i) low network data transmission rate; (ii) high speed vehicles can acheive on a highway; and (iii) decision-making that changes the device's route [11]. Therefore, it is currently a challenge to smoothly change access points in a way that the user does not notice any inconsistency in his/her application [12].

2.2   Mobility Management

Mobility management is the module responsible for maintaining the mobile nodes connection, and it contains two main components [13]: location management and handover management. The location management allows the system to track the location of mobile nodes between two consecutive communications. The handover management allows mobile devices to exchange the network keeping the connection alive.

When a device connected to an access point (AP) moves away from the coverage area, the signal level of the device suffers degradation. When approaching another access point with a stronger signal level, a mechanism is needed to keep the network connection status of the device, transferring the responsibility for communicating to the new access point [14].

There are two types of handovers [15]. Handovers that occur between access points of the same technology are called horizontal handovers. Handovers that occur between access points belonging to different networks (e.g. Wi-Fi to 3G) are called vertical handovers. Thus a vertical handover occurs between heterogeneous cells of access networks that differ in many aspects such as bandwidth, signal frequency, etc. These particular characteristics of each network make the implementation of vertical handovers more difficult when compared with that of horizontal handovers. In this scenario, it is difficult to integrate various network technologies due to the limitations of each technology to ensure the minimum requirements for the application. Therefore, to jointly run a simulation environment as a collaboration of various network technologies and protocols that change over time turns into a major challenge.

2.3   Vertical Handover

In order to help in vertical handovers, the IEEE 802.21 provides a standard to assist the implementation of vertical handovers. The IEEE 802.21 [16] is a recent effort to allow the transfer and interoperability between heterogeneous network types. The goal of IEEE 802.21 is to improve and facilitate the use of mobile nodes, providing uninterrupted transmission in heterogeneous networks. To achieve this objective, the delivery procedures may use information collected from the mobile terminal and / or network infrastructure. At the same time, several factors may determine the decision of delivery: continuity of service, application class, quality of service, negotiated quality service, security, etc. The most important tasks of the IEEE 802.21 are: the discovery of new networks in the environment and the selection of the most appropriate network for a given need.

The core of the 802.21 is the Media Independent Handover Function (MIHF). The MIHF has to be implemented in all devices compatible with the IEEE 802.21 (in hardware or software). This function is responsible for communicating with different terminals, networks and remote MIHFs, and also for providing information services to higher layers. The MIHF defines three different services: Media Independent Event Service (MIES), Media Independent Command Service (MICS), and Media Independent Information Service (MIIS) [17].

The MIES provides sorting, filtering, and event report corresponding to the dynamic changes that occur in the link, such as its features, condition, and quality. The MICS enables MIH users to manage and control relevant features of the link for handover and mobility. The MIIS provides the ability to obtain necessary information for the handover, such as a neighborhood map, information about the link layer, and availability of services through the information elements (IE) to assist in decision making of the handover.

3   Related Works

Horizontal and vertical handover issues have received substantial attention. In particular, many of the recent projects are dealing with handover in heterogeneous wireless networks (vertical handover). This section presents some proposals for mechanisms and architectures that, in some way, perform vertical handover to integrate wireless networks transparently to the mobile user, vehicular or not.

Yang et al. [18] used a cross-layer protocol designed for WiMax mesh networks, called Coordinated External Peer Communication (CEPEC), to provide Internet access services in a motorway environment. To support Internet access, CEPEC separates the road in Multi-segments, and uses the shared channel to retransmit packets. Each segment has a Segment Head (SH) to perform gathering of local packets and retransmission of aggregated packets.

Mussabbir et al. [19] extended the FMIPv6 with the IEEE 802.21 networks on vehicle networks. The authors proposed an improvement in the FMIPv6 mechanism to support Network Mobility (NEMO) in vehicular environments, and used the IEEE 802.21 protocol to achieve better performance in the transmission through the use of a cache to store and maintain the network information.

Chiu et al. [20] presented a cross-layer design to accelerate base station changes, called Vehicular Fast Handover Scheme (VFHS), where the physical layer information is shared with the MAC layer to reduce delay. The VFHS main idea is to use the vehicles approaching from the opposite side to accumulate information from the physical layer and MAC that flows to relay vehicles, which in turn transmit the information to vehicles that are temporarily disconnected. Inactive vehicles can thus perform a fast delivery when they enter the transmission range of an approaching relay vehicle.

Lee et al. [21] proposed an improved multicast handover procedure that optimizes multicast group management by utilizing the context of consumer mobile node running multicast applications. They developed analytical models to evaluate the proposed multicast handover procedure compared with the base one. The authors demonstrated that the proposed multicast handover procedure minimizes the service interruption time and prevents the multicast packet loss during handovers.

In the proposed architecture, we use mechanisms to benefit from network monitoring resources from the 802.21 protocol. These mechanisms capture information from the network to make the best decision in performing the handover, always taking into consideration the network requirements as well as vertical handover techniques. This is done by extending the 802.21 protocol, adding more information to its information service in order to know what kind of application users are running.

4   The Proposed Architecture for Mobility Management

The proposed architecture considers a common infrastructure for multiple access technologies in a transparent way. We created a multi-access wireless network architecture using the Wi-Fi, Vehicular, WiMax, and LTE technologies, providing a continuous and transparent connection for the user to obtain low inconsistency in the virtual world. The architecture is intended to provide connectivity to the application and ensure that its requirements are guaranteed. To accomplish this, the architecture inputs are the state of the network and application requirements. The requirements are: throughput of the network, packet delay, transmission time, and number of lost packets.

4.1 Protocols Used

Information on the state of the network is obtained through the 802.21 protocol, used as a base in the architecture. This information is used to choose the best network for performing the handover. Unlike other protocols, the 802.21 protocol is not tied to any wireless network technology. It can interact with any network interface to obtain the status of networks, both locally and globally, i.e., the node can know the states of its links as well as the state of other nodes through exchange of messages between nodes. The Proxy Mobile IP version 6 (PMIPv6) is also part of the proposed architecture, handling with addresses of each node in the completion of the handover, thereby informing the base station the need for a redirection of messages. Differently from Mobile IPv6 and some protocols based on MIPv6, such as NEMO protocol, the PMIPv6 has a lower overhead on the wireless link than the MIPv6 [22]. Besides this, the PMIPv6 reduces the signaling delay and removes the movement detection time present in NEMO protocol [23].

The 802.21 protocol is supported by PMIPv6. While 802.21 captures the network state information and verifies if the base station is available for a new connection, the PMIPv6 performs the exchange of the node address and handles the mechanisms necessary to perform the redirection of these packets to this new address. We used UDP as the transport protocol, which needs no confirmation on receipt of messages, thereby decreasing the amount of traffic on the network.

4.2 Proposed Architecture

The proposed architecture differs from the existing ones by extending the 802.21 protocol. We added another field to the 802.21 protocol that defines what applications the node is using, thus allowing faster searches for nodes that are part of the same application.

The architecture is divided into two modules: a module embedded in the vehicle (Figure 1(a)) and another module that acts in the access points (Figure 1(b)).

The focus of the architecture is on applications that need to show representations of virtual environments to multiple mobile users. Besides gaming, another application of the architecture is on rescue or hostile environments, where teams can be assisted by mobile applications that mimics a disaster map or a hostile territory.

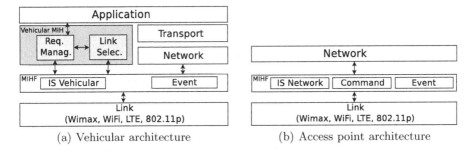

(a) Vehicular architecture   (b) Access point architecture

Fig. 1. Components of the proposed architecture

A mobility management module, called Vehicle MIH, contains a requirement management module, which receives the minimum network requirements that the application needs to run, and also stores information about users who are using the same application. The Vehicle MIH module (Figure 1(a)) has also a module for link selection, which receives the network status information and decides whether it will perform a handover and, if so, to which network it should connect. Both the requirement management module and the link selector module send commands to the MIHF module. An MIHF module is an extension of the functions of the 802.21 protocol. This module has the vehicle network information service (Vehicle IS), which contains information about the vehicle network state as well as the proposed additional field that informs what applications the node is currently using. The MIHF also features the standard Event module of the 802.21 protocol to inform whether the link is active or not. In the link layer, we can use Wi-Fi, WiMax, LTE, or 802.11p (for communication between vehicles).

In the access point architecture (Figure 1(b)), the network layer has the PMIPv6 protocol for handling node addresses and the prefix of the access point required for routing messages. It also has an MIHF module that has the standard functions of the 802.21 protocol, but with the additional field that identifies applications that nodes are using. In the link layer we can also use Wi-Fi, WiMax, LTE, or 802.11p.

4.3   Architecture Operation

Figure 2 shows the steps performed when the application is started. First of all, the requirement manager receives the application requirements (step 1), then transmits these requirements to the link selector (step 2), and the link selector sends all the settings to the MIHF (steps 3 to 7). After this first stage, the application will look for other participants by sending a request to the management module, which registers it in MHIF and also sends a search request for the application information (steps 8 to 10). The MHIF sends an information search to base stations, which checks if there are any nodes connected to them that are attending the same application. If there exist connected nodes using the same application, the base station sends a request to such nodes in order to verify whether they are still participating (step 11). The nodes receive this information, forward it to the MHIF, which forwards it to the management. Then, the management creates its participant table (steps 11 and 12).

After the completion of the search for participants in a particular application, the verification for participants who are in the same area of interest is started. The application sends a message to all participants to check who is sharing the same area of interest and, after receiving the responses, it sends the request to all participants who have confirmed their request to receive and send the information of the environment update. Figure 2 shows these steps.

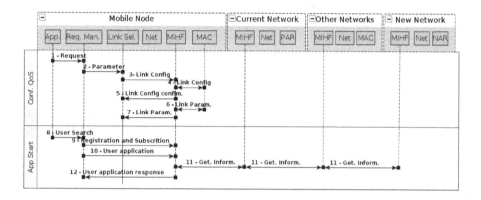

Fig. 2. Steps performed when an application starts

Figure 3 illustrates the steps when a handover is necessary. In this case, the model of link selection receives an event of going down of the MHIF (step 14), then the node sends a request to its base station, which in turn sends requests to other base stations. After that, the base stations respond with information about their states, and then the current base station forwards it to the node that made the request (steps 15 to 17). The node, through the link selector, verifies which is the best base station that complies with the application requirements. The application is responsible for providing its priorities so the link selector is able to decide to which network to connect. The base station that has the lowest levels and complies with the limitations of delay and throughput of the application is to be chosen. After that, the node sends a connection request to its base station that will transfer the request to the selected station (steps 18 and 19). If the selected station responds with a confirmation, the PMIPv6 protocol will terminate the handover process, and the MIHF model will inform that the link is ready for use (steps 20 to 22).

To maintain the active nodes, the requirement manager periodically sends an information request to the MHIF, which forwards it to all access points to find information about the network status. In other words, the requirement manager verifies the type field to check which applications are running, to make sure

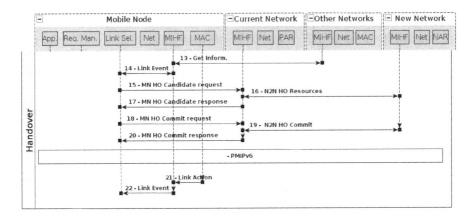

Fig. 3. Steps performed when a handover is necessary

that the nodes are sharing the same game or simulation. To exit the game or simulation, the requirement manager sends a release message that goes through the whole architecture removing all the information about that application. This message is also passed to all access points so they can inform their connected nodes that the participant left the game/simulation.

5 Simulation Environment and Result Analysis

The proposed architecture has been implemented in the Network Simulator (NS-3). We used the PMIPv6 model that was developed by Hyon-Young Choi [24], and the 802.21 model [25].

As application, we modified the overlay support for collaborative virtual environments on vehicular networks [26], which is based on Gnutella [27]. In this scenario, it is assumed that the collaborative virtual environments are divided into hexagons of equal size, generating a set of cells. Users in the same cell form a group of participants with the same interest, being part of what is known as an *area of interest*. This division of the virtual environment aims to reduce the amount of messages that will travel across the network, thereby facilitating the achievement of the networking requirements of a collaborative virtual environment. These network requirements of the application, such as delay, throughput and packet loss, were used in the experiments to make a decision to handover. They were drawn from previous experiments [26] and from the work of Tonguz et al. [28]. In our simulations the link selector will choose the network which provides the following characteristics, in this order: network with lowest message delay; network with highest throughput; network with lowest packet loss in all base stations.

Simulations aimed to evaluate the average handover time and the distribution of connections among network interfaces. Therefore, we chose to not have any node out of reach of any access point. The architecture was evaluated using four metrics: throughput, packet loss, packet delay time, and the handover time.

For the simulation scenario we used: the RandomWaypoint mobility model, 50 vehicles using the overlay support for collaborative virtual environments, as well as a wired node and a router connecting two base stations (one Wi-Fi and one LTE). We used the default parameters of the modules NS3 to configure both the LTE and the WI-FI base stations. These base stations were in the middle of the map, which is 5,000 x 5,000 meters. We conducted several tests with the speed of the vehicles set to 5, 10, 15, 20, and 25 meters per second. At the beginning of each test, all nodes were connected to the LTE access point. We performed 10 simulations for each scenario and we calculated 99% confidence intervals. Some intervals do not appear in the figures because they are too small, though.

Figure 4 shows the average throughput of each interface. We observe that the proposed architecture has a better balance between wireless networks, because the extension of 802.21 protocol provided more relevant information about the state of the network. In other words, the extension of 802.21 provided important data for the best selection of the network, so that the application requirements could be guaranteed. However in the case where we only use the PMIPv6 protocol, most of the connections were managed by the LTE, since the handover mechanism did not have enough information to make the best network choice.

As shown in Figure 5, the mechanism that uses the extension of 802.21 protocol provides a little better throughput in the network due to the low packet loss at the time of the handover, and also due to low packet loss during the exchange between areas of interest in the virtual environment. We also observe a drop in network throughput when the speed increases to 25 m/s. This occurs because there is an increase in the number of lost packets, as seen in Figure 6.

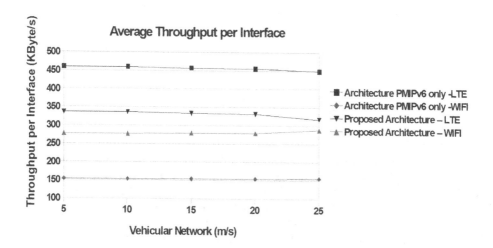

Fig. 4. Throughput per Network Interface

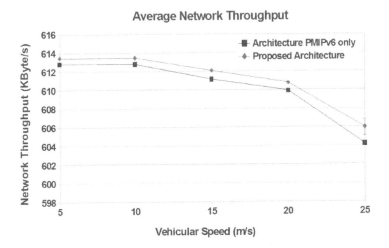

Fig. 5. Throughput

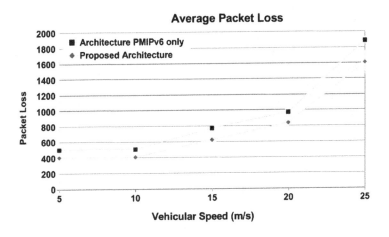

Fig. 6. Packet Loss

The amount of lost packets over the network was higher when using only the PMIPv6. It presented more packet losses during the exchange from an area of interest to another in the virtual environment, and also during handover. This occurs because the architecture with only the PMIPv6 protocol spends more time in searching who is using the same application, besides the higher handover time compared to our architecture, as shown in Figure 7.

Besides the data shown in the figures, we also observed in the simulations that for vehicles with a speed of 20 m/s there was an average of 96 disconnections due to the handover, with an average disconnection time of 0.008s. The mechanism that uses only the PMIPv6 protocol presented 54 percent more packet loss on

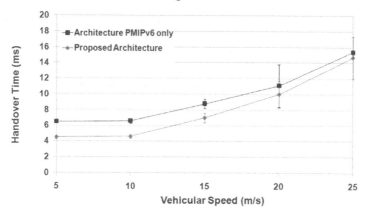

Fig. 7. Handover Time

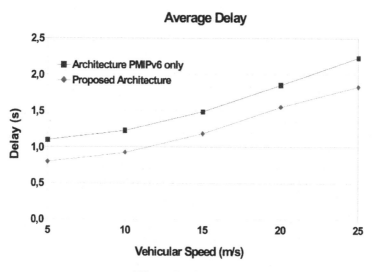

Fig. 8. Packet Delay

average than the 802.21 protocol at the time of handover, with an average delay of more than 1.7s.

Figure 7 shows that the handover time of the proposed mechanism, which uses the extension of 802.21 protocol, is smaller than the other mechanism, because the extension of 802.21 protocol eliminates the need for some messages at the time of changing to a new network. The handover time caused a small impact on the packet delay, as shown in Figure 8. We can observe from this figure that the mechanism that used only the PMIPv6 presented greater delay in the delivery of packets than the proposed mechanism. This occurs due to the different handover times and also due to the amount of lost packets, which require some retransmissions.

In summary, the graphs showed that the proposed architecture achieved a better balance between connections, a shorter handover time, and also smaller packet delay compared to the architecture that only has the PMIPv6 protocol. This improvement is fundamental for the interactivity, which refers to the delay between the generation of an event in a node and the time at which other nodes become aware of that event. Also, it influences consistency, which regards to uniformity of the current virtual world state viewed by all participants.

6   Conclusion

We present and evaluate a wireless multi-access network architecture for vehicular networks to support collaborative virtual environments. The architecture considers people on the move using applications of virtual world representation without losing the connection, switching between different access networks.

The architecture and the proposed extension of the 802.21 protocol presented a better performance than using only the PMIPv6 protocol, showing shorter handover times and lower packet loss due to elimination of some messages when performing the search for new networks. An increase of packet losses in the PMIPv6 occurs during the periods of disconnection, as well as during handover. With the management and use of the extension of the 802.21 protocol and its additional information, a better balance between networks was obtained. Thus, the link selection mechanism can make better decisions when performing handover.

As future work we intend to perform new simulations to verify the impact in the time inconsistency of the virtual environment. The next handover mechanism will be the diagonal, which allows to use more than one network interface simultaneously, thereby increasing the rate of packet delivery.

Acknowledgment. The authors would like to thank CNPq, CAPES, and FAPESP (2009/15008-1) for the financial support.

References

1. Karagiannis, G., Altintas, O., Ekici, E., Heijenk, G., Jarupan, B., Lin, K., Weil, T.: Vehicular networking: A survey and tutorial on requirements, architectures, challenges, standards and solutions. IEEE Communications Surveys Tutorials 13(4), 584–616 (2011)
2. Asgari, M., Jumari, K., Ismail, M.: Analysis of routing protocols in vehicular ad hoc network applications. In: Zain, J.M., Wan Mohd, W.M.B., El-Qawasmeh, E. (eds.) ICSECS 2011, Part III. CCIS, vol. 181, pp. 384–397. Springer, Heidelberg (2011)
3. Gerla, M., Maggiorini, D., Palazzi, C., Bujari, A.: A survey on interactive games over mobile networks. Wireless Communications and Mobile Computing (2012)

4. Zhou, S., Cai, W., Lee, B.S., Turner, S.J.: Time-space consistency in large-scale distributed virtual environments. ACM Trans. Model. Comput. Simul. 14, 31–47 (2004)
5. Faezipour, M., Nourani, M., Saeed, A., Addepalli, S.: Progress and challenges in intelligent vehicle area networks. Communications of the ACM 55(2), 90–100 (2012)
6. Lee, U., Gerla, M.: A survey of urban vehicular sensing platforms. Computer Networks 54(4), 527–544 (2010)
7. Kakarla, J., Sathya, S.S.: Article: A survey and qualitative analysis of multi-channel mac protocols for vanet. International Journal of Computer Applications 38(6), 38–42 (2012)
8. Feng, W.C., Chang, F., Feng, W.C., Walpole, J.: A traffic characterization of popular on-line games. IEEE/ACM Trans. Netw. 13(3), 488–500 (2005)
9. Tonguz, O.K., Boban, M.: Multiplayer games over vehicular ad hoc networks: A new application. Ad Hoc Netw. 8(5), 531–543 (2010)
10. Gupta, P., Kumar, P.: The capacity of wireless networks. IEEE Transactions on Information Theory 46(2), 388–404 (2000)
11. Tayal, S., Tripathy, M.: Vanet-challenges in selection of vehicular mobility model. In: 2012 Second International Conference on Advanced Computing Communication Technologies (ACCT), pp. 231–235 (January 2012)
12. Prakash, A., Tripathi, S., Verma, R., Tyagi, N., Tripathi, R., Naik, K.: A cross layer seamless handover scheme in ieee 802.11p based vehicular networks. In: Ranka, S., Banerjee, A., Biswas, K.K., Dua, S., Mishra, P., Moona, R., Poon, S.-H., Wang, C.-L. (eds.) IC3 2010. CCIS, vol. 95, pp. 84–95. Springer, Heidelberg (2010)
13. Akyildiz, L., McNair, J., Ho, J., Uzunalioglu, H., Wang, W.: Mobility management in current and future communications networks. IEEE Network 12(4), 39–49 (1998)
14. Chen, Y.C., Hsia, J.H., Liao, Y.J.: Advanced seamless vertical handoff architecture for wimax and wifi heterogeneous networks with qos guarantees. Computer Communications 32(2), 281–293 (2009)
15. Yusof, A., Ismail, M., Misran, N.: Handoff architecture in next-generation wireless systems. In: Asia-Pacific Conference on Applied Electromagnetics, APACE 2007, pp. 1–5 (December 2007)
16. Dutta, A., Das, S., Famolari, D., Ohba, Y., Taniuchi, K., Fajardo, V., Lopez, R.M., Kodama, T., Schulzrinne, H.: Seamless proactive handover across heterogeneous access networks. Wirel. Pers. Commun. 43, 837–855 (2007)
17. Taniuchi, K., Ohba, Y., Fajardo, V., Das, S., Tauil, M., Cheng, Y.H., Dutta, A., Baker, D., Yajnik, M., Famolari, D.: Ieee 802.21: Media independent handover: Features, applicability, and realization. IEEE Communications Magazine 47(1), 112–120 (2009)
18. Yang, K., Ou, S., Chen, H.H., He, J.: A multihop peer-communication protocol with fairness guarantee for ieee 802.16-based vehicular networks. IEEE Transactions on Vehicular Technology 56(6), 3358–3370 (2007)
19. Mussabbir, Q., Yao, W., Niu, Z., Fu, X.: Optimized fmipv6 using ieee 802.21 mih services in vehicular networks. IEEE Transactions on Vehicular Technology 56(6), 3397–3407 (2007)
20. Chiu, K.L., Hwang, R.H., Chen, Y.S.: Cross-layer design vehicle-aided handover scheme in VANETs. Wireless Communications and Mobile Computing (2009)
21. Lee, J.H., Ernst, T., Deng, D.J., Chao, H.C.: Improved pmipv6 handover procedure for consumer multicast traffic. IET Communications 5(15), 2149–2156 (2011)
22. Kim, J., Morioka, Y., Hagiwara, J.: An optimized seamless ip flow mobility management architecture for traffic offloading. In: 2012 IEEE Network Operations and Management Symposium (NOMS), pp. 229–236 (April 2012)

23. Lee, H.B., Han, Y.H., Min, S.G.: Network mobility support scheme on pmipv6 networks. International Journal of Computer Networks and Communications 2(5), 206–213 (2010)
24. Choi, H.Y., Min, S.G., Han, Y.H., Park, J., Kim, H.: Implementation and evaluation of proxy mobile ipv6 in ns-3 network simulator. In: 5th Intl. Conference on Ubiquitous Information Technologies and Applications, pp. 1–6 (December 2010)
25. Salumu, M.: ns3 - 802.21, http://code.nsnam.org/salumu/ns-3-mih/ (accessed in 2012)
26. Meneguette, R.I.: Overlay network to support collaborative virtual environments in vehicular networks. Master's thesis, Universidade Federal de São Carlos (2009) (in portuguese)
27. Kirk, P.: Gnutella protocol development, http://rfc-gnutella.sourceforge.net (accessed in 2012)
28. Tonguz, O.K., Boban, M.: Multiplayer games over vehicular ad hoc networks: A new application. Ad Hoc Networks 8(5), 531–543 (2010)

ISAAR
(Internet Service Quality Assessment and Automatic Reaction) a QoE Monitoring and Enforcement Framework for Internet Services in Mobile Networks

Marcus Eckert and Thomas Martin Knoll

Chemnitz University of Technology, Reichenhainer Str. 70, 09126 Chemnitz, Germany
{marcus.eckert,knoll}@etit.tu-chemnitz.de

Abstract. In order to achieve acceptable service quality, the broad spectrum of Internet services requires differentiated handling and forwarding of the respective traffic flows within increasingly "Internet Protocol (IP)" based mobile networks. The "3rd Generation Partnership Project (3GPP)" standard based procedures allow for such service differentiation by means of dedicated "GPRS Tunnelling Protocol (GTP)" tunnels, which need to be specifically setup and potentially updated as the mixture of client initiated service consumption changes. The ISAAR (Internet Service quality Assessment and Automatic Reaction) framework augments existing quality of service functions in mobile networks by flow based network centric quality of experience monitoring and enforcement functions. The following chapters state the current situation followed by the explanation of the ISAAR architecture in chapter 3 and its internal realisation in chapters 4, 5 and 6. Chapter 7 gives an overview of the required signalling procedures and interfaces followed by a summary and outlook chapter 8.

Keywords: ISAAR, QoE framework, QoE, quality of experience, QoS, quality of service, measurement, estimation, monitoring, enforcement, DPI classification, traffic manipulation, flow-based QoE enforcement.

1   Introduction

Internet based services have become an essential part of private and business life and the user experienced quality of such services is crucial for the users' decision to subscribe and stay with the service or not. However the experienced service quality results from the whole end-to-end line-up from participating entities. It is starting from the service generation, covering potentially several transport entities and finishing up in the application displaying or playing the result on the end device's screen or audio unit. However, the contributing performances of the individual service chain parties can often not be separately assessed from the end user perspective. Sluggish service behaviour can thus stem from slow server reaction, transport delay or losses due to congestion along the potentially many forwarding networks as well as

A. Timm-Giel et al. (Eds.): MONAMI 2012, LNICST 58, pp. 57–70, 2013.
© Institute for Computer Sciences, Social Informatics and Telecommunications Engineering 2013

from the end device capabilities and load situation during the result processing and output. More insight can be gained from the mobile network perspective, which potentially allows for a differentiated assessment of the packet flow transport together with a transparent and remote "Quality of Experience (QoE)" estimation for the quality observed on the end device.

User satisfaction and user experienced service quality are strongly correlated and lead - from an Internet service provider point of view - either to an increase in subscription numbers or to customer churn towards competitors. Neither the capabilities and load situations on end devices nor the performance of content provider server farms nor the transport performance on transit links can be influenced by the Internet service provider of a mobile network. Therefore, this QoE framework will concentrate on the monitoring and enforcement capabilities of today's mobile networks in terms of differentiated packet flow processing and forwarding. Since all competing providers will face similar conditions on either end of the service chain, the emphasis on the provider own match between service flow requirements and attributed mobile network resources in a cost efficient manner will be key for the mobile operator success.

The "Internet Service quality Assessment and Automatic Reaction (ISAAR)" quality of experience framework takes this situation into account and leverages the packet forwarding and traffic manipulation capabilities available in modern mobile networks. It focuses on "Long Term Evolution (LTE)" and LTE Advanced networks, but is applicable to the packet domains in 3G and even 2G mobile networks as well. Since different services out of the broad variety of Internet services will ideally require individual packet flow handling for all possible services, the ISAAR Framework will focus only on the major service classes for cost and efficiency reasons. The set of tackled services is configurable and should sensibly be limited to only the major contributing sources in the overall traffic volume or the strong revenue generating services of the operator network. The current Sandvine Internet statistic report [1] for instance shows, that only "Hypertext Transfer Protocol (HTTP)", Facebook and YouTube services alone cover about 65% of the overall network traffic.

2   State of the Art

The standardization of mobile networks inherently addresses the topic of "Quality of Service (QoS)" and the respective service flow handling. The 3GPP defined architecture is called "Policy and Charging Control (PCC) architecture", which started in Release 7 and applies now to the "Evolved Packet System (EPS)" [2]. The Figure 1 depicts the logical architecture and shows, that the "Policy and Charging Rules Function (PCRF)" is being informed about service specific QoS demands by the "Application Function (AF)". Together with the "Traffic Detection Function (TDF)" or the optionally available PCRF intrinsic "Application Detection and Control (ADC)", traffic flow start and end events should be detected and indicated to the PCRF. This in turn checks the "Subscription Profile Repository (SPR)" or the "User Data Repository (UDR)" for the permission of actions as well as the "Bearer Binding and Event Reporting Function (BBERF)" for the current state of already established dedicated bearers. As can be seen here, the 3GPP QoS control relies on the setup of QoS reserving dedicated bearers. These bearers need to be setup, torn down for service flows or modified in their resource reservation, if several flows are being bundled into the same bearer [3]. Nine "QoS Class ID (QCI)" have been defined by 3GPP for LTE networks, which are associated with such dedicated bearers. Today, "IP Multimedia Subsystem (IMS)" based external services and or provider own services make use of this well defined PCC architecture and setup dedicated service flow specific reservations by means of those bearers. Ordinary Internet services, however, are often carried in just one (default) bearer without any reservations and thus experience considerable quality degradations for streaming and real time services.

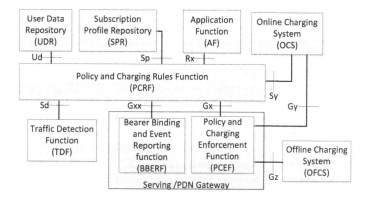

Fig. 1. 3GPP PCC logical architecture after [2] and [4]

Non-IMS based ordinary Internet services, most notably video streaming services, have a high impact on customer satisfaction and overall provider service experience. Therefore, current network operators need to address and differentiate service flows besides the standardized QoS mechanisms of the 3GPP. HTTP based adaptive streaming video applications currently amount the highest traffic share (see [1]), which need to be investigated for their application behaviour and appropriate actions should be incorporated in any QoS enhancing framework architecture. An overview of HTTP based streaming services can be found in [5].

There are many approaches found in the literature, which address specific services and potential enhancements. "HTTP Adaptive Streaming Services (HAS)" [6] for instance is a new way to adapt the video streaming quality based on the observed transport quality.

Other approaches target the increasing trend of "Fixed-Mobile Convergence (FMC)" and network sharing concepts, which inherently require the interlinking of PCRF and QoS architecture structures and mechanisms (see e.g. [7]). This architectural opening is particularly interesting for the interlinking of 3GPP and non-3GPP QoS concepts, but has not yet been standardized for close QoS interworking.

The proposed interworking of "Worldwide Interoperability for Microwave Access (WiMAX)" and LTE networks [8] and the „Session Initiation Protocol (SIP)" based "Next Generation Network (NGN)" QoE Controller concept [9] are just examples of the recent activities in the field.

The ISAAR Framework presented in this paper follows a different approach. It aims for service flow differentiation within single bearers without PCRF support as well as 3GPP inclined flow treatment triggering dedicated bearer setups using the Rx interface towards the PCRF. This way it is possible to use ISAAR as a standalone solution as well as aligned with the 3GPP PCRF support.

The following chapters document the ISAAR Framework structure and work principle in detail.

3   QoE Framework Architecture

The ISAAR Framework has the logical architecture as shown in figure 2. The framework architecture is 3GPP independent but closely interworks with the 3GPP PCC. This independent structure generally allows for its application in non-3GPP mobile networks as well as in fixed line networks also. ISAAR provides modular service specific quality assessment functionality for selected classes of services combined with a QoE rule and enforcement function. The assessment as well as the enforcement is done for service flows on packet and frame level. It incorporates PCC mechanisms as well as packet and frame prioritisation in the IP, Ethernet and potentially the "Multiprotocol Label Switching (MPLS)" layer . Its modular structure in the architecture elements allows for later augmentation towards new service classes as well as a broader range of enforcement means as they are defined and implemented. Service Flow Class Index and Enforcement Database register the available detection, monitoring and enforcement capabilities to be used and referenced in all remaining components of the architecture.

ISAAR is divided into three functional parts which are the "QoE Monitoring (QMON)" unit, the "QoE Rules (QRULE)" unit and the "QoE Enforcement (QEN)" unit. These three major parts are explained in detail in the following chapters.

The interworking with 3GPP is mainly realized by means of the Sd interface [10] (for traffic detection support), the Rx interface (for PCRF triggering as application function and thus triggering the setup of dedicated bearers) and the Gx / Gxx interface [10] (for reusing the standardized "Policy and Charging Enforcement Function (PCEF)" functionality as well as the service flow to bearer mapping in the BBERF).

Since ISAAR is targeting default bearer service flow differentiation also, it makes use of "Differentiated Services (DiffServ) Code Point (DSCP)" markings, Ethernet prio markings as well as MPLS "Traffic Class (TC)" markings as available. This is being enforced within the QEN by Gateway and Base Station (eNodeB) initiated packet header priority marking on either forwarding direction inside as well as outside of the potentially deployed GTP tunnel mechanism. This in turn allows all forwarding entities along the packet flow path through the access, aggregation and backbone network sections to treat the differentiated packets separately in terms of queuing, scheduling and dropping. No matter whether the entities are switches or routers.

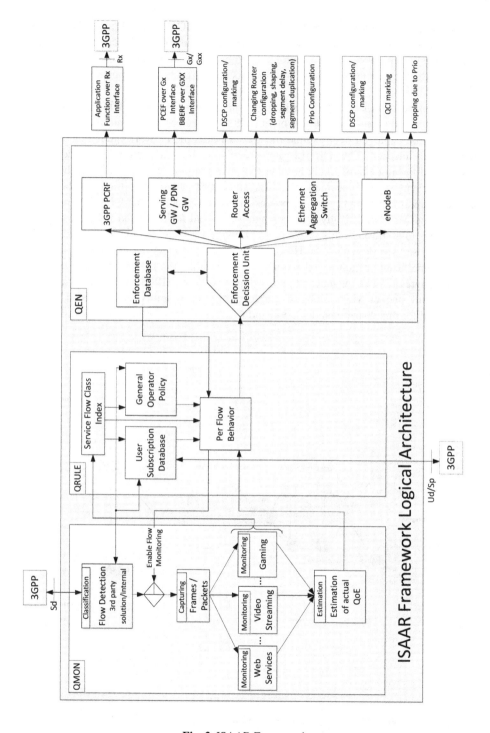

Fig. 2. ISAAR Framework

The modular structure of the three ISAAR units (QMON, QRULE and QEN) allow for a more or less decentralized deployment and placement of the functional elements. Given the common network topology of today's mobile networks as shown in figure 3, the placement of ISAAR components can be done on the potential locations (1) to (6).

QoE enforcement is the prominent functionality, which could profit the most from a distributed and harmonized deployment right from the access (1) into the core (5). It could also be deployed even behind the core towards the network interconnection to the public Internet. The QRULE unit seems to be sufficiently deployed in a centralized fashion - most likely number (5). The monitoring unit QMON is the most difficult element for placement decision since this becomes a trade-off between service flow route pinning and the processing performance of the QMON device(s). Positioning QMON in (5) gives the advantage, that all traffic to and from the mobile node needs to go through this single point allowing for the complete monitoring of all exchanged service flow packets. However, the interface speed in this central location will become faster, which might require to decentralize the monitoring functionality into the aggregation or even access network part. GTP or MPLS tunnelling could still provide full packet view along a single path, but mobility effects need to be considered for this distributed detection and monitoring ISAAR mode of operation.

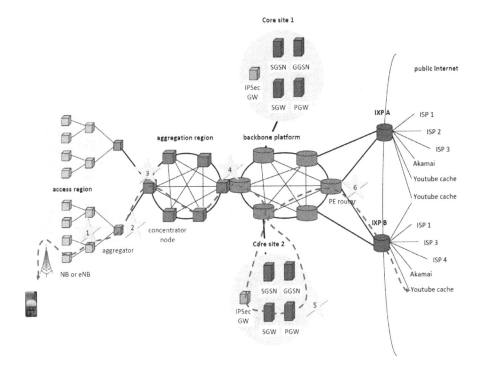

Fig. 3. Today's common network topology of mobile networks

4   QoE Monitoring (QMON)

Today's mobile networks carry a mix of different services. Each traffic type has its own requirements to meet the expectation of the user. The Internet Service Provider wants to satisfy the needs of their customers. Therefore the monitoring of the QoE of the users is necessary. Since the end user's quality of experience of a service is not directly measurable, a network based method is required, which can calculate a QoE "Key Performance Indicator (KPI)" value out of measurable QoS parameters. The most challenging and at the same time most rewarding service QoE estimation method is the one for video streaming services. Therefore, the paper will focus on video quality monitoring and estimation, not limiting the more general capabilities of ISAAR for all sorts of service KPI tracking. YouTube is the predominant video streaming service in mobile networks and ISAAR is consequently delivering a YouTube based QoE solution first. Within this YouTube monitoring we are able to detect and evaluate the QoE of MP4 as well as "Flash Video (FLV)" in "Standard Definition (SD)" and "High Definition (HD)" format.

There are some client based video quality estimation approaches around (e.g. the YoMo application [11]), but we consider such end device bound solutions as being cumbersome and prone to manipulation. Therefore, ISAAR will not incorporate client-side solutions but concentrates on simple, transparent, network-based functionality only.

Some monitoring solutions follow a similar track, like the "Passive YouTube QoE Monitoring for ISPs" [12] and "Network Monitoring in EPC" [13] system, but rely on "Self Organizing Networks (SON)" features only.

The flow monitoring which is used in the ISAAR Framework is explained in chapter 4.2. However, before the QoE of a service can be estimated, the associated data flow needs to be identified. Chapter 4.1 explains the flow detection and classification in detail.

4.1   Flow Classification

The ISAAR Framework is meant to work with and without support by an external "Deep Packet Inspection (DPI)" device. Therefore it is possible to use a centralized DPI solution like the professional devices provided by Sandvine [14]. For unencrypted and more easily detectable traffic flows, it is possible to use a cheaper and more minimalist DPI algorithm which is provided within the ISAAR Framework. The two possibilities could be seen in figure 3. For a distributed solution, the DPI nodes could be located on location (1) to (6), in a centralized case, location (5) or (6) have to be chosen. In an distributed classification architecture, the classification load could be managed by each node. In a first demo implementation, the classification is limited to "Transmission Control Protocol (TCP)" traffic, focussing on YouTube video stream detection within the traffic mix.

In the centralized architecture the flow detection and classification is most suitably done by a commercial DPI solution, in the demonstrator a Sandvine PTS8210 is used.

In this case the measurement nodes have to be informed, that a data stream was found and the classification unit has also to tell them the "five tupel". Contained in the five tupel are the source and destination IP address as well as the source and destination port, the last information element is the used transport protocol. The measurement starts, as soon as the node gets the identification information of the flow.

4.2   Flow Monitoring

The flow monitoring within the ISAAR Framework is application specific. For each service, which should be monitored, there has to be a specific measurement algorithm. The first part of the monitoring section is the Video QoE estimation (e.g. for YouTube) that was presented at the EuroView 2012 [15], [16]. Like all for the framework planned measurement algorithms the video estimation is a network based algorithm. The advantage is that they are working transparently and fully independent from the user's end device. Therefore, no tools have to be installed and no access on the end device has to be granted.

The approach presented is focusing on video stalling events and their re-buffering timings as a quality metric for the QoE instead of fine grained pixel and block structure errors. To determine the number and duration of re-buffering events it is necessary to comprehend the fill level of the play out buffer at the client. Focusing on YouTube video incurs TCP encoded HTTP streaming transport. The detailed description of our method can be found in [15] and [16]. It contains 3 variants of estimation methods - an exact method, an estimation method and a combination of these.

4.3   Location Aware Monitoring

Due to the fact that it is probably not possible to measure all streams within a provider network a subset has to be assigned in a random way. But the distribution of the samples could be mapped to the tracking areas. So it is possible to draw a random set of samples which is normal distributed to all tracking areas. If it is also possible to map the eNodeB cell "Identifications (IDs)" to a tracking area, it becomes possible to draw the samples in a regionally distributed fashion. With the knowledge of that it could be decided whether a detected flow is monitored or not due to the respective destination region. If there are enough samples within the destination area of the flow, further flows will not be selected for measurement. If there are no or few measurements in this area, the flow would be observed.

5   QoE Policy and Rules (QRULE)

In chapter 5 the QoE Policy and Rules entity of the ISAAR Framework is presented. The QRULE gets the flow information and the estimated QoE of the corresponding stream form the QMON entity. It also contains a service flow class index in which all measurable service flow types are stored. In interaction with the user subscriber

Database and the general operator policy, where the operator's policy for each service and the information for what service a user has subscribed is stored, the flow behaviour is appointed. Also the enforcement database within the QEN, which is explained in chapter 6, is taken into account. In combination with all this information the QRULE maps the KPIs to the forwarding and routing rules for each data stream managed by ISAAR. The "Per Flow Behaviour (PFB)" is implemented by marking of packets and frames. Therefore the each PFB has to be specified. Table 1 shows an example of PFB configuration settings for e.g. video streaming, voice traffic and Facebook traffic.

Table 1. Per Flow Behaviour table

Media Type	Key Performance Indicator	IP DSCP	Ether net Prio	MPLS Traffic Class	3GPP QCI	Action
Video	Buffer Level in Sec. Th1 < t < Th2	CS5 101 000	101	101	6 (or 4)	Mark in S/P-GW and eNodeB with high priority
	Buffer Level in Sec. t < Th1	"Expedited Forwarding (EF)" 101 110	111	111	1	Mark in S/P-GW and eNodeB with highest priority
	Buffer Level in Sec. Th2 < t	"Best Effort (BE)" 000 000 or even Lower Effort LE 001 000	000	000	9	Mark in S/P-GW and eNodeB with default priority or even start dropping packets
Voice	Delay in ms	EF 101 110	111	111	1 or 2	Mark in S/P-GW and eNodeB with highest priority or even Create dedicated bearer with QCI 1 or 2
Facebook	Page load time	CS5 101 000	101	101	6	Mark in S/P-GW and eNodeB with high priority
...						

In the video section are three possible modes which are depending on the buffer fill level calculated in the QMON. According to the information from QoE monitoring different markings are chosen. In the example shown in figure 5 the two buffer fill level thresholds are defined to th1 = 5 seconds and th2 = 42 seconds. If the QoE is poor, that means the video buffer fill level is below Threshold 1 (t < th1), the EF class or the equivalent class of the other technologies is used to improve the video QoE. Lies the fill level between Threshold 1 and 2 (th1 < t < th2) a DSCP value like CS5 (101 000) should be chosen, because the QoE is ok and needs not to be treated in a special way. For the third case if the fill level exceeds Threshold 2 (th2 < t) QRULE

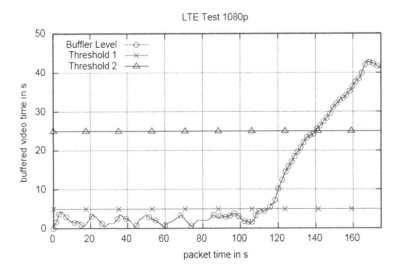

Fig. 4. Per flow Behaviour dependent on the buffer fill level in a YouTube example

has to choose a DSCP value with a lower prioritization (like BE 000 000 or LE 001 000), so the freed resources could be occupied by other flows.

QRULE also decides which kind of marking is deployed depending on the available technology. So it is possible to use the DSCP marking for IP routing, Prio for Ethernet forwarding, the MPLS class for "Label Switched Path (LSP)" switching and the QCI tunnel mapping for 3GPP. Due to the reason that these mechanisms are used in combination in provider networks, there must be a consistent mapping between them. This mapping is also done by the QRULE. Further details on the mapping can be found in [17].

For future investigation ISAAR is prepared to incorporate the interworking of GTP and MPLS LSP tunnels in a transparent fashion. Further details on the interworking can be found in [18].

6   QoE Enforcement (QEN)

The third function block in the ISAAR Framework is the QoE Enforcement. In this block the flow manipulation is done. For example if there is an internet service data stream which is estimated with a low QoE then the QEN has to react and e.g. prioritize the flow. To do this we assume some methodologies to influence the transmission of the involved data frames or packets. One possibility is to take advantage of a PCRF/PCEF with dedicated bearers where it is applicable and trigger the setup via the Rx interface.

The second method we propose to be located within the eNodeB and the "Serving Gateway/Packet Data Network Gateway (SGW/PGW)". It is based on layer 2 and 3 marking within the GTP tunnel as well as outside. How the marking is transferred from inside the GTP to outside is discussed in detail in chapter 5. With the GTP outside marking the stream can be prioritized over other streams along the forwarding and routing path using commonly available priority and DiffServ mechanisms. So the stream is preferentially handled by the network elements without any new configuration within those elements. The marking has to be done by the SGW/PGW for the downstream and the eNodeB has to mark the upstream packets. To be able to mark all packets of a flow, the flow information (five tupel) must be transmitted from the QMON block to all involved elements in this case the SGW/PGW and the eNodeBs which the flow will pass through. This could e.g. be realized via the "Mobility Management Entity (MME)" and the flow state could automatically be transferred during handover using the standard user state procedure.

The outer tunnel marking has also to be transferred to the "Internet Protocol Security (IPSec)" so that the priority of an encrypted stream can also be changed. Therefore the DSCP value of the outer tunnel IP packet header is set to the same value. This leads to the possibility to handle encrypted traffic streams without decryption. The network element need not to know what kind of flow is within the tunnel they only handle the IP packets by their DSCP configuration.

The marking mentioned above has to be done within IP, Ethernet Priority, MPLS Priority and the QCI classes. To get a comprehensive QoE Enforcement, the flow has to be classified and measured in the QMON, the priority of that flow has to be determined by the QoE Ruler and then the QoE Enforcement takes place and does the marking. But the marking has to be valid in the whole operator's network, where the mentioned priority markings were used in a mixed way. To overcome that, the markings have to be converted to each other which is also explained in detail in chapter 5. Marked packets or frames could be routed or forwarded with operator configured per hop behaviour, which results in different queuing and dropping strategies. With this option the QEN does not have to change the router or switch configuration within the operator's network. Because such priority based forwarding and routing is handled automatically by prio enabled Switches and "Label Switch Routers (LSRs)" as well as DSCP enabled routing devices.

But the ISAAR Framework should be also able to do a fully automated router configuration [19]. For that case the enforcement function optionally changes the router behaviour for a specific flow. Thus the packet dropping is influenced. To do this the QEN has to be aware of the actual router configuration and has to change it in a way that the stream's needs are met. After the configuration is changed it must be transferred back onto the router. There are two conceivable ways how the QEN could be aware of the actual router configuration. The first one is to read the information from the router in at first. But with this option the signalling load is increased and it takes a lot of time. A second approach is that the router configuration of all routers is known in a configuration database. In this variant ISAAR only changes the configuration send it to the corresponding devices and save the new configuration in this database.

7   QoE Framework Signalling and Interfaces

The ISAAR Framework consists of different entities and devices. The framework itself could be distributed across the whole provider network. For example the QMON and QRULE could be located in the PGW/SGW and the QEN could be distributed over eNodeBs and routers within the network. To ensure the function of ISAAR there must be a information exchange between the different functional parts. The reasons why the communication between the distributed entities is necessary will be shown in the following example.

If the flow detection is located within the SGW/PGW the information about a detected flow (e.g. the five tupel) has to be transmitted to the policy enforcement entities which could be located in the eNodeBs. The results out of the measurement in the eNodeBs have to be processed in the central QRULE to decide how a stream has to be treated. The Information about the treatment (e.g. handling of the different DSCP values determined by the QEN) could also be transmitted back to the routers and eNodeBs. Also the QRULE must announce the DSCP marking. If the DSCP treatment is statically configured within the routers the QRULE does not have to share this information and the signalling load is reduced.

Maybe there are some other entities within the concept e.g. a KPI collector which gathers the information measured by the probes within the eNodeBs and creates a statistical summary to minimize the transmitted data. Also due to the distributed character of ISAAR it has to be ensured, that all entities know from each other. For that reason all probes, collectors and other distributed entities need to be configured accordingly.

In order to enable the more sophisticated location aware monitoring, ISAAR has to map the cell ID to a specific IP and also to a specific probe address. Therefore the framework needs access to the MME. With the help of the MME it is possible to locate a specific cell ID and together with the former mapping from cell ID to probe to IP address, the localization of a flow destination, the probe in charge for this location can be found. This way, ISAAR can delegate the measurement load into the respective area.

In case an observed and treated flow gets lost for any reason ISAAR has to inform all involved framework parts. Therefore it has to be signalled, that the measurement of the lost stream should be stopped and also all DSCP rules and markings.

The ISAAR Framework has some replicated functionalities with the PCC architecture from 3GPP [2]. Therefore, it is possible to use some of the PCC functional blocks if they are available. The ISAAR Flow Detection could be aligned with 3GPP's "Traffic Detection Function (TDF)", the User Subscription Database has a similar functionality as the "Subscription Profile Repository (SPR)" and some parts of the QEN from ISAAR could also be done from the BBERF, the PCEF and the "Application Function (AF)".

8   Summary

The ISAAR (Internet Service quality Assessment and Automatic Reaction) framework presented in this paper addresses the increasingly important quality of experience management for Internet based services in mobile networks. It takes the network operator's position to optimize the transport of packet flows belonging to most popular video streaming, voice, Facebook and other web services in order to satisfy the customers and their service quality expectation. The framework is aware of the 3GPP standardized PCC functionality and tries to closely interwork with the PCRF and PCEF functional entities. However, 3GPP QoS control is mainly based on dedicated bearers and observations in today's networks reveal that most Internet Services are carried undifferentiated within the default bearer only.

ISAAR therefore sets up a three component logical architecture, consisting of a classification and monitoring unit (QMON), a decision unit (QRULE) and an enforcement unit (QEN) in order to selectively monitor and manipulate single service specific flows with or without the standardized 3GPP QoS support entities. This is mainly achieved by priority markings on (potentially encapsulated) service flow packets making use of the commonly available priority and DiffServ capabilities in layer two and three forwarding devices. In the case of LTE networks, this involves the eNodeBs and SGWs/PGWs for selectively bidirectional marking according to the QRULE determined service flow behaviour.

More sophisticated mechanisms for location aware service flow observation and steering as well as direct router configuration access for traffic engineered flow routing are optionally available within this modular framework.

Due to the strong correlation between achieved video streaming QoE and customer satisfaction for mobile data services, the high traffic volume share of YouTube video streaming services are tackled first in the ongoing ISAAR implementation activity. An optimized network-based precise video QoE estimation mechanism is coupled with automated packet flow shaping and dropping means guided by a three level play out buffer fill level estimation. This way, a smooth play out with reduced network traffic demand can be achieved.

Since ISAAR is able to work independently of 3GPP's QoS functionality, it can be used with reduced functionality in any IP based operator network. In such setups, the service flow QoS enforcement would rely on IP DiffServ, Ethernet priority and MPLS LSP traffic class marking only.

References

1. Sandvine: Global Internet Phenomena Report (2011)
2. 3GPP: TS 23.203 Policy and Charging Control Architecture. 3GPP standard (2012), http://www.3gpp.org/ftp/Specs/archive/23_series/23.203/23203-b60.zip
3. Ekström, H.: QoS Control in the 3GPP Evolved Packet System. IEEE Communications Magazine, 76–83 (February 2009)

4. Balbas, J.P., Rommer, S., Stenfelt, J.: Policy and Charging Control in the Evolved Packet System. IEEE Communications Magazine, 68–74 (February 2009)
5. Ma, K.J., Bartos, R., Bhatia, S., Naif, R.: Mobile Video Delivery with HTTP. IEEE Communications Magazine, 166–175 (April 2011)
6. Oyman, O., Singh, S.: Quality of Experience for HTTP Adaptive Streaming Services. IEEE Communications Magazine, 20–27 (April 2012)
7. Ouellette, S., Marchand, L., Pierre, S.: A Potential Evolution of the Policy and Charging Control/QoS Architecture for the 3GPP IETF-Based Evolved Packet Core. IEEE Communications Magazine, 231–239 (May 2011)
8. Alasti, M., Neekzad, B., Hui, L., Vannithamby, R.: Quality of Service in WiMAX and LTE Networks. IEEE Communications Magazine, 104–111 (May 2010)
9. Sterle, J., Volk, M., Sedlar, U., Bester, J., Kos, A.: Application-Based NGN QoE Controller. IEEE Communications Magazine, 92–101 (January 2011)
10. 3GPP: TS 29.212 Policy and Charging Control (PCC) over Gx/Sd reference point. 3GPP standard (2011)
11. Wamser, F., Pries, R., Staehle, D., Staehle, B., Hirth, M.: YoMo: A YouTube Application Comfort Monitoring Tool (March 2010)
12. Schatz, R., Hossfeld, T., Casas, P.: Passive YouTube QoE Monitoring for ISPs. In: 2nd International Workshop on Future Internet and Next Generation Networks, Palermo, Italy (June 2012)
13. Wehbi, B., Sankala, J.: Mevico D5.1 Network Monitoring in EPC. Mevico Project (2009-2012)
14. Sandvine Incorporated ULC: Solutions Overview (2012),
http://www.sandvine.com/solutions/default.asp
15. Rugel, S., Knoll, T.M., Eckert, M., Bauschert, T.: A Network-based Method for Measurement of Internet Video Streaming Quality. In: European Teletraffic Seminar Poznan University of Technology, Poland (2011),
http://ets2011.et.put.poznan.pl/index.php?id=home
16. Knoll, T.M., Eckert, M.: An advanced network based method for Video QoE estimation based on throughput measurement. In: EuroView 2012,
http://www.euroview2012.org/fileadmin/content/euroview2012/abstracts/05_04_abstract_eckert.pdf
17. Knoll, T.M.: Cross-Domain and Cross-Layer Coarse Grained Quality of Service Support in IP-based Networks, http://archiv.tu-chemnitz.de/pub/2009/0165/
18. Windisch, G.: Vergleich von QoS- und Mobilitätsmechanismen in Backhaul-Netzen für 4G Mobilfunk (2008)
19. Eckert, M.: Analyse und automatisierte Konfiguration klassenbasierter Paketvermittlung (2010)

User-Centric Network-Application Interaction for Live HD Video Streaming[*]

Thomas Zinner, Dominik Klein, and Tobias Hossfeld

Chair of Communication Networks, University of Wuerzburg
{zinner,dklein,hossfeld}@informatik.uni-wuerzburg.de

Abstract. Applications and resource allocation within the network become more and more flexible in supporting divergent user demands. This is reflected by state-of-the-art video codecs like H.264/SVC which allow a dynamic adaptation of the video quality and therewith the required network resources. Within the network, techniques like network virtualization and multipath data transport allow flexible allocation of network resources based on application demands. This paper outlines the potential of the interaction between application and network with an example of a scalable video streaming service and a multipath transport network.

1 Introduction

Internet applications are becoming more and more flexible and support divergent user demands and network conditions. This is reflected by technical concepts, which provide new adaptation mechanisms to allow fine grained adjustments of the application quality.

To overcome network resource limitations, a service has to adjust its demands to the available network resources in order to provide the best possible user perceived quality, denoted to as *Quality-of-Experience* (QoE) [7]. In particular, this is of high importance for applications with stringent requirements like high-quality video streaming or cloud gaming. Accordingly, such applications have to use the available resources efficiently with respect to the user perceived quality. This requires a continuous QoE management of the video streaming service including the monitoring of the current network state as well as control mechanisms to dynamically adapt the video system to deliver the optimal QoE. Typically, the required bandwidth of a video stream depends on the frame rate, the video quality, and its resolution. The dynamic adaptation of these parameters at the involved devices and within the network can be achieved for instance by the scalable extension of the state of the art video codec H.264/AVC. Applications

---

[*] The work has been conducted in the project G-Lab, funded by the German Ministry of Educations and Research (Förderkennzeichen 01 BK 0800, G-Lab) and within the G-Lab project COMCON, funded by the German Ministry of Educations and Research (F"oerderkennzeichen 01BK0918, G-Lab). The authors alone are responsible for the content of the paper.

A. Timm-Giel et al. (Eds.): MONAMI 2012, LNICST 58, pp. 71–83, 2013.

which monitor the network and adapt themselves to the current state are called
network-aware applications.

Within the network and transport domain, new technologies have evolved during the last years providing a more flexible and efficient usage of data transport and network resources. The most promising technologies are *Network Virtualization* (NV), which is seen as an enabler to overcome the ossification of the Internet stack [5], and multipath transport, i.e., the simultaneous data transfer via multiple available transport paths.

NV promises to overcome the limitations of the current Internet and its protocols [11] by providing means to simultaneously operate multiple logical networks on a single physical substrate. Physical resources can be easily added to virtual networks to cope with high demands or removed to reduce operational expenditures during times of low workloads. This enables a flexible and efficient allocation of network resources based on the demands of specific virtual networks.

Multipath transport allows the concurrent usage of network resources and thus provides higher capacities for end devices. Accordingly, this technique allows faster downloads or video streaming with higher quality as compared to the utilization of only a single network resource. Both techniques allow the network to react on application demands, denoted as *application-aware networks.*

The combination of both approaches may be beneficial for both sides, the network and the application. On the one hand, network resources can be utilized more efficiently and on the other hand, applications can easily adapt their demands to the available resources. In this work, we detail the management of application and network interaction with the example of multipath video streaming using the scalable video codec H.264/SVC and show the potential of such an interaction.

The remainder of this paper is structured as follows: In Section 2 we provide background and requirements for scalable video streaming. This includes an introduction to QoE assessment. The benefit of interaction between network and application for multipath video streaming based on H.264/SVC is evaluated in Section 3. Section 4 discusses future work and in Section 5, the paper is concluded.

2   Scalable Live HD Video Streaming

In this section we briefly outline QoE for video streaming before we discuss user, network, and application requirements.

2.1   Background on QoE for Video Streaming

First we summarize different objective and subjective methods to evaluate QoE for video streaming. After that we detail the Provisioning Delivery Hysteresis which describes fundamental relationships between Quality-of-Service measures and QoE.

Objective and Subjective QoE. QoE is in its nature a subjective measure of the quality a user experiences when using a service such as Voice-over-IP, video streaming, or browsing the web. It combines non-technical parameters such as user perception, experience, and expectations with technical parameters on application and network level.

The QoE of an application is a characteristic that is highly subjective to a user's perception, experience and expectations. Thus, the obvious way to measure it is to vary the network Quality of Service (QoS) and investigate its impact on the user perception by asking the users themselves. Based on the user ratings, the QoE can be calculated as, e.g., the average user rating, the Mean Opinion Score (MOS). The QoE assessment based on user surveys is called *subjective* QoE (sQoE) throughout this work.

On the other hand, it is possible to compare the original video clip with the received video clip based on signal and frame processing techniques. Thus, the distortion of the received video clip can be evaluated and the received video quality can be calculated. Based on the video quality, an approximation of the user perception can be estimated. Such an approximation of the user-perceived quality based on computational metrics is called *objective* QoE (oQoE) throughout this work.

The perceived quality can be investigated in subjective tests, where presented stimuli—such as impaired video sequences—are rated by subjects under controlled conditions. However, the assessment of results from these tests is difficult, since the individual scoring depends on daily form and mood of the human subject, as well as on generally overly pessimistic or overly optimistic users. For the purpose of having comparable and uniform tests, the International Telecommunication Union has created a recommendation for standardized user tests concerning video and image quality in ITU-R BT.500-11 "Methodology for the subjective assessment of the quality of television pictures" [8]. The recommendation gives guidelines to normalize the viewing conditions for a subjective study, in terms of room illumination, display position and parameters (resolution, contrast, brightness), hardware to use, the selection of test materials and the length of test sessions. Typical methods for assessing the sQoE are Double-Stimulus Continuous Quality Scale (DSCQS), Double-Stimulus Impairment Scale (DSIS) and Single-Stimulus Continuous Scale Quality Evaluation (SSCQE), as discussed in detail in [8].

The grades of the scale are mapped for instance to numerical values from 1 (bad quality) to 5 (excellent) or 1 to 100, and the mean of the scores, the MOS value, is obtained for each test condition. The obtained rating expresses the subjective Quality of Experience (sQoE).

The presented methods differ in their objectives. Whereas DSCQS is used to measure the remaining quality of an impaired video relative to the reference video, DSIS focuses on the distortions and rates impairments. SSCQE measures the overall satisfaction of the user with his experience regardless of a reference. Another criterion for the selection of a specific method is available equipment, budget, and time.

The results of such surveys reflect the user's perception and thus have a high significance. However, due to different quality judgment of human observers, multiple subjects are required to participate in a subjective study [13]. According to [8], at least 15 observers should asses stimuli in order to gain significant results. Tests are conducted manually in a controlled environment which is time-consuming and costly. Thus, it should be used as base data for objective video quality algorithms which automatically predict the visual quality of a video clip.

Objective video quality metrics can be classified into three categories by the required amount of reference information [15]: *Full-Reference* (FR) metrics are based on frame-by-frame comparison between a reference video and the video to be evaluated; *No-Reference* (NR) metrics have to make assumptions about the video content and distortions, e.g. by evaluating the blockiness of a frame, as a common artifact in block-based compression algorithms such as MPEG; *Reduced-Reference* (RR) metrics evaluate the test video based on a subset of features previously extracted from the reference video. Based on the complex nature of cognitive aspects and the human visual system, objective quality metrics do not capture its entire complexity and focus on aspects, which have been shown to correlate well with human perception in subjective tests. For our studies we use publicly available full reference metrics, i.e., the Peak Signal to Noise Ratio (PSNR), Structural Similarity Index Metric (SSIM), and Video Quality Metric (VQM). These mechanisms range in their complexity and their correlation with human perception.

To evaluate the impact of video distortion on the user experience, we use the SSIM metric and the SSIM to MOS mapping function presented in [4]. This exponential fitting function $f(x) = 13.91 \cdot e^{1.715 \cdot x}$ is intended to map SSIM values, ranging from 0 to 1, to a mean opinion score ranging from 0 to 100. It has to be noted that the used mapping function allows for MOS values $MOS \in [f(0); f(1)] = [13.91; 77.29]$. Accordingly, the results are presented on a scale of 1 to 100 instead of 1 to 5.

Provisioning Delivery Hysteresis. The QoE-Provisioning Delivery Hysteresis (PDH) is introduced in [6] and describes fundamental relationships between QoE and Quality of Service (QoS) parameters. The PDH reveals that the impact of a controlled reduction of application demands and thus an adaptation to the available network resources outperform the uncontrolled adaptation to insufficient network resource, e.g., like packet loss. For both types of degradation we consider the goodput as joint parameter. For the controlled degradation or the *provisioning*, the relative goodput ratio is defined as the ratio between the current capacity compared to the capacity required for the optimal quality. For the uncontrolled degradation, the *delivery*, the goodput is defined as $1 - p_l$ where p_l is the packet loss rate.

Figure 1 sketches the hysteresis as a set of functions of the goodput ratio. While specific relationships between QoE and goodput ratio depend amongst others on application and context, we observe two fundamentally different areas. Controllable quality distortion allows to keep the QoE rather high in view of considerable savings, i.e. goodput ratios much smaller than one. Significant

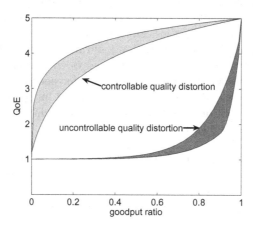

Fig. 1. Illustration of the QoE Provisoning-Delivery Hysteresis

decreases in QoE are observed for rather small goodput ratios. Uncontrollable quality distortion, however, yields a completely different behaviour. Small decreases in the goodput ratio imply large decreases in the QoE values, while that decrease flattens out at the lower edge of the QoE scale as the goodput ratio sinks. This implies that, in order to ensure good QoE, it is better to apply controlled actions than to suffer from problems that appear in an uncontrolled way.

2.2 Requirements for Scalable Live HD Video Streaming

First, we discuss the user requirements for the video streaming use case and derive requirements to the application which can be mapped to network requirements.

User Requirements. The presented use case considers live streaming services. The user expects high video quality and a high resolution for watching e.g. a soccer match in HD resolution at home. Furthermore, the contents are to be delivered in real-time to guarantee the live experience during watching. Based on these user requirements, the network and application requirements are derived.

Requirements to the Network. Due to the real-time nature of TV, only a small video buffer is available at the application which is in the order of a few seconds only. Hence, the network has to deliver the data with low delay and also low jitter that the video buffer can cope with. If data packets in the network get lost, retransmissions are often not possible without violating the real-time constraint. Typically, connectionless transport protocols are used therefore. However, data packets still should arrive in order at the video client so that the video player on application layer does not need to take care about the order of frames. Thus, in-order transmission and reception of frames is a network requirement.

As the user demands high video quality and high resolution, the network has to be capable of providing sufficient bandwidth to carry the video contents. Since video streaming is prone to packet loss and small packet loss rates already lead to a strong impairment of QoE [6], the packet loss ratio should be fairly low. Such insufficient network resources, e.g., too little bandwidth or packet loss, result in a strong impairment of the video service in form of video decoding errors and frame drops. Controlled quality adaptation e.g. by reducing image quality/resolution or frame rate allows considerable bandwidth savings while having only minor impact on user perceived quality [6, 17].

Requirements to the Application. Typically, a video clip can be encoded in different qualities with respect to the frame rate, the resolution and the image quality. In case of limited network resources, these properties should be adapted so that the user still perceives a good quality. At least a minimum resolution, quality and frame rate, which also depends on actual usage context, has to be provided. Otherwise the user will not accept the video service. Higher quality-related layers will increase the QoE further, but also require a higher bandwidth.

Current research on the impact of packet loss on user perceived quality indicates a strong impairment of the video already at small packet loss rates of less than 2 % [18]. This motivates mechanisms able to protect a video stream against packet loss, such as Forward Error Correction (FEC) methods. These techniques provide means to correct corrupted or lost packets and thus allow an exchange of bandwidth against packet loss protection.

3   Benefit of Interaction for Multipath Video Streaming Using H.264/SVC

At first, this section highlights the impact of controlled quality degradation on the user perceived quality. Then, the effect of increasing the network capacity by using multipath transport is discussed. Finally, it presents the benefit of an interaction of both adaptation mechanisms, one on application and the other on network layer.

3.1   Adaptation to Network Resources on Application Layer Using H.264/SVC

In order to optimize the Quality of Experience (QoE) for live video streaming by real-time adaptation of video bitrate and thus video quality to the current network situation (i.e., available bandwidth or unreliable links with packet losses), it is necessary to know the bandwidth requirements of the different layers and their impact on QoE. Therefore, we conducted an intensive measurement study with different network conditions. For evaluating the user perceived quality, we use a full-reference video quality metric SSIM [2] and map it to subjective mean opinion scores (MOS). For our investigations we rely on H.264/SVC, the scalable extension of H.264/AVC [9], which provides an effective way to reduce the

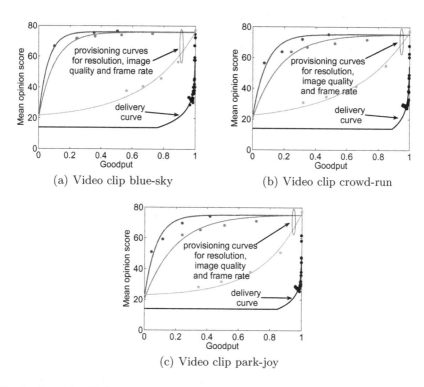

(a) Video clip blue-sky

(b) Video clip crowd-run

(c) Video clip park-joy

Fig. 2. Provision-Delivery Hysteresis for the video clips blue-sky, crowd-run and park-joy

required bandwidth and adjust the video quality within the network. This extension enables the encoding of a video file at different qualities within the same layered bit-stream. Besides of different resolutions, this also includes different frequencies (frames displayed per second) and image qualities with respect to Signal-to-Noise Ratio (SNR), which is referred to as spatial, temporal and quality scalability. In particular we investigate the resolution 1920x1080, 1280x720, 960x540, 640x360, and 480x270, different image qualities according to the quantization parameter ranging from 30 to 38 in steps of 2, and the frame rates 30, 15, 7.5 and 3.75 The impact of a bandwidth reduction, either by packet loss or by a graceful reduction of the video quality is shown for three different video clips in Figure 2. The x-axis denotes the *goodput ratio*, i.e. the relative capacity perceived on application layer as compared to the capacity for which the QoE is maximal. The y-axis denotes the user perceived video quality, respectively. As can be seen, a reduction of the quality in order to adapt the video bandwidth to insufficient network resources in terms of end-to-end throughput results in still a high good QoE. As indicated by the results, resolution and quality adaptation outperform temporal adaptation in terms of user perceived quality. However, as soon as packet loss appears, the video quality is strongly impaired. In order to cope with packet loss, additional mechanisms have to be provided, e.g., forward error correction (FEC) mechanisms. In order to evaluate such a mechanism, we implemented Luby codes [12] and evaluated the interaction of packet loss protection bandwidth reduction. In the investigated scenario, packet loss protection is implemented by adding additional redundancy while bandwidth reduction is performed by reducing the video resolution. More details can be found in [20].

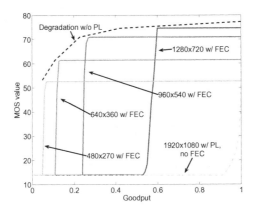

Fig. 3. Guideline for selecting the resolution of the SVC video stream depending on the available network capacity. In case of packet loss due to unreliable transmission, forward error correction is suggested to achieve high QoE, which increases the need for goodput.

The results of our study are depicted in Figure 3 with the user perceived quality in terms of MOS on the y-axis. The x-axis denotes the relative goodput, i.e. the application-perceived throughput, which is equal to one if the maximum quality can be streamed. In case of packet loss p_l the resulting goodput is $1 - p_l$. For streaming a video in 1920×1080 resolution with no FEC, the QoE decreases rapidly and becomes minimal for packet loss rates larger than 2 %, i.e. a goodput of 98 %. This is shown by the lower dashed line. In case of controlled quality reduction (lower resolutions) but no packet loss, QoE decreases much slower and maintains a tolerable value even for small resolutions at 480×270 pixels. This is illustrated by the upper dashed line. In that case, only 15 % of the bandwidth compared to the maximum resolution is required. Hence, in case of bandwidth shortage, SVC is a powerful mechanism for reducing the QoS requirements of the application without compromising QoE too much.

The other cases in Figure 3 denote controlled service degradation with FEC mechanisms. As an example, streaming a video with a resolution of 1280×720 with FEC is considered. Switching to this resolution reduces the required goodput by 60%. We add a FEC mechanism which adds an overhead of 50 %, resulting in a relative goodput of 60 %. By transmitting more symbols, it is now possible to cope with packet loss rates up to 40 % and still ensuring a very good quality of the video stream and not allocating more bandwidth than before. For lower video stream qualities, more bandwidth can be used to protect the video stream. The results in Figure 3 provide clear guidelines how to optimize QoE for live TV streaming according to the current network situation.

3.2 Adaptation of the Network Capacity to Application Demands Using Multipath Transport

The split-up of a data flow on multiple paths towards a common sink has recently attracted a lot of attention since it allows to utilize different access networks, e.g., 3G and WLAN which are usually available on today's smart phones. Techniques like transport virtualization [14] or multipath transport protocols like Multipath-TCP [10] or SCTP-CMT [16] allow a flexible usage of these parallel network resources. A multi-path transmission is initiated by a *splitting* component that splits up the data on disjoint paths. In contrast to Equal-Cost-Multi-Path (ECMP), the splitter is not bound to simple packet-wise or flow-wise load balancing but might be able to make use of knowledge on the structure of the transmitted data, i.e., a scalable video stream. Finally, the multiple transmission paths end in an *assembling* component. Thereby, the assembler not only has to join but also needs to synchronize corresponding data streams by means of buffering and has to prevent reordering of packets.

3.3 Benefit of Mutual Adaptation and Interaction

If network and application are flexible and can adapt to application demands or network state, the question arises how such an adaption should be done. In the following, we discuss this question for the example of a video streaming service based on H.264/SVC and an exemplary network setup with two available paths. A discussion how to implement such a mechanism within a virtual network can be found in [3]. Each path is able to provide resources for a number of x video streams, e.g., for the equivalent of 1.5 video streams. We assume that the capacity of both paths can be bundled by a multipath transmission mechanism. We study four different policies, (1) no service or network interaction in case of insufficient resources, (2) the network reacts to the bottleneck by increasing the capacity with a concurrent transmission via a second path, (3) the service reacts by reducing the quality of the video stream, (4) first the network reacts by providing additional capacity, then the service decreases its demands.

For this study we use the clip *crowd-run* as reference as illustrated in Section 3.1. For the delivery curve, i.e., for the case of packet loss we use the illustrated fitting function, for the provisioning part we use the fitting function for the quality degradation by reducing the resolution. The results of the study are depicted in Figure 4. The x-axis denotes the number of customers using the video streaming service, the y-axis the average quality per customer. For the case of no interaction between applications and network, the application quality is sufficient for one customer, but already for two customers, the quality per customer drops rapidly. The network resources are insufficient and neither the

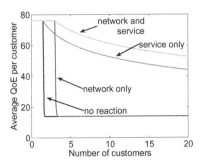

Fig. 4. Average QoE per customer for a varying number of customers and different adaptation mechanisms

application nor the network adapt to the congestion state. Thus, a huge amount of packets are lost, resulting in low service quality. If the network reacts to the congestion by providing additional resources, the application can be provided to more customers without impairments. However, for more than three customers, the service quality drops rapidly. Again, the available network resources are not sufficient, congestion and packet loss occur resulting in a low service quality per customer. Otherwise, the service can adapt to the congestion by reducing the service requirements, i.e., reducing the quality of the video stream. Thus, the network can be relieved and recover from the congestion. Accordingly, no packets are lost and the huge impact of packet loss on video streaming can be avoided. However, in case of service quality adaptation, the quality of the video stream is reduced due to the adaption to the available resources. As illustrated by Figure 4, the best quality for customers can be achieved if both, service and network, adapt to the rising number of customers. In this case the network first reacts to the congestion and ensures that the service quality can be kept to the maximum. However, if further customers join the system no additional network resources can additionally be provided. The network may signal this to the service which then reduces its demands by reducing the service quality. Thus, the average service quality per customer can be maximized.

The results indicate a high potential to increase the user perceived quality for the interaction between networks and applications. To show the capabilities of multipath video streaming based on H.264/SVC, we implemented a software framework enabling multipath functionality either at the edge or within the network. We integrated the implemented multipath streaming framework into the demonstration of the COMCON [1] project at the GLab Status Meeting during the Euroview 2012 event [19]. During the course of the demonstration, the capabilities of a dynamic Network Virtualization Infrastructure based on GMPLS and of an elaborated service provisioning architecture, the multipath SVC streaming architecture, were shown.

4   Future Work

Future work in the area of service and network interaction may investigate the following issues:

- Monitoring: In order to be able to adjust network capabilities and application demands an appropriate monitoring of the varying application and network conditions is necessary. This includes a discussion of the trade-off of monitoring accuracy and the resulting monitoring and signaling overhead. Further, appropriate sampling techniques might be necessary if the data rates are too high.
- Control: How shall application and network react to changing conditions? On the one hand, the video quality should be maximized with respect to the current network resources, on the other hand frequent changes of the video quality also disturb the user experience.
- Decision Component: A detailed investigation where to place the decision entity including communication protocols between these entities as well as a discussion of the benefits for the application and network are required.
- Flow of Information: The necessary information, their impact on the user perceived quality as well as the information exchange between network and application have to be discussed. Taking video streaming into account, the impact of network distortion on the user perceived quality typically varies for each video scene. Thus, the question arises if a MOS value of a layer for the whole video is enough? Or if it is necessary to provide the MOS value for each scene of a layer?

5   Conclusions

This paper investigated the potential of network and service interaction for multi-path transport in the network and service adaptation for H.264/SVC. It derives guidelines how the video streaming service should react in case of insufficient network resources.

In principle, the network can adapt to a congestion state by providing additional resources and thus support more customers. However, if no additional resources can be provided, congestion and packet loss occur, resulting in a strong impairment of the service quality. If the service adapts to the congestion in the network by reducing its requirements, the service quality is reduced gracefully. Thus, the perceived quality of a customer is reduced compared to the maximum available service quality, but still is much higher than in case of delivery failures and packet loss. Further, we have seen that the best service quality can be provided if both, network and service react together.

Current work in the area of future networks discusses a tighter interaction of applications and networks by providing unified interfaces between applications and networks. The design as well as the operation of such interfaces are objectives for future research.

References

1. COMCON - COntrol and Management of COexisting Networks (2011),
   http://www.german-lab.de/phase-2/comcon//
2. Brunet, D., Vrscay, E.R., Wang, Z.: A class of image metrics based on the structural similarity quality index. In: Kamel, M., Campilho, A. (eds.) ICIAR 2011, Part I. LNCS, vol. 6753, pp. 100–110. Springer, Heidelberg (2011)
3. Duelli, M., Meier, S., Wagner, D., Zinner, T., Schmid, M., Hoffmann, M., Kiess, W.: Experimental Demonstration of Network Virtualization and Resource Flexibility in the COMCON Project. In: 8th International ICST Conference on Testbeds and Research Infrastructures for the Development of Networks and Communities, Thessaloniki (June 2012)
4. Engelke, U., Kusuma, M., Zepernick, H.-J., Caldera, M.: Reduced-reference metric design for objective perceptual quality assessment in wireless imaging. Signal Processing-Image Communication, 525–547 (2009)
5. Feldmann, A., Kind, M., Maennel, O., Schaffrath, G., Werle, C.: Network virtualization - an enabler for overcoming ossification. ERCIM News 77, 21–22 (2009), invited article; Special theme: Future Internet Technology,
   http://ercim-news.ercim.org/content/view/574/763/
6. Hoßfeld, T., Fiedler, M., Zinner, T.: The QoE Provisioning-Delivery-Hysteresis and Its Importance for Service Provisioning in the Future Internet. In: Proceedings of the 7th Conference on Next Generation Internet Networks (NGI), Kaiserslautern, Germany (June 2011)
7. Hoßfeld, T., Hock, D., Tutschku, K., Fiedler, M.: Testing the IQX Hypothesis for Exponential Interdependency between QoS and QoE for Voice Codecs iLBC and G.711. In: 18th ITC Specialist Seminar on QoE, Karlskrona, Sweden (May 2008)
8. ITU-R Rec. BT.500, Recommendation 500-10: Methodology for the subjective assessment of the quality of television pictures (2000)
9. ITU-T Recommendation, H.264 : Advanced video coding for generic audiovisual services (2010)
10. Iyengar, J., Amer, P., Stewart, R.: Concurrent multipath transfer using SCTP multihoming over independent end-to-end paths 14(5), 951–964 (2006)
11. Kofman, D., Lefévre, J.-P.: First update of the Euro-NF vision regarding the network of the future - D.SEA.10.1.1 (2009), http://www.euronf.org
12. Luby, M.: LT Codes. In: 43rd Annual IEEE Symposium on Foundations of Computer Science (2002)
13. Seshadrinathan, K., Soundararajan, R., Bovik, A.C., Cormack, L.K.: Study of subjective and objective quality assessment of video. IEEE Transactions on Image Processing 19(6), 1427–1441 (2010), http://dx.doi.org/10.1109/TIP.2010.2042111
14. Tutschku, K., Zinner, T., Nakao, A., Tran-Gia, P.: Network virtualization: Implementation steps towards the future internet. Electronic Communications of the EASST 17 (March 2009)
15. Winkler, S.: Video Quality and Beyond. In: Proc. European Signal Processing Conference (2007)
16. Wischik, D., Handley, M., Braun, M.B.: The resource pooling principle. ACM SIGCOMM Computer Communication Review 38(5), 47–52 (2008)
17. Yamagishi, K., Hayashi, T.: Parametric Packet-Layer Model for Monitoring Video Quality of IPTV Services. In: IEEE International Conference on Communications, ICC 2008, pp. 110–114 (2008)

18. Zinner, T., Abboud, O., Hohlfeld, O., Hoßfeld, T., Tran-Gia, P.: Towards QoE Management for Scalable Video Streaming. In: 21th ITC Specialist Seminar on Multimedia Applications - Traffic, Performance and QoE, Miyazaki, Jap (March 2010)
19. Zinner, T., Klein, D., Meier, S., Wagner, D., Hoffmann, M., Kiess, W., Singorzan, V., Schmid, M.: Dynamic Topology Adaptation enabled by Network Virtualization: A Use-Case for the Future Internet. In: 12th Wuerzburg Workshop on IP: ITG Workshop "Visions of Future Generation Networks (EuroView 2012) (July 2012)
20. Zinner, T., Liers, F., Hoßfeld, T., Rauscher, D., Reuther, B., Günther, D., Volkert, T., Fiedler, M.: Prospects for Realizing User-Centric Network Orchestration: FEC-protected SVC Streaming. In: 7 GI/ITG KuVS Fachgespräch 'Future Internet', München (January 2012)

Evaluating User-Centric Multihomed Flow Management for Mobile Devices in Simulated Heterogeneous Networks

Xi Li[1,*], Olivier Mehani[2], Ramón Agüero[3], Roksana Boreli[2,4],
Yasir Zaki[1], and Umar Toseef[1]

[1] University of Bremen, Bremen, Germany
{xili,yzaki,umr}@comnets.uni-bremen.de
[2] Nicta, Eveleigh, Sydney, NSW, Australia
{olivier.mehani,roksana.boreli}@nicta.com.au
[3] University of Cantabria, Santander, Spain
ramon@tlmat.unican.es
[4] University of New South Wales, Sydney, NSW, Australia

Abstract. We implemented approaches to solve the multihomed flow management problem using the OPNET simulator. We formulate a quality-aware decision method as a binary integer problem and use it (with the CPLEX solver) to drive the network selection and flow distribution in the simulated scenarios. We compare the behaviour of application flows with our approach and the most commonly implemented nowadays. This allows us to more accurately evaluate these approaches' potential when applied to real network scenarios, where adaptation loops in protocols and algorithms in the network stack may alter the expected performance. We show that, even uncalibrated, the quality-aware multihomed flow management allows to make better trade-offs between different user criteria and identify improvement directions.

1 Introduction

Accessing the Internet on the move is now the rule rather than the exception. On the one hand, new wireless network technologies provide higher capacities to cater for the increasing number of users and their needs. On the other hand, user equipments now support several of these technologies. Yet, no clear consensus exists on how to balance their use to provide "always best connected" devices [1], and the simplest method ("everything on Wi-Fi if available, or cellular otherwise") is widely implemented [2].

Most of the research work tends to focus on selecting the network(s) with the highest quality estimates. A subset of these approaches also considers using more than one interface at the same time (see Section 5), with various levels of granularity. Nonetheless, these estimated metrics are based on technical parameters of the communication. Various ITU recommendations [3], [4], [5] however

---

* This work was conducted while Xi Li was a visiting researcher at Nicta.

A. Timm-Giel et al. (Eds.): MONAMI 2012, LNICST 58, pp. 84–98, 2013.

showed that the quality a user perceives (quality of experience, QoE [6]), is in no way linearly dependent on such technical metrics.

In earlier work [7], it was proposed to pay closer attention to the metrics most relevant to the user, such as the QoE, the power consumption and the access price. The generic *multihomed flow management problem* (MFM) was defined, and several approaches were tested. Results showed that directly basing optimisation decisions on user-centric metrics improved the resulting perceived quality. However, the evaluation of the results was only based on objective models applied to QoS estimates; in essence, the ideal outcome of the decision mechanism.

Here, we therefore propose to lift this shortcoming by implementing the described approach in a network simulator, in order to evaluate the behaviour of application flows when distributed to the selected networks. We implemented the main framework in OPNET and linked it to the CPLEX solver in order to implement the decision methods, and more accurately evaluate their potential. We confirm the results from [7] and show that the quality-aware multihomed flow management allows to make better trade-offs between user-visible metrics. We also identify directions to further improve these results.

The remainder of this paper is organised as follows. In the next section, we remind the reader to the multihomed flow management problem, and present our binary integer programming (BIP) formulation of the user-centric solution. In Section 3, we present the relevant performance metrics, as well as the simulation scenarios. The results of the comparison to a standard technique are presented and discussed in Section 4. We present related work in Section 5, and finally conclude and describe future work in Section 6.

2   LP Formulation of the User-Centric Flow Management

The multihomed flow management problem is that of selecting the network association for each interface, distributing the flows over the active links and adjusting application parameters to the best matching set [7]. Its user-centric solution consists in maintaining a high application quality while keeping reasonable power consumption and access prices. It was expressed as a constrained optimisation problem in [7], but solving times proved to be prohibitive. We therefore reformulate it as a BIP, which were shown to be faster to solve (*e.g.*, [8]).

We want to distribute flows in set F over a set of possible links, formed by the association of a local interface i, from set I, to a remote network n, from set N. As the associations between interfaces and networks are limited to within the same technology, only a subset of $I \times N$ is actually valid. We address this limitation later. It is assumed that the capacity C_{in} and delay D_{in} of a link can be reliably obtained through the use of frameworks such as IEEE 802.21 [9], OConS [10], [11] (developed within the SAIL project [12]) or actively measured [13], [14], [15]. Additionally, the flows are assumed to have several parameter sets (*e.g.*, codecs) selectable from set C.

This creates $|F| \times |C| \times |I| \times |N|$ binary variables of the form

$$x_{fcin} = \begin{cases} 1 & \text{if flow } f \text{ with configuration } c \text{ is distributed on link } i\text{-}n \\ 0 & \text{otherwise} \end{cases} \quad (1)$$

to optimise a given objective. Our model is defined by the following constraints

$$\begin{cases} \forall f, c, i, n, & x_{fcin} \in \{0, 1\} & \text{(binary variables)} & (2a) \\ \forall f, & \sum_{c,i,n} x_{fcin} = 1 & \text{(one parameter set per flow)} & (2b) \\ \forall i, n, & \left(\sum_{f,c} x_{fcin} C_{fc} \right) \le C_{in} & \text{(capacity limitation).} & (2c) \end{cases}$$

It is necessary to be able to express the fact that a link is active. This is done through the use of an auxiliary variable,

$$a_{in} = \begin{cases} 1 & \text{if a link from } i \text{ to } n \text{ is active} \\ 0 & \text{otherwise} \end{cases} \quad (3)$$

with additional constraints

$$\begin{cases} \forall i, n, & a_{in} \in \{0, 1\} & \text{(binary variables)} & (4a) \\ \forall f, c, i, n & x_{fcin} \le a_{in} & (a_{in} = 1 \text{ if any } x_{fcin} = 1) & (4b) \\ \forall i, & \sum_{n} a_{in} \le 1 & \text{(one association per interface).} & (4c) \end{cases}$$

The goal for the user-centric flow management approach is to maximise the QoE of flows, while minimising the energy and monetary costs incurred. The general objective function is therefore

$$\max \sum_{f,c,i,n} \left(\alpha Q(f, c, C_{fc}, D_{in}) - (\beta E'_{in} + \gamma M'_{in}) C_{fc} \right) x_{fcin} -$$

$$\sum_{i,n} (\beta E_{in} + \gamma M_{in}) a_{in}, \quad (5)$$

where α, β and γ are scaling and priority weights, $Q(f, c, C, D, \dots)$ is the expected QoE as computed by objective models based on the offered QoS (as defined by ITU's E-Model [3], [4], [5], see [7] for more details), and E_{in} and M_{in} (resp. E'_{in} and M'_{in}) are the time-based and (resp. data-based) energy and monetary costs for link i-n. However, $Q(\cdot)$ is not a linear function of its arguments, and this objective cannot be used directly by the solver. To address this problem, we precompute a part of it, for each possible configuration, as utility value

$$u_{fcin} = \alpha Q(f, c, C_{fc}, D_{in}) - (\beta E'_{in} + \gamma M'_{in}) C_{fc}. \quad (6)$$

These precomputed utility values can then be used in the new linear optimisation objective,

$$\max \sum_{f,c,i,n} u_{fcin} x_{fcin} - \sum_{i,n} (\beta E_{in} + \gamma M_{in}) a_{in}. \tag{7}$$

The next section presents how this model and approach are implemented in the OPNET network simulator

3   Simulations

We implemented a basic mobility scenario with a UE moving between multiple wireless access points (WAP) under the coverage of a single LTE eNodeB using the OPNET discrete-event simulator.[1] The decision aspect is done through the use of a linear programming solver integrated within the control code of the mobility model.

3.1   OPNET Model

3GPP has specified an architecture that allows mobile users to roam between 3GPP and non-3GPP access technologies [16]. To provide users with seamless mobility, Proxy Mobile IPv6 (operator-based mobility [17]) and Dual-stack Mobile IPv6 (host-based mobility [18]) are proposed [16]. The work presented in this paper proposes an extension to the the integration of LTE and trusted non-3GPP access technology (*e.g.*, 802.11g), where the host-based mobility solution is considered. One of the issues that are not supported in the current 3GPP specification is the use of multihoming: a user can use either LTE or WLAN but not simultaneously. We therefore developed an extension which can provide users with multihoming capabilities. This is achieved by extending the implementation of MIPv6 to support multiple care-of addresses [19] and flow management functionalities [20], [21].

Fig. 1 shows an overview of the simulation network implemented in OPNET. The model is built as an extension of our previous work in LTE networks modelling [22, which include channel model details] with additional support for the integration of WLAN, extending the standard OPNET WLAN implementation to support link adaptation to user movements and changing channel conditions. Moreover, the standard OPNET MIPv6 implementation has been integrated after extending it to support multihoming and flow management. The final model includes all relevant entities that are necessary to carry out the multihoming scenario. Following [16], the home agent (HA) functions are located at the PDN gateway. The remote server in the figure acts as a correspondent node (CN). Users receive router advertisements from the eNodeB and the WLAN access points so that they can configure their care-of addresses. They then register with the HA through standard MIPv6 signalling. In this way all user traffic is tunnelled from the HA to the user, and vice-versa.

---

[1] http://www.opnet.com

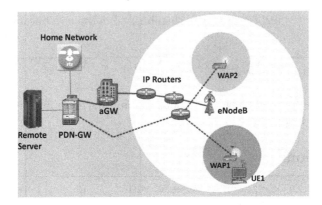

Fig. 1. OPNET simulation model. A User Equipment roams between two WAPs covered by a single LTE cell. Host-based mobility is supported within the home network through the use of MIPv6, with the MCoA extensions.

3.2   CPLEX Integration

CPLEX[2] provides a large set of APIs for various languages. We used the CPLEX Callable C Library for the integration with OPNET. After adding this library in the OPNET repository, the available CPLEX functions can be called directly from OPNET.In this work, we need to solve a BIP to decide the flow and network associations (see Section 2). We used CPLEX's MIP optimiser to compute the solutions to our MFM problem.

This allowed us to implement a practical online decision method in the user device. With this method, the proposed decision function can be called at any time, and the decision results obtained from the solver directly. They are then used to enforce the network selection and flow distribution in the simulated environment. Currently, a periodic triggering method calls the solver at regular intervals. The periodicity should be chosen properly; if too large, this may lead to performance degradation due to late adaptation, but too small a value will cause changes to happen too frequently, creating higher overheads for the network managements. Finding an optimised setting of this interval, or using a more dynamic triggering algorithm (*e.g.*, based on new arrivals or departures of flows), is left for future work.

To support correct decision-making, we rely on having proper estimates of all access network conditions such as their availability, the link capacity (C_{in}) and delays (D_{in}). The network capacity depends on the user's distance from the base stations and is thus estimated inside the mobility model.

The WLAN link capacity is estimated based on the selected PHY model, depending on the distance to the WAP. Similarly, we estimate the available capacity of the LTE network based on the measured average SINR and the

---

[2] http://www-01.ibm.com/software/integration/optimization/
   cplex-optimizer/

amount of available radio resources (*i.e.*, number of physical resource blocks). A more accurate estimation of per-user link capacity for multi-user scenarios, by considering resource scheduling at the WAPs and eNodeBs, is left for future work. Given the link capacity per network, we are able to estimate the probable per-flow capacities (C_{fc}), in order to derive potential utility values. For elastic traffic (*e.g.*, TCP-based traffic), it is assumed that each flow will get an equal share. We therefore calculate the flow capacities by dividing the link capacity C_{in} by the total number of active elastic flows of the user. However, for real time traffic, the flow capacity C_{fc} depends on the application codec rate. The link delays are estimated based on the measured RTTs. With the estimated flow capacity, link capacities and delays, the per-flow QoE can be estimated following ITU's objective models. Alongside the data-based energy and monetary costs, this allows to evaluate the utilities following (6). These pre-computed utilities and resultant objective function (7) are then expressed in a form suitable for CPLEX's MIP solver.

3.3   Performance Metrics

Several metrics are relevant to our study. First, we implemented the ITU QoE objective models, following our description in [7], to be computed based on actual network conditions experienced by the flows, such as flow throughput or packet delay, reported from the simulator. The two other important user metrics are the power consumption, and the monetary price.

We use simple models for these costs, where some comes from having an interface up and connected to a network, and some comes from transferring data over the thus created link. For each run, we can therefore determine how much battery has been used, and how much the network usage has cost. Table 1 shows the base values we have chosen for this paper, based on power data from [23], and arbitrary estimates for access costs (\$5 for 500 MB is reasonably common). All are expressed per time unit as the solver is called at a periodic interval. It is however important to note that these parameters are not hardcoded, and that other values are possible.

Delays are an important factor in the quality perception, and is indeed already taken into account for voice [3] and web traffic [4]. Yet, it is interesting to consider it separately as it also gives an indication of the load along the end-to-end path, with higher load creating fuller buffers and queues, and larger packet delays. As

Table 1. Battery and monetary costs used in the scenarios

Technology	Power		Price	
	E [%/s]	E' [(%/B)/s]	M [\$/s]	M' [(\$/B)/s]
Cellular	6.5×10^{-3}	2.3×10^{-13}	0	1×10^{-8}
WLAN	3.6×10^{-3}	9.9×10^{-14}	0	0

it also gives an indication of the load along the end-to-end path, it is however interesting to consider it separately too.

3.4 Comparison Approach

In this paper, we are mostly interested in presenting and validating our simulation model to confirm its proper behaviour. Rather than comparing the proposed approach to many techniques, we selected the most common one, where a mobile device senses the networks around it, and favours any WLAN and uses the cellular link as a last resort [2], which we call 3GPP-HO [24]. In essence, this means that the mobile device will always be connected to the LTE network, but switch to the WLAN link shortly after it becomes available, and keeps using it until it becomes virtually unreachable.

3.5 Simulation Scenarios

We chose to study two different scenarios to evaluate our proposed quality-aware approach for different application types and compare it to the 3GPP-HO approach.

Real-time video four different codec rates (400 kbps, 600 kbps, 800 kbps and 1000 kbps); fixed frame rate of 30 fps;
Elastic Web traffic 1 MB web objects; inter-arrival time of 100 s.

In both scenarios, the user stays within the coverage of a single LTE eNodeB as shown in Fig. 1. However, in the first scenario the user is moving from WAP1 to WAP2, experience vertical handovers between cellular network and WLAN. In the second scenario, the user is only moving with WAP1 and can always connect to either or both WLAN and LTE networks.

For the quality-aware multihomed flow management approach, the time interval of triggering the decision function is set to 1 s. To calculate the utility and objective function, the scaling and priority weights for the QoE, energy and cost are all set to 1 (calibrating these values is left for future work). The battery and monetary costs per network are defined in Table 1.

4 Results and Discussion

This section presents the results for both the real-time and elastic scenarios, then some timing information about the solver is given.

4.1 Real-Time Video Traffic

We recall that our proposed quality-aware multihomed flow management (QA-MFM) adjusts the bitrate of the video flows to match the available capacities. Fig. 2 compares our approach to the 3GPP-HO approach with respect to the selected metrics. In essence, the QA-MFM achieves a lower delay, slightly lower

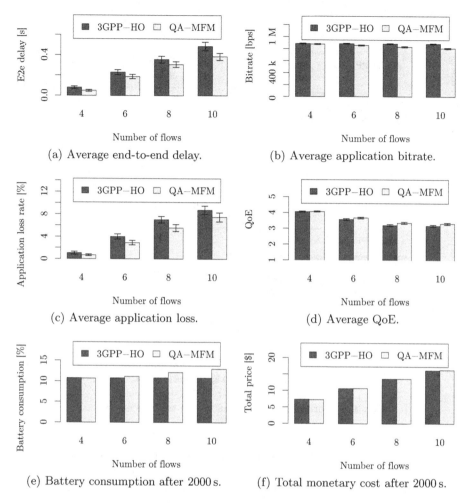

Fig. 2. Metrics for the real-time video scenario for a varying number of flows. Error bars are placed at $1.96SE$ as an estimate of the 95% CI for the mean.

bitrate, lower application loss-rate and slightly better QoE at the cost of a higher battery consumption and very slightly higher cost for one-way real-time video traffic.

The results for the QoE, battery consumption and price are coherent with the predictions of [7]. However, the difference in quality of experience (Fig. 2d) is much smaller than expected. We hypothesise it is due to the packetisation of application data units tending to fragment one video frame into several UDP packets. Losing only one of many packets therefore results in the loss of the entire video frame; for a packet loss rate of p, this means that the application-layer loss

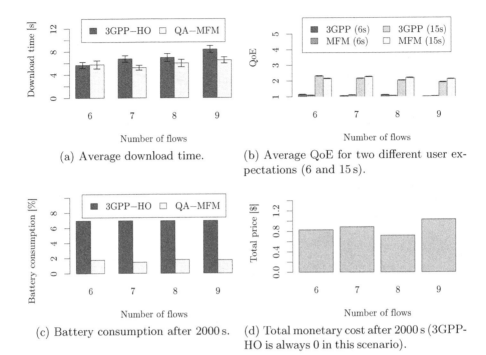

(a) Average download time.

(b) Average QoE for two different user expectations (6 and 15 s).

(c) Battery consumption after 2000 s.

(d) Total monetary cost after 2000 s (3GPP-HO is always 0 in this scenario).

Fig. 3. Performance for the elastic web traffic scenarios

rate would be $(1 - p)^n$, where n is the number of UDP packets a video frame is fragmented in. In addition, we did not take header overhead into account. This has led to overestimating the available capacity, even with the QA-MFM approach. This explains the application losses shown in Fig. 2c.

An interesting effect of our proposed approach is that, reducing the bitrate of the video flows to match the networks' capacities, it creates less congestion at the intermediate routers, which in turns allows to reduce the packet delay, as shown in Fig. 2a. We believe that addressing the capacity estimation problems mentioned previously would also allow to further reduce these delays.

4.2   Elastic Web Traffic

The comparison results for the web traffic scenario are shown in Fig. 3. At a higher price, the QA-MFM delivers shorter download times and lower battery usage. Even though our approach tends to achieve a higher quality than the 3GPP-HO, the QoE is lower than expected. We believe it could be further improved with a proper calibration of the optimisation weights, which we keep as future work.

We recall from Section 3.5 that, in this scenario, the UE remains within range of both the LTE network, and one wireless access point. It is therefore expected that, in order to improve the performance, the QA-MFM would use the LTE network in addition to the WLAN network that the 3GPP-HO would always choose. This therefore explains that our approach costs some money, also using the cellular network in this case (Fig. 3d). Another key advantage of the QA-MFM approach is to save the battery by switching off the interfaces in case there is no data transfer required by the user, given the ON-OFF behaviour of the web traffic, while the interfaces were always on with the 3GPP-HO approach, the QA-MFM simply deactivated them. The QA-MFM approach therefore consumed much less battery than the 3GPP-HO (Fig. 3c).

While the download time is shortened by the quality-aware approach (Fig. 3a), the QoE is not very much improved (almost at its worst in the 6 s cases). Fig. 3b shows two estimates of this QoE, depending on the expectation of the user with respect to the session duration. In this scenario, we only transferred 1 MB objects, for which the expectations of 6 and 15 s may have been a bit too great. Internally, the decision mechanism only used a 6 s-based estimation, regardless of the transfer size. This highlights a problem in calculating the QoE for elastic traffic based on [4] for the QA-MFM approach, as it becomes necessary to estimate what the expectations of the user would be in order to make the proper decision. It is the subject of future work to address this question.

4.3   Solving Time

The solving time is the time needed by the CPLEX LP solver for one iteration of calculation of the decisions on network selections, flow distributions and choosing proper application parameter per application flow. The problem size is determined by the number of constraints and variables, which increases with the number of active flows, the number of networks, and configurable flow parameters. As the QA-MFM problem is to be solved per user, the time to solve the BIP does not dependent on the number of users in the network. The average solving time for all our presented scenarios are shown in figure 4. It exhibits a sub-linear trend with an increasing number of constraints and variables. For our largest scenario (9 web flows), the mean solving time lies within $(186, 296)$ ms with 95% confidence.

As mentioned in Section 3.5, we used a periodic trigger to call the linear solver every second. With a grand maximum of 0.39 s, this means that this optimisation-based technique is well-suited and feasible for making real-time decisions in real systems.[3]

---

[3] Simulations for this work were run on 2.67 GHz Xeon X5550 machines. However, with the increasing CPU power of mobile devices, it seems reasonable that our approach can scale.

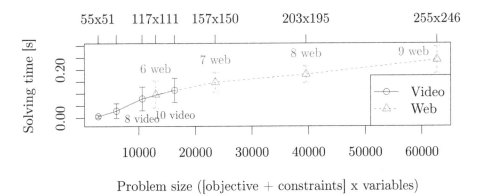

Fig. 4. Average solving time depending on the problem size (10 random samples). Error bars show a 95% CI for the mean. Labels indicate the scenario.

5   Related Work

This section reviews work related to metrics used for network selection as well as various decision techniques. A more detailed version of this review can be found in [25, chap. 2, sec. 2.3].

5.1   Criteria for Network Selection

A large range of criteria has been proposed to discriminate access links and networks in order to select the best ones to connect to. The simplest mechanisms are based on measuring the quality of the radio signal (*e.g.*, signal-to-noise ratio or received signal strength) and comparing it to a threshold [26]. The same thresholding approach can be applied to more precise metrics from the access link such as the delay or data rate [27], [28], [29], [30].

More relevant than the link layer properties for communication facilitated by transport protocols like TCP, end-to-end parameters such as network path capacities or RTTs are important to support feature-rich applications [27], [28], [30], [31], [32], [33], [34], [35], [36], [37]; some proposals also specifically take the application requirements into account in this phase [29], [38]. Additionally, some networks only provide limited connectivity to the rest of the infrastructure or require specific credentials to grant access; the reachability of the Internet [33] has also been proposed as a criteria in this case.

As we argue in this paper, battery life is important in a mobile context, and trade-offs have been considered to preserve it [23], [34], [35], [36]. Similarly, multiple approaches take monetary considerations into account [29], [31], [32], [35], [36], [39]. The currently observed application layer performance, as observed by already connected nodes, can also be used as an indication of the "health" of a network link [39]. However, QoE is still very rarely used for such tasks.

5.2   Flow Distribution

The distribution of application flows over multiple uplinks active at the same time could be seen as a superset of the network selection schemes just presented. However, the flow scheduling problem has to accommodate additional constraints such as that only the networks to which the device is associated can be used, some of which are mutually exclusive. Two main classes of solutions can be distinguished.

The first group applies traffic classification and load balancing approaches of conventional wired technologies after network uplinks have been selected and established. Simple policies, based on flows' destinations or port, to decide which network is the most appropriate are often seen [40]. However, more complex techniques proposed distribute new flows with more elaborate heuristics (*e.g.*, random or load balancing) [30], [41].

Approaches in the second class take a more holistic approach by performing network selection and flow distribution at the same time. A number of solutions rely on knowledge of the applications' requirements to select the network which most closely matches them [31], [35]. These approaches however come at the cost of a larger solution space to search. To address this issue, the problem was modelled as a Markov chain [42] to leverage decision process techniques of that field. Binary integer programming techniques have also been proposed [36].

5.3   Multi-criteria Selection Techniques

To enable a finer selection of an access network, it may also be argued that considering a single criterion is not sufficient. Therefore, a number of more recent proposals use some sort of multi-objective optimisation technique where the various criteria can be composed and compared.

Common approaches use utility functions in order to create a weighted compound variable for each network, to be compared to a threshold or that of other networks [38], [43]. The analytic hierarchy process (AHP) [44], a more formal way of ranking choices according to multiple criteria, is also proposed to find the highest ranked options [27], [45].

A number of proposals introduce sub-optimal but computationally efficient algorithms [32], [34]. Linear programming techniques have been proposed to find optimal solutions for specific formulations of the problems [8], [36].

Finally, weights or scaling factors are an important parameter in multi-objective optimisations, as the input variables need be mapped to comparable ranges. Genetic algorithms [29] or the grey relational analysis [27], [46] can be used to derive these weights. This preprocessing is also often done using fuzzy logic approaches [28], [29], [45].

6   Conclusion and Future Work

In this paper, we presented our integration of a linear programming solver with a discrete-event network simulator. This allows us to drive the multihomed flow management by optimising user-level metrics such as the quality of experience, battery life or access price. We also presented comparison results, using this system, that show that the QA-MFM performs better than the legacy techniques of only choosing one best network, however slightly.

It is important to note that the version of the QA-MFM we evaluated here was not calibrated. It is the subject of future work, enabled by the system presented in this paper, to investigate questions about the QA-MFM approach such as properly setting the weights of the objective function—or exploring other forms for this function altogether—the implementation of more cross-layer signals to inform the transport protocols to the decision, or other optimisation triggering approaches, amongst others. This model will also enable simulations in more realistic scenarios and, more specifically, with a higher number of users, to evaluate the load this approach creates on the visited networks.

Acknowledgements. This research work has been supported by funding from NICTA. research initiatives through Australian Research Council (ARC). This work is being carried out in collaboration with the SAIL FP7 EU Project under Grant Agreement Number 257448.

References

[1] Gustafsson, E., Jonsson, A.: Always Best Connected. IEEE Wireless Communications 10(1) (2003)

[2] Wasserman, M., Seite, P.: Current Practices for Multiple-Interface Hosts, RFC 6419 (2011)

[3] ITU-T: The E-Model, a Computational Model for Use in Transmission Planning. Recommendation G.107 (2005)

[4] ITU-T: Estimating End-to-End Performance in IP Networks for Data Applications. Recommendation G.1030 (2006)

[5] ITU-T: Opinion Model for Video-Telephony Applications. Recommendation G.1070 (2007)

[6] Kilkki, K.: Quality of Experience in Communications Ecosystem. Journal of Universal Computer Science 14(5) (2008)

[7] Mehani, O., Boreli, R., Maher, M., Ernst, T.: User- and Application- Centric Multihomed Flow Management. In: LCN 2011 (2011)

[8] Choque, J., Agüero, R., Hortigüela, E.-M., Muñoz, L.: Optimum Selection of Access Networks within Heterogeneous Wireless Environments Based on Linear Programming Techniques. In: Pentikousis, K., Agüero, R., García-Arranz, M., Papavassiliou, S. (eds.) MONAMI 2010. LNICST, vol. 68, pp. 135–149. Springer, Heidelberg (2011)

[9] Piri, E., Pentikousis, K.: IEEE 802.21. The Internet Protocol Journal 12.2 (2009)

[10] Agüero, R., Caeiro, L., Correia, L.M., Ferreira, L.S., García-Arranz, M., Suciu, L., Timm-Giel, A.: OConS: Towards Open Connectivity Services in the Future Internet. In: Pentikousis, K., Aguiar, R., Sargento, S., Agüero, R. (eds.) MONAMI 2011. LNICST, vol. 97, pp. 90–104. Springer, Heidelberg (2012)

[11] Diez, L., Mehani, O., Suciu, L., Agüero, R.: Design and Implementation of the Open Connectivity Services Framework. In: Timm-Giel, A., Strassner, J., Agüero, R., Sargento, S., Pentikousis, K. (eds.) MONAMI 2012. LNICST, vol. 58, pp. 1–12. Springer, Heidelberg (2013)

[12] SAIL project. Architectural Concepts of Connectivity Services. Deliverable FP7-ICT-2009-5-257448-SAIL/D-4.1(D-C.1) (2011)

[13] Shalunov, S., et al.: A One-way Active Measurement Protocol (OWAMP). Tech. rep. 4656 (2006)

[14] Hedayat, K., et al.: A Two-Way Active Measurement Protocol (TWAMP), RFC 5357 (2008)

[15] Constantine, B., Forget, G., Geib, R., Schrage, R.: Framework for TCP Throughput Testing, RFC 6349 (2011)

[16] Architecture Enhancements for Non-3GPP Accesses. TS 23.402 (2012)

[17] 3GPP: Proxy Mobile IPv6 (PMIPv6) Based Mobility and Tunnelling Protocols; Stage 3. TS 29.275 (2010)

[18] Johnson, D., Perkins, C.E., Arkko, J.: Mobility Support in IPv6, RFC 3775 (2004)

[19] Wakikawa, R., et al.: Multiple Care-of Addresses Registration, RFC 5648 (2009)

[20] Tsirtsis, G., Giaretta, G., Soliman, H., Montavont, N.: Traffic Selectors for Flow Bindings, RFC 6088 (2011)

[21] Tsirtsis, G., et al.: Flow Bindings in Mobile IPv6 and Network Mobility (NEMO) Basic Support, RFC 6089 (2011)

[22] Zaki, Y., Weerawardane, T., Görg, C., Timm-Giel, A.: Long Term Evolution (LTE) Model Development Within OPNET Simulation Environment. In: OPNETWORK 2011 (2011)

[23] Petander, H.: Energy-aware Network Selection Using Trafic Estimation. In: MIC-NET 2009 (2009)

[24] Toseef, U., Zaki, Y., Timm-Giel, A., Görg, C.: Uplink QOS Aware Multi-homing in Integrated 3GPP and non-3GPP Future Networks. In: Timm-Giel, A., Strassner, J., Agüero, R., Sargento, S., Pentikousis, K. (eds.) MONAMI 2012. LNICST, vol. 58, pp. 114–127. Springer, Heidelberg (2013)

[25] Mehani, O.: Contributions to Mechanisms for Adaptive Use of Mobile Network Resources. PhD thesis (2011)

[26] Mohanty, S., Akyildiz, I.F.: A Cross-Layer (Layer 2 + 3) Handover Management Protocol for Next-Generation Wireless Systems. IEEE Transactions on Mobile Computing 5(10) (2006)

[27] Song, Q., Jamalipour, A.: Network Selection in an Integrated Wireless LAN and UMTS Environment Using Mathematical Modeling and Computing Techniques. IEEE Wireless Communications 12(3) (2005)

[28] Wilson, A.L., Lenaghan, A., Malyan, R.: Optimising Wireless Access Network Selection to Maintain QoS in Heterogeneous Wireless Environments. In: WPMC 2005 (2005)

[29] Alkhawlani, M., Ayesh, A.: Access Network Selection Based on Fuzzy Logic and Genetic Algorithms. In: Advances in Articial Intelligence 2008 (2008)

[30] Kandula, S., Lin, K.C., Badirkhanli, T., Katabi, D.: FatVAP: Aggregating AP Backhaul Capacity to Maximize Throughput. In: NSDI 2008 (2008)

[31] Gazis, V., Alonistioti, N., Merakos, L.: Toward a Generic "Always Best Connected" Capability in Integrated WLAN/UMTS Cellular Mobile Networks (and Beyond). IEEE Wireless Communications 12(3) (2005)

[32] Adamopoulou, E., Demestichas, K., Koutsorodi, A., Theologou, M.: Intelligent Access Network Selection in Heterogeneous Networks - Simulation Results. In: ISWCS 2005 (2005)

[33] Nicholson, A.J., et al.: Improved Access Point Selection. In: MobiSys 2006 (2006)

[34] Xing, B., Venkatasubramanian, N.: Multi-constraint Dynamic Access Selection in Always Best Connected Networks. In: MobiQuitous 2005 (2005)

[35] Bonnin, J.-M.: La diversité technologique au service des terminaux et routeurs multiconnectés. Mémoire d'habilitation à diriger des recherches (2008)

[36] Zafeiris, V.E., Giakoumakis, E.A.: Mobile Agents for Flow Scheduling Support in Multihomed Mobile Hosts. In: IWCMC 2008 (2008)

[37] Pang, J., et al.: Wi-Fi reports: Improving Wireless Network Selection with Collaboration. In: MobiSys 2009 (2009)

[38] Liu, X., Li, V.O.K., Zhang, P.: Joint Radio Resource Management through Vertical Hando s in 4G Networks. In: GlobeCom 2006 (2006)

[39] Piamrat, K., Viho, C., Ksentini, A., Bonnin, J.-M.: QoE-aware Network Selection in Wireless Heterogeneous Networks. Tech. rep. RR-7282 (2010)

[40] Tsukada, M., Mehani, O., Ernst, T.: Simultaneous Usage of NEMO and MANET for Vehicular Communication. In: TridentCom 2008 (2008)

[41] Nicholson, A.J., Wolchok, S., Noble, B.D.: Juggler: Virtual Networks for Fun and Profit. IEEE Transactions on Mobile Computing 9(1) (2010)

[42] Singh, J., Alpcan, T., Agrawal, P., Sharma, V.: A Markov Decision Process Based Flow Assignment Framework for Heterogeneous Network Access. Wireless Networks 16(2) (2010)

[43] Aust, S., Görg, C., Pampu, C.: Policy Based Mobile IPv6 Handover Decision (POLIMAND). Internet-Draft draft-iponair-dna-polimand-02.txt (2005)

[44] Saaty, T.L.: Fundamentals of Decision Making and Priority Theory with the Analytic Hierarchy Process. vol. 6 (2000)

[45] Chan, P.M.L., et al.: Mobility Management Incorporating Fuzzy Logic for Heterogeneous a IP Environment. IEEE Communications Magazine 39(12) (2001)

[46] Liu, S., et al.: Introduction to Grey Systems Theory. In: Grey Systems—Theory and Applications, ch.1, vol. 68 (2011)

On the Equilibrium of Pricing Assignment for Heterogeneous Wireless Access Networks

Carmen López[1], Johnny Choque[1], Ramón Agüero[1],
Joan Serrat[2], and Luis Muñoz[1]

[1] Universidad de Cantabria, Santander, Spain
[2] Universidad Politécnica de Catalunya, Barcelona, Spain
{clopez,jchoque,ramon,luis}@tlmat.unican.es, serrat@tsc.upc.edu

Abstract. Next generation networks and service providers are rapidly evolving in order to satisfy the demands of an increasing number of users. Nowadays, one of the most relevant research lines in the Heterogeneous Wireless Access Networks realm is the use of procedures and mechanisms so as to provide intelligence to the network, with the main goal of optimizing its performance. Furthermore, mobile communication users are becoming more demanding, and thus it becomes essential for the providers to be able to offer a competitive value for money. This paper pursues the objective of obtaining, from an analytical perspective, the optimum price assignment strategy according to the characteristics of a particular scenario, analyzing the improvement attained with such optimum pricing policy as compared to a more traditional one. Game theory techniques, which are gathering the interest within the communications scientific community, are used for the analysis.

Keywords: pricing, game theory, heterogeneous networks.

1 Introduction

In the latest years we have seen a significant evolution of the wireless communication realm, embracing both the subjacent technologies as well as their operation and management. In addition, this has come together with an increase of the user's degree of responsibility when selecting a network to connect to.

During the early days of telephony, the market was a monopoly. However, this situation has remarkably evolved and new operators have appeared, turning the market into a very competitive environment. In such scenario, operators must compete amongst them in different aspects, such as the services which are offered to the users, the corresponding Quality of Service (QoS) and/or prices. It goes without saying that, from the users' perspective, one of the most significant elements is the price to be paid. At the time of writing, the most common pricing policy is the flat-rate, where the user pays a monthly fee in exchange of various services. However, the emergence of new operators has led to a situation where churning (i.e. change between operators) needs to be considered. One potential solution to this problem is to better accomodate the pricing models, so that

A. Timm-Giel et al. (Eds.): MONAMI 2012, LNICST 58, pp. 99–113, 2013.

they are more suitable to the new scenarios. In this sense, it is now believed that modulating the offered price depending on the particular context might be sensible; it is worth saying that with context we refer to a relatively large number of aspects, such as the number of operators sharing the same coverage area, their capacity, number of users demanding connectivity, etc. Another assumption is that the end-user would select the cheapest alternative[1]. The main goal is to increase operators' benefit while not damaging (or even improving) users' satisfaction.

Besides, one tool which has recently gained a lot of relevance in the wireless communication research area is game theory. It is mainly used to analyze the behavior of different techniques, mechanisms or procedures, when various entities have conflicting interests and it usually has the goal of obtaining the *best-they-can-do*. In this work we propose analyzing (by means of game theory) various price assignment policies to be used by wireless Access Elements (AEs). We will obtain the potential strategies which can be established by each of the AEs, deriving the benefits associated to each of them. From those, we will propose a non-cooperative game, which will be solved so as to obtain the Nash Equilibrium Point. Finally, and to demonstrate the benefits of using this *optimal* strategy, we will compare the corresponding performances (in terms of the operators' benefit) with those which result when the AEs use a naive policy, establishing a fixed price.

There are some works which have previously addressed (*partially*) the combination of pricing, wireless heterogeneous networks and game theory. In [5] Niyato and Hossain depict various pricing-based situations over networks where only one wireless technology is available. In addition, they propose two models for price competition in a heterogeneous scenario, formulating two non-cooperative games: a *simultaneous-play*, whose solution is the Nash Equilibrium Point, and a *leader-follower game*, which is solved with the Stackelberg equilibrium. The same authors consider, in [6], the case where providers cooperate, posing a simultaneous game and introducing a scheme for revenue sharing between the service providers, based on a N-person coalition game.

Another approach to tackle the pricing problem is to analyze the situations from the point of view of the players involved in the game. Using that approach some works consider both operators and users, while others only focus on the operators. Illustrative examples of the first group are [7] and [8]. The first one mainly proposes a theoretical non cooperative game to investigate the conflict between wireless service providers and users for varying QoS requirements. On the other hand, the authors of [8] develop a framework to analyze service providers' strategies to attract users, by offering competitive prices. As a combination of these two approaches, [2] presents both non-cooperative and cooperative games, to tackle optimal pricing and network selection, respectively.

---

[1] This is actually a simplification and we could add as well more parameters into the decision process; however, by limiting this study to price, we will be able to focus on the impact that these new pricing policies might have on system performance.

Finally, it is also worth mentioning that there exist other works addressing pricing policies, but without game theory. Amongst these, we could highlight [1], where the authors analyze (*in general*) service management policies, including pricing, which are used by the operators to maximize their benefit; in addition, they also analyze various access selection procedures, emphasizing the role of the price to pay for a connection.

In this context, the most relevant novel contributions of this work can be summarized as follows.

- Analysis of price strategies where the operators can only establish a discrete *and finite* set of fees.
- Deploy heterogeneous network deployments, comprising access elements with different capacities and coverages.
- Use of discrete load units, bounding the capacity of the access elements, which can not accept more connections than their available capacity.
- An extensive performance analysis, comprising different scenarios and multiple instances of them.

The paper is structured as follows. Section 2 presents a theoretical analysis, which aims at modeling the dynamic pricing situation and settles the rationale for the rest of the paper. The network model and the game which is posed are depicted in Section 3, while Section 4 describes how the game was solved. The achieved results are discussed in Section 5, which identifies the benefits brought about by the optimum strategies. Finally, Section 6 concludes the paper, advocating some items which are left for future work.

2   Analysis of Dynamic Pricing Schemes

In this work we consider a network scenario over a squared area where a set of N AEs, characterized by their capacity and coverage, are deployed. In this environment, each AE wants to maximize its benefit; this is to say, serve as many users as possible. In order to achieve this goal, the AEs aim to motivate/encourage the users to connect to it, even if they have more alternatives.

From the point of view of the users, the motivation to select one of the options over the others is the corresponding price[2]. In this sense, users will select the cheapest alternative, from the available ones. Note that we further assume that any available connection alternative (provided it has enough capacity) would fulfil the requested QoS level.

Starting from the previous assumptions, and using a simple scenario, this section aims at identifying the strategy which each of the operators shall use, provided that they are aware of the *rational* behavior of the users, which only depends on the price offered by the AEs. We will study two different pricing policies, namely legacy/conventional and novel/dynamic. In the former scheme,

---

[2] Throughout this work we will restrict to situations in which users base their decisions only on price.

AEs do not change the offered fee, while in the dynamic policy, AEs are able to adapt their fees according to the particular context, entailing them to implement various strategies to attract more users. We will assume two particular scenarios, whose results could be extended to more complex environments: one in which there is one traditional AE competing with a novel one and another one in which two AEs are able to modify their fees.

2.1   Dynamic vs. Traditional Pricing Policies

First of all, lets assume that the traditional operator establishes a generic and fix price P_t, while the non-conventional operator is able to settle any price within a particular set. We can thus define a vector $P = \{p_1, p_2, \ldots p_{t-1}, p_t, \ldots p_m\}$, sorted in ascending order, where p_t equals the fee fixed by the traditional operator and p_m is the maximum price allowed by the market. We also suppose that these prices are per user and connection (this is, they are average prices per service).

The analysis is carried out over the scenario shown in Figure 1, comprising two AEs, each belonging to any of the two aforementioned operators, with an overlap area where they try to attract as many users as they can afford. As can be seen, there exist three different areas: A (only covered by the non conventional operator), B (covered by the two AE) and C (in which the only access alternative is the traditional operator); we define u_A, u_B and u_C as the number of users within each of these areas, respectively. Under these circumstances, the users who are within the non-overlap areas can be seen as *preferred* users for the corresponding operator (the one which covers such area). This assumption is sensible, since they would surely select such operator (being the only access alternative).

In this sense, once u_A and u_C have already connected to the corresponding AEs, the two operators can offer the rest of their resources, C_t and C_{nc} for the traditional and non-conventional operators, respectively, to those users within

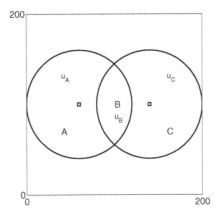

Fig. 1. Scenario used for the analysis

the overlap area. Three different situations can be identified, depending on the available resources for each of the AEs, as depicted below.

1. $C_t = C_{nc}$

   We will focus on the benefit obtained by the non-conventional operator, represented in terms of the number of users within area B (u_B). In this case, as can be seen in Figure 2(a), we can further distinguish two possibilities:
   - The non-conventional operator assigns a smaller price than the traditional one (in this analysis we will assume that it sets the maximum fee fulfilling such requirement, i.e. p_{t-1}. As can be seen in Figure 2(a), the users will therefore select the non conventional operator and therefore the benefit equals ($u_B \cdot p_{t-1}$). Furthermore, the maximum achieved benefit will be bounded by the AE's capacity, ($C_{nc} \cdot p_{t-1}$). In this sense, if the number of users is greater than the non conventional operator resources, some of them would select the traditional alternative.
   - The non-conventional operator establishes a price higher than p_t, (in this case, it fixes the maximum one, i.e. p_m). Since it provides a cheaper alternative, users would select the traditional operator, but when its available resources are fewer than the number of users, the rest of users would choose the non conventional operator.

   The upper line in Figure 2(a) represents the maximum benefit that the non-conventional operator can obtain for each value of u_B. It is worth highlighting u_x, which determines the decision threshold (in the number of users) for deciding upon the fee to establish. This value is the point on which the two aforementioned benefits are the same, an can be calculated as follows:

   $$(u_x - C_t) \cdot p_m = C_{nc} \cdot p_{t-1} \to u_x = \frac{p_{t-1}}{p_m} \cdot C_{nc} + C_t \qquad (1)$$

   Hence, the intervals and the optimum prices to be used are:

   $$u_B < u_x \Rightarrow P = p_{t-1} \qquad (2)$$

   $$u_B > u_x \Rightarrow P = p_m \qquad (3)$$

2. $C_t < C_{nc}$

   As happened before, we can also distinguish two cases, depending on the point where the benefit functions of the non-conventional operator get the same value.
   - If ($u_x > C_{nc}$). The analysis is depicted in Figure 2(b) (and is similar to the one described for the former case) and the intersection point is calculated as follows.

   $$(u_x - C_t) \cdot p_m = C_{nc} \cdot p_{t-1} \Rightarrow u_x = \frac{p_{t-1}}{p_m} \cdot C_{nc} + C_t \qquad (4)$$

   - If ($u_x < C_{nc}$). This case is also shown in Figure 2(c), and the corresponding intersection point can be derived as follows.

   $$(u_x - C_t) \cdot p_m = u_x \cdot p_{t-1} \Rightarrow u_x = \frac{C_t \cdot p_m}{p_m - p_{t-1}} \qquad (5)$$

3. $C_t > C_{nc}$

Following a similar analysis as before we can obtain the benefit shown in Figure 2(d), and the point in which the non-conventional operator shall shift its strategy (u_x) is calculated as follows.

$$(u_x - C_t) \cdot p_m = C_{nc} \cdot p_{t-1} \Rightarrow u_x = \frac{p_{t-1}}{p_m} \cdot C_{nc} + C_t \tag{6}$$

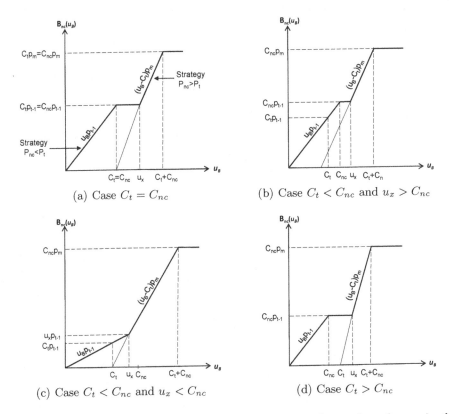

(a) Case $C_t = C_{nc}$

(b) Case $C_t < C_{nc}$ and $u_x > C_{nc}$

(c) Case $C_t < C_{nc}$ and $u_x < C_{nc}$

(d) Case $C_t > C_{nc}$

Fig. 2. Benefit of the non conventional operator against the number of users in the overlap area for the different cases

2.2   Two Dynamic Pricing Strategies

In this situation, both operators use dynamic pricing, and we also assume that none of them knows, *a priori*, the price which the other one assigns. For the analysis, we will study the behavior of the operators for all the potential combinations of prices, so as to select the one which leads the highest benefit. The scenario will be the same as the previous one, although we will have additional assumptions so as to limit the complexity of the analysis.

- The two AEs have the same capacity.
- We will use three illustrative use cases, depending on the percentage of users which are within the overall area; in particular we will assume that these are 80%, 50% and 20% of the overall number of users.

For each of the three aforementioned situations we have obtained the benefit for each of the two AEs as we increase the overall number of users studying two complementary situations, which are explained below.

- The benefit which is achieved when the two AEs use dynamic pricing, but we prioritize AE_1, forcing AE_2 to establish the fee which maximizes AE_1 benefit (Figure 3(a)).
- For comparison purposes we will also assume that AE_2 uses a fixed fee, while AE_1 is able to modulate its price, as was discussed in the analysis presented before (Figure 3(b)).

From the results presented in Figure 3(a) some interesting conclusions can be derived. First of all, if the overlap area is small, we can see that the benefits of the two AEs are almost alike. The reason is that becomes more sensible for both operators to establish the average price and share the users evenly. If any of the two operators assigns the maximum price, a lower benefit would be assessed, since users would select the cheapest operator. If the AEs establish the cheapest fee, this would encourage the users within the overlap area, but globally it would lead to a lower benefit from those areas where users can only access one AE. Besides, when the overlap areas is bigger, AE_1 obtains a higher benefit. Furthermore, we can also see that the benefits of both operators get equal only when the number of users is large enough so as to allow them establishing the highest fee and get their capacity fully occupied.

On the other hand, Figure 3(b) shows the benefits which were obtained when one of the operators uses a static fee. Again, if the percentage of users within the overlap areas is small, the benefits are almost the same. Besides, when the size of

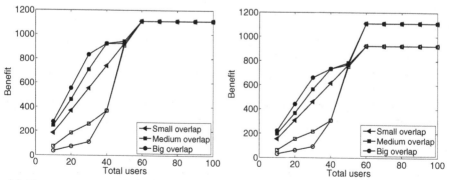

(a) Two operators with dynamic pricing   (b) One operator with dynamic pricing

Fig. 3. Overall benefit for AE_1 and AE_2. *Solid markers represent the benefit obtained by the AE_1, while the empty ones are for AE_2.*

the overlap area gets higher, we can see that the operator assigning the optimum strategy gets higher benefits. In this case, since the traditional operator does not change the established fee, it never uses the highest price and, thus, its benefit would not equal the one obtained by the dynamic operator, as it happened in the previous case.

To conclude, it can be said that the dynamic pricing leads to a higher benefit. As can be seen, a thorough analysis of all the situations might be too complex to achieve (especially if we increase the number of overlap areas, AEs, etc); in order to solve these situations we will use *game theory* techniques, as explained in the following sections.

3   Network Model and Non Cooperative Game

In this section we bring about a more realistic approach for assessing the benefits of using dynamic pricing strategies. We consider a square area in which there exist N access elements, which are characterized by their coverage and capacity, $AE = \{1, 2, \ldots, N\}$. Their position within the scenario under analysis will be done according to two different models: random and deterministic. The position of AEs and end-users leads to the definition of a set of m areas, result of the overlapping of the various AEs coverage, $\Gamma = \{1, 2, \ldots, m\}$.

We assume that each AE has a particular capacity, for which a generic and discrete unit will be used, the so-called *Traffic Unit* (TU) [3], no matter it refers to code, sub-carriers, time slots, etc. Anytime an end-user connects to a particular AE, one of its resources is consumed, and thus they could eventually get extinguished.

Furthermore, we also need to establish the way an end-user selects an AE, whenever she has different connection alternatives; in the framework of this work, we have considered that the users will choose the AE which offers the best price between the available choices, and if there are various AEs with the same price the users selects one randomly.

Considering the presented network model, we introduce herewith the non-cooperative game which will allow the operators to find the optimum price to impose. It is assumed that the *players* are the AEs which are deployed within the scenario and that their *strategy spaces* will be determined by the various possibilities they have so as to assign a price from their possibilities; thus, $(x_i)^j$ would represent the prices that the ith AE assigns to all areas under its coverage in the jth strategy.

Furthermore, the overall set of strategies can be obtained as the cartesian product of the individual ones (per AE).

$$\mathbb{X} = \mathbf{x}_1 \times \mathbf{x}_2 \times \ldots \times \mathbf{x}_N \tag{7}$$

Hence, we can define a strategy profile[3] (s) as an element of the space strategy

$$s \in \mathbb{X}, s = (s_1, s_2 \ldots s_N) \text{ with } s_i \in \mathbf{x}_i \tag{8}$$

---

[3] We will use the words strategy and strategy profile indifferently.

For each of the strategy profile, we obtain the benefits for all AEs and, after that, we can finally pose the finite game to be solved. The corresponding maximization problem can be strictly set out to maximize the following expression:

$$B_i = \sum_{\forall k:\ i \in k} \overline{(b_i)_k} \tag{9}$$

where $\overline{(b_i)_k}$ would be the average expected benefit by the ith AE in the kth area.

For the specified selecting model, the average number of users selecting an AE will depend on both the price such AE assigns and the fees fixed by the rest of AEs. As mentioned before, if various AEs assign the same price and they are giving coverage at the same area, users will make their choice randomly, so the AE more likely to be selected is that which has more available resources within such area [4].

There exits three situations which bring about different benefits, as discussed below.

1. Case $p_i < p_t\ \forall\ AE_t \in k$

$$\overline{(b_i)_k} = \begin{cases} u_k \cdot p_i & if \quad u_k < r_i \\[2mm] r_i \cdot p_i & if \quad u_k > r_i \end{cases} \tag{10}$$

where p_i and r_i are the price assigned and the available resources of AE_i, respectively, and u_k are the users deployed in the area k. When AE_i has the lowest price of all the connection alternatives within such area, the users would select AE_i until all its resources are exhausted.

2. Case $p_i > p_t\ \forall\ AE_t \in k$

$$\overline{(b_i)_k} = \begin{cases} (u_k - r_j) \cdot p_i & if \quad (u_k - r_j) < r_i,\ \sum_{\forall j \neq i:\ j \in k} r_j < u_k \\[2mm] r_i \cdot p_i & if \quad (u_k - r_j) > r_i,\ \sum_{\forall j \neq i:\ j \in k} r_j < u_k \\[2mm] 0 & if \quad \sum_{\forall j \neq i:\ j \in k} r_j > u_k \end{cases} \tag{11}$$

where $\sum_{\forall j \neq i:\ j \in k}$ is the overall resources from all AEs available in the k_{th} area with a lower price than AE_i. In this case, the price established by AE_i is higher and thus, users would only select it if the resources from the rest of alternatives is not enough for satisfying all users in the area.

---

[4] We do not assume that AEs are limiting their resources within a particular area, since this would change the strategy space, by adding another dimension to the strategy profile, but we refer to the remaining resources once the users within the single areas (only covered with an AE) have already established their connectivity.

3. Case $p_i = \min p_t \; \forall \; AE_t \in k$

$$\overline{(b_i)_k} = \begin{cases} \dfrac{r_i}{\sum_{\forall j:\, j \in k} r_j} \cdot u_k \cdot p_i & if \quad u_k < \sum \forall j \neq i:\ j \in k \\ r_i \cdot p_i & if \quad u_k > \sum_{\forall j:\, j \in k} \end{cases} \qquad (12)$$

In this case the price of AE_i is the minimum one within the area, but there are more AEs which have establihed such fee. In this case the benefit obtained (users would select one alternative on a random way) depends on the number of resources offered by AE_i, as compared with those offered by the AEs which established the same price.

We could also think on a situation merging cases 2 and 3, when two or more AEs establish the same price, but it is not the minimum amongst those offered in such area, but the demand can not be satisfied by those access alternatives (the cheapest AEs).

Once we have obtained the benefits, we can pose the Price Assignment Game *(PAG)* as follows, where s is a strategy profile:

$$PAG = \{N, \mathbb{X}, \{b_i(s)\}_{i \in N}\} \qquad (13)$$

The following definition (see e.g. [9] for a deep treatment of *Game Theory*), establish the solution of the corresponding problem.

Definition 1. *A strategy profile s is a pure Nash Equilibrium if*

$$b_i(s_i, s_{-i}) \geq b_i(s_i', s_{-i}) \qquad (14)$$

for all $s_i' \in S$ and each player i, where $s_{-i} = s_1, s_2, \ldots s_{i-1}, s_{i+1}, \ldots s_n$.

4   Implementation

In order to solve the aforementioned problem, two separated phases are followed: the first one (`getStrategies`) establishes the strategy space, sets out the corresponding game and obtains its *Nash Equilibrium*, while the second one (`compareStrategies`) studies the benefits which are brought about by such optimum solution as compared to a situation where the AEs always assign a fixed price.

Both phases share some common steps, which are briefly described below.

1. **Scenario setup.** Both AEs and end-users are deployed within the area under analysis. Random as well as deterministic deployments are supported. For the `compareStrategies`, only deterministic positioning is used, since the scenario must be the same as the one which was used during the `getStrategies`.
2. **Connectivity.** Once end-users and AEs are deployed within the scenario, we establish the existing links between them (whenever an end-user lies within the coverage area of a particular AE.).

3. **Area establishment.** In the framework of this work, an area is defined by a group of users which might be able to connect to the same group of AEs. Furthermore we can distinguish between two types of areas: *single* and *overlap* areas; the former group corresponds to those areas where there is only one reachable AE, while for the second group more than one AE would be reachable.

After these common procedures, the execution for the `getStrategies` and `compareStrategies` differs.

In the case of the `getStrategies` we implemented some functions so as to identify all possible strategies and, afterwards, process them to obtain the benefit for each AE, with the goal of finding the optimum strategy. The concrete steps which are undertaken are briefly depicted below.

1. **Getting strategies.** The first step is to actually obtain the strategy space; strategies are established for each of the AEs. Each AE will have as many strategies as prices it can assign. For obtaining our results AEs can impose three prices but it can be assigned as many prices as we want. Finally, to find the overall set of strategies, we obtain the combinations which can be established from the strategies of all AEs applying the cartesian product.
2. **Obtain benefits.** Once the strategy space has been obtained, we calculate the average benefit obtained by the AEs for each strategy. For this purpose, strategies are processed so as to derive the corresponding benefit in each one of the areas applying equations 10, 11 or 12 depending on the situations. Finally we accumulate all the benefits over those areas for every AE.
3. **Solve the game.** In this point, having in mind the strategies and their benefits, we can already pose a *finite* game to be solved. The pure *Nash Equilibrium Point* (NEP) is obtained with the *Gambit* software [4].

Regarding the `compareStrategies` method, the goal is to analyze the benefits which would be obtained by imposing the *optimum* strategy (i.e. using the previously found NEP in the `getStrategies` procedure), comparing them with those which would be achieved when the AEs use the medium price. In either of the two cases, we go through all the end-users, who use the aforementioned connecting decision (until they establish a connection or they do not have any available possibility). The order in which end-users are processed has a clear impact on the resulting connectivity, so we randomly shuffle them, repeating the same process for a sufficiently big number of times.

5   Discussion of Results

In this section, we present and discuss the results which were obtained by implementing the procedure which was previously depicted. We assume a squared area (200 m side) in which we deploy 7 different AEs, belonging to three types of Radio Access Technology (RAT), whose characteristics are shown in Table 1. Note that for RAT_1 we fix a sufficiently large coverage so as to ensure that it always cover the complete scenario, no matter the position of the AE is. We consider two complementary network deployments: deterministic and random; the topology of the former can be seen in Figure 4(a), while Figure 4(b) shows an illustrative example of a random deployment.

We increase the number of users from 10% to 200% of the overall network capacity (i.e. from 7 to 130 users) and for each case we execute 100 independent analysis (so as to ensure the statistical validity of the results). For the random deployment, both AEs, as well as end-users' positions, are changed every time, while for the deterministic case, it is only the users' position which changes in all runs. In all cases we compare the results achieved between the NEP and the naive strategy (the latter corresponding to the situation in which AEs assign the medium price).

First, Figures 5(a) and 5(b) show the benefit achieved by the whole network. The *better* distribution of AEs in the deterministic topology is clearly reflected in the obtained results, since the benefit by the overall network is always larger in this case. Comparing both network topologies, we can see that the greater gain is achieved when the number of users equals the network capacity, being this difference lower in the edge cases. The gain which the NEP strategy yields is also more relevant for the deterministic scenario, being around 36% when the offered load (number of users) equals the overall network capacity. Another interesting aspect is that there is not any particular gain when the offered load is low (end-users are below 40% of the overall network capacity).

In order to get a better understanding of the differences between the NEP and the naive strategies, Figures 5(c) and 5(d) depict the benefit for the three RAT types which are being used (we still use the same two network deployments). First of all, it is worth highlighting that the highest capable RAT (RAT_1) gets the greater gain after applying the NEP strategy, but for situations in which users are fewer than the 40% of the network capacity, where the benefit is very similar (or even slightly worse). Comparing both network topologies, it can be seen that the results are rather similar for RAT_1. On the other hand, for both RAT_2 and RAT_3, we can see the consequences of having a better deployment, since the gain is, in most cases, higher than the one assessed in the random scenario.

Table 1. Types of RAT used during the analysis

RAT ID	Range (m)	Capacity (TU)	# of AEs in the scenarios
1	*full*	20	1
2	50	10	3
3	30	5	3

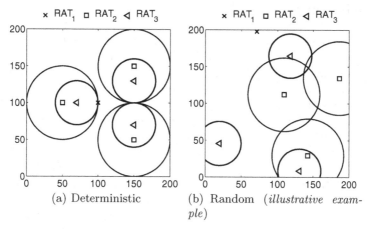

(a) Deterministic

(b) Random (*illustrative example*)

Fig. 4. Network topologies used during the analysis

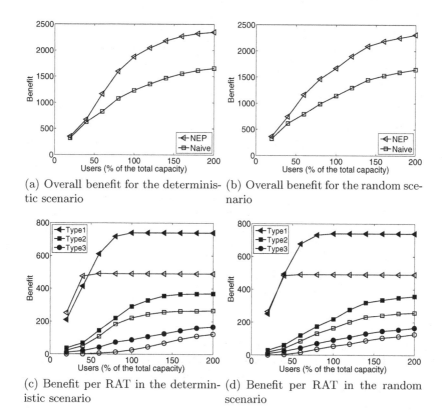

(a) Overall benefit for the deterministic scenario

(b) Overall benefit for the random scenario

(c) Benefit per RAT in the deterministic scenario

(d) Benefit per RAT in the random scenario

Fig. 5. Overall benefit and benefit per RAT type for the two scenarios. *Solid markers are the ones obtained with the NEP strategy, and the empty ones are those corresponding to the naive assignment.*

6 Conclusions

In this work we have proposed a dynamic pricing model to be used by operators over heterogeneous wireless networks and we have used *Game Theory* techniques so as to study the optimum strategies.

In particular, two different analysis have been carried out. On the one hand we have made a theoretical study about the expected behavior of the system in some illustrative situations. Since the complexity of the subjacent scenario might get too high, we have carried out a more realistic analysis so as to corroborate the benefits of using dynamic pricing strategies. For this purpose, we have posed a finite game, in which the players are the available AEs. The obtained results show that the use of the optimum strategies (the Nash Equilibrium of the games) brings about additional revenue to the operators, which would obtain a higher benefit than that assessed with more traditional policies. Furthermore, two complementary network deployments were analyzed and it was shown that the deterministic network deployment yields slightly better results, since it somehow reflects an optimum distribution of the AEs.

The work presented in this paper sets the basis for a wide range of research lines, some of them have already started. We will also use another approach, by means of an event-driven simulator [3] so as to see how the proposed scheme works when including both user movement and different traffic patterns. Other analysis types, such as linear programming, can also be followed in future work. In addition, we could increase the complexity of the pricing policies, by allowing the AEs to provide differentiated prices per user; besides, the developed framework might be combined with other parameters like resource allocation from the operators.

Acknowledgements. The authors would like to express their gratitude to the Spanish government for its funding in the following project: "Cognitive, Cooperative Communications and autonomous SErvice Management", C3SEM (TEC2009-14598-C02-01). The authors also acknowledge the European Commission for its funding through the "Scalable and Adaptive Internet Solutions", SAIL Project (FP7-ICT-2009-5-257448).

References

1. Baliosian, J., Rubio-Loyola, J., Salazar, P., Ag R.: Gestión de políticas y precios en entornos de acceso heterogéneos. X Jornadas de Ingeniería Telemática (2011)
2. Chen, Q.B., Zhou, W.G., Chai, R., Tang, L.: Game-theoretic approach for pricing strategy and network selection in heterogeneous wireless networks. IET Communications 5(5), 676–682 (2011)
3. Choque, J., Agüero, R., Muñoz, L.: Simulation framework for the evaluation of access selection algorithms over heterogeneous wireless networks. In: 3rd International ICST Conference on Mobile Networks and Management, MONAMI (2011)
4. McKelvey, et al.: Gambit: Software tools for game theory, version 0.2010.09.01 (2010), http://www.gambit-project.org

5. Niyato, D., Hossain, E.: Competitive pricing in heterogeneous wireless access networks: Issues and approaches. IEEE Network 22(6), 4–11 (2008)
6. Niyato, D., Hossain, E.: A game theoretic analysis of service competition and pricing in heterogeneous wireless access networks. IEEE Transactions on Wireless Communications 7(12), 5150–5155 (2008)
7. Sengupta, S., Anand, S., Chatterjee, M., Chandramouli, R.: Dynamic pricing for service provisioning and network selection in heterogeneous networks. Physical Communication 2(1-2), 138–150 (2009)
8. Sengupta, S., Chatterjee, M., Kwiat, K.: Pricing-based service and network selection in overlaid access networks. In: 2007 6th International Conference on Information, Communications Signal Processing, pp. 1–5 (December 2007)
9. Watson, J.: Strategy, An Introduction to Game Theory, 2nd edn. W. W. Norton & Company (2002)

Uplink QoS Aware Multi-homing in Integrated 3GPP and non-3GPP Future Networks

Umar Toseef[1,2], Yasir Zaki[2], Andreas Timm-Giel[1], and Carmelita Görg[2]

[1] Institute of Communication Networks
Hamburg University of Technology Schwarzenbergstr. 95E, 21073 Hamburg, Germany
{umar.toseef,timm-giel}@tuhh.de

[2] TZI ComNets, University of Bremen, 28359 Bremen, Germany
{umr,yzaki,cg}@comnets.uni-bremen.de

Abstract. Future wireless networks will consist of a mixed heterogeneous 3GPP and non-3GPP access technologies. The 3rd Generation Partnership Project 3GPP has already facilitated the integration of non-3GPP access by standardizing the System Architecture Evolution (SAE) where non-3GPP access technologies can co-exist with 3GPP access networks. In such heterogeneous networks though the seamless vertical handovers can be performed between the available access networks, the question still remains whether the Quality of Service (QoS) demands of user applications can be satisfied from QoS unaware non-3GPP access technologies? Within the context of the Open Connectivity Services (OConS) of the SAIL European project[1], this work investigates the effects of the integration of two network types on user Quality of Experience (QoE) in the uplink direction. In order to realize QoS guaranteed service from non-3GPP access technologies, this paper proposes two novel resource estimation and management algorithms. With the help of simulation it is shown that integration of non-3GPP technologies in the existing 4G networks extends the network capacity without compromising the user QoE when the proposed schemes are deployed.

Keywords: Integrated 3GPP and non-3GPP networks, User QoE optimization, resource management in heterogeneous networks, QoS aware flow management.

1 Introduction

The EU-funded research project SAIL (Scalable & Adaptive Internet Solutions) research the design of the Networks of the Future, investigating new architecture for the future internet. The SAIL project is part of the European Commission's 7th Framework Program [1]. 24 operators, vendors and research institution are working together since 2010 on the research and development of novel networking technologies using proof-of-concept prototypes to lead the way from current networks to the Network of the Future .

In SAIL there are 3 technical work packages (WPs) covering different aspects of future networks: NetInf - Network of Information (WP-B) aims at developing

A. Timm-Giel et al. (Eds.): MONAMI 2012, LNICST 58, pp. 114–127, 2013.

a general information centric networking architecture, OConS - Open Connectivity Services (WP-C) targets the efficient use of multi-path, multi-protocol and multi-layer networking over any fixed and mobile networks, and CloNe - Cloud Networking (WP-D) combines both Cloud Computing and Network Virtualization together.

1.1 OConS Architecture and Multi-P

The work of this paper falls within the solutions that the OConS work package is providing. The work ranges from concepts of OconS architecutre framework and Multi-P transmissions in LTE systems. OconS proposes an open and flexible architectural framework to handle the connectivity of networks. To fulfill the network requirements, keep the flexibility and openness of OconS, a component-based architecture frame-work is proposed, in 3 steps: (1) information collection; (2) decision making; (3) decision enforcement. These steps are handled by three functional entities:

- Information Management Entity (IE) is in charge of gathering information required by decision making, e.g. link quality, power limitation, load and congestion of the networks. IE also pre-processes and filters the gathered information before it is delivered to the other entities.
- Decision Making Entity (DE) uses the information from IE to make the decision to fulfill some pre-defined metrics. For example, the final enforcements can be handover, load balancing and flow splitting. The goals of improving system performance can be maximizing the network throughput, load balancing, flow management, or even a mixture of them.
- Execution and Enforcement Entity (EE) finally executes or performs the decision made by DE.

The Multi-P mechanism of OConS has multiple meanings of Multi-Path, Multi-homing and Multi-Protocol. The Multi-P transmission tries to simultaneously employ multiple wireless networks/interfaces to enhance the transmission reliability, data rates and the network resource utilization. The key part of this Multi-P transmission strategy is the decision process of DE to fulfill different transmission strategies and that is where this paper will focus on.

1.2 Motivation and Contributions

Nowadays end-user equipments are more powerful and normally have more than one interfaces which can connect to different wireless networks, e.g. mobile sytems or WLAN. On the other hand, the network resources are always scarce for supporting a huge number of users running different applications. The Multi-P algorithm, enables the interconnection of LTE and WLAN, so that end users can exploit all of the available wireless resources. In addition, mobile operators can also flexibly balance the traffic load among multiple access networks.

In this presented work, the focus is put on developing a simulation model that can be used to realize the Mult-P transmissions of 3GPP LTE and WLAN. This involves development of simulation model according to 3GPP specifications, implementation of MIPv6 extensions to realize multi-homing and flow management techniques, as well as, the integration of user QoE evaluation tools in the simulator. With the help of the intelligent resource management schemes proposed by this paper, it is shown that network capacity improvements and user QoE enhancement can be achieved.

The rest of this paper is organized as follows: Section 2 introduces the details of the OPNET[1] [14] simulation model for Multi-P. The traffic flow splitting strategies and the detailed mechanisms are described in Section 3. For proof of concept, Section 4 shows simulation results of different scenarios to reveal the advantages of our approach. At the end, Section 5 concludes this work and points out some possible points for our future works.

2   System Models

2.1   Applying OCons Multi-P in Integrated 3GPP LTE and WLAN Networks

The goal of the presented work is to investigate the Interconnection (and cooperation) of 3GPP (e.g. LTE) and non-3GPP systems (e.g. Wireless Local Area Network (WLAN)) by means of the Multi-P transmission. The key part of this approach is the decision process: selection of the UE interfaces and access alternatives (at the network side) that should be used for the transmission and how to split the traffic flows.

From an architectural point of view as depicted in Fig. 1, the interconnection between 3GPP and non-3GPP (in this paper, LTE and WLAN were chosen as case study) is possible at the Packet Data Network Gateway (PDN GW). Hence, it becomes a reasonable location for the DE/EE of the Network controlled Multi-P decision. For the LTE side, the IEs are located at the eNodeB (eNB) and the serving gateway (S-GW). For the WLAN side, the IE is located at the Wireless Access Point (WAP). Each UE also has IEs, EEs and DEs, so that it can gather the downlink information for the Multi-P decisions, as well as, make and execute the Multi-P transmission decisions.

2.2   OPNET Simulation Model

3GPP specified SAE [13] architecture allows a mobile user to roam between 3GPP and non-3GPP access technologies. In order to provide users with seamless mobility Proxy Mobile IPv6 (network based mobility) and Dual stack Mobile IPv6 (host based mobility) have been proposed [13]. This proposal is followed

---

[1] OPNET Modeler®is a commercial network simulator which accelerates the R&D process for analyzing and designing communication networks, devices, protocols, and applications.

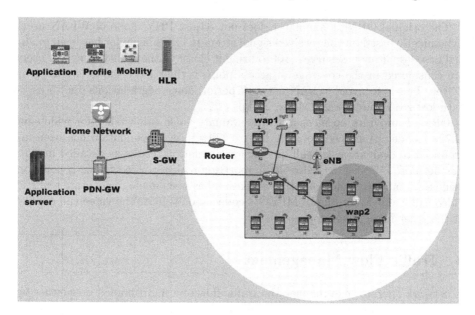

Fig. 1. OPNET simulation model example scenario. The large circular area shown is the coverage of LTE network while smaller circular areas represent the WLAN coverage. The user movement has been restricted to the rectangular area.

in the integration of 3GPP access technology (namely LTE) and trusted non-3GPP access technology (namely legacy WLAN 802.11g) where host based mobility solution i.e. Dual stack Mobile IPv6 is considered. According to current 3GPP specification multi-homing is not supported. This implies that the user can either be associated to LTE network or WLAN network but cannot connect to both networks simultaneously. This work extends the 3GPP specified architecture to give users multi-homing capabilities. This is achieved by extending the implementation of MIPv6 to support multiple care-of address [9] and flow management functionality [7][8].

Fig. 1 shows an overview of the example simulation network implemented in OPNET. All entities of SAE architecture which are necessary to carry out multi-homing scenario have been implemented. As per 3GPP proposal home agent (HA) function is located at PDN gateway. All users are considered to be out of their home network during the complete simulation time. The application server acts a correspondent node (CN) from where mobile users access application services like VoIP, Video and FTP. Users receive router advertisements from the eNB and possibly from the WLAN access point to configure care-of addresses. These care-of addresses are then registered with their HA through standard MIPv6 signaling. In this way all user traffic is tunneled up to the HA.

The focus on this paper is only on the is only on the uplink access for LTE and WLAN. This implies that no downlink transmissions are performed for WLAN during the whole simulation time. Instead all downlink traffic (e.g. TCP ACK packets etc.) is transmitted by the user through the LTE access link.

The original OPNET simulator does not adjust PHY mode of WLAN users dynamically based on the received signal strength. This behavior has been modified based on literature survey [10] to bring it closer to the reality. However users are considered in the coverage of access point if their PHY mode is 6Mbps or better. This is to avoid WLAN network performance degradations due to users with low PHY modes e.g. 1Mbps, 2Mbps etc.

OPNET provides no mechanism to evaluate voice call quality for wideband G.722.2 codec. A procedure according to ITU-T recommendation has been introduced to evaluate voice call quality for simulation results as detailed in [12]. Furthermore OPNET has also no support for realistic video traffic generation using any standard codec. Another extension has been made to generate realistic video call traffic according to MPEG-4 codec and evaluate the video call quality at the receiving end as proposed in [11].

3   Traffic Flow Management

A network operator can manage the traffic flow of a multi-homed user either by switching the complete traffic flow from one path to another or by splitting it into multiple sub flows so that each path carries one sub flow. These sub flows are then aggregated at the destination to reconstruct the original traffic flow of the application. Though the option of splitting a traffic flow involves more sophisticate techniques, it provides greater flexibility in network load balancing. That's why in this work, flow management with flow splitting option is implemented and analyzed with the help of simulations.

A very basic question that arises when deciding for flow splitting option is: What is an appropriate size of sub flows transported over each path to a multi-homed user? In other words how much traffic should be sent to user on each available access link? And a straightforward answer would be: each path or link should be loaded according to its bandwidth capacity. Another important question is: how sub-flows will be aggregated at the receiving end. In the following sub-sections answers to these two questions are addressed.

From the architecture viewpoint the flow management functionality is split into two functional parts. One part resides at the network and the other part is implemented at user side. Each functional part receives the necessary information from "Information Management Entities", forwards the information to "Decision Making Entities" and then executes the decisions with the help of "Execution and Enforcement Entities". The flow management functional part on UE side (named as flow management client function) has the additional responsibility to respond to the information queries and decision execution commands sent by the flow management function residing at the network.

3.1   Estimation of WLAN Link Capacity

Most modern wireless LAN access networks follow IEEE 802.11 standards, marketed under the name of Wi-Fi. In the infrastructure mode of 802.11 typically a number of stations are associated to an access point (AP) (which is normally a router) that serves as a bridge to a wired infrastructure network. 802.11 MAC uses one of the following three techniques to provide channel access control mechanisms.

1. Point coordination function (PCF): resides on the access point to coordinate the channel access for all associated stations through polling. A polled station can communicate with the access point in a contention free manner within a time slot. PCF is not part of the Wi-Fi Alliance interoperability and therefore is rarely found implemented on a portable device.
2. Distributed coordination function (DCF): is a random access scheme based on the Carrier Sense Multiple Access with Collision Avoidance protocol (CSMA/CA) with a binary exponential back-off algorithm. The DCF has two operating modes: the basic channel access mode and the RTS/CTS (Request-to-Send/Clear-To-Send) mode. DCF does not provide a contention free medium access and therefore collisions can occur during the transmission if other stations also start transmitting at the same time. DCF is the de-facto default setting for Wi-Fi hardware.
3. Hybrid coordination function (HCF): has been designed to provide a differentiated medium access. Though HFC does not provide service guarantees, it establishes a probabilistic priority mechanism to allocate bandwidth based on traffic categories. HCF was introduced for the 802.11e standard, but it is hard to find complaint hardware. In recent time the 802.11n standard has incorporated HCF, which though becoming increasingly popular, is still available for a limited number of portable devices.

From the above description it can be deduced that a dominant percentage of today's portable Wi-Fi capable devices operate in the DCF mode of 802.11a/b/g. Three flavors of 802.11, i.e. a,b&g, follow very similar procedures in medium access mechanism therefore in this work we focus only on one of the flavors i.e. 802.11g. The readers are encouraged to refer to [16],[17] for further details on 802.11 specifications and performance.

In 802.11g network where a number of users are contending for medium access, the network capacity and the individual user throughput is highly variable due to several time varying factors like number of active users, type of traffic flow (TCP or UDP), user channel conditions, as well as, mobility pattern of the users. This makes it extremely difficult if not impossible to mathematically compute individual user throughput in such a network. This work proposes two approaches with the help of which an estimation of the the user throughput can be performed along the time.

Approach 1 - Random Access: In this approach a metering function, as a part of information management entity (IE), is introduced at the WLAN MAC layer buffer of the user device. This metering function is responsible for measuring the outlet data rate from the buffer, as well as, the buffer occupancy level. These two values are obtained periodically and sent to flow management client function residing at UE. In the beginning, flow management client function directs a sufficient amount of user traffic to WLAN MAC for transmission. This data stays at the MAC layer buffer before transmission over the radio interface. The flow management client function now continuously receives the buffer occupancy level reports and adjusts the size of traffic flow to the WLAN network path to keep the buffer occupancy at the original level. In this way, if buffer occupancy level increases, it hints a reduction in available WLAN path capacity due to some reason e.g. congestion, poor channel conditions etc. Therefore flow management function accordingly reduces the traffic flow amount directed towards the WLAN path. The opposite is true if a reduction in MAC buffer occupancy is observed which suggests an improvement in the path capacity and flow management client function takes advantage of this by sending more traffic towards the WLAN path. Following this approach time varying WLAN network path capacity can be tracked and used by the flow management function.

The practical implementation of the suggested approach is straightforward as, it does not require any modification in the UE hardware or WLAN MAC protocol. However an appropriate amount of the MAC buffer occupancy μ for a smooth operation of this approach still has to be determined. For this purpose following relation is used for every user i i.e.

$$\mu_i = \beta_i^{WLAN} \cdot \tau, \tag{1}$$

where β_i^{WLAN} is the throughput estimation of WLAN path. For a TCP based application flow $\tau = \tau_{tcp}$ which is the TCP re-ordering timer and will be discussed in further details later. For real time applications like, VoIP or video, $\tau = \tau_{\text{de-jitterbuffer}}$ (which is the length of de-jitter buffer in units of seconds) is used for that particular application.

Approach 2 - Round Robin: This approach involves a quasi-scheduling of the WLAN network resources. The main idea behind this approach is to save the network resources which are otherwise wasted due to contention in channel medium access and packet collisions when multiple users are transmitting simultaneously. By saving these network resources the user throughput can be improved and the network capacity can be increased. To realize this approach flow management function residing in the network collects the information about the users who are associated with a hotspot. This information is periodically sent by the flow management client function residing at the user device through the fast LTE signalling. The flow management function at the network builds a list of active users and assigns them time slots to transmit in a round robin manner. In order to minimize the signalling traffic the scheduling decision is communicated to the user in the form of ON-OFF periods. A user transmits only during the indicated ON period of self repeating scheduling interval and halts the transmissions otherwise. For example, if two users are associated to a hotspot, they share the network resources in a round robin way so that one user transmits for a fixed time period determined by its allocated time slot. During the transmission time of the first user, the second user does not transmit anything and waits for the first user's time slot to end. When the time slot of the first user elapses, the channel access time for the second user starts lasting for a duration equal to its time slot during which the first user stops its transmissions over the WLAN. This cycle is repeated until any change happens in the network e.g. a new user joins the WLAN network or a existing user leaves the WLAN network etc. In response to such events, the flow management reschedule the users and sends updated schedule of transmissions to the flow management client function of the active users.

This approach assumes that the participating users are precisely time synchronized which could be hard to achieve in real world. If this condition is not met, there could be some contention for medium access during the overlapped period of the two adjacent time slots. However, if the length of the time slot is much larger than this overlapping period, the users will still be able to enjoy sufficient contention free time period for their transmission. Moreover, during the overlapping period only two users will be competing for the medium access which is still better than the situation where all actives users are contending for the medium access and hence degrade the network performance.

Another problem associated with this approach is related to the WLAN MAC buffer contents at the user equipment. Owing to the fact that WLAN MAC function is unaware of the proposed approach, it will try to transmit the existing buffered data even when the user time slot has elapsed. If the WLAN radio transmitter is switched off after transmission and switched on again when the next time slot for transmission approaches, the user will not contend for the channel during the time slot for other users but in this case the packets already lying in the MAC buffer will be lost. To avoid this packet loss and minimize the contention period, flow management client function at the user equipment sends only two IP packets to WLAN MAC for the transmission. When WLAN MAC function takes out one packet from the buffer for transmission, a software interrupt is sent to client function which responds by delivering another IP packet to the MAC buffer. In this way, at any time instant during the transmission time slot of a user there are maximum two packets lying in the buffer. As soon as the time slot of the user elapses, the flow management client function stops sending new packets to WLAN MAC and therefore the user contends the medium access with the user of adjacent time slot to transmit only two packets. Another possible way to circumvent this problem could be to use guard time between two adjacent time slots.

The quasi-scheduling decisions are conveyed to the users using LTE signalling in order to avoid any excessive delays. Due to the fact that each user follows its time slot for transmission, there are very few events of packet collision or medium access contention involved. As a result an improvement in the network capacity is expected. This mechanism of the proposed approach resembles the famous token ring protocol, however it does not require any modification on the WLAN MAC protocol. Though in this work simple round robin schemes is used, the proposed quasi-scheduling approach is general enough to accommodate other resource sharing schemes. This work considers a constant time slot value of 100 ms for each user, however a complete sensitivity analysis of slot time length on achievable performance is a future work item. Once a user is given a certain time slot for transmission, its effective throughput depends on the its channel conditions which are mapped to PHY speed of the user device. Based on the PHY speed information and excluding the protocol overheads an accurate estimation of WLAN path can be made.

It should be noted that approach 1 for WLAN link capacity estimation can be used by both network centric and user centric flow management schemes. However approach 2 can only be used with the help of network functions and is therefore suitable only for network centric flow management scheme.

3.2   Estimation of LTE Access Link Capacity

In case of LTE, the bandwidth capacity available to a user depends on several factors e.g. MAC scheduler type, channel conditions of all users, QoS requirements of traffic from all users, cell load level etc. The throughput estimation is therefore performed by using the same solution as discussed in 3.1. That is a metering function is introduced between PDCP and RLC layers at UE. This metering function reports the average throughput of the user data flowing from PDCP to RLC layer in uplink direction. The reported throughput value is then taken as LTE link capacity of that particular user. Similar to the mechanism explained in 3.1 the deployed metering function also provides occupancy level of user PDCP buffer where LTE data for transmission over radio interface is stored. The flow management client function based on the PDCP buffer occupancy level adjusts the user throughput for the path. In LTE case the target PDCP buffer occupancy ε_i of a user i is also computed in the same way as shown in equation 1 i.e.

$$\varepsilon_i = \beta_i^{LTE} \cdot \tau, \tag{2}$$

where β_i^{LTE} is the throughput estimation of LTE path. This approach of link capacity estimation can be used by user centric as well as network centric flow management.

3.3   Sub-flow Aggregation Function

In multi-path communication packet may arrive out of order at the destination [6]. Real time applications usually deploy a play-out (or de-jitter) buffer which is intended to get rid of jitter associated with packet delays. However it can also perform packet reordering if packets arrive within time window equal to play-out buffer length. In this way, real time applications face no problems when receiving out of order packets in multi-path communication unless delay of all paths is less than play-out buffer length $\tau_{\mathrm{de-jitterbuffer}}$.

On the other hand TCP based applications are very sensitive to packet reordering. This is because an out-of-sequence packet can lead to TCP overestimate the congestion of the network which results in a substantial degradation in application throughput and network performance [5]. A literature survey shows that there are several proposals to make TCP robust against packet re-ordering. However, the analysis and implementation of such schemes are currently not within the focus of this research work. Instead we implement a simple TCP re-ordering buffer at the user side which is very similar in functionality to a play-out buffer. Simulation analysis shows that the re-ordering buffer length must be less than the TCP protocol time out value. In this work the re-ordering buffer length has been kept between 100ms to 500ms. TCP re-ordering buffer length τ_{tcp} is a key factor in deciding target PDCP buffer occupancy level ε_i and WLAN MAC buffer occupancy level μ_i for a user i as explained earlier. With the help of this strategy WLAN and LTE link delay is controlled not to exceed the TCP re-ordering buffer length and hence avoid unnecessary TCP time-outs.

4   Simulation Scenarios and Results

The target of this section is to highlight the gains that can be achieved by extending the 3GPP inter-working architecture to support the simultaneous use of the multi interfaces. In this section, two main scenarios are compared against each other, that is, the 3GPP default architecture, where multi-homing is not supported however the users can perform seamless Handover (HO) between the multiple wireless networks, and this will be referred to as "3GPP HO". In this scenario the users communicate through LTE network when they are away from a hotspot and make handover to the WLAN network as soon as they are in its coverage. Whereas, the second scenario is the novel proposal of this paper where the simultaneous use of multiple wireless interfaces is supported, this will be referred to as "Multi-P". In this scenario the users in the overlapped coverage of the WLAN and the LTE networks can simultaneously make use of the two network interfaces. The distribution of user traffic over the two network paths is performed by the flow management function. When the users are away from hotspot they have only the LTE network access to communicate.

In "3GPP HO" scenario the users make handover between two access technologies without following make-before-break approach, i.e. the connection is broken from one network, and a new connection is established to the other one. Though MIPv6 keeps all IP layer connections alive through seamless handover, the user might lose data packets buffered at the lower protocol layers of the previously in use network interface. For example, LTE buffers the received IP packets at PDCP, RLC and MAC layers while WLAN keeps all the data buffered at MAC layer before transmission over the radio interface. Therefore when making complete handover from one access technology to another, this buffered data is discarded and have to be recovered by upper layers through retransmissions. This behavior leads to applications performance degradation for both TCP and UDP based applications.

The "Multi-P" scenario the users are allowed to use the WLAN access when it is in the coverage, and can still keep the LTE connection alive and use it at the same time. In the coverage of WLAN access, the flow management client function sends user traffic on WLAN link only when user PHY mode is 9Mbps

Table 1. Simulation configurations

Parameter	Configurations
Total Number of PRBs	25 PRBs (5 MHz specturm)
Mobility model	Random Direction (RD) with 6 km/h
Number of users	5 VoIP, 4 Skype video call and 11 FTP downlink users
LTE Channel model	Macroscopic pathloss model [2], Correlated Slow Fading [3]
LTE MAC Scheduler	TDS: Optimized Service Aware, FDS: Iterative RR approach [4]
WLAN access technology	802.11g, RTS-CTS enabled, coverage $\approx$ 100 m, non-overlapping channel, uplink data transmissions only
VoIP traffic model	G.722.2 wideband codec, 23.05kbps data rate and 50 fps
Skype video model	MPEG-4 codec, 512kbps, 30fps, 640x480 resolution, play-out delay: 250 ms
FTP traffic model	FTP File size: constant 10 MByte, as soon as one file upload finishes the next FTP file starts immediately.
Simulation run time	1000 seconds, and 14 seeds with 98% Confidence interval

or higher. This is because when a user enters in 6Mbps mode it implies that the user is almost at edge of coverage which is a strong indication that loss of WLAN link is imminent. Hence no new traffic data is scheduled for WLAN link which gives user a chance to transmit already buffered data to the access point before the loss of link happens. Moreover "Multi-P" approaches, in contrast to "3GPP HO" scenario, keep buffered data at the minimal required level through the use of network path capacity estimations.

In this section two simulation setup are investigated. The first setup is composed of 20 users with mixed traffic of: Voice over IP (VoIP), File Transfer Protocol (FTP) and Skype video call. The users move within one LTE eNodeB cell, and within this cell two wireless access points or hot-spots are present as shown in Fig. 1. The second setup is a special case where 7 FTP users are moving within the restricted coverage of a wireless access point where no LTE access is available. The motivation behind the second setup is to show the advantages of using "Round robin" approach over "Random access" approach. The simulation configuration parameters are shown in Table 1.

4.1 Mixed User Traffic

In this subsection, the mixed traffic setup investigations are shown. Fig. 2 shows the mean IP uplink throughput as experienced by a FTP user. It can be seen that the "3GPP HO" scenario has the highest FTP file upload time and "Multi-P - Round Robin" scenario achieves the lowest file transfer time. Similarly "Round Robin" approach also manages to provide approximately 35% higher IP throughput compared to "3GPP HO" scenario. Furthermore, approximately 27% gain in uplink IP throughput is observed for users following "Random access" approach compared to the "3GPP HO" scenario. This indicates that "Multi-P" approaches outperform the "3GPP HO" approach by making better use of aggregated bandwidth resources through network path capacity estimation. As far

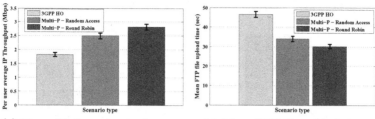

(a) Mean IP throughput of an up-   (b) Mean FTP file upload time
link FTP user

Fig. 2. FTP uplink performance

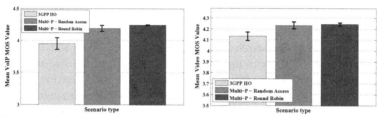

(a) Mean MOS value of wideband (b) Mean value of MOS computed
VoIP application   for Skype video application

Fig. 3. VoIP and video application performance

as UDP based application e.g. VoIP and video are concerned their performance
is evaluated by comparing the Mean Opinion Score (MOS)[15] values as shown
in Fig. 3(a) and Fig. 3(b). The results show that the "Multi-P" algorithms also
provide very good performance for the VoIP, as well as, for video conference
traffic type. The "3GPP HO" scenario achieves lower MOS value because when
the users move from one access network to the other (from LTE to WLAN, and
vice versa), there is a chance of some data loss as explained earlier, and this
affects the quality of the real time services (as reflected in the MOS value). Furthermore when VoIP and video traffic is transmitted over LTE, it is prioritized
over FTP to achieve required QoS (i.e. throughput and delay). But in "3GPP
HO" scenario when this traffic type is handed over to the WLAN the required
QoS cannot always be achieved due to lack of QoS differentiation support by
802.11g. Thanks to algorithms of "Multi-P" scenario which estimates and manages 802.11g resources in a way that not only the required QoS for real time
traffic is met but also an enhanced throughput performance of WLAN access
point is accomplished.

4.2 FTP User Traffic

In this subsection, a special setup is investigated in order to highlight the advantages of using WLAN resource management approach "Round Robin" as

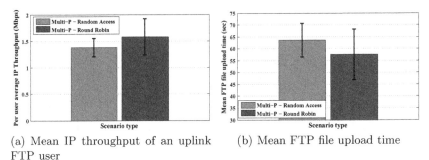

(a) Mean IP throughput of an uplink FTP user

(b) Mean FTP file upload time

Fig. 4. FTP uplink performance

discussed in Section 3.1. The scenario comprises of 7 FTP users, all moving within the coverage of the wireless access point without having LTE access. In both scenarios, the FTP users upload constant 10MByte file size one after the other. Fig. 4 shows the FTP uplink performance for both scenarios. The results show that "Round Robin" algorithm of WLAN resource management does its job to increase overall network throughput and enhance user QoE. It achieves a lower FTP file upload time and higher IP throughput compared to the other scenario where no management of WLAN resources is performed. The performance gain is approximately 13% in this particular scenario with 7 users. However this gain depends on the number of active users associated with a hotspot. The larger the number of users, the higher the gain obtained by minimizing the contention periods. It should be noted that the users in this simulation scenario were perfectly time synchronized therefore no overlapping of the adjacent time slots happens. Fig. 4 shows that there is a larger deviation around the mean user throughput in the "Round Robin" scenario. This is because in "Round Robin" scenario users are given a fixed time slot for transmission therefore the users with the high PHY speed manage to achieve higher throughput compared to the users suffering from bad channel conditions and transmitting with lower PHY speed.

5   Conclusion

3GPP SAE architecture specifies how non-3GPP access technologies can be integrated in 3GPP networks and a seamless handover between these access technologies can be performed. This work proposes an extension to the specifications to allow a user benefit from all available access technologies by connecting to them simultaneously. The legacy WLAN does not provide QoS guarantee and therefore not suitable for real time interactive applications. However through the use of suggested algorithms for resource management and accurate bandwidth capacity estimation WLAN bandwidth resources can be utilized for multi-homed users running QoS sensitive applications. In order to validate the proposed algorithm and procedures an implementation of integrated network of LTE and legacy WLAN access technologies in OPNET simulator has been carried out. The simulation results provide proof of the concept where proposed scheme succeeds not only in providing QoS aware service to multi-homed users but also improves the network bandwidth resource utilization. By outperforming the current 3GPP proposal, the new scheme assures a win-win situation for network operators as well as for users in future wireless networks.

References

1. SAIL project official website, http://www.sail-project.eu/
2. 3GPP Technical Report TS 25.814, Physical layer aspects for E-UTRA, 3rd Generation Partnership Project, v.7.1.0 (September 2006)
3. Zaki, Y., Weerawardane, T., Görg, C., Timm-Giel, A.: Multi-QoS-Aware Fair Scheduling for LTE. In: Vehicular Technology Conference, VTC Spring (2011)
4. Marwat, S.N.K., Weerawardane, T., Zaki, Y., Goerg, C., Timm-Giel, A.: Performance Evaluation of Bandwidth and QoS Aware LTE Uplink Scheduler. In: 10th International Conference on Wired/Wireless Internet Communications, Santorini, Greece, June 6-8 (2012) (in press)
5. Laor, M., Gendel, L.: The Effect of Packet Reordering in a Backbone Link on Application Throughput. IEEE Network 16(5), 28–36 (2002)
6. Blanton, E., Allman, M.: On Making TCP More Robust to Packet Reordering. ACM Computer Communication Review 32(1) (January 2002)
7. Tsirtsis, G., Giaretta, G., Soliman, H., Montavont, N.: Traffic selectors for flow bindings (RFC 6088) (2011)
8. Tsirtsis, G., Soliman, H., Montavont, N., Giaretta, G., Kuladinithi, K.: Flow bindings in mobile IPv6 and NEMO basic support (RFC 6089) (2010)
9. Wakikawa, R., Devarapalli, V., Tsirtsis, G., Ernst, T., Nagami, K.: Multiple care-of addresses registration (RFC 5648) (2009)
10. Gast, M.S.: 802.11 Wireless Networks, The Definitive Guide, 2nd edn. O'reilly publications
11. Klaue, J., Rathke, B., Wolisz, A.: EvalVid - A Framework for Video Transmission and Quality Evaluation. In: Proc. of the 13th International Conference on Modeling Techniques and Tools for Computer Performance Evaluation, Illinois, USA, pp. 255–272 (September 2003)
12. Toseef, U., Li, M., Balazs, A., Li, X., Timm-Giel, A., Görg, C.: Investigating the Impacts of IP Transport Impairments on VoIP service in LTE Networks. In: 16. VDE/ITG Fachtagung Mobilkommunikation, Osnabrück, Germany (May 2011)
13. 3GPP Technical Report TS 23.402, Architecture enhancements for non-3GPP accesses, 3rd Generation Partnership Project, v10.6.0 (December 2011)
14. OPNET official website, http://www.opnet.com (as accessed in March 2012)
15. Recommendation P.800, Methods for subjective determination of transmission quality. Approved (August 1996)
16. Wireless LAN Medium Access Control (MAC) and Physical Layer (PHY) Specifications ISO/IEC 8802-11:1999(E); ANSI/IEEE Std 802.11, 1999 edn., USA
17. Bianchi, G.: Performance Analysis of the IEEE 802.11 Distributed Coordination Function. IEEE Journal on Selected Areas in Communications 18(3), 535–547 (2000)

Wireless Multi-access Delivery
for SVC-Based Video Applications

Rui Costa[1], Telemaco Melia[1], Lucas Eznarriaga[2,3], Fabio Giust[2,3],
Antonio de la Oliva[3], and Carlos J. Bernardos[3]

[1] Alcatel-Lucent Bell Labs, Paris, France
{rui_pedro.ferreira_da_costa,telemaco.melia}@alcatel-lucent.com
[2] Institute IMDEA Networks, Madrid, Spain
{lucas.eznarriaga,fabio.giust}@imdea.org
[3] University Carlos III of Madrid, Spain
{aoliva,cjbc}@it.uc3m.es

Abstract. Optimized video delivery, Quality of Experience (QoE) and customer satisfaction are key issues to be addressed by mobile network operators while providing next generation video services to their users. The sharp increase in video traffic, the diversity of video applications and the availability of advanced smart-phones create new challenges that require a closer cooperation between the different layers of the IP protocol stack. Specifically, in this paper we explore the combination of heterogeneous wireless access (3G and WiFi) with intelligent video transport mechanisms implemented at the core network. Experiments demonstrate that implementing Scalable Video Coding (SVC) awareness at the mobility anchors can greatly enhance the video delivery process, increasing the QoE perceived at the users while reducing the cost per bit carried over the wireless network. Leveraging our prior work on IP flow mobility, we conduct experimental tests of SVC-based applications and report the perceived QoE over a sample of 25 people. The results show that the combination of 3G and WiFi coverage enhance the video delivery close to locally played video streams.

Keywords: Mobility, Wireless Video Streaming, 3G, WiFi, SVC, PMIPv6, Quality of Experience.

1 Introduction

In the past decade, mobile users have drastically changed their habits with respect to the content they consume, where it is consumed and, above all, when it is consumed. The availability of always connected mobile phones and flat rate data plans encourages the users to enjoy data services in a plethora of different manners: the common denominator is that the way contents are consumed has changed over time, being now part of everyday life helped by a proliferation of free to download applications, in particular video applications, which have gained great interest in the *smart-phone* community. Video on demand,

A. Timm-Giel et al. (Eds.): MONAMI 2012, LNICST 58, pp. 128–141, 2013.

Mobile TV, Video calling are just examples of the rich and constantly evolving landscape.

Networking technologies to enrich media delivery are also rapidly evolving. On the one hand we witness the increasing number of solutions based on HTTP adaptive streaming, usually over the top service, aiming at enhancing the Quality of Experience (QoE) of the user by combining intelligent caching (Content Delivery Networks, CDN) and opportunistic feedback from the mobile handset. On the other hand, the availability of new encoding mechanisms (e.g., Scalable Video Coding, SVC) carried over real time protocols such as RTP makes live media delivery more efficient and opens the floor for a new set of optimizations. The combination of these technologies with the ALL IP-based network defined by the 3GPP standardization body creates new opportunities for industrial manufacturers to provide efficient and cost effective solutions to overcome the sharp rise in mobile video traffic and associated costs per bit.

In this paper, we study innovative and efficient video delivery methods for dual mode handsets implementing cellular and WiFi technology in a network-based mobility management architecture using Proxy Mobile IPv6 (PMIPv6). By exploiting the characteristics of the SVC mechanisms and the possibility to be simultaneously connected to both cellular and WiFi networks, we show how policies can steer video traffic across both wireless access technologies. Media encoded with SVC has the peculiar property of generating different IP packets each containing a different quality layer. The reception of low quality layers enables the player to still play the video, at the mobile side, even if at a lower quality than planned. The experiments conducted in this paper confirm that it is possible to split the video flow across different wireless access technologies and that the WiFi connection can be used to boost the received video quality without negative impact on the overall playback experience. The authors, starting from previous work on the IP flow mobility subject, further describe how the very same architecture and protocol extensions can be tuned to efficiently handle video traffic exploiting the SVC encoding techniques.

The remainder of this article is organized as follows. Section 3 recalls IP flow mobility principles and introduces the Proxy Mobile IPv6 technology. Section 4 summarizes the properties of SVC techniques used later on in the paper. Section 5 describes the extensions of the IP flow mobility technology with video aware policies for flow marking and flow routing, while Section 6 shows the results obtained from real case testing. In Section 7 we extend the framework of our architecture by transposing it into the current 3GPP EPC design. We conclude in Section 8.

2   Related Work

There are some publications that relate to our own in several aspects. One of these works is [1], which describes a client server architecture for optimized video stream delivery over heterogeneous wireless networks. Defined in the SCALNET project, the architecture addresses single interface mobile devices and explores a number of extensions for multi interface support. The server is capable of handling multiple interfaces and IP addresses and generate a different RTP session for each SVC layer.

The server is also capable of receiving feedback from the clients and network elements. Client feedback concerns wireless connectivity and received QoS/QoE, while network elements send information about network congestions and available resources. With such information the server is capable of producing RTP sessions on different wireless access technologies aiming to optimize the client's perceived QoE.

The described experimental evaluation does not include any mobility support and features a special purpose video server and video client. Another feature is the use of SDP messages between the server and client to exchange information about the video streams.

While this paper shows that SVC video delivery over heterogeneous networks is a hot topic, it does not address cross layer interaction between application layer and IP layer. Furthermore, integration with IP Mobility Infrastructure would require more research and more emphasis should have been given to network intelligence. In conclusion, the fact that this solution is implemented over the top is its main drawback.

Another publication worth mentioning is [2]. It describes the challenges and open research issues while delivering video flows over wireless networks. Although a broad spectrum of issues is addressed we will focus only on the most relevant that have impact in our research work. First, the paper acknowledges the need to introduce more robust codecs. Second, it identifies the SVC extensions of the H.264/AVC standard as a key advance, although issues concerning protection of video frames differentiation by importance and priority still need to be addressed. Third, treating packets with sensitive information would allow improvements by checksum error correction schemes. Furthermore it identifies the need of cross layer interaction between MAC and IP layers, in order to adjust transmission rates depending on class services as well as to drop layers depending on priority. It concludes that packet dropping should not follow random algorithms, but rather be adaptive to terminal feedback to minimize the the perceived distortion. In this work it is also identified the need for terminal interaction and capability reporting to the network elements. Finally bandwidth estimation and cross layer provisioning are seen as key open features for the successful deployment of enhanced video delivery platforms.

This [2] paper, among others, identifies some of the technologies studied in our own work, namely smart packet marking, network congestion detection and terminal feedback reporting. The functionalities will be further detailed as they come up in our work.

In [3] is described a mobility platform to support quality driven handover procedures. Handover decisions take into account several metrics including QoS, QoE, Cost, Power efficiency and User preferences. By giving the right weight to each of the five parameters the mobile device is capable of selecting at any given time the best access satisfying the application requirements. To perceive the work's impact an evaluation is done in comparison form. This comparison opposes the author's solution results from a simple simulation scenario to well know management schemes such as Mobile IP , Mobile SIP and DDCP. The lack of detail in the description of the SASHA framework is its drawback, which makes it very hard to compare with other well known protocols. In addition, all the added value proposed by the SASHA framework is more focused on handover preparation and selection rather than handover execution. We argue that the authors could have implemented the same handover decision logic on top of any other mobility mechanism. Nevertheless the importance of terminal feedback and resource monitoring in the access and the terminal are taken as key points.

This will be further discussed in the remainder of this paper.

3   Wireless Multi-Access

This article leverages the multi-access capabilities of mobile devices and shows how video delivery can be enhanced across heterogeneous wireless technologies aiming at maximizing the perceived QoE by the user. The use of simultaneous wireless accesses is a feature of the latest release of 3GPP specifications defining the functionalities of both network components and mobile devices. In particular for a given mobile device it is possible, using the same Access Point Name (APN), to configure IP connectivity across the LTE/3G cellular network and the WLAN access. The simultaneous access is called IP flow mobility support since it enables tracking of IP connections belonging to a specific application and the routing of these selected flows to a specific technology. For example, a mobile device, having both a Voice over IP (VoIP) call and a video download ongoing at the same time, can keep the VoIP call over LTE and move the video download to the WLAN network. The mobile node will be always be reachable at the same IP home address on both networks.

The authors already gave an overview of IP flow mobility technology in [4]. Since we aim at presenting experimental results and real case scenarios we selected the already implemented network based IP mobility solution (PMIPv6 technology) extended with IP flow mobility capabilities. For exhaustive details on the technology, the interested reader can refer to [5], while we provide a short recall to ease the reader in understanding the rationale of the paper.

Mobility management in PMIPv6 [6] is network-based, meaning that the MN's mobility support is located on the network. The MN's mobility is then supported without its direct involvement. In fact, movement detection and IP signaling operations are performed by a new functional entity called Mobile Access Gateway (MAG), which usually resides in the access router for the MN (see Fig. 2). In a Localized Mobility Domain (LMD), which is the area where the network provides mobility support, there are multiple MAGs. The MAG learns through standard terminal operation, such as router and neighbor discovery or by means of link-layer support, about an MN's movement and coordinates routing state updates without any specific IP mobility support from the MN.

The IP prefixes (Home Network Prefixes – HNPs) used by MNs within an LMD are anchored at an entity called Local Mobility Anchor (LMA), which plays the role of local HA of the LMD. Bi-directional tunnels between the LMA and the MAGs are set up, so the MN is enabled to keep the originally assigned IP address despite its location changes within the LMD. Through the intervention of the LMA, packets addressed to the MN are tunneled to the appropriate MAG within the LMD, making the MN oblivious of its own mobility.

Current PMIPv6 provides basic multi-homing capabilities, enabling the MN to attach to the network using multiple interfaces. This triggers the LMA to create a different mobility session per attached interface and provide one or multiple HNPs to each interface. With current PMIPv6, the LMA can only move the complete set of HNPs from one interface to another, not allowing the movement of a single HNP or a sub-set of the allocated prefixes, and therefore disabling the possibility of supporting full flow mobility granularity. Hence, PMIPv6 must be extended to: i) span one mobility session across multiple MN interfaces, ii) allow the MN to configure the same HNPs on multiple interfaces and iii) transfer the policies between the MN and the network to install the required filters in the LMA/MAG for flow routing.

Some ideas to tackle this subject have been discussed in the IETF[1] NETEXT WG[2] as described in [7] and impact the MN, the MAG and the LMA. To support flow mobility, the MN must be able to send and receive traffic to/from any prefix associated to it through any of its interfaces. At the IETF, mechanisms such as Weak Host Model [8] and the Logical Interface (LIF) [9] have been studied as possible solutions on this subject. Taking into account that the MN's unawareness of mobility is paramount in PMIPv6, the IETF prefers the use of the LIF, since the Weak Host Model relies on changing the conditions of the packet admission process of the MN's IP stack.

On the other hand, the MAG must be able to forward packets addressed to any HNP associated to the MN, even if this HNP was delegated by a different MAG. The subject is being tackled in the IETF through the addition of extra signaling to the standard PMIPv6 so that the MAGs can be configured appropriately. Finally the LMA requires extensions to its binding cache, being able to simultaneously delegate the same set of prefixes to both access networks and install routing rules taking into account the per flow granularity.

4   Encoding, Streaming and Marking SVC Video

Scalable Video Coding (SVC) is the scalable extension of the Advanced Video Coding (AVC) MPEG-4 AVC/H.264 standard. It is developed by the Joint Video Team (JVT) of the ISO/IEC Moving Pictures Experts Group (MPEG) and the ITU-T Video Coding Experts Group (VCEG). Therefore, it is defined in both Amendment 3 to MPEG-4 Part 10 (AVC) [10] and in Annex G of the ITU-T Recommendation H.264 [11].

---

[1] Internet Engineering Task Force: http://www.ietf.org/
[2] http://datatracker.ietf.org/wg/netext/

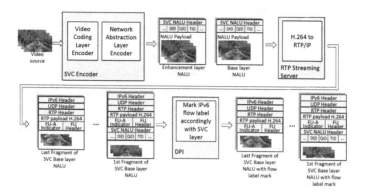

Fig. 1. Encapsulation of SVC video at different stages

SVC additions to MPEG-4 AVC/H.264 enable the partial multi-layered transmission and decoding of video bit streams hierarchically organized in the so-called SVC layers (or sub-streams). This allows their adaptation by including or excluding layers at the source, in-network, at the destination or in a cross-layer fashion to face the heterogeneity of devices, e.g., screen resolution, processing capabilities; and network conditions, such as bandwidth, jitter, errors, etc.

An SVC stream consists on a base layer of the lowest quality and bit rate which is H.264/AVC compliant and several enhancement SVC sub-streams. Scalability is provided by partially decoding an SVC stream which allows to increase the received quality as higher enhancement layers are completely received. It also allows to decrease it, in a graceful way, down to the base layer quality. Hence, the base layer transmission must be protected over the enhancement layers, e.g., being sent over the best link or employing more robust error protection techniques.

As for H.264/AVC, SVC bit streams are encapsulated in Network Abstraction Layer Units (NALUs) which are designed for transmission in packet oriented networks. SVC extends the H.264/AVC by defining new types of NALUs and extending the standard H.264/AVC NALU header with the fields to identify the scalability layer carried by the payload of the SVC NALU. The above explanation regarding the encapsulation of the different SVC flows is shown with higher detail in Fig. 1.

There are different types of scalability dimensions for SVC video bit streams:

- **Spatial scalability** is provided by encoding layers with different image sizes (picture resolution). The use of this feature is identified by the field *dependency_id* (DID) of the SVC NALU header.
- **Temporal scalability** is provided by encoding the video with different frame rate (temporal resolution). The use of this feature is identified by the *temporal_id* (TID) field.

– **Signal-to-Noise Ratio (SNR) scalability** is provided by encoding layers
with different quantization parameters (QPs) which determine the video
quality, i.e., the higher the QP the lower the quality. Two types of encoding
can be selected for this mode; *i)* Coarse-Grain Scalability (CGS) which allows
per-layer adaptation and *ii)* Medium-Grain Scalability (MGS) which allows
to progressively refine the quality by dropping certain NALUs. The use of
this feature is identified by the *quality_id* (QID) field.

Hence, an SVC layer is formed by SVC NALUs having the same (DID, TID,
QID) in the SVC NALU header.

RTP payload format for SVC [12] extends the one for H.264/AVC and allows
SVC streams to be transmitted over single or several RTP sessions: single-session
transmission (SST) or multi-session transmission (MST).

Depending on the size of the NALUs and other constraints, an RTP streaming server can encapsulate each NALU in an RTP packet (Single NALU Packet),
aggregate multiple NALUs in the payload of a unique RTP packet (Aggregation
Packet) or fragment them into several RTP packets or Fragmentation Units
(FUs) in which case only the first fragment contains the SVC header and therefore the SVC layer information. This limitation, specially when using SST transmission mode, increases the complexity of the network mechanisms in charge of
the adaptation of the SVC stream, as it does not allow for per-packet stateless inspection of the stream, being Deep Packet Inspection (DPI) techniques required
to keep the current SVC layer information state for FUs. For the experiments
performed in this work, we take advantage of DPI in order to set the flow label
field in the IPv6 header with a mark according to the SVC layer. In this way, at
next stages of the transmission, the routers can exploit the flow label to route
or redirect packets according to their policies (see Fig. 1).

5   IP Flow Mobility Management and SVC

Quality of Experience has become a hot topic while delivering media content over
heterogeneous wireless access networks. The combination of cellular technology,
by nature a centralized and managed wireless medium with guaranteed QoS, with
WiFi, by nature an unmanaged and distributed technology, requires different
ways of assessing the video quality perceived by the end user. QoE evaluation is
a key tool and this article shows how QoE can be augmented by leveraging the
multi access connectivity of mobile devices.

5.1   Architecture and Key Components

Fig. 3 depicts the key building blocks while also giving an understanding of the
physical mapping of our architecture:

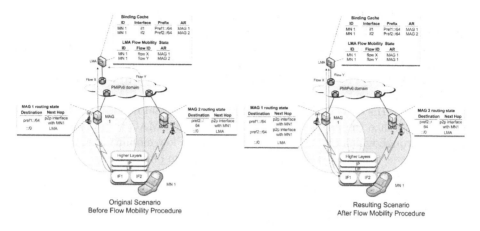

Fig. 2. PMIPv6 flow mobility operation

MN - LIF. The Logical Interface (LIF) is commonly implemented as part of the connection manager software of the MN, which is in charge of handling and automatically configuring the different network interfaces. Although the implementation of the LIF requires some changes on the client side, those are part of an already required terminal component (the connection manager), and does not have any impact on the IP stack, which remains standard. The LIF is a software entity that hides the real physical interface implementation to the host IP layer. Its use allows the MN to provide a single and permanent interface view to IP and higher layers, that can bind to this interface in order to establish any remote communication. Internally the logical interface is able to leverage several functionalities such as inter-technology handover, multi-homing or flow mobility, while presenting always the same IP address (or set of IP addresses) to higher layers. The LIF hides to the IP layer the physical interface used to actually send each packet, hence the movement of a flow from one physical interface to another is transparent to the IP and higher layers. Even more, it supports sequential attachment of interfaces as they come up, so the flow mobility features can be started in order to offload some interface or network (e.g., 3G offload) as soon as a new interface becomes active (e.g., a WiFi interface associates with an Access Point), without the higher layers being aware of it. In this way, the use of the LIF, sometimes referred to as Virtual Interface, enables the MN to suffer no drawbacks from the split of the SVC packet flow through different access technologies.

MAG - PMIPv6 Extended for Flow Mobility. As explained above, signaling extensions to PMIPv6 are required in order to provide the MAGs with the information regarding the different prefixes used by the MN. This information exchange is needed since, in general, a MAG will not forward traffic from/to a prefix that has not been delegated by it to the MN. In [7] several cases showing the possible configurations for the combinations of prefixes and interfaces

are detailed. The IETF is mainly focusing on two scenarios: *i)* the so-called
"handover with full flow granularity", which consists in the movement of a specific flow from one interface to another (e.g., a video-conference where the voice
is going through a reliable interface such as 3G and the video through a high
bandwidth link such as WiFi, but both flows are addressed to the same prefix),
and *ii)* the movement of a complete prefix and all the communications using it,
to another interface, scenario often referred to as "partial handover".

Both cases face the problem of requiring the target MAG to be aware of the
prefixes through which the MN is receiving traffic. Flow mobility signaling takes
place whenever the LMA decides to move a flow from one access to another. At
the time of movement, either the prefix is already known at the target MAG or
the LMA must advertise it to the MAG which is going to receive traffic addressed
to this prefix. In the case the MAG already knows the target prefix, the LMA
simply switches the flow to the target MAG, and no extra signaling is required.
In the case signaling is required, the IETF is defining new messages to manage
the notification to the MAG of the new flow/prefix to be forwarded.

Fig. 2 shows an example of the initial and resulting routing state of the network upon a flow mobility procedure is completed. Let us suppose the following
scenario: an MN (MN 1) is attached to the network through two interfaces `if1`,
connected to MAG1, and `if2`, connected to MAG2 and each one receives a prefix,
`pref1::/64` for `if1` and `pref2::/64` for `if2` respectively. The MN is receiving
two flows, Flow X and Y. Flow X is addressed towards `pref1:lif` (being `lif`
the resulting EUI64 identifier of the Logical Interface) and is forwarded through
MAG1, while Flow Y is addressed to `pref2:lif` and is forwarded though MAG2.
Following this configuration, the LMA has a conceptual data structure called the
Flow Mobility Cache containing the mapping of flows and corresponding MAGs.
This mapping can be based on any of the flow identifiers defined in [13].

At some point in time the LMA decides to move Flow Y from MAG2 to
MAG1. The decision can be based on application profiles, or traffic type oriented policies triggered due to network congestion, for instance. In order to do
so, the LMA needs to signal MAG1 that Flow Y is going to be forwarded through
it. Using dedicated signaling, the LMA is able to install state in MAG1 regarding the identification of the flow and the identity of MN 1. Once this state is
installed on MAG1, the LMA modifies the mapping stored in its Flow Mobility
Cache, indicating that Flow Y is routed through MAG1 and starts forwarding
the packets towards MAG1. The final state after flow mobility completion of the
routing configuration on the network is also presented on Fig. 2.

This flow routing mechanism can be used to influence how an SVC encoded
packet flow is routed. This means that marked packets with a certain flow label
(i.e., containing the same video layer) will be routed according to the quality
layer they contain, and therefore through a different technology if necessary.

LMA - FM. The key addition is the intelligence in the Flow Manager to
understand the SVC video layers and to take decisions according the predefined
policies. In particular the flow manager is capable of splitting a single video flow
across two different wireless access technologies. By means of specific information

contained in the IPv6 header (the flow label field) the flow manager can route the packets containing the different video layers on the most appropriate wireless medium. The key idea is that the Flow Manager receives information about traffic load, network congestion and can react accordingly. By leveraging on the complement of WLAN access it can therefore deliver different video quality sub-streams on different wireless access media. By nature low quality layers have low bandwidth requirements while high quality layers are more greedy in terms of bit rate. To this end, dynamic decision can be taken. If the MN has only cellular technology and the stream is badly played, the quality can be lowered (high quality layers dropped) to preserve customer satisfaction. In case the MN has both cellular and WLAN coverage (and the cellular network is overloaded) the LMA can send low quality layers on the cellular connections and route high quality layers over the WLAN connection. Thus a flow can be split across different access technologies according to routing and policy rules, allowing the evaluation of the perceived feedback to be done by the network.

SVC Server. The SVC server transmits SVC encoded streams. In addition, it marks the outgoing packets to embed in the IPv6 header the information related to the carried quality layer. This packet marking could also be performed by a network entity, like the LMA, so no direct interaction between the video service provider and the network video provider is required (in case they are not the same).

6   Experimental Setup

The benefits that can be obtained from the use of a combined SVC and flow mobility approach are shown through an experimental analysis, which setup is depicted in Fig. 3.

The testbed features an MN implementing the LIF over 3G (USB dongle) and WiFi interfaces . The 3G part relies on an in-house UMTS network while the WiFi link is provided by an IEEE 802.11b/g Access Point. Each access technology is connected to a different MAG: WLAN is configured for direct IPv6 connectivity between MAG and MN while over the 3G access a VPN (Open-VPN[3]) IPv6-in-IPv4 tunnel is built, due to the limited availability of IPv6 in 3G access. The MAGs implement the IP flow Mobility extensions developed for [5], while the LMA box includes flow mobility management software. The video server is based on the Live555[4] library, which supports SVC streaming through RTSP encapsulation. Also, the video server runs a tool to mark the packets according to the explanation given in Section 4. As video client, the MPlayer[5] application was selected, since it supports the SVC codec through Open SVC Decoder[6] library.

---

[3] http://www.openvpn.net/
[4] http://www.live555.com
[5] http://www.mplayerhq.hu/
[6] http://sourceforge.net/projects/opensvcdecoder/

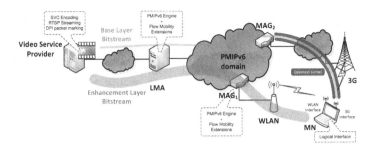

Fig. 3. Experimental setup

The video used for our tests is a two minutes-long scene taken from an animation movie[7] with resolution 640x360 encoded with JSVM[8] software, using SNR MGS mode with two layers: *basic*, with $QP = 46$ resulting in an average bit rate of 150 Kbps, and *enhancement*, with $QP = 26$ and rough average bit rate of 900 Kbps. The overall video stream is hence transmitted at more than 1 Mbps on average, and we argue these characteristics are typical for streaming good quality videos on hand-held devices.

Our experiment consists in streaming the SVC coded video, which in the remainder will be referred as SVC local, from the server outside the PMIPv6 domain to the MN, under three different conditions, which depend on the availability of connectivity options for the MN:

– SVC 3G scenario: the MN is attached to the 3G MAG only, and both SVC video sub-streams are delivered to the client, as no policy is defined at the flow manager;
– SVC 3G base scenario: the MN has only the 3G link active, but, according to an operator's decision (e.g., due to congestion), the flow manager at the LMA drops the flow related to the enhancement layer, based on the assumption that the 3G network cannot cope with a satisfactory delivery of both layers, or that it is consuming too many resources on the access;
– SVC 3G/WiFi scenario: the MN is connected to the network through the 3G and WiFi links. The attachment to multiple MAGs is detected by the LMA and the FM, which installs routing rules to forward the low quality sub-stream via the 3G MAG, and the high quality layer through the WiFi MAG.

The system can automatically switch among any of the described scenarios, as the flow manager, Mplayer and the LIF run custom tools to react promptly to a change in the network conditions (which are simulated in our platform), producing the proper adjustments smoothly. From the user's perspective, no manual intervention is required, as MPlayer can seamlessly switch between SVC layers, by using an ad-hoc LIF-to-MPlayer API based on flow and interface

---

[7] http://www.bigbuckbunny.org/
[8] http://ip.hhi.de/imagecom_G1/savce/downloads/SVC-Reference-Software.htm

Table 1. Video ratings summary

Video	MOS	95% confidence interval
SVC 3G	2.44	±0.30
SVC 3G base	1.36	±0.22
SVC 3G+WiFi	3.36	±0.27

information (it can be easily extended to allow sending commands to the NICs, e.g., to power up and/or to associate to an ESSID/APN).

In order to assess the validity of our proposal, we conducted a Double Stimulus Impairment Scale (DSIS) test. Following ITU-R Rec. BT 500-11 for the subjective evaluation of video and audio quality, we showed to 25 users the 3 videos related to the corresponding test scenarios against SVC local, which is taken as reference. After watching the videos, the people involved in the test were asked to rate the degree of impairment with respect to the reference on the standard discrete five-level scale: *Very annoying* (mark 1), *Annoying* (2), *slightly annoying* (3), *Perceptible, but not annoying* (4) and *Imperceptible* (5).

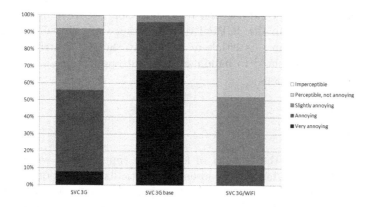

Fig. 4. Marks distribution for the video samples

The results obtained are summarized in Table 1, where the Mean Opinion Score (MOS) and the 95% confidence interval are shown. The complete distribution of the ratings collected for each video sample is depicted in Fig. 4.

We can observe from the stacked histogram that the video started on the 3G interface does not produce a good experience at the user. Also, it causes a considerable resource consumption, hence after a network's decision, the packets belonging to the enhancement layer are dropped. Unfortunately, the video with the base SVC-layer only (SVC 3G base) was rated the poorest, meaning that there was a sensible deterioration in the user's QoE. However, the bandwidth availability can be augmented by establishing an additional link using WiFi. The PMIP+Flow Mobility intelligence is now able to re-direct the video layers through both paths to the terminal, therefore restoring a video quality that is equal or better to what experienced with the 3G only. More, a key-aspect in this latter scenario, is that the resource consumption in the 3G network (the most critical for an operator) is kept identical as that in scenario 2, where the enhancement layer is dropped.

7   3GPP Considerations

The experimental platform depicted in Section 6 has been implemented using the IETF standard for network based mobility, namely PMIPv6. PMIPv6 has also being adopted by 3GPP[9] as alternative to the GPRS Tunneling Protocol (GTP) protocol. In the 3GPP architecture, both protocols can be used to implement tunneling mechanisms between the Serving Gateway (S-GW) and the PDN Gateway (P-GW) to handle user mobility. The S-GW includes the MAG functionality while the P-GW implements the LMA functionality. We argue that the results presented for the PMIPv6 case hold also in the case of a GTP based network, being the terminal not impacted by any mobility signaling. In addition, the mapping of the flow management functionality to the 3GPP architecture concerns the Policy Charging and Rules Function (PCRF), an already well established component in the 3GPP Evolved Packet Core. To summarize, the concepts demonstrated in this article nicely fit into the 3GPP architecture and the intelligence implemented to handle SVC based applications is added value for mobile service providers.

8   Conclusions

In this article we show the benefits of leveraging simultaneous wireless access technologies while receiving video content. In particular the use of cellular and WiFi networks combined with SVC based applications has been experimentally demonstrated. The vertical integration of these technologies allows mobile service providers to reduce the cost per bit while maximizing the perceived QoE by the end user. Starting from previous work on IP flow mobility, we extended the experimental framework for SVC based applications. A packet marking function is proposed to intelligently mark SVC payloads and video aware rules are installed in the mobility anchors to reach mobile users on both cellular and WiFi networks. The experiments confirm that the proposed technology outperforms current solutions achieving a better performance than current approaches. Finally, as next steps we plan to design and implement a better feedback mechanism, relaying more information from the mobile device to the network so to more efficiently adapt the stream and therefore the perceived QoE. The impact of additional parameters, such as the range of access technologies, number of SVC layers, number and class of streaming users will be further explored.

---

[9] http://www.3gpp.org/

Acknowledgment. The research leading to these results has received funding from the European Commission's Seventh Framework Programme (FP7-ICT-2009-5) under grant agreement n. 258053 (MEDIEVAL project). Antonio de la Oliva has also received funding from the Spanish Government, MICINN, under research grant TIN2010-20136-C03.

References

1. Sutinen, T., Rivas, H.: Multi-interface Extension to a Scalable Video Streaming Architecture. Journal of Communications 6(9), 700–710 (2011)
2. Hsiao, Y., Lee, J., Chen, J., Chu, Y.: H.264 video transmissions over wireless networks: Challenges and solutions. Computer Communications 34(14), 1661–1672 (2011)
3. Ciubotaru, B., Muntean, G.-M.: SASHA-A quality-oriented handover algorithm for multimedia content delivery to mobile users. IEEE Trans. Broadcast. 55(2), 437–450 (2009)
4. de la Oliva, A., Bernardos, C.J., Calderon, M., Melia, T., Zuniga, J.C.: IP Flow Mobility: Smart Traffic Offload for Future Wireless Networks. IEEE Communications Magazine (October 2011)
5. Melia, T., Bernardos, C.J., de la Oliva, A., Giust, F., Calderon, M.: IP Flow Mobility in PMIPv6 Based Networks: Solution Design and Experimental Evaluation. Wireless Personal Communications Journal (October 2011), doi:10.1007/s11277-011-0423-3
6. Gundavelli, S., et al.: Proxy Mobile IPv6. RFC 5213 (Proposed Standard), Internet Engineering Task Force (August. 2008)
7. Bernardos, C.J.: Proxy Mobile IPv6 Extensions to Support Flow Mobility. draft-bernardos-netext-pmipv6-flowmob-02, Internet Engineering Task Force (February 2011)
8. Braden, R.: Requirements for Internet Hosts - Communication Layers. Internet Engineering Task Force, RFC 1122 (Standard) (October 1989)
9. Melia, T., Gundavelli, S.: Logical Interface Support for multi-mode IP Hosts, Work in Progress, draft-ietf-netext-logical-interface-support-01, Internet Engineering Task Force (October 2010)
10. ISO/IEC, Information technology – Coding of audio-visual objects – Part 10: Advanced Video Coding, 14496-10:2005
11. ITU-T Recommendation H.264, Advanced video coding for generic audiovisual services (November 2007)
12. Wenger, S., Wang, Y.-K., Schierl, T., Eleftheriadis, A.: RTP Payload Format for Scalable Video Coding, RFC 6190, Internet Engineering Task Force (May 2011)
13. Tsirtsis, G., Giarreta, G., Soliman, H., Montavont, N.: Traffic Selectors for Flow Bindings. RFC 6088 (Proposed Standard), Internet Engineering Task Force (January 2011)

On the Performance of LTE UL Power Control in Realistic Conditions

Maria A. Lema, Mario Garcia-Lozano, Silvia Ruiz, and Joan Olmos*

Universitat Politecnica de Catalunya (UPC),
C/ Esteve Terradas, 7 - 08860 Castelldefels, Spain
maria.lema@tsc.upc.edu

Abstract. This paper deals with the interference control in the uplink (UL) of Long Term Evolution (LTE) systems. Although the multiple access technique allows an almost null intra-cell interference, the system is still sensitive to the inter-cell component caused by neighbouring cells. The UL power control proposed by the 3GPP is a means to reduce this interference. In this sense, user equipments (UE) establish an operation point (open loop power control or OLPC) to compensate the mean path loss and its slow variations. Additionally, this may be fine tuned by specific commands (closed loop). The current paper focuses on the performance of OLPC when deployed in realistic scenarios where heterogeneity is a key feature, both in the deployment of sites and in the concentration of users. The investigation is done in a comparative way, against a classic synthetic and regular scenario. Results indicate that the performance of the OLPC differs from the theoretical environment, due to the difference in the scenario nature. The summation of indoor coverage and guided path-loss results the urban scenario OLPC optimal point to lie in between two limits, one established by the reduced transmitted power fixed by the OLPC and the other by the interferences.

Keywords: Long Term Evolution, Uplink Power Control, Realistic Scenario, Interference Managemenr.

1 Introduction

The Long Term Evolution (LTE) of Universal Mobile Telecommunications System (UMTS) arise in a context of constant growth of user demand towards mobile data services. In order to assure quality of service (QoS) to the subscribers it is necessary to design mechanisms that accurately manage the radio resources. Specifically, power efficient techniques which permit reducing interference, and hence, obtain higher speed rates. For this reason they have a paramount importance in radio network deployments.

Regarding interference, the particular medium access technique in LTE allows an almost null intra-cell interference. The use of Single-Carrier Frequency

---

* This work is supported by the Spanish National Science Council through the project TEC2011-27723-C02-01 and by the European Regional Development Fund (ERDF).

A. Timm-Giel et al. (Eds.): MONAMI 2012, LNICST 58, pp. 142–155, 2013.

Division Multiple Access (SC-FDMA) implies that channels used by different users are orthogonal [1]. On the other hand, it is desirable to reuse all available channels in every cell to achieve higher throughput levels. This implies interferences between adjacent cells jeopardize the performance of certain users. For this reason, the power control mechanism presented by 3GPP plays an important role in maintaining the required Signal to Interference Noise Ratio (SINR) while reducing the interferences caused among the cells in the scenario.

Traditional power control algorithms assure that users with the same service are received at the eNodeB (eNB) with the same SINR. This approach fully compensates the particular path-loss of every link, for this reason it is known as Full Compensation power control. In this scheme cell edge users transmit higher power levels to meet the requirements, as they are making up for a high path-loss. In order to avoid this situation, the PC formula defined for the LTE Uplink (UL) enables the use of Fractional Power Control (FPC). This means that the User Equipment (UE) can compensate for a fraction of its path-loss, so a given UE with higher losses will operate at lower SINR values and hence, generate less interference [2].

Several previous studies were done regarding this topic. In [3] authors analyse and compare the uplink OLPC against two reference mechanisms. Results show that FPC is beneficial when compared to traditional full-compensation algorithms. Authors in [2] present an accurate study of the FPC regarding the impact of the OLPC parameter set on the resulting SINR distribution. Also, it evaluates the impact on the interference generated when setting the OLPC variables. Further work is presented in [4] where parting from the uplink LTE PC formula, it adapts the total transmitted power density so as to compensate for the variation in the allocated bandwidth by maintaining the OLPC constants. In fact, PC variables may not be optimal for all load situations. In [5], authors analyse the influence of uplink power control on system performance in an indoor scenario. Regarding the closed-loop PC, in [6] and [7] the authors compare the performance between both OL and closed-loop PC. Closed-loop variables also are the objective in [8], where authors use the closed-loop constants to control the interference generated by other users and obtain high gains compared to the OLPC results. All these studies are centred on the performance evaluation of the PC formula in synthetic scenarios. Realistic scenarios present new and interesting challenges when assessing performances, also in other contexts as it is downlink inter-cell interference coordination [9], where authors conclude that schemes for realistic networks can not be done by simply extending classical approaches.

Rising upon the dependency on the scenario distribution and on the users' position, the novelty of this work is the analysis of LTE UL OLPC under realistic conditions. It is also done an investigation on the optimal adjustments of the OLPC parameters by evaluating first the impact on the parameter variation. This research has been done in a comparative way, against a classic layout with hexagonal distribution of eNBs.

This paper is organized as follows: Section II explains the power control defined in LTE. Section III describes the system model that assumed in the simulations and Section IV presents the results. Finally in Section V some conclusions are extracted.

2   UL Power Control in LTE

The UE performs the OLPC based on the path-losses estimation, broadcast system parameters, and dedicated signalling. Equation 1 from [10] establishes the criteria to adjust the power. Note that there is no signalling associated to OLPC on the Physical Downlink Control Channel of LTE.

$$P = \min(P_{\max}, P_0 + 10 \log M + \alpha \cdot PL + \Delta_{\mathrm{TF}} + \Delta_{\mathrm{i}}) \tag{1}$$

Where,

- $P_{\max}$: Maximum allowed transmission power for all UEs (dBm).
- M: is the number of Physical Resource Blocks (PRBs)[1] allocated in the Physical Uplink Shared Channel (PUSCH). Regardless of the allocated bandwidth the power per PRB remains constant
- P_0: This parameter is used to control the SINR target. It has an important impact on the system performance. Intuitively, an increase in P_0 would provoke a rise in the transmitted power density, and as a consequence global SINR could decrease (dBm).
- α: is a broadcasted cell-specific path loss compensation factor for FPC. The basics of the OLPC is to compensate for a fraction α of the PL and slow variations, determining the basic operating point. The path loss compensation factor variation would bring the system into a trade-off between total UL capacity and cell-edge data rate.
- PL: is the downlink path-loss estimated by the UE. This estimation is done based on the reference signal received power (dB).
- Δ_{TF}: is a UE specific parameter that allows a finer tuning of transmission power considering the transport format that is allocated to the user. Without loss of generality, UEs do not consider any additional offset in the current work.
- Δ_{i}: is a closed loop correction that can be accumulative or absolute and it is signaled by the eNB. Since the focus of this work is to analyse the performance of the system under OLPC conditions this parameter is just set to zero.

From the previous paragraphs it is clear that P_0 and α are not only the most important parameters, but also those with major impact in the system performance. Both must be adjusted at a time, setting an optimal combination to assure an interference operating point in the scenario to accomplish the Block Error Rate (BLER) and SINR requirements. It is important to bear in mind

---

[1] A PRB is the minimum allocable BW defined in LTE.

Table 1. Realistic Scenario SystemModel

Parameter	Value
Pixel size	5 m
UTM upper left coordinates	600500 m X 5340500 m Y
Area	500 x 500 pixels
Transmitters	16 sites (Trisectorial antennas)
Propagation model	COST 231-Walfisch–Ikegami
Indoor losses	15 dB

that when modifying any of both parameters the cell capacity and the cell-edge performance varies. So, it is necessary to tune them and find the combination that suits the most with the scenario definition.

3   System Model and Methodology

With the aim of studying the performance of the OLPC, the algorithm is studied under a realistic scenario obtained from the MORANS initiative developed during the European COST Action 273 [11] and whose aim was the definition of scenarios with different levels of realism so that researchers were able to test and compare radio resource management algorithms at the planning and system level with a more realistic distribution of the base stations. The propagation model considered in this system model is the COST 231-Walfisch-Ikegami[12].

The model comprises a dense urban area composed by a fraction of the city of Vienna. In particular the following inputs are provided by the MORANS scenario:

- Area of simulation: UTM-30 coordinates of the selected area.
- Building information: Represents the height at a given pixel. This information is used to compute the streets direction and it also is an input to the propagation model that realistically considers these buildings as a source of diffraction.
- Site and transmitter information: physical location, height and antenna patterns.

System model parameters regarding this area are summarized in Table 1.

The other scenario considered in this investigation is a conventional synthetic one. The system model comprises 24 tri-sectorial cells equally distributed along 56 km^2. Other system aspects are listed in Table 2.

To carry out the analysis a System level Simulator programmed in C# language in a .NET framework has been implemented, which involves most of the RRM functionalities considered in 3GPP LTE.

Table 2. Synthetic Scenario SystemMode

Parameter	Value
Pixel size	15 m
Area	500 x 500 pixels
Transmitters	8 sites (Tri-sectorial antennas)
Propagation model	L = 35,5+37,6log(d); d = distance in meters
Shadow fading	Log-normal, 8 dB standard deviation

The different blocks implemented are:

- A channel state information (CSI) manager, which is in charge of allocating bandwidth parts to be used by the UEs to transmit sounding reference signals (SRS). Indeed, this module is also in charge of collecting this SRS and computing the corresponding sounded SINR.
- The link adaptation unit works in conjunction with the CSI manager. Specifically, it selects the appropriate Modulation and Coding Scheme (MCS) according to the sounded SINR values.
- The last main block implemented is the Packet Scheduler which is proportional fair based and includes a HARQ controller based on the specifications given in [10]. The packet scheduler attends a maximum of 8 UEs per TTI. Users are modelled with full buffers during the entire simulation. This has a direct impact on the quantity of PRBs that can be allocated to each user. Since the eNB will intend to allocate the entire system bandwidth, the fixed transmission bandwidth scheduled to each UE will initially be equal. In the case when no UE can accomplish the power requirements for that bandwidth then is reduced one PRB, until all users are allocated or the number of PRBs arrives to zero.

Users are randomly set in the area, even though a fixed number of users per eNB is considered.

Simulations are dynamic in time, considering realistically long and short-term fading. In particular, spatially correlated log-normal variations are introduced following the approach in [13]. An extended typical urban power delay profile is assumed considering a UE speed of 3 km/h and following the model in [14]. Main simulation parameters are listed in Table 3.

The methodology employed to analyse both scenarios was to run several simulations for each one changing α and P_0 parameters. In fact as α only takes values from 0.4 to 1, every value of α is simulated for all the range of $P_0[-126, +23] \, dBm$ [10].

4   Results

The OLPC algorithm is strongly dependent on the simulation environment, as the resulting transmitted power is directly related to the path-loss each user

Table 3. Simulation Parameters

Parameter	Value
Carrier frequency	2 GHz
Simulated BW	20 MHz [84 PRB, 16 used for control]
SC-FDMA symbols	6; 1 reserved for sounding transmissions
Fast fading	ITU Typical Urban (3km/h)
Users per cell	20
Number of scheduled users per TTI	8
UE traffic model	Full (infinite) buffers
Maximum UE TX power	250 mW
HARQ	Synchronous and adaptive
Transmission delay	8 ms
BLER target	10 %
AMC formats	Defined in [10] Table 8.6.1-1
Channel estimation	Real (SRS sounding)
SRS sounding BW	24 PRB
SRS sounding periodicity	1 TTI
MCS index	17 MCSs (64-QAM not supported)

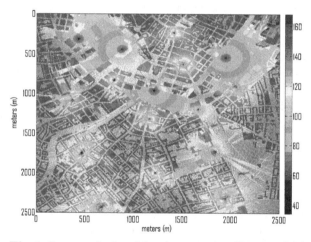

Fig. 1. Losses calculated for the scenario of Vienna (dB)

experiences. The system behaviour is determined by the configuration of the OLPC parameters. As stated before, these are mainly α and P_0. The selected pair of values will be those that, while maintaining a reasonable level of interference, maximizes the cell and user throughput.

As explained when introducing the core topic of this paper, the OLPC algorithm is studied in a dense urban realistic environment and in the context of our benchmark, the synthetic case.

The realistic environment presents many sources of losses, as it is seen in Figure 1. This figure also shows the transmitter position in the area under test.

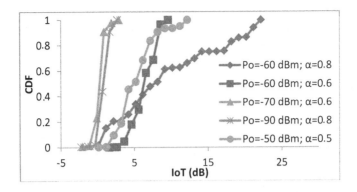

Fig. 2. IoT levels in the realistic scenario

The analysed transmitters are the central ones. The areas with no line of sight are the most attenuated ones, as signals are attenuated by diffractions from the buildings nearby; also indoor communications are severely affected by the large attenuations. This would lead to user transmission power limits, as they would have to compensate for a larger path-loss. Also, as users must transmit at maximum levels of power, the OLPC configuration must be accurately selected. Cell-edge users must reach the minimum SINR to be scheduled, and at the same time do not generate much interference in the scenario.

The comparison between both scenarios is done with different configurations of the OLPC parameters because the behaviour of both systems to the same values is not comparable. Despite the absolute values of P_0 and α, what is interesting to analyse is the overall behaviour of the system to a change in both parameters.

Figure 2 presents the IoT (Interference over Thermal[2]) levels for several combination of parameters. In general, values of interference are low bearing in mind that the analysis is done under a dense urban area. As P_0 lowers for a fixed value of α ($P_0 = -60$ dBm, $\alpha = 0.6$ and $P_0 = -70$ dBm, $\alpha = 0.6$) the interference does as well; the same happens with the path-loss compensation factor ($P_0 = -60$ dBm, $\alpha = 0.8$ and $P_0 = -60$ dBm, $\alpha = 0.6$). This happens because these two parameters are directly related to the transmitted power. However, a change in P_0 lowers the total IoT level, as it regulates the global SINR level, whereas a change in α causes a more spread IoT level, as the latter regulates the fairness in the eNB radius. Interference is not so high when compared to the thermal noise, and except for the case in which $P_0 = -90$ dBm or $P_0 = -70$ dBm the IoT is just some units above the noise power.

On the other hand, in the benchmark scenario, interferences are clearly the limiting aspect of the power control modelling. Almost all the configurations simulated for the synthetic case show higher levels of interference, an example of it is shown in Figure 3. The values selected are interesting in the sense that a

---

[2] Interference plus noise divided by noise.

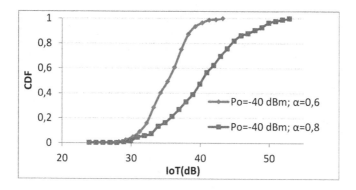

Fig. 3. IoT levels in the synthetic scenario

small variation on the fractional path-loss compensation parameter leads to an increase on the IoT levels. In this sense, the system aims at keeping IoT below 16 dB in all the scenario. This way a correct functioning of the eNB is assured [2]. Both variables must be tuned in order to find this interference level. When tuning P_0 and α for both scenarios, the most interesting points of analysis are different due to the changes in the scenario configuration.

Despite the low levels of interferences reached in the realistic case, there are some OLPC configurations that leave a great number of users without any transmission, lowering also the overall cell throughput, as it can be observed in Figure 4 (a). When $P_0 = -60$ dBm and $\alpha = 0.8$ cell edge users cannot transmit enough power to surpass the interferences and achieve a SINR value higher than the minimum required by the least MCS index. This configuration generates a high level of interference and in these conditions cell edge users cannot be scheduled. Hence, a high percentage of users are devoured of transmission. The same graph shows an improved cell average throughput because the transmitted power is reduced due to the fractional path-loss compensation variable.

Figure 4 (b) depicts the percentage of users that do not transmit during the entire simulation for different configurations of OLPC variables. Besides the previous case, there is also a high percentage of users with no successful transmissions when $P_0 = -90$ dBm and $\alpha = 0.6$. In this case, a high number of users cannot reach the minimum SINR requirements because the transmitted power lowers. Only cell centre users are scheduled as their sounded SINR values are the highest ones. Also, one RTT later, the received SINR is low to accomplish the established BLER and after many retransmissions, all packets are discarded. Clearly this is another limitation in the scenario: the power capabilities to deal with the path-losses in non line of sight conditions. Based on the results, the selected pair of values should be the one that maximizes the cell throughput and assures the maximum number of successful transmissions, taking into account both limitations presented: interference generation and transmitted power capabilities.

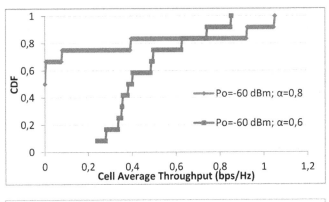

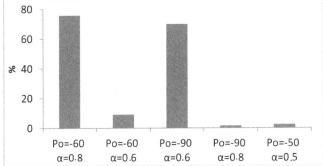

Fig. 4. Throughput evaluation in the realistic scenario (a) Cell CDF throughput, (b) Percentage of users that have no successful transmissions

The synthetic scenario has a similar performance, however it just presents one of both limitations studied in the previous case. Figure 5 pictures the cell throughput for two pair of variables. When the transmission power rises, cell-edge users are not able to transmit because interferences are too high. Users are power limited and their transmission power is not enough to overcome the interference level and obtain a higher MCS. However, when the fractional path-loss compensation factor reduces, transmission power lowers and the fairness increases, and with it the overall eNB throughput rises as well.

In order to appreciate more the effect of both limits above explained, Figure 6 shows two graphics that compare both environments. The OLPC variables in the horizontal axis is ordered from higher to lower average transmitted power. Values presented in this graphic are the most significant ones resulting from tuning P_0 and α. Again, values employed in both scenarios are different because the limitations on the performance of both scenarios are at different combination of values of the OLPC variables.

In this sense, for the highest value of transmitted power the user average throughput is zero. This means that only a few number of them are allowed to transmit, those near the eNB. Since users are transmitting at very high values of

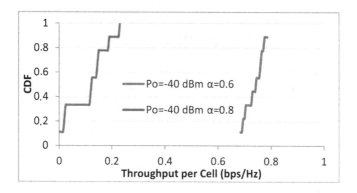

Fig. 5. Throughput evaluation in the synthetic scenario

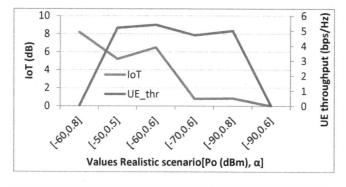

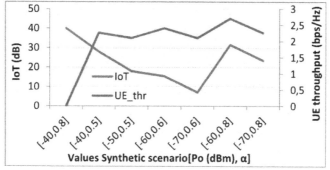

Fig. 6. Scenarios comparison in terms of limitations. (a) realistic (b) synthetic

Table 4. Realistic Scenario: Parameter Selection

α	0.5
Po	-50 dBm
Mean IoT	5.21 dB
Mean UE Throughput	5.2 bps/Hz

Table 5. Synthetic Scenario: Parameter Selection

α	0.6
Po	-60 dB
Mean IoT	15 dB
Mean UE Throughput	2.4 bps/Hz

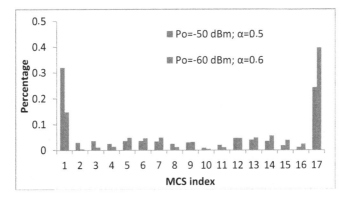

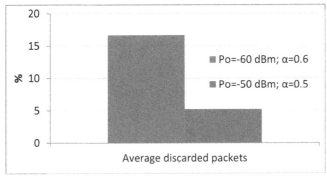

Fig. 7. Realistic environment. (a) MCS index allocated (b)Percentage of discarded packets over the allocated ones.

power, maximum interference is generated. As the transmission power lowers so does the interference and there are more users scheduled because most of them are capable of achieving the SINR levels for the MCS indexes. However, when the OLPC variables set a very low SINR level (by reducing P_0) transmission power reduces. As users must compensate high path-losses many retransmissions are required. Average user throughput can still be maintained (as it can be seen in Figure 6, for values of -70 or -90 dBm) as cell centre users can be scheduled high MCS due to the reduced level of IoT, however, as it was explained before, average cell throughput is abruptly reduced due to the high number of retransmissions. The realistic environment presents this limitation as the power lowers, but the synthetic scenario does not. Although the tendency is to reduce both interferences and average UE throughput, the limitation is not as abrupt as in the realistic case, due to the difference in path-loss.

The two couples of variables that reach better performance in the scenario of Vienna are $[-60, 0.6]$ and $[-50, 0.5]$. Both values are attractive as the transmitted power is correct for assuring fairness and, at the same time it does not generate high levels of interference. As it was seen in Figure 4, average user throughput can be high although a certain number of users remain with no successful transmissions, jeopardizing the system's throughput (less users transmit at higher bit rates, rising the average). These values are further analysed in terms of MCS allocation and discarded packets, as it is shown in Figure 7. When users compensate less for their path-loss, $\alpha = 0.5$, transmission power lowers. This is reflected on the MCS selected. Users SRSs are received at lower SINR values and the probability of being allocated a higher MCS lowers. On the other hand, when $\alpha = 0.6$, users are allocated most frequently the highest MCS indexes. Intuitively, this should show an increase in the system throughput. However, as transmitted power rises, interferences does as well. So, the result is that the estimated SINR is higher than the real one, and in consequence more packets are discarded. This effect lowers the cell average throughput, as more retransmissions are required. The parameter setting that shows better performance is summed up in Table 4. Values of throughput and mean IoT are also presented.

Table 5 represents the final configuration for the benchmark environment in this case. In addition, the values of average user throughput and interferences are listed. The resulting value of P_0 is higher in the realistic case, to assure that the transmissions are received and less packets are discarded. Also, α must be lower to assure that users have available power to be scheduled. In the case of the realistic conditions, transmission power can be higher as the path-loss experienced by the users is also higher.

5 Conclusions

A detailed performance study of the LTE uplink OLPC has been presented, considering a realistic scenario and comparing it to a classic hexagonal based distribution of base stations; both environments are very similar in the number of transmitters analysed and cell radius. The OLPC is dependent on the path-loss each user estimates, so the environment is a key issue when investigating the performance at the system level. To assure the optimum functioning of the RRM algorithms, the OLPC parameters must be adjusted. Both scenarios present different limits. The realistic case is sensitive to the interference generation and the availability of the transmission power, while the synthetic case presents high sensitiveness to the interferences. Therefore, the PC algorithm must be adjusted in a different manner. The versatility presented by the algorithm allows finding suitable configurations for each specific case.

Results show that the OLPC adjustment at a given environment needs a special analysis of the system performance due to a change on the OLPC parameters. For instance, both scenarios presented in this work require a different parameter adjustment.

To conclude, the power control formula is a quite versatile way of optimizing cell networks that share frequency carriers. Still it has to be studied separately in each case, taking into account several factors within the area. As the system is brought into a trade-off when applying the OLPC formula, the performance evaluated for one environment may not work for another, maybe similar, but with totally different assumptions, as seen in the presented study.

As an outcome of this work it can be concluded that the performance of the studied system should be further improved with the open loop corrections. This would charge the system with more signalling, however the UEs can save even more power and make their communications more power efficient.

References

1. Myung, H.G.: Introduction to Single Carrier FDMA. In: Proceedings of the 15th European Signal Processing Conference, EUSIPCO 2007 (2007)
2. Castellanos, C., Villa, D., Rosa, C., Pedersen, K., Calabrese, F., Michaelsen, P., Michel, J.: Performance of Uplink Fractional Power Control in UTRAN LTE. In: Vehicular Technology Conference, VTC Spring 2008, pp. 2517–2521. IEEE (2008)
3. Simonsson, A., Furuskar, A.: Uplink Power Control in LTE-Overview and Performance, Subtitle: Principles and Benefits of Utilizing rather than Compensating for SINR Variations. In: IEEE 68th Vehicular Technology Conference, VTC 2008-Fall, pp. 1–5. IEEE (2008)
4. Boussif, M., Rosa, C., Wigard, J., Müandller, R.: Load Adaptive Power Control in LTE Uplink. In: 2010 European Wireless Conference (EW), pp. 288–293 (April 2010)
5. Muehleisen, M., Walke, B.: Analytical Evaluation of LTE Uplink Performance in the IMT-Advanced Indoor Hotspot Scenario. In: Proceedings of PIMRC 2011, Toronto, Canada, p. 6 (September 2011)
6. Müllner, R., Ball, C.F., Ivanov, K., Lienhart, J., Hric, P.: Performance Comparison between Open-Loop and Closed-Loop Uplink Power Control in UTRAN LTE Networks. In: Proceedings of the 2009 International Conference on Wireless Communications and Mobile Computing: Connecting the World Wirelessly, pp. 1410–1416 (2009)
7. Müllner, R., Ball, C., Ivanov, K., Lienhart, J., Hric, P.: Contrasting Open-Loop and Closed-Loop Power Control Performance in UTRAN LTE Uplink by UE Trace Analysis. In: IEEE International Conference on Communications, ICC 2009, pp. 1–6 (June 2009)
8. Boussif, M., Quintero, N., Calabrese, F., Rosa, C., Wigard, J.: Interference Based Power Control Performance in LTE Uplink. In: IEEE International Symposium on Wireless Communication Systems, ISWCS 2008., pp. 698–702 (October 2008)

9. González G, D., García-Lozano, M., Ruiz, S., Olmos, J.: On the Performance of Static Inter-cell Interference Coordination in Realistic Cellular Layouts. In: Pentikousis, K., Agüero, R., García-Arranz, M., Papavassiliou, S. (eds.) MONAMI 2010. LNICST, vol. 68, pp. 163–176. Springer, Heidelberg (2011)

10. 3GPP: Physical Layer Procedures. TS 36.213, 3rd Generation Partnership Project (3GPP) (September 2009)

11. Verdone, R., Buehler, H.: MORANS White Paper. Technical Report TD-03-057, COST-237 (January 2003)

12. 231, C.: Propagation Prediction Models. In: COST-231 Final Rep. 17–22

13. Fraile, R., Lazaro, O., Cardona, N.: Two Dimensional Shadowing Model. Tr available as td(03)171, COST 273 (2003)

14. 3GPP: Evolved Universal Terrestrial Radio Access (E-UTRA); User Equipment (UE) conformance specification; Radio transmission and reception; Part 1: conformance testing. TS 36.521-1, 3rd Generation Partnership Project (3GPP)

Physical Cell ID Allocation in Multi-layer, Multi-vendor LTE Networks

Péter Szilágyi[1], Tobias Bandh[2], and Henning Sanneck[3]

[1] Nokia Siemens Networks Research
Budapest, Hungary
peter.1.szilagyi@nsn.com
[2] Network Architectures and Services
Technische Universität München, Germany
bandh@net.in.tum.de
[3] Nokia Siemens Networks Research
Munich, Germany
henning.sanneck@nsn.com

Abstract. The evolution of radio access technologies and the user demand for increased capacity drives network deployments towards multiple cell layouts, often referred to as Heterogeneous Networks. With the ongoing rollout of commercial Long Term Evolution (LTE) networks, not only different radio access technologies are offered but LTE networks can also be multi-layered by themselves, consisting of differently sized cells providing coverage in overlapping areas. This comes with increased complexity of network management, which is even more relevant in common multi-vendor deployments, where coordinated configuration and operation of network elements provided by different vendors is essential. In this paper, we investigate and evaluate possible allocation schemes of an LTE radio parameter, the Physical Cell Identity. Results indicate that a particular allocation strategy, the range separation provides an elegant and efficient solution, which makes PCI management in multi-layer, multi-vendor networks easier. The standardization relevance of the range separation scheme is also discussed.

Keywords: LTE, multi-layer networks, PCI, physical cell identity, range separation, self-configuration, self-organizing networks.

1 Introduction

The increasing user demand for low latency, high speed mobile networks drives the evolution of radio access technology. Network operators deploy new radio access technologies (RAT) such as Long Term Evolution (LTE) to provide the required high data rates to mostly Internet based applications such as interactive web browsing or streaming video. LTE deployments may consist of differently sized cells (i.e., *resource layers*), usually referred to as macro, micro, pico, etc. cells, which may cover geographically overlapping areas in order to provide not only basic coverage but increased capacity where it is needed. Deployments

A. Timm-Giel et al. (Eds.): MONAMI 2012, LNICST 58, pp. 156–168, 2013.
© Institute for Computer Sciences, Social Informatics and Telecommunications Engineering 2013

making heavy use of overlapping differently sized cells are commonly referred to as Heterogeneous Networks (HetNet). Within one RAT, resource layers may use different or the same frequency band, the latter option being referred to as co-channel deployment. Additionally, HetNets may contain co-existing RATs including legacy Global System for Mobile Communications (GSM), High Speed Packet Access (HSPA) or Evolved HSPA technologies next to LTE. The scope of this paper focuses on the allocation of an LTE specific radio parameter; therefore, we focus on LTE deployments with multiple resource layers, which will be referred to as multi-layer LTE networks. However, the principles and concepts presented in this paper are applicable to different parameters in other RATs with multiple resource layers as well.

In LTE networks, Physical Cell Identity (PCI) is a low-level cell identifier broadcasted in the System Information Block Type 1 (SIB1), which is accessible after decoding the Master Information Block (MIB) of a cell [5]. There are 504 possible PCI values in the range of 0–503, divided into 168 PCI groups containing 3 IDs each [2]. The PCI is used in various radio related and mobility procedures such as handover, the configuration of physical layer measurements or Self-Organizing Network (SON) [8] use case Automatic Neighbor Relation (ANR) [3].

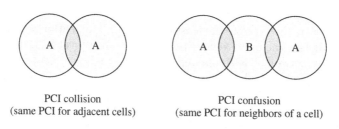

PCI collision
(same PCI for adjacent cells)

PCI confusion
(same PCI for neighbors of a cell)

Fig. 1. Illustration of PCI collision and confusion, both of which should be avoided

The PCI serves as the primary identifier for handover procedures, which are prepared and initiated based on the PCIs reported by the user equipment (UE). In order to allow successful handovers, the PCI allocation in a network has to fulfill two requirements: it has to be both *collision-* and *confusion-free*, i.e., scenarios illustrated in Fig. 1 must be avoided. Collision-free means that adjacent cells must not have the same PCI and confusion-free means that a cell must not have two neighbors configured with the same PCI. If there is PCI confusion, e.g., the serving cell of the UE has two neighbors with the same PCI, there is no unambiguous way to provide the UE with the identity of either of those cells as handover targets and such handovers may fail. Conflicting PCIs also make handovers impossible in case the source and target cells share the same PCI as it would be interpreted by the UE as a command to handover to the same cell to which it is currently connected. Therefore, proper PCI allocation is essential but due to the limited number of PCIs, it is a non-trivial task; proposals exist that aim at the extension of the available PCI range by considering time synchronization information along with the PCI together as the cell identity, effectively increasing the available number of different identities by 1024 times PCIs [9]. However, such solutions are not transparent to the network management and require UE support as well.

Proper PCI assignment in a network is challenging not only due to the limited number of PCIs compared to the large number of cells in different resource layers but also if different network elements are provided by multiple vendors (in particular, the case where each of the resource layers is provided by a different vendor); such multi-vendor setups are very common but often complicate configuration tasks if the required interfaces are not standardized or incompatible algorithms are implemented by vendors to find or assign optimal values to configuration parameters such as the PCI. For proper network operation, the PCI configuration of adjacent cells hosted by base stations from different vendors have to be closely aligned, which is a non-trivial task. A common network planning strategy is to deploy base stations from different vendors to separate geographical areas, which limits the number of adjacent cells on vendor boundaries in case a single resource layer is considered. On the other hand, if different resource layers (i.e., macro, pico, etc. cells) are deployed over the same geographical area to provide overlapping service and the resource layers are provided by different vendors, inter-vendor cell boundaries become very common, making PCI allocation especially complex.

In this paper, we investigate the feasibility of a PCI allocation scheme that can effectively deal with the multi-vendor problems in multi-layer LTE networks. The solution is fully network-based, making cell identity management transparent to UEs. The solution splits the entire PCI range into disjoint ranges and assigns each range to one of the resource layers, which may only use PCIs from their respective PCI range. The number of PCIs required by this range separation method is compared to the number of PCIs in a continuous allocation, i.e., if cells from the different resource layers are allocated PCI from the entire PCI range in a coordinated way so that collision and confusion-free requirement is fulfilled. The comparison is based on simulations of eight multi-layer LTE network scenarios, each having a macro and a pico layer.

The rest of this paper is organized as follows. In Section 2, different PCI allocation scheme for multi-layer networks are discussed and the motivations for using range separation are detailed. Section 3 describes the multi-layer LTE network scenarios taken for comparing the performance of range separation with the continuous allocation. Section 4 describes the simulation setup and Section 5 gives the result and the evaluation of the simulations. Finally, Section 6 concludes the paper.

2   Multi-layer PCI Allocation Schemes

Basically, three different PCI allocation techniques may be considered in multi-layer networks, as illustrated in Fig 2 and detailed below. All strategies assume the existence of an *algorithm* that is able to provide a proper PCI allocation within a single layer.

Layer independent: this is a straightforward but somewhat inaccurate scheme where the entire PCI range (0–503) is used independently to allocate PCIs in each layer. Although the PCI allocation within a given layer satisfies the collision- and confusion-free criteria, the same PCI may be allocated to cells in different layers with inter-layer adjacency (e.g, overlapping with each other); therefore, reactive conflict detection and resolution is required to provide also proper inter-layer allocation, which must be executed in the live network, possibly causing service disruption due to the PCI reconfiguration.

Continuous with cross-layer coordination: cells in the different resource layers can be given PCIs from the entire available range but in a way that the PCI allocation is coordinated between layers at run-time, ensuring that inter-layer adjacencies also satisfy the proper PCI allocation requirements.

Range separation: the entire PCI range is split a priori into disjoint ranges, each of them dedicated to one resource layer and cells from each layer may only be assigned PCIs from the corresponding PCI range at run-time. This facilitates fully independent PCI allocation in the different layers, at the same time ensuring that no PCI collision or confusion may occur provided that the PCI allocation is proper within each layer. On the other hand, the range separation cannot be adapted at run-time, i.e., it can happen that while one layer runs out of PCIs, the other layer underutilizes its allocated PCI range.

The layer independent allocation scheme is not effective as it trades the complexity of providing proper intra- and inter-layer PCI allocation for the complexity of reactive collision and confusion resolution in the operational network. Despite causing potential service interruption, the conflict resolution has the same multi-vendor issues as if the allocation would have to be coordinated among various layers in case they are provided by different vendors. The continuous allocation with cross-layer coordination has the same complexity (where complexity lies in the coordination), with an advantage of being free from operational-time PCI conflict resolution. However, from multi-vendor point of view, the same constraints apply.

Range separation has two advantages over the other allocation methods: it has lower complexity and it facilitates multi-vendor allocation in case the resource layers are provided by different vendors; however, single vendor deployments are also supported. A requirement for using range separation is the ability to split the entire range into suitable ranges and to convey the configuration to the network entities performing the PCI allocation, which is required to support both centralized and distributed approaches [4]. Defining the PCI ranges is possible only if the sum of the PCIs required to provide the proper allocation in each of the layers is less than 504, i.e., the total number of PCIs. In this study, it is investigated whether a feasible separation can be created in case of different multi-layer LTE scenarios; for comparison, the continuous cross-layer coordinated technique is also evaluated. The number of PCIs required by the

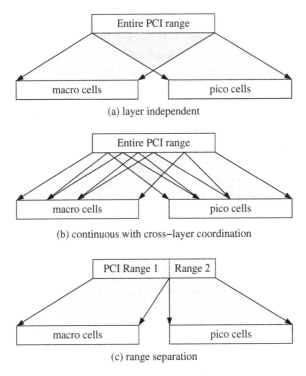

Fig. 2. PCI allocation techniques

layer independent allocation is theoretically the same as that of the coordinated allocation as both methods use the entire PCI range and consider all resource layers at the same time; therefore, it is enough to use the coordinated allocation as the reference.

3 Scenario Description

In this paper, eight LTE HetNet scenarios have been studied, each of which having two different cell layers: a macro layer and a pico layer. These scenarios are based on research of the characteristics of the anticipated macro network evolution together with selective deployment of pico cells taking place in Nokia Siemens Networks. The scenario description consists of the location of the macro and pico sites along with a few radio parameters. Each macro site had three or six cells with 46 dBm maximum transmission power and specific antenna bearing and tilting. The pico cells were assumed to be omnidirectional with 30 dBm transmission power. In these scenarios, pico cells are deployed for capacity enhancements as an addition to good macro coverage.

In order to obtain the adjacency information, a simulation has been conducted based on the Okumura-Hata path loss model complemented by horizontal and vertical antenna characteristics for macro cells according to [1]. The deployment area has been traversed with a 1×1 m resolution to find the best cell s at each position P having the highest Reference Signal Received Power (RSRP), denoted by $\mathrm{RSRP}_s^{(P)}$. Besides the best cell, each cell $i^{(P)}$ was identified and added to a set $N^{(P)}$ at each position for which

$$\mathrm{RSRP}_i^{(P)} > \mathrm{RSRP}_s^{(P)} - \mathrm{HO}_{\mathrm{offset}} - \mathrm{HO}_{\mathrm{hyst}} \tag{1}$$

where $\mathrm{RSRP}_i^{(P)}$ is the RSRP of cell i at position P and $\mathrm{HO}_{\mathrm{offset}} = 3$ dB and $\mathrm{HO}_{\mathrm{hyst}} = 0.5$ dB were the handover offset and hysteresis values. Finally, pairwise adjacencies were added between cells in set $N^{(P)}$.

The properties of the adjacency graph built for each scenarios are shown in Table 1. Besides the total number of cells and edges, the number of macro and pico cells as well as the intra- and inter-layer edges are also given separately.

Table 1. Properties of the adjacency graph in the studied scenarios

scenario	cells (graph nodes)			estimated adjacencies (graph edges)			
	macro	pico	all	macro–macro	pico–pico	macro–pico	all
A1	160	40	200	1042	6	139	1187
A2	236	40	276	2346	6	192	2544
A3	236	100	336	2338	54	454	2846
B1	99	20	119	418	7	53	478
B2	135	20	155	528	6	72	606
B3	129	20	149	496	6	72	574
B4	99	70	169	413	43	209	665
B5	99	55	154	413	27	146	586

It is important to note that all cells are assumed to be co-channeled, i.e., deployed in the same or overlapping bandwidth, which means that in case two cells are neighbors from radio propagation point of view, they are potentially conflicting from PCI allocation point of view. In real deployments, separate frequency spectrum may be allocated to overlapping cells, which decreases the adjacencies needed to take into account for proper PCI allocation. Therefore, this study gives an upper bound for the number for PCIs and in case a proper PCI allocation was feasible in the considered scenarios it would be likewise feasible in real deployments. Fig. 3 and Fig. 4 show the layout of two networks, both of them illustrating different evolutionary stages, having fewer or more pico cells and in Fig. 3 even showing the expansion of macro cells as well.

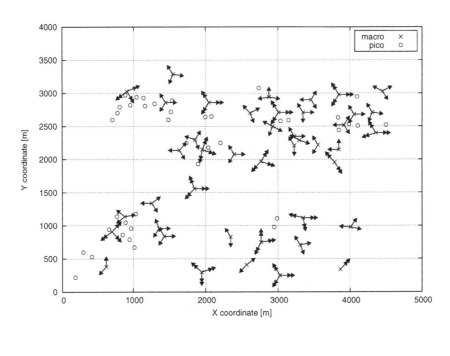

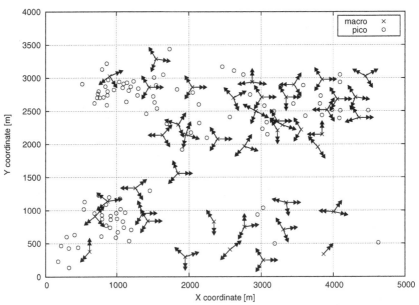

Fig. 3. Two evolutionary stages of the same multi-layer network, scenario A1 (top) and scenario A3 (bottom). Note that the extended layout was also subject to macro cell evolution, switching to 6-sectored cells at all macro sites.

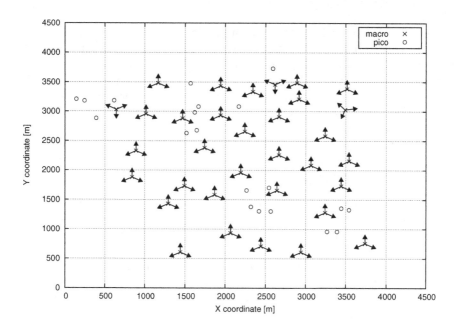

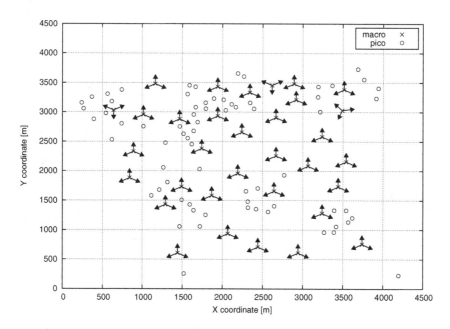

Fig. 4. Overlaying the same macro layer with pico cells having different level of expansion in scenario B1 (top) and scenario B4 (bottom)

4   Simulation Setup

The output of the air interface simulation was the adjacency graph of each scenario. This graph can be taken by a PCI allocation algorithm to find the number of PCIs required to properly allocate the IDs, i.e., in a collision and confusion free way. The algorithm used in this study was the graph coloring based PCI assignment technique explained in [7]. This algorithm takes a graph with cells as nodes and adjacencies as edges and outputs the number of PCIs required for allocation.

In order to compare the number of required PCIs with the continuous allocation and the range separation methods, the PCI allocation algorithm was executed on three different graphs as follows.

1. For the continuous allocation, the graph containing all cells (macro and pico) and all (both intra- and inter-layer) edges was used. The required number of PCIs for the continuous allocation is given directly by the algorithm.
2. For the range separation, the algorithm was run on two subgraphs: the first one containing only the macro cells (and the intra-macro adjacencies as edges) and the second subgraph consisting of the pico cells and the intra-pico adjacencies. The number of PCIs required for the range separation allocation is given by the sum of the PCIs used in the macro and pico layers separately.

Besides the cells and the adjacency information, the graph coloring based PCI allocation algorithm has an extra parameter called the *safety margin* (SM). It gives specifies a range around each cell (in terms of number of hops in the adjacency graph) in which the same PCI cannot be assigned more than once. Specifically, SM = 1 means only collision- but not confusion-free PCI allocation as it mandates that a PCI allocated to a cell must not be reused in any of the direct neighbors of the cell but permits its repeated usage otherwise. The SM = 2 means collision- and confusion free PCI allocation (i.e., this is the minimum SM fulfilling the requirements for proper PCI allocation) as it prohibits the usage of the same PCI not only among the direct neighbors of a cell among but its second level neighborhood as well. Choosing a SM higher than the required minimum 2 as although it results in more number of required PCIs, this also provides additional safety "buffer" in the PCI allocation by means of assuring that even in case new adjacencies are formed later in the operational network (due to neighbor relation discovery via ANR [3], additional cell deployment, etc.), still no or significantly less PCI reconfigurations are needed than with the minimum SM = 2.

5   Evaluation and Results

The performance of the continuous PCI allocation and the range separation approach was compared in scenarios A1–A3 and B1–B5 with different safety margin values. The required number of PCIs for proper allocation for the minimum SM = 2 are shown in Fig. 5.

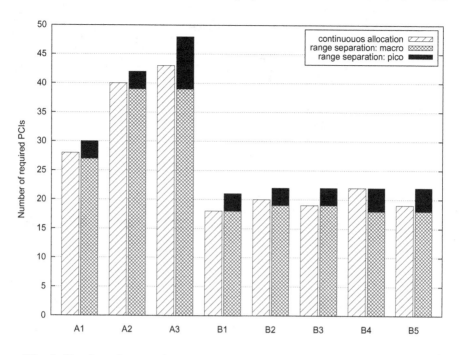

Fig. 5. Number of required PCIs with SM = 2 (collision and confusion free)

The results for higher safety margins (i.e., with additional safety buffer) is given in Fig. 6 for SM = 3 and in Fig. 7 for SM = 5. The latter is a relatively large safety margin to see whether a proper allocation is still possible even in that case. For the given scenario, in practice SM = 3 or 4 would be chosen to on the one hand leave some "headroom" for adding new cells in the same area (SM > 2) and on the other hand to avoid exhausting the full range of the available PCIs.

As the SM increases, range separation results in significantly lower number of PCIs (up to 30% less) in case there is a high number of inter-layer adjacencies (e.g., scenario A3 with 100 pico cells). The inter-layer adjacencies do not increase the connectivity of the per-layer subgraphs used by the range separation scheme, thus an increasing number of inter-layer adjacencies has no effect on the number of PCIs required by using range separation. However, inter-layer adjacencies may heavily increase the connectivity of the whole adjacency graph that has to be taken into account by the continuous cross-layer allocation.

With high SM, the adjacency graph extended with additional level of neighbors can even reach full mesh stage, i.e., each cell is connected with all other cells (e.g., scenario A3 with SM = 5). For the continuous allocation case, this may result in the same number of PCIs as the number of cells (including all layers) due to the inter-layer connections that make the graph fully connected. However, in case of range separation, only intra-layer meshes can be formed as the inter-layer adjacencies are not taken into account. Accordingly, in the macro

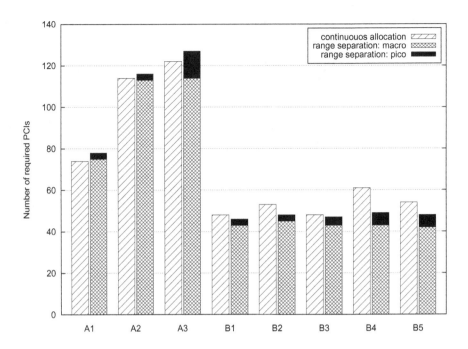

Fig. 6. Number of required PCIs with SM = 3 (collision and confusion free with extra buffer of 1)

layer, there can also be a full mesh due to its dense connectivity; however, in the pico layer, due to the sparser deployment, no full mesh is formed as the pico layer is not a connected graph in the beginning. As a result, with higher SM, the PCI range separation results in less number of PCIs due to the savings realized in the pico layer.

Based on the number of PCIs required for the proper allocation of the macro and pico layers using the range separation method, the splitting of the entire PCI range into macro and pico ranges is straightforward even considering high SM. An example range definition could be to allocate the range [0–399] for the macro cells and range [400–503] for the pico cells.

The PCI range separation scheme requires not only the definition of the PCI ranges but also their signaling to the appropriate network entity running the PCI algorithm. In case of a standardized solution, this information has to be sent via the Northbound management interface (Itf-N) standardized by the 3rd Generation Partnership Project (3GPP). The communication of the ranges requires a PCI list Information Element (IE); such an IE is currently defined in [6] as the `pciList` as an attribute of the `EUtranGenericCell` abstract information object class. However, the shortcomings of the current definition of `pciList` is that it requires the enumeration of all PCI values allowed to be used by the PCI allocation algorithm. A potential improvement would be to allow the definition of consecutive PCI ranges by specifying only the first and last PCI in

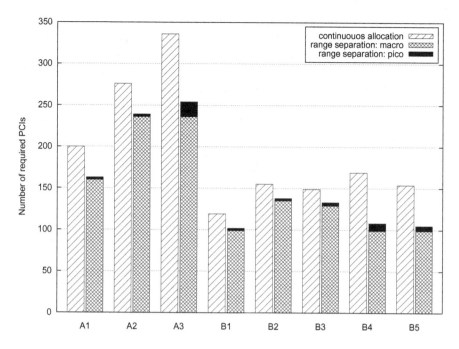

Fig. 7. Number of required PCIs with SM = 5 (collision and confusion free with extra buffer of 3)

the range, making their configuration more effective. The definition of multiple ranges should also be permitted.

The evaluation covered the comparison of the continuous PCI allocation and the range separation techniques. Considering the layer independent allocation with reactive conflict resolution, it can be anticipated that since each inter-layer edge is a potential conflict, the number of reconfigurations required in the live network in that case is proportional to the number of inter-layer edges. Given the number of inter-layer edges in Table 1, it can turn out to be significantly high. An improvement to the layer independent allocation method and partial solution to this problem could be the introduction of an OAM-based cross-layer "auditing" of the initial PCI configuration to spot and resolve obvious inter-layer conflicts offline before the cells are gone operational and thus minimize the required live reconfigurations.

6   Conclusion

In this paper, the PCI allocation was evaluated in eight multi-layer LTE network deployments considering the continuous cross-layer coordinated and the range separation allocation schemes.

The PCI range separation performs similarly to the continuous allocation already at the minimum SM = 2, i.e., satisfying the collision- and confusion free criteria without additional safety buffer. With higher SM, the range separation requires even less number of PCIs than the continuous allocation. This is due to the higher SM creating increased number of inter-layer dependencies, which on the one hand turn into additional constraints for the continuous allocation but on the other hand can be completely ignored by the range separation scheme, making it a more scalable solution. In summary, range separation is a feasible allocation scheme, providing the additional benefits of allowing independent PCI allocation schemes on each layer, which is an enabler for multi-vendor PCI allocation. For the considered scenarios, which are believed to be realistic in the time frame until 2020, even for higher SM, the choice of the ranges provided to be fairly simple. The limit of the ranges was not exceeded in any cases.

References

1. 3GPP. Physical layer aspect for evolved Universal Terrestrial Radio Access (UTRA). TS 25.814 Rel-7, 3rd Generation Partnership Project (3GPP) (October 2006)
2. 3GPP. Evolved Universal Terrestrial Radio Access (E-UTRA); Physical channels and modulation. TS 36.211 Rel-10, 3rd Generation Partnership Project (3GPP) (December 2011)
3. 3GPP. Telecommunication management; Automatic Neighbour Relation (ANR) management; Concepts and requirements. TS 32.511 Rel-11, 3rd Generation Partnership Project (3GPP) (September 2011)
4. 3GPP. Telecommunication management; Self-Organizing Networks (SON); Concepts and requirements. TS 32.500 Rel-11, 3rd Generation Partnership Project (3GPP) (December 2011)
5. 3GPP. Evolved Universal Terrestrial Radio Access (E-UTRA); Radio Resource Control (RRC); Protocol specification. TS 36.331 Rel-10, 3rd Generation Partnership Project (3GPP) (March 2012)
6. 3GPP. Telecommunication management; Evolved Universal Terrestrial Radio Access Network (E-UTRAN) Network Resource Model (NRM) Integration Reference Point (IRP); Information Service (IS). TS 32.762 Rel-11, 3rd Generation Partnership Project (3GPP) (March 2012)
7. Bandh, T., Carle, G., Sanneck, H.: Graph coloring based physical-cell-ID assignment for LTE networks. In: Proceedings of the International Conference on Wireless Communications and Mobile Computing: Connecting the World Wirelessly, IWCMC 2009, Leipzig, Germany, pp. 116–120. ACM (June 2009)
8. Hämäläinen, S., Sanneck, H., Sartori, C. (eds.): LTE Self-Organising Networks (SON): Network Management Automation for Operational Efficiency. John Wiley & Sons (December 2011)
9. Kwon, S., Lee, N.-H.: Virtual extension of cell IDs in a femtocell environment. In: 2011 IEEE Wireless Communications and Networking Conference (WCNC), pp. 428–433 (March 2011)

Evaluation of Dense Cooperative Relay Deployments for Autonomic Emergency Communications

Michał Wódczak

Ericsson, ul. Umultowska 85, 61–614 Poznań, Poland
michal.wodczak@ericsson.com

Abstract. The consideration of the concept of autonomic cooperative networking is very well justified in the context of emergency communications. Emergency networks are instantiated on demand in the areas of incident and are formed by First Responders who are coordinated by Chief First Responders. This way, the the entire networked emergency system might attempt to adapt accurately to the changing conditions and requirements. Specifically, it is possible to employ cooperative transmission between different Chief First Responders so that, for resilience purposes, they would be in a position to mutually support the transmission of the same data. This paper provides an analysis of cooperative set-ups of this type allowing to quantify potential gains which would result from autonomic switching among densely populated Chief First Responders.

Keywords: cooperative transmission, autonomic networking, emergency communications.

1   Introduction

The world of emergency communications provides a very desirable field for the integration of the rationale behind cooperative transmission and autonomic networking [12], [3]. Obviously, when commercial networks are designed, it is almost impossible to assume the option of exploiting a given user's device(s) for the purposes of instantiating cooperative relaying in order to support somebody else's data transfer(s). Such an approach could result immediately in an increased battery drainage. To alleviate such an inconvenience, the commercial users would have to be offered certain incentives encouraging them to participate in cooperation [15]. Thankfully, in the case of emergency systems such limitations seem non-existent as it is necessary to handle the crisis situation in the first place despite increased cost of the above-mentioned sort [19]. Consequently, it is possible to devise convergent solutions that would be properly tailored to the requirements of emergency communications [18]. It is especially driven by the ad hoc nature of such set-ups where the network is formed on demand and it needs to adapt to the existing and rapidly changing situation [17]. The notion of adaptation means that the whole system may be more resilient to specific features

A. Timm-Giel et al. (Eds.): MONAMI 2012, LNICST 58, pp. 169–182, 2013.

of a harsh environment it is supposed to operate in [20]. It might be achieved through the integration of both the notion of cooperative transmission and the paradigm of autonomic networking, as outlined in the remainder of this paper. Cooperative transmission aims to improve the reliability of mobile communications through the application of transmission diversity introduced by additional Relay Nodes. Autonomic system design, in turn, is expected to provide the ability to self-manage without any explicit intervention during most of the time of its operation.

The paper is organised as follows. First, the rationale behind cooperative relaying and autonomic networking is generally presented in Section 2. Following, the analysed scenario is detailed together with the investigated deployments of Chief First Responders in Section 3. Finally, the functioning of the system is detailed in Section 4, while the performance evaluation is provided in Section 5. The paper is concluded in Section 6.

2   Cooperative Relaying and Autonomic Networking

Cooperative transmission aims to improve the reliability of wireless communications in terms of robust data transfer. It may be done very neatly with the aid of the transmission diversity provided by Relay Nodes (RNs) assisting in the conveyance of radio data between the Source Node (SN) and the Destination Node (DN). This is feasible as the rationale behind spatio-temporal processing can be directly mapped onto networking [21], [13]. Most certainly, a sufficiently tight synchronisation must be guaranteed to this end. Consequently, the network nodes can be perceived as elements of a Virtual Antenna Array (VAA) [6] and they can preform the operation of a Distributed Space-Time Encoder [10], as outlined in Figure 1. The transmission takes two stages. First, the SN broadcasts the data to be delivered to the DN. The relevant information is also received by the intermediary node(s) while each of them may become an RN. During the second phase, only such nodes are entitled to resend the received data towards the DN.

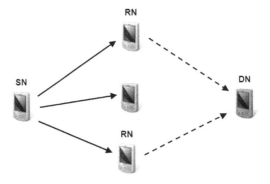

Fig. 1. Generalised virtual antenna array concept

Obviously, one might take different spatio-temporal processing techniques into account and, in this paper, the emphasis is laid on space-time block coding [21], [13]. The basic space-time block code G_2 is defined below (1) to outline the operation of spatio-temporal processing and to better illustrate its relation to the concept of VAAs.

$$G_2 = \begin{bmatrix} x_1 & x_2 \\ -x_2^* & x_1^* \end{bmatrix} \tag{1}$$

The operation of a space-time block encoder for the presented case code can be described in the following way. In the first time slot the x_1 and x_2 symbols are sent by the first and second transmit antenna, respectively. Then, in the second time slot, the $-x_2^*$ and x_1^* symbols are transmitted alike. This operation can be translated to VAA-aided cooperative transmission by simple substitution of antennas with network nodes. The addition of certain network logic, able to provide the notion of cooperative processing, is necessary, too.

Based on the increased complexity of a networked system of this type there is a need for the provision of a certain level of automation. This may be achieved with the aid of the aforementioned autonomic system design for self-managing networks [5]. Such an autonomic system is characterised by the ability to self-configure without any need for an external intervention. Moreover, its inherent feature is the necessity of continuous monitoring. This way the network should be able to self-configure according to the imposed policies and taking into account additional information about incidents that through proper fault-management can improve the service resilience [2]. The resulting system is then continually driven by a very large number of parallel processes running on their own but remaining in relevant relations. Currently, certain effort is undertaken in the area of standardisation to facilitate the application the relevant network engineering mechanisms in this area [4], [22]. In particular, the idea of control loops is

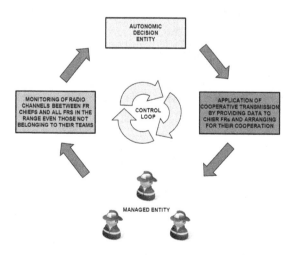

Fig. 2. Control loop

applicable to such systems, where a Decision Element (DE) is controlling a Managed Entity (ME) based on a closed information flow and with the use of external monitoring and policies related data, as outlined in Figure 2.

3   Investigated Scenario

The analysed scenario is based on a Relay Enhanced Cell (REC) comprising one floor of the height of 3 m located in a building and containing two corridors each of dimensions 5 m x 100 m. Specifically, there are 40 rooms of dimensions 10 m x 10 m [14], [7]. Thus the scenario is very demanding and specific because the transmitted signals become severely distorted by numerous walls crossing the paths the radio waves are traversing. For this reason specific dense deployments of Chief First Responders (CFR) are investigated as depicted in Figure 3 and Figure 4. The configurations of CFRs are denoted by the numbers placed next to them. The presented system follows the general assumptions for the indoor environment, as outlined in [8], [14]. In particular, it assumes fixed modulation and coding scheme consisting of QPSK modulation and the (4, 5, 7) convolutional code. Besides, Additive White Gaussian Noise (AWGN) radio channel is employed while either a Line-of-Sight (LOS) or Non Line-of-Sight (NLOS) radio propagation model [8] is used, depending on the presence or absence of walls between the end points of a given radio link. In particular, the LOS model is defined as follows:

$$PL_{LOS}[dB] = 18.7\log_{10}(d) + 46.8 + \sigma, \tag{2}$$

where d denotes the distance in meters between the transmitter and the receiver and σ represents the standard deviation of the shadow fading and is equal to 3 dB. The NLOS propagation model, in turn, is defined as:

$$PL_{NLOS}[dB] = 20.0\log_{10}(d) + 46.4 + 5n_w + \sigma, \tag{3}$$

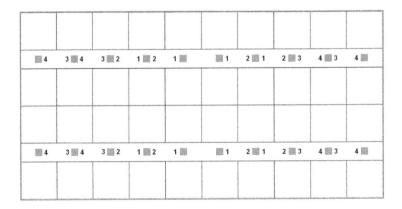

Fig. 3. Deployment I

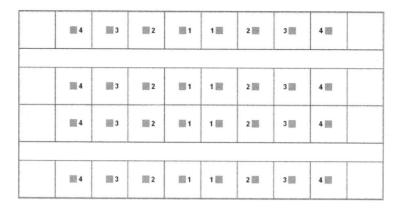

Fig. 4. Deployment II

where n_w denotes the number of walls between the transmitter and the receiver and $\sigma = 6$dB, meaning that all the walls are of the same light type. Additionally, the average interference power level of -125 dBm per subcarrier is assumed while no outdoor users are taken into account. OFDMA is employed and TDD mode is used at the carrier frequency of 5.0 GHz with the channel bandwidth of 100 MHz. Each user, i.e. FR, is assigned the amount of radio resource equal to one chunk, i.e. 8 subcarriers and 15 OFDM symbols [14], [21].

4   Emergency System Functioning

One of the main entities orchestrating the operation of an Emergency System is the Mobile Emergency Operations Centre (MEOC). MEOC is responsible for controlling the CFR(s) who are feeding data towards a given FR. In case it is to be done by means of cooperative transmission, as postulated in this paper, then the hierarchy among the CFRs and FRs cannot be disregarded [19]. In fact, logically, a given FR is allowed to communicate with one Chief FR only which may form a serious bottleneck. This is because a given FR might become exposed to severe radio channel impairments resulting either from obstacles or too big a distance towards their CFR. In such a case, another CFR may effectively support the process of communication by exploiting the diversity gain offered by a Virtual MISO channel in a way invisible and transparent to the aforementioned hierarchy. In particular, when necessary, the destination FR may be served cooperatively by two CFRs as outlined in the diagram presented in Figure 5 [21]. This would obviously require the application of the distributed spatio-temporal encoding. To control such a deployment one would employ the entities allowing for autonomic decisions. This way the links between CFRs and their respective FRs would be monitored in a control loop (Figure 2).

Table 1. System parameters

Parameter	Value	Comments
Carrier frequency	5.0 GHz	TDD mode
Channel bandwidth	100 MHz	OFDMA
Spatial processing	Distributed STBC	CFR-CFR cooperation
CFR antennas	1	Omnidirectional
FR antennas	1	Omnidirectional
CFR transmit power	21 dBm	7 dBi antenna gain
FR transmit power	21 dBm	0 dBi antenna gain
Channel modelling	AWGN channel	A1 NLOS Room-Room model used for CFR-FR links
Link adaptation	Fixed code and modulation scheme	QPSK and (4, 5, 7) convolutional code
Mobility	Yes	FR random movement
Resource scheduling	Fixed	1 chunk (15 OFDM symbols and 8 subcarriers) for each FR
RAP selection	Signal power	At the destination
Traffic model	Constant bit rate	CBR

To accommodate such a concept in emergency systems it would be necessary to employ the rationale behind the Generic Autonomic Network Architecture (GANA) [5]. This way, each network node would become logically composed of a number of Decision Elements (DEs). In particular, there would arise a need for a Cooperative Processing Decision Element (CP_DE) which would be responsible for controlling the aspects of distributed spatio-temporal block encoded cooperative transmission [16]. Such a Decision Element would be responsible for the processing of the relayed signals according to the relevant column of the space-time block matrix. Obviously, it would need to interact with the a specifically designed Resilience and Survivability Decision Element RS_DE, as well as the Fault Management Decision Element FM_DE [21]. In this case, the former would be assumed to specifically cover the aspects such as service resilience and survivability, while the later would control the symptoms suggesting that a failure, e.g. in terms of service continuity, may be imminent [20].

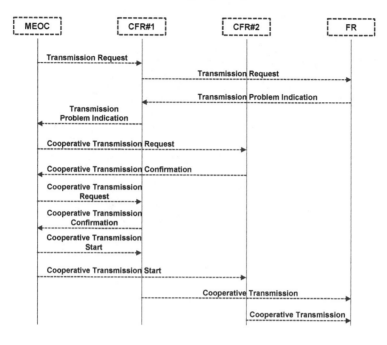

Fig. 5. Cooperative transmission initialisation diagram

5 Performance Evaluation

The performance evaluation is done with the use of the previously described cooperative transmission in two stages as depicted in Figure 1. Here, the MEOC broadcasts the data to be delivered to the destination FR. The relevant information is also received by the CFR(s) being the potential RNs. In fact, during the second phase only the eventually chosen CFRs resend the received data towards the FR. In this paper, the spatio-temporal block coding is employed with the use of the G_2 code (1) [1]. The signal received by a receiving antenna j may be expressed as (4) [1], [11]:

$$r_t^j = \sum_{i=1}^{N} h_{i,j} s_t^i + \eta_t^j, \tag{4}$$

where $h_{i,j}$ denotes a channel coefficient, s_t^i represents the symbol transmitted by antenna i and the noise samples η_t^j are modeled by the complex Gaussian process with zero mean and $N_0/2$ variance per dimension. The equation (4) describes the superposition of the signals coming from different transmitting antennas, including channel coefficients and noise. In the investigated case, as indicated in Table 1, the AWGN channel is assumed and so the channel coefficients are equal to one. The decoding process is based on a maximum-likelihood detection, which aims to minimise the decision metric given by the formula (5) [11],[9].

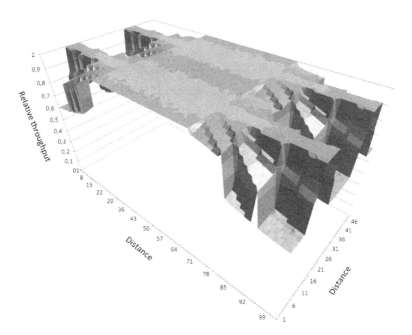

Fig. 6. Relative throughput for Deployment I.1

$$z = \sum_{t=1}^{L}\sum_{j=1}^{M}\left| r_t^j - \sum_{i=1}^{N} h_{i,j}s_t^i \right|^2 \qquad (5)$$

It means that, for a given code, the symbols minimising this metric are chosen. In fact, this is a generalised metric and its expanded and computationally efficient one was applied during the simulation evaluation, as originally proposed in [11].

The presented results pertain to the deployments outlined in Figure 3 and Figure 4. The simulations were performed in such a way that a given FR is served cooperatively[1] by two CFRs able to provide signal of best quality. It means that the two CFRs are chosen which provide the strongest signal. FR mobility is modeled by random movements as long as the whole area is sufficiently convered. The switching is done in an autonomic way and it is transparent to the system. There are two levels of autonomic operation. First, autonomic DEs are deployed to choose the cooperating CFRs on the basis of the information acquired in control loops. Second, the network level DE switches between the groups of FRNs, i.e. 1 - 4, within each of the two evaluated set-ups. To visualise the results, the relative throughput graphs are presented in three-dimensional figures to highlight the fluctuations arising from the repositioning of the CFRs. It is clearly visible that there is no one optimum deployment and autonomic

---

[1] In case the reader is interested in a comparison between cooperative and non-cooperative set-ups they are referred to [14] and [8].

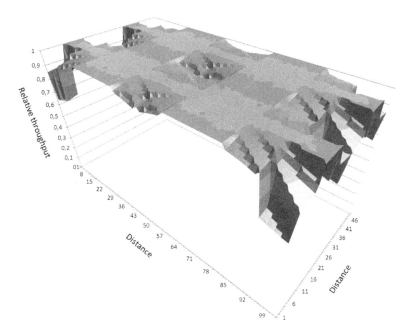

Fig. 7. Relative throughput for Deployment I.2

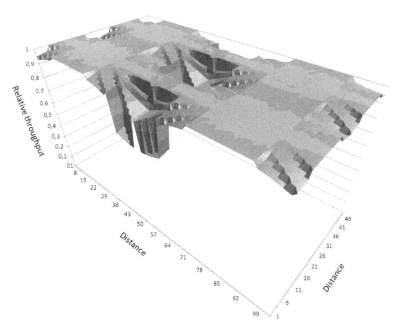

Fig. 8. Relative throughput for Deployment I.3

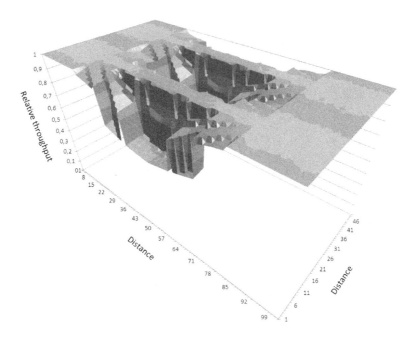

Fig. 9. Relative throughput for Deployment I.4

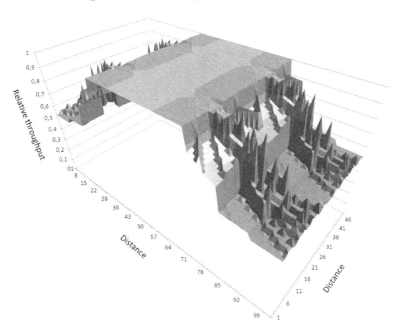

Fig. 10. Relative throughput for Deployment II.1

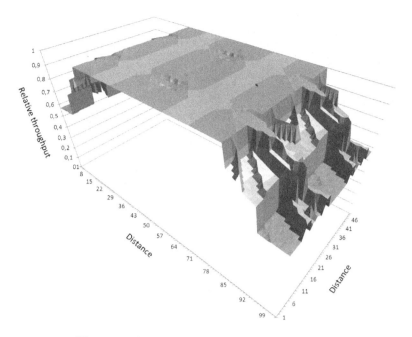

Fig. 11. Relative throughput for Deployment II.2

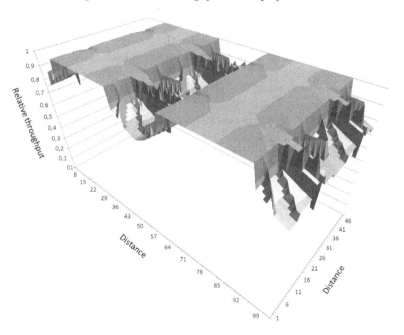

Fig. 12. Relative throughput for Deployment II.3

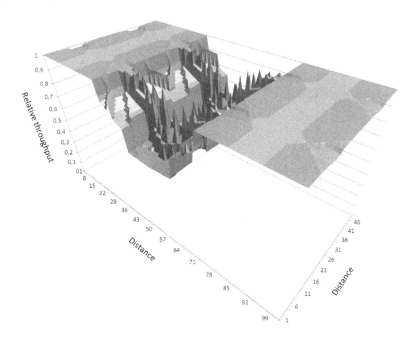

Fig. 13. Relative throughput for Deployment II.4

switching is necessary. Further work includes the incorporation of both the CFR mobility models and various traffic models together with QoS requirements so that different cooperative and non-cooperative transmissions may be going on depending on the requirements. One should note that both the scenarios contain the same number of nodes but in the case of Deployment I some of them overlap. The target solution is to deploy network layer routines such as the ones provided, for example, by the Optimised Link Static Routing protocol interfacing directly with the autonomic network overlay.

6   Conclusion

The presented work was placed in the context of autonomic cooperative networking for emergency communications. In particular, the evaluation of different deployments of Chief First Responders was carried out involving autonomic formation of cooperating CFRs and autonomic switching among their groups. The presented results show that the positioning of CFRs is crucial and not all the deployments may function equally well so there is a need for them to complement and another. It is then justified to further investigate the autonomic design of an emergency communication system where specific routines would allow for the use of more unstructured, and so natural, deployments to best adjust to the existing situation determined, for example, by the CFR mobility model, traffic models, and QoS requirements.

Acknowledgment. This paper has been prepared on the basis of the investigations in the area of autonomic cooperative communications carried out by the author in EU FP7 project E-SPONDER as a follow-up to the previous work performed in EU FP7 project EFIPSANS and EU FP6 project WINNER.

References

1. Alamouti, S.: A Simple Transmit Diversity Technique for Wireless Communications. IEEE Journal on Selected Areas in Communications 16(8), 1451–1458 (1998)
2. Liakopoulos, A., Zafeiropoulos, A., Polyrakis, A., Grammatikou, M., Gonzalez, J.M., Wódczak, M., Chaparadza, R.: Monitoring Issues for Autonomic Networks: The EFIPSANS Vision. In: European Workshop on Mechanisms for the Future Internet (2008)
3. Calarco, G., Casoni, M., Paganelli, A., Vassiliadis, D., Wódczak, M.: A Satellite based System for Managing Crisis Scenarios: the E-SPONDER Perspective. In: 5th Advanced Satellite Multimedia Systems Conference, Cagliari, Italy, September 13-15 (2010)
4. Chaparadza, R., Ciavaglia, L., Wódczak, M., Chen, C.-C., Lee, B.A., Liakopoulos, A., Zafeiropoulos, A., Mancini, E., Mulligan, U., Davy, A., Quinn, K., Radier, B., Alonistioti, N., Kousaridas, A., Demestichas, P., Tsagkaris, K., Vigoureux, M., Vreck, L., Wilson, M., Ladid, L.: ETSI Industry Specification Group on Autonomic network engineering for self-managing Future Internet (ETSI ISG AFI). In: Vossen, G., Long, D.D.E., Yu, J.X. (eds.) WISE 2009. LNCS, vol. 5802, pp. 61–62. Springer, Heidelberg (2009)
5. Chaparadza, R., Papavassiliou, S., Kastrinogiannis, T., Vigoureux, M., Dotaro, E., Davy, K.A., Quinn, M., Wódczak, M., Toth, A.: Towards the Future Internet - A European Research Perspective. In: Tselentis, G., Domingue, J., Galis, A., Gavras, A., Hausheer, D., Krco, S., Lotz, V., Zahariadis, T. (eds.) Creating a viable Evolution Path towards Self-Managing Future Internet via a Standardizable Reference Model for Autonomic Network Engineering. IOS Press (May 2009) ISBN: 978-1-60750-007-0
6. Dohler, M., Gkelias, A., Aghvami, H.: A resource allocation strategy for distributed MIMO multi-hop communication systems. IEEE Communications Letters 8(2), 99–101 (2004)
7. Doppler, K., Redana, S., Wódczak, M., Rost, P., Wichman, R.: Dynamic resource assignment and cooperative relaying in cellular networks: Concept and performance assessment. EURASIP Journal on Wireless Communications and Networking (July 2007)
8. Dottling, M., Irmer, R., Kalliojarvi, K., Rouquette-Leveil, S.: System Model, Test Scenarios, and Performance Evaluation. In: Dottling, M., Mohr, W., Osseiran, A. (eds.) Radio Technologies and Concepts for IMT-Advanced. Wiley (December 2009) ISBN: 978-0-470-74763-6
9. Goldsmith, A.: Wireless Communications. Cambridge University Press (2005)
10. Laneman, J.N., Wornell, G.W.: Distributed space-time-coded protocols for exploiting cooperative diversity in wireless networks. IEEE Transactions on Information Theory 49(10), 2415–2425 (2003)
11. Tarokh, V., Jafarkhani, H., Calderbank, A.R.: Space-time block coding for wireless communications: performance results. IEEE Journal on Selected Areas in Communications 17(3), 451–460 (1999)

12. Vassiliadis, D., Garbi, A., Calarco, G., Casoni, M., Paganelli, A., Morera, R., Chen, C.-M., Wódczak, M.: Wireless Networks at the Service of effective First Response Work: the E-SPONDER Vision. In: EEE International Symposium on Wireless Pervasive Computing, Modena, Italy, May 5-7 (2010)
13. Wódczak, M.: On Routing information Enhanced Algorithm for space-time coded Cooperative Transmission in wireless mobile networks. PhD thesis, Faculty of Electrical Engineering, Institute of Electronics and Telecommunications, Poznań University of Technology, Poland (September 2006)
14. Wódczak, M.: Cooperative Relaying in an Indoor Environment. ICT Mobile Summit, Stockholm, Sweden, June 10-12 (2008)
15. Wódczak, M.: Future Autonomic Cooperative Networks. In: Pentikousis, K., Agüero, R., García-Arranz, M., Papavassiliou, S. (eds.) MONAMI 2010. LNICST, vol. 68, pp. 71–78. Springer, Heidelberg (2011)
16. Wódczak, M.: Aspects of Cross-Layer Design in Autonomic Cooperative Networking. In: IEEE Third International Workshop on Cross Layer Design, Rennes, France, 30 November - 1 December (2011)
17. Wódczak, M.: Autonomic Cooperation in Ad-hoc Environments. In: 5th International Workshop on Localised Algorithms and Protocols for Wireless Sensor Networks (LOCALGOS) in Conjunction with IEEE International Conference on Distributed Computing in Sensor Systems (DCOSS), Barcelona, Spain, June 27-29 (2011)
18. Wódczak, M.: Convergence Aspects of Autonomic Cooperative Networking. In: IEEE Fifth International Conference on Next Generation Mobile Applications, Services and Technologies, Cardiff, Wales, UK, September 14-16 (2011)
19. Wódczak, M.: Deployment Aspects of Autonomic Cooperative Communications in Emergency Networks. In: 3rd International Congress on Ultra Modern Telecommunications and Control Systems (IEEE ICUMT), Budapest, Hungary, October 5-7 (2011)
20. Wódczak, M.: Resilience Aspects of Autonomic Cooperative Communications in Context of Cloud Networking. In: IEEE First Symposium on Network Cloud Computing and Applications, Toulouse, France, November 21-23 (2011)
21. Wódczak, M.: Autonomic Cooperative Networking. Springer, New York (2012)
22. Wódczak, M., Meriem, T.B., Chaparadza, R., Quinn, K., Lee, B., Ciavaglia, L., Tsagkaris, K., Szott, S., Zafeiropoulos, A., Radier, B., Kielthy, J., Liakopoulos, A., Kousaridas, A., Duault, M.: Standardising a Reference Model and Autonomic Network Architectures for the Self-managing Future Internet. IEEE Network 25(6), 50–56 (2011)

Service for Management of Connectivity in Spontaneous Community-Based Wireless Mesh Networks

Lúcio Studer Ferreira and Luís M. Correia

Instituto de Telecomunicações/Instituto Superior Técnico
Technical University of Lisbon, Lisbon, Portugal
{lucio.ferreira,luis.correia}@lx.it.pt

Abstract. Spontaneously deployed wireless mesh networks raise challenging connectivity aspects. Based on an organizational framework and on an open connectivity service architecture, an opportunistic resources management service is proposed, which exploits network conditions and node capabilities to improve connectivity. This service is able to orchestrate adequate connectivity mechanisms, such as access provisioning, mesh forwarding and Internet gateway ones, in multi-radio nodes. The service is evaluated for a spontaneous neighbourhood community-based Wireless Mesh Network scenario, where a flash crowd of end-users with heterogeneous terminals is explored. It is shown that network performance is improved, increasing overall coverage and capacity.

Keywords: Wireless Mesh Network, Connectivity, Management, Opportunism.

1   Introduction

Internet has become a key player in modern society. More than simple consumers, end-users have become producers of information (so-called "prosumers"), community-based networking having gained an important role in the development and growth of the Internet. One of the key technical drivers is the increasing pervasiveness of wireless technologies, enabling ubiquity of access to the Internet. In fact, the availability of community-based wireless networks is already a reality among us. A successful example is FON [1], where each member shares its home WiFi Access Point (AP) with the community, having access to the hotspots of other members around the world. Still, each AP needs connectivity to the fixed Internet infrastructure. A natural evolution is the flexible wireless interconnection of APs, building a mesh of hotspots, where only a sub-set is connected to the Internet, which is the Wireless Mesh Network (WMN) paradigm. Classical WMNs follow a two-tiered architecture, where the first one consists of Wireless Mesh Routers (WMRs) forming a self-organized wireless backhaul, and the second of Wireless Mesh Clients (WMCs), end-user terminals. WMRs act as APs, covering a region where they offer connectivity to WMCs. Aggregated traffic flows travel between WMN's gateways and aggregating WMRs. Classical two-tier WMNs are typically deployed in an organized way within a specific area [2] guaranteeing seamless connectivity to

A. Timm-Giel et al. (Eds.): MONAMI 2012, LNICST 58, pp. 183–195, 2013.

Clients. Still, using WMNs for the spontaneous formation of community-centric wireless networks raises several challenges:

- Self-organization: users need to organize themselves, cooperating to provide means for the network to survive.
- Heterogeneity: it is likely that end-user terminals are heterogeneous in many aspects (communication and computational capabilities, location and visibility from other nodes, persistence and mobility).
- Opportunism: conditions and properties of the network, as well as the specificities of each node and its neighbours, must be explored dynamically.

Adaptive and flexible solutions for network formation and maintenance are needed. The Ambient Networks project [3] addressed heterogeneity in radio access networks, proposing a novel architecture to deal with access selection; still, it does not address multi-hop backhaul WMNs architectures. The OpenFlow framework [4] aims at making networks programmable; still, it is mostly designed for fixed networks, advances towards wireless networks still being needed. The 4WARD project [5] developed an architecture based on the generic-path concept, the main objective being to support communication needs in highly mobile and dynamic networking conditions; still the architecture is clean slate, its implementation being very complex. In [6] a WMN organizational framework is proposed to include flexibility in the assignment of roles to nodes, relaxing the strict rules in which nodes are either routers or clients. Any node may collaborate into the mesh infrastructure: depending on its capabilities, appropriate network functionalities may be assigned to it, enhancing network availability and usability. This framework is adopted in the current paper. An Open Connectivity Service (OConS) architecture [7], developed within the SAIL Project [8], supports the flexible orchestration of nodes connectivity resources, functionalities and mechanisms (both legacy and novel ones), being also used in here.

In the current paper, a novel OConS Service is proposed for the opportunistic management of connectivity of multi-radio nodes in spontaneous community WMNs, based on the organizational framework [6] and OConS architecture [7]. Considering the network conditions and capabilities of each node, this OConS service suggests the node to orchestrate one or multiple connectivity mechanisms: a) client access provisioning, b) multi-radio mesh forwarding connectivity, c) Internet gateway provisioning mechanism. This OConS service is made available to the WMN community, every joining node being suggested to use it, according to its capabilities.

The remaining paper is structured as follows: in Section 2, a WMN organizational framework and architecture is presented, used in Section 3 to define an Opportunistic WMN resources management service. In Section 4, this service is evaluated in a spontaneous community-based WMN scenario with a flash crowd of end-users. Conclusions are drawn in Section 5.

2   Organizational WMN Framework and OConS Architecture

In this section, two reference concepts supporting the implementation of the proposed OConS Service are presented. First, a WMN organizational framework that proposes functional roles to nodes based on their capabilities is reminded. Secondly, the

OConS architecture is highlighted, that enables the orchestration of a service implementing such functionalities.

2.1   Flexible Organizational Framework for WMNs

A flexible organizational framework for the opportunistic WMN formation and maintenance is proposed in [6], breaking the rigidness of the traditional WMN architecture. The nodes' role separation constraint into clients or mesh routers is relaxed, and the case of spontaneous network formation, relying in the concept of self-organization, is considered. The main idea is that the network takes advantage of the specific resources and characteristics of the nodes in an opportunistic fashion, where any node (routers and clients) can perform any network functionality, if they *can* and if they *wish*. For this, it is proposed that nodes are assigned tasks based on what they really are, as depicted in Fig. 1.

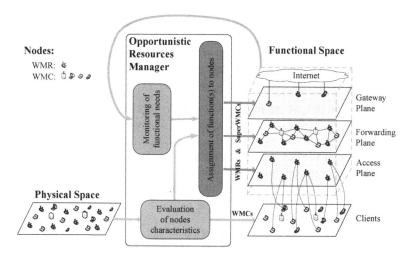

Fig. 1. Flexible organization framework of a WMN thanks to the opportunistic management of nodes' capabilities and network' functional needs (extracted from [6])

This assignment is decomposed into two main spaces:

- **Physical space** - It is composed of all nodes willing to participate in the community, identifying their characteristics and resources. A number of resources and nodes' characteristics are identified as having an impact on their ability to perform a given task, such as, communication capabilities, surrounding environment, mobility pattern (helping, e.g., in the dissemination of information), persistence (evidencing the confidence one can have on a node to remain connected to the network), position awareness, energy autonomy, computational capabilities, memory, and storage space.
- **Functional space** - It identifies the minimum set of tasks that guarantee the proper operation of the network. Note that, in this space, there is a notion of requirement, which specifies the characteristics of the nodes that should

perform the tasks. Several network functions can be identified, such as, resources management (requests persistent nodes with low mobility or energy constrains and high connectivity), network access connectivity (requests the nodes to be equipped with a wireless interfaces working as an AP), forwarding (requests one or two wireless interfaces working as mesh forwarders), gateway access (requests a connection to Internet) location service (requests position awareness, persistence and low mobility, storage space). The efficiency of these functionalities is influenced by the characteristics of the nodes performing them.

These two spaces are regulated by an opportunistic resources manager, a centralized or distributed entity, which identifies the set of nodes in the physical space that, due to their characteristics, would perform efficiently tasks identified in the functional space. The basic WMN infrastructure is provided by the interconnection of WMRs forming the core of the network. In order to join this infrastructure, and also extend it, nodes shall run a minimal communication protocol, allowing them to exchange information on their capacities and characteristics. This information is collected by the opportunistic resources manager that, besides general information, gathers information relative to the different network functionalities and task requirements. It suggests specific functionalities and/or tasks that the nodes are free to accept or not. In such a context, three types of nodes are defined:

- **WMR** - Nodes whose main purpose is to form the core infrastructure and perform all the tasks necessary for minimal network functioning and provide the primary community services. These nodes correspond to the traditional definition of WMRs, yet, they are able to hand out some tasks to other nodes, on request of the opportunistic resources manager.
- **WMC** - Nodes that do not fulfil the requirements to contribute in enhancing the infrastructure, or are not willing to do it. They represent the traditional definition of WMCs.
- **SuperWMC** - Nodes that are WMCs, but that have enough resources (communication capabilities, persistence, etc.), and are willing to actively contribute in enhancing the core infrastructure. These nodes reply to the opportunistic resources manager entity, accepting to perform tasks that are useful to the community, thus, improving the existing network.

2.2   Open Connectivity Service Architecture

The above framework needs an architecture and communication protocol to support such exchange information, as well as to implement network functionalities in nodes. The Open Connectivity Service (OConS) architecture [7] is ideal for this task, being flexible and modular in the description of connectivity resources and mechanisms, based on the identification of functional entities and their interfaces. It enables the orchestration of both legacy and enhanced connectivity mechanisms, which can be dynamically adapted and orchestrated into OConS Services offered to the network. The OConS architecture is built on top of three functional entities, defined as the building blocks of any OConS mechanism:

- Information Entity (IE), for information gathering and monitoring.
- Decision Making Entity (DE), where decision algorithms are implemented.
- Execution and Enforcement Entity (EE), which implements the decisions.

An OConS mechanism is a process made of one or multiple DEs, and zero or multiple IEs and EEs. These are pieces of software, available in an OConS node, enabling basic configuration functions and their interfacing among them supported by a specified Intra-/Inter-Node Communication (INC) process.

This approach allows the implementation, instantiation and launching of any OConS mechanism, and its integration with other OConS mechanisms to form an OConS Service. Any mechanism (legacy or novel) can be defined as an OConS mechanism, as long as it is modelled by the Functional Entities and OConS interfaces. Besides this, the networking elements that constitute the OConS architecture are:

- OConS node: infrastructure node (e.g., end-user terminals, base-stations, and routers) providing computing, storage, and networking resources to the OConS entities. It is the place where OConS entities are residing, instantiated, and executed, enabling the launch of OConS services. It can be an OConS enabled node, or a node originally without OConS capabilities, upgraded with OConS-related software.
- OConS domain: set of OConS nodes. It provides connectivity services to applications, by implementing a given set of OConS services.

The Orchestration is the functionality that supports the OConS architecture. It serves an explicit request by a user, or an implicit request triggered by a network state. From a set of available OConS mechanisms, the Orchestration dynamically identifies the most appropriate ones, launching an OConS service to address the connectivity requirements. It relies on the following elements:

- OConS Registry (OR), an IE where available OConS entities, mechanisms, and created OConS services are registered.
- Service Orchestration Process (SOP), responsible for the coordination of the orchestration of OConS entities, mechanisms, and services, a central point locally within an OConS node. It is based on a set of rules, needed for mapping demand profiles, connectivity requirements, network states, and a selection of mechanisms to compose an OConS service. The SOP provides various functionalities: a) bootstrapping, where available OConS entities and mechanisms are discovered in a node, and default OConS services launched; b) response to an OConS user connectivity request; c) response to a modification in the network state; d) OConS Service monitoring.

3   Opportunistic WMN Resources Management OConS Service

An Opportunistic WMN Resources Management (OWRM) OConS service is proposed for spontaneous community-based WMN, based on the WMN organizational framework and the OConS architecture presented in Sections 2.1 and 2.2. This service is available in the community-based WMN, an OConS domain, being offered to every node of the community. This is a distributed and self-organized service. Members willing to collaborate take tasks in the network according to their capabilities. In fact, the heterogeneity of multi-radio nodes characteristics opens a wide set of connectivity possibilities, which go much beyond the classical two-tier WMN architecture. The OWRM OConS service explores the capabilities of each node and the network functional needs, suggesting one or multiple of the following OConS mechanisms:

- **Internet gateway provisioning mechanism:** this is a legacy mechanism, where the node has an interface (radio or Ethernet) with connectivity to the Internet. This mechanism enables the node to provide gateway connectivity to the WMN.
- **Client access provisioning mechanism:** this is a classical mechanism, where the node acts as a classical radio access network, covering a region where it offers connectivity to WMCs. It optimizes the operating bit rate, power and channel resources. To be triggered, the node needs to have an available radio interface capable to offer such service.
- **Mesh forwarding connectivity mechanism:** this is a novel mechanism, described in [9], for multi-radio nodes that optimizes rate, power and channel radio resources, guaranteeing a max-min fair capacity, R_{fair}, to all aggregating nodes. To be triggered, one or more radio interfaces must exist, capable of forwarding traffic. The OConS mechanism that implements this mechanism is described in detail in [7], being in the current paper only considered its orchestration with the other two mechanisms to build the OWRM OConS.

Next, the orchestration of the proposed OWRM OConS service is described. Every WMR of the OConS domain has the knowledge of the functional networking needs within its neighbourhood, see Fig. 1. It has also registered, in its OR (so-called domain OR) the three above mechanisms that may compose the OWRM connectivity service (gateway, access, and forwarding), with the associated requirements. The service is offered to members of the community. Depending on the node's capabilities and functional network needs, the service suggests specific network functionalities that the node is free to accept or not; to be noted that in the classical WMN architecture, WMCs would never implement such functionalities.

For a new member of the community, two phases exist: bootstrapping, and orchestration of the OWRM OConS service. It is considered that the bootstrapping phase has been successful. A new member of the community that is not an OConS node is upgraded with OConS-related software by the SOP of a neighbouring WMR. Each node is aware of the available OConS entities.

To orchestrate the OWRM OConS service in a new member of the community, various interaction procedures are needed, Fig. 2:

1. **Monitoring of functional needs:** a neighbouring WMR informs the node about the state of the network and the functional networking needs.
2. **Subscription of candidate OConS mechanisms:** subscription, by the node's SOP towards a domain OR, of the OConS mechanisms available in the OConS domain. The domain OR publishes in the node's SOP the available mechanisms (gateway, access, and forwarding ones).
3. **Physical space characteristics request:** The network state information is subscribed by the SOP towards IEs, as well as OConS entities capabilities, to specify the node's physical space characteristics, namely communication capabilities (one or several radio interfaces, of similar or different standards,

Ethernet connection), surrounding environment (e.g., geographic position, propagation environment, and nodes in communication range), mobility pattern, persistence, energy autonomy, and computational capabilities.

4. **Validation of OConS mechanisms:** the physical space characteristics and available OConS entities will validate which candidate OConS mechanisms are supported by the node.

5. **Selection of OConS mechanisms:** Within these mechanisms, based on a set of rules for mapping connectivity requirements into mechanisms capabilities, the ones that satisfy the connectivity requirements are selected.

6. **Composition and configuration of OConS service:** SOP instantiates the DEs of OConS mechanism's to be created, launched and put in relation to work together. Resources and some mechanisms may need to be configured.

7. **Registration of instantiated OConS mechanisms and OConS service** in the OR.

These orchestration steps enable to implement, in any OConS node, the adequate OWRM service's connectivity mechanisms.

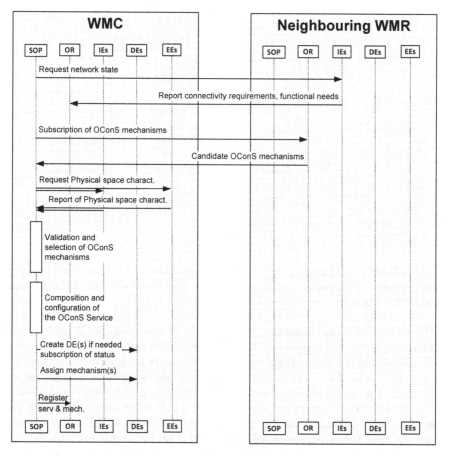

Fig. 2. Orchestration of an OWRM OConS Service in a Wireless Mesh Client

4   Performance Evaluation of the Proposed Service in a Community-Based WMN with a Flash Crowd Scenario

4.1   Scenario

For the evaluation of the proposed OWRM OConS service, a residential neighbourhood scenario is considered, with an area of 300×200 m^2, as depicted in Fig. 3. A spontaneous community-based WMN, of 12 randomly deployed WMRs, where two of them are also gateways to the Internet, provides connectivity to WMCs. Urban outdoor propagation environment conditions are considered. A flash crowd situation is considered, where a large number of end-users with heterogeneous multi-radio WMCs congregate, all willing to simultaneously access the Internet. Thanks to the OWRM OConS service, some of these may become SuperWMCs, also providing access, forwarding or gateway functionalities.

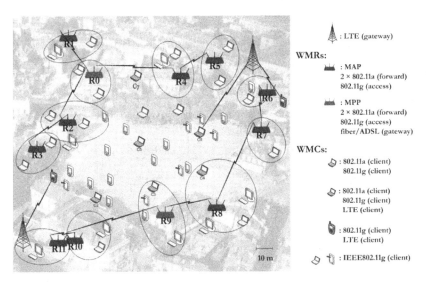

Fig. 3. Spontaneous community-based WMN reference scenario, with a flash crowd of clients. If the traditional role separation constraint into mesh routers and clients is followed, many clients are not served.

The OPNET Modeler simulation platform [12] is used to evaluate the proposed OConS service for the proposed WMN scenario. Multi-radio WMRs models were developed, equipped with two IEEE 802.11a [10] radios for mesh forwarding, one IEEE 802.11g [10] radio for client access provisioning, and some with gateway access (considered of unlimited capacity, not to bias the evaluation of the maximum capacity of the WMN). They implement the described mechanisms, also optimizing and controlling the operating channel, rate and power of each radio. IEEE 802.11a was chosen for mesh forwarding, as more channels are available than in 802.11g (11 vs 3, respectively), essential for interference free multi-hop communications. For access, 3 channels can be efficiently reused when small coverage ranges are dimensioned.

Although the operating band is higher for IEEE 802.11a than for 802.11g (5.5 Ghz vs 2.4 Ghz), resulting in higher attenuations, this is compensated with higher maximum allowed transmission power levels, $P_{tx\,max}$, for outdoor communications (30 vs 20 dBm, respectively). Possible P_{tx} levels range between 9 and 30 dBm with steps of 3 dB, for IEEE 802.11a, and between -1 and 20 dBm with steps of 3 dB, for IEEE 802.11g. Values of achieved throughput, maximum urban outdoor communication range, $d_{rx\,max}$ (for $P_{tx\,max}$) and interference range, d_i, are presented for some bit rates in Table 1. The crowd of end-users is equipped with WMCs terminals of heterogeneous connectivity capabilities, willing to use the Internet. Most of them are equipped with an 802.11g radio, used to access the WMN, but many WMCs have two or more interfaces of other systems, such as 802.11a and LTE [11], as represented in Fig. 3.

Table 1. Throughput, communication and interference ranges for some bit rates

Bit rate	Throughput	$d_{rx\,max}$ [m] (for $P_{tx\,max}$)		d_i/d_{rx}
[Mbps]	[Mbps]	802.11a	802.11g	
6	5.3	149.3	122.8	1.4
9	7.6	139.2	114.6	1.6
12	9.8	121.1	99.6	1.7
18	13.7	105.3	86.7	2.0
24	17.0	74.3	61.1	2.9
36	22.6	64.6	53.2	3.2
54	29.0	45.6	37.5	4.8

Optimal routes are pre-determined. For each aggregating node (WMR or SuperWMC), a downlink flow of UDP packets of 1500 bytes is sent via the nearest gateway with a specific inter-arrival time, determining the offered load. UDP is used, as it enables the study of the network under stress conditions, not limited by a congestion control mechanism. Depending on the WMN capacity, the achieved aggregated throughput at the aggregating node is similar or inferior to the offered load. For each aggregating node, the max-min fair aggregated throughput and the corresponding gateway-to-node delay are evaluated.

4.2   Performance Evaluation

The reference scenario is evaluated in terms of coverage and capacity. It is first considered that the WMN operates according to the classical architecture, where the crowd of WMCs gets Internet access via WMRs, a multi-hop wireless backhaul with some gateways to the Internet. Although many WMCs have multiple radio interfaces, the rigid architecture only exploits the 802.11g one. The resulting simulated max-min fair aggregated throughput, R_{fair}, and gateway-to-WMR delay, per WMR, is depicted in Fig. 4. This corresponds to the maximum supported aggregated throughput per WMR. The gateway WMRs naturally achieve the maximum throughput, as they are directly connected to the gateway. For the remaining nodes, the announced capacity R_{fair} could be offered in the access network using an 18 Mbps bit rate in the 802.11g. With a range up to 86 m for IEEE 802.11g at 18 Mbps, every WMC of the crowd is within communication range of at least one WMR. Still, the limited number of orthogonal channels (only 3 orthogonal IEEE 802.11g) to be used by all WMRs and the associated interference range (2 times the communication distance, for 18 Mbps), do not allow to have the entire capacity of all WMRs used simultaneously, as nodes would interfere. To reduce interference ranges, lower power levels have to be used, reducing also the coverage range of each WMR, a large number of WMCs of the flash crow remaining uncovered, as represented in Fig. 3.

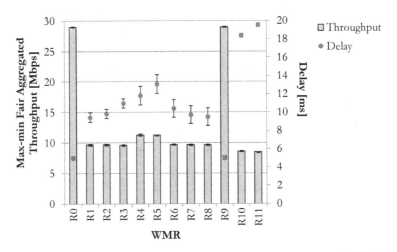

Fig. 4. Performance of the WMRs for the classical WMN without the proposed OWRM service

The performance of the same scenario is evaluated when the OWRM OConS service is offered to WMCs willing to join the community-based WMN. In this case, besides WMRs, some WMCs opportunistically assume network functionalities thanks to the proposed OWRM OConS service, becoming SuperWMCs, as shown in Fig. 5. SuperWMCs capabilities are explored by the service in the most advantageous way. Many provide access and forwarding network functionalities, enabling to provide coverage to all WMCs and increase the offered capacity.

An analysis of various improvements brought by SuperWMCs, depicted in Fig. 5, is presented next. SuperWMC C1 has both an LTE and an 802.11g interface. After accepting an invitation to join the community, it is upgraded with OConS-related software, and starts the orchestration process described in Fig. 2. It receives the conditions of the network, and the available OWMR OConS service mechanisms. Based on its capabilities, the SOP validates two mechanisms it can assume: gateway and access provisioning, with the 802.11g and LTE interfaces, respectively, accepting to become a SuperWMC and launch the OWMR OConS service, starting to provide Internet access to end-users over the 802.11g interface. As C2 has both 802.11g and 802.11a interfaces, the SOP suggests to launch an OWRM OConS service with access and forwarding mechanisms, providing access to end-users via its 802.11g, while the 802.11a forwards traffic to R9. For C3, SOP does not suggest to become SuperWMC as it is not necessary for the network. For C5, SOP launches and OWRM OConS service, using its LTE connection as a gateway to the Internet, its 802.11g to provide access to uncovered end-users, and its 802.11a interface to forward traffic to C5 and C4. C7 will forward the traffic between R0 and R4, reducing the hop distance, thus, enabling to use a higher bit rate. C8 will provide a nearer and faster access to the Internet to R6 and R7.

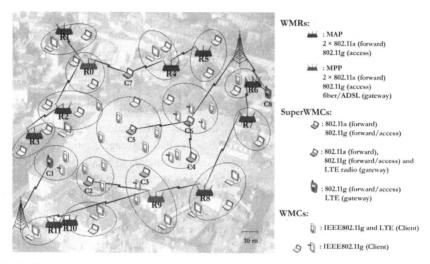

WMRs:

🏭 : MAP
2 × 802.11a (forward)
802.11g (access)

🏭 : MPP
2 × 802.11a (forward)
802.11g (access)
fiber/ADSL (gateway)

SuperWMCs:

📱 : 802.11a (forward)
802.11g (forward/access)

📱 : 802.11a (forward),
802.11g (forward/access) and
LTE radio (gateway)

📱 : 802.11g (forward/access)
LTE (gateway)

WMCs:

📱 : IEEE802.11g and LTE (Client)

📱 📱 : IEEE802.11g (Client)

Fig. 5. Spontaneous community-based WMN, where the proposed OWRM service enables some WMCs to become SuperWMCs, enhancing coverage, connectivity and capacity

The simulation results for the WMN with the OWRM OConS service are depicted in Fig. 6. It can be seen that offered capacity has increased for many WMRs, as more gateways to the Internet are available and the ranges between many forwarders is shorter, thanks to the SUperWMCs. SuperWMCs also provide coverage extension to many WMCs that originally were not covered. It is concluded that, in opposition to the

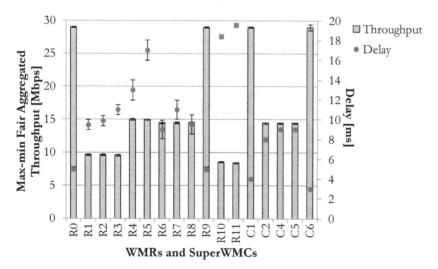

Fig. 6. Performance of the aggregating nodes (WMRs and SuperWMCs) of the opportunistic WMN, when the OConS service assigns networking tasks to many WMCs

classical WMN, where more WMCs represent more congestion and reduced resources for all, when the OWRM service is used, a flash crowd of heterogeneous WMCs brings large benefits in terms of connectivity, coverage and capacity to the overall WMN.

5   Conclusions

Spontaneous community-based WMNs networks, of random deployment and distributed management, present many connectivity and coverage challenges. When a flash crowd of end-users with heterogeneous devices intends to access such a network these limitations are evidenced even more. A WMN organizational framework, which exploits conditions and properties of the network as well as capabilities and specificities of each node, is explored. Recurring to an OConS open connectivity architecture, an opportunistic WMN resource management OConS service is proposed. It is able to orchestrate, in nodes with adequate capabilities, networking functionalities, such as end-users access provisioning, Internet gateway connectivity, and mesh forwarding connectivity. It is shown through simulation how this OConS service, when offered by the community-based WMN, can be orchestrated in nodes willing to join the community WMN by cooperating. It is shown how the presence of an end-users flash crowd in a community-based WMN scenario can be beneficial in the improvement of coverage, capacity, and connectivity, when the proposed OConS service is offered by the community to joining members.

Acknowledgement. The support of the European Commission by partially funding this work via the FP7-ICT-2009-5-SAIL project, Grant Agreement Number 257448, is acknowledged.

References

1. FON, http://www.fon.com/en
2. Seattle Wireless, http://seattlewireless.net
3. Niebert, N., Schieder, A., Zander, J., Hancock, R.: Ambient Networks: Co-operative Mobile Networking for the Wireless World. John Wiley & Sons, London (2007)
4. McKeown, N., Anderson, T., Balakrishnan, H., Parulkar, G., Peterson, L., Rexford, J., Shenker, S., Turner, J.: Openflow: enabling innovation in campus networks. ACM Computer Communication 38(2), 69–74 (2008)
5. Correia, L.M., Abramowicz, H., Johnsson, M., Wunstel, K. (eds.): Architecture and Design for the Future Internet. Springer, Berlin (2010)
6. Ferreira, L.S., Amorim, M.D., Iannone, L., Berlemann, L., Correia, L.M.: Opportunistic Management of Spontaneous and Heterogeneous Wireless Mesh Networks. Wireless Communications Magazine 17(2), 41–46 (2010)
7. Agüero, R., Caeiro, L., Correia, L.M., Ferreira, L.S., García-Arranz, M., Suciu, L., Timm-Giel, A.: OConS: Towards open connectivity services in the future internet. In: Pentikousis, K., Aguiar, R., Sargento, S., Agüero, R. (eds.) MONAMI 2011. LNICST, vol. 97, pp. 90–104. Springer, Heidelberg (2012)

8. SAIL-Scalable and Adaptive Internet Solutions, EC FP7 ICT Project,
   `http://www.sail-project.eu`
9. Ferreira, L.S., Correia, L.M.: Efficient and Fair Radio Resources Allocation for Spontaneous Multi-Radio Wireless Mesh Networks. In: Proc. of ISSSE 2012: International Symposium on Signals, Systems and Electronics, Potsdam, Germany (October 2012)
10. IEEE, Local and metropolitan area networks - Specific requirements Part 11: Wireless LAN MAC and PHY Specifications, IEEE 802.11 WG (June 2007)
11. 3GPP, UTRA-UTRAN Long Term Evolution (LTE) and 3GPP System Architecture Evolution (SAE) (May 2008)
12. OPNET Modeler Wireless Suite, `http://www.opnet.com`

A Cognitive Management Framework for Smart Objects and Applications in the Internet of Things

Dimitris Kelaidonis[1], Andrey Somov[2], George Poulios[1], Vassilis Foteinos[1],
Vera Stavroulaki[1], Panagiotis Vlacheas[1], and Panagiotis Demestichas[1]

[1] University of Piraeus, Department of Digital Systems,
Karaoli & Dimitriou Str. 80, 185 34 Piraeus, Greece
{dkelaid,gpoulios,vfotein,veras,panvlah,pdemest}@unipi.gr
[2] CREATE-NET
Via alla Cascata 56/D, 38123 Povo di Trento, Italy
asomov@create-net.org

Abstract. This paper proposes a cognitive management framework for the Internet of Things (IoT). The framework includes three levels of functionality: virtual object (virtual representation of real object enriched with context information), composite virtual object (cognitive mash-up of semantically interoperable virtual objects), and user/stakeholder levels. Cognitive entities at all levels provide the means for self-management (configuration, healing, optimization, protection) and learning. The paper also presents the implementation of the proposed framework, comprising real sensors and actuators. The preliminary results of this work demonstrate high potential towards self-reconfigurable IoT.

Keywords: Internet of Things, Cognitive Management, (Composite) Virtual Object, Self-Management, Smart Object.

1 Introduction

The "7 trillion devices for 7 billion people" paradigm [1] yields that the handling of the amount of objects that will be part of the Internet of Things (IoT) requires suitable architecture and technological foundations. Internet-connected sensors, actuators and other types of smart devices and objects need a suitable communication infrastructure.

The appearance of RFID [2] and Wireless Sensor Network (WSN) [3] technologies allowed the users to capture and identify Real World Objects (RWOs) automatically [4]. Due to distributed and autonomous nature of WSNs, a user can capture a RWO everywhere at any time.

The next research problem, which appeared with the evolution of the IoT domain, was 'how a RWO can be represented in a virtual world?'. A *Virtual sensor* approach is described in [5] that hides the implementation details from the user, but at the same time represents and includes a number of real devices, e.g. sensor, mobile phone, actuator, video camera. A lot of approaches, such as [5], have focused on the

A. Timm-Giel et al. (Eds.): MONAMI 2012, LNICST 58, pp. 196–206, 2013.

virtualization of the real devices. These works, however, lack smart management functionality of virtualized RWO, which is essential to overcome the technological heterogeneity and complexity of pervasive networks, to enhance context-awareness, to provide high reliability for reliable service provision, to support energy-efficiency of services.

The research works in [6] and [7] describe their efforts in the enrichment of each single virtual object with augmented smart functions to communicate with people and other virtual objects and are aware of context, situation, and past actions. A similar approach has been proposed in [8] where smart objects, support users in making decisions and taking mature and responsible actions. The research in multi-agent systems also tackles *smart environment* problem [9].

A distinctive feature of CASAGRAS approach consists in the real object identification rather than its representation [10]. More specifically, the CASAGRAS derives an ontology for automatic real object identification in physical layer. This is a key requirement in the framework for the interfacing between real and digital world. The identified and digitized objects can be grouped in the networks and are then transmitted to the information management system through a gateway layer to provide the functional platform for application and services.

Another research works are focused on various technical aspects (hardware, software, etc.) as well as on application domains. For example, the SOFIA project [11] attempts to create a semantic interoperability platform to make information in the physical world available for smart services - connecting the physical world with the information world. In [12] the authors investigated how ontologies, runtime task models, Belief-Desire-Intention (BDI) models, and the blackboard architectural pattern may be used to enable semantic interaction for pervasive computing. In the approach presented in [13] the authors used explicit semantics to design abstracted models of connections between devices in a smart home environment. An architectural framework with three different levels of abstraction is the core concept of the SENSEI project [14]. The digital world has been classified into three abstractions: (a) resources (representations of the instruments), (b) entities (representations of people, places, and things), and (c) resource users (representations of real users which interact with resources and entities).

In response to the requirement of overcoming technological heterogeneity this paper proposes a cognitive management framework which aims to provide the means to realize the principle that any real world object (RWO) and any digital object, which is available, accessible, observable or controllable, can have a virtual representation in the IoT, which is called Virtual Object (VO). As opposed to [6][7][8], basic VOs can be composed in a more sophisticated way by forming Composite VOs (CVOs), which provide services to high-level applications and end-users. Essentially, a CVO is a mash up of different types of VOs. A CVO may be considered as a smart object that has functionality, and can communicate with other smart objects and/or applications. Moreover, a CVO may be used by the users in order to interact with other available smart objects.

The rest of this paper is structured as follows. Section 2 introduces a reader to the proposed cognitive framework for IoT. Section 3 presents an indicative scenario of the operation of the cognitive management framework applied in a smart home (assisted living) use case. Section 4 provides a detailed description of the framework implementation. Finally, concluding remarks and description of future work are provided in Section 5.

2   Framework Overview and Key Definitions

There are two key issues that need to be addressed for the successful realization of the IoT namely: (a) the abstraction of the technological heterogeneity that derives from the vast amounts of heterogeneous objects, while enhancing reliability and energy efficiency of network services and infrastructures; (b) the consideration of the views of different users/stakeholders (owners of objects & communication means) for ensuring proper application provision, business integrity and, therefore, maximization of exploitation opportunities.

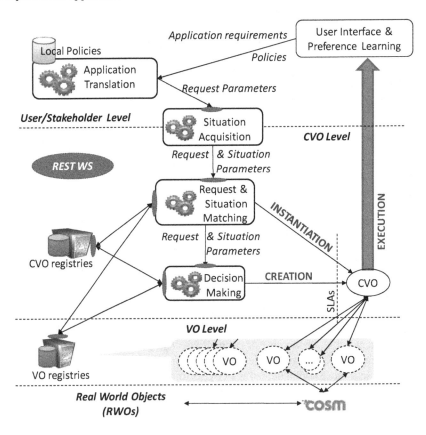

Fig. 1. An indicative operation scenario

In this direction, the solution proposed in this paper is a cognitive management framework comprising three levels of functionality, reusable for various and diverse applications. The levels under consideration (Figure 1) are: (a) Virtual Objects (VOs) level. VOs are virtual representations of devices or digital objects (e.g. sensors, actuators, smartphones, music players, etc) associated to everyday objects or people (e.g. a table, a room, an elderly, etc) that hide the underlying technological heterogeneity. (b) Composite virtual objects (CVOs) level. Composite Virtual Objects exploit the Virtual Objects. They are cognitive mash-ups of semantically interoperable VOs, delivering services in accordance with the user/stakeholder requirements. Essentially, the CVO is a smart object with cognitive capabilities. (c) User/stakeholder level. User/ stakeholder related objects will convey the respective requirements.

Cognitive entities at all levels provide the means for self-management (configuration, healing, optimization, protection) and learning. In this respect, they are capable of perceiving and reasoning on their context (e.g., based on event filtering, pattern recognition, machine learning), and of conducting associated knowledge-based decision-making (through associated optimization algorithms and machine learning). In the next subsections, the key concepts and the cognitive mechanisms of the three levels of functionalities are described in more detail.

2.1   Virtual Objects Level

The main entities at the Virtual Object (VO) level are the VOs (representing various RWOs) and VO registries which store VO descriptions and provide information on available VOs.

2.1.1   Virtual Object

A Virtual Object (VO) is the virtual representation of Real-World Objects (RWOs). RWOs may be either digital objects with Information and Communication Technologies (ICT) capabilities or non-ICT objects. ICT objects include objects such as sensors, actuators, smart phones, etc. ICT objects may have a physical location and may offer various functions such as environmental condition measurements, location of objects/person, monitoring of places for security reasons, etc. Non-ICT objects are tangible objects of the physical world that do not have any direct ICT capabilities such as furniture, a room, fruits, a person, etc. Non ICT objects can be implicitly represented in the virtual world through their association with one or more ICT objects, which in turn are represented through VOs.

2.1.2   VO Registry

The VO registry includes information about VOs that are available in the system. The information describes the associations between the VOs with ICTs and non-ICTs as well as the related data with these. Each VO is identified by a Uniform Resource Identifier (URI) and contains information on the association with an ICT object. The ICTs are also identified by a specific URI, have a specific physical location that is described with the coordinates and offer one or more functions. A function description provides information on its inputs and outputs and is also identified by a URI. Furthermore, each function has a set of costs and a set of utilities that are considered by the decision making process when targeting any specific policy enforcement. Moreover, information about associations between ICT objects with non-ICTs is included in the VO registry whilst the description of a non-ICT comprises of a URI and a non-ICT name.

2.2   Composite Virtual Object Level

The CVO level contains CVOs, the CVO registry, which contains information on the available CVOs, the Request and Situation Matching, and the Decision Making mechanisms.

2.2.1   Composite Virtual Objects

CVOs exploit the functions provided by VOs. A CVO is a cognitive mash-up of semantically interoperable VOs that renders services in accordance with user/stakeholder perspectives and application requirements. CVOs are self-managed, self-configurable components, which exploit cognitive mechanisms to enable the mash-up and re-use of existing VOs and CVOs by various applications, also outside the context and domain for which they were originally developed. CVOs are smart objects created dynamically in an autonomous manner taking into account requirements deriving from the user, application and objects levels.

2.2.2   CVO Registry

The CVO registry contains all information regarding the components of CVOs, how they are interconnected and the situation as well as the actual request parameters under which they were created or instantiated. In addition, it holds any explicit or implicit user feedback that is associated with the CVO lifecycle. Such records are exploited in forthcoming requests to improve the performance of the CVO deployment phase as well as the service quality for either the particular stakeholder or others requesting similar services.

2.2.3   Request and Situation Matching

The goal of the Request and Situation Matching functional entity is to identify past application requests that match closely enough to the present, incoming ones and the situations under which they were issued, so that the task of VO composition from scratch can be avoided under certain circumstances. In order to compare between past and present situations and requests, parameters that describe them have been identified. Request parameters consist of the set of functions requested and the costs or utilities specified to be maximized or minimized. Situation parameters consist of the time of day the request occurred, the area of interest, and the available VOs at that time. In order to enhance the filtering process, the requested functions can be matched with approximate ones, e.g. a video capture function can satisfy a requirement for an image capture function. The result of this mechanism is performance gain, as the process of creating a CVO from scratch is more complex. Moreover, reusability of resources is introduced in the system.

2.2.4   Decision Making

The Decision Making entity is triggered by the Request and Situation Matching mechanisms interacts with the VO registry and its objective is to find the optimal composition of VOs that fulfils the requested functions and policies. It receives as input a set of available VOs, a set of functions for each VO, a set of utility and cost values for these VOs and finally weights for these utilities and costs. A correlation matrix provides the suitability level of an offered function of a VO with the requested ones. The result of the decision making process is the creation and activation of a new CVO. The description of the newly instantiated CVO is recorded in the CVO registry in order to be available for future requests.

2.3   User / Stakeholder Level

Users interact with the system via interfaces, and may request, configure and use applications or consume services. In order to enhance, among others, user experience, the system maintains user profiles that hold a collection of parameters regarding their preferences. Their feedback is used to build knowledge so that future preference estimations can potentially be derived. Further description of the user/stakeholder level mechanisms that the specification of the proposed framework designates follows in the next paragraphs.

2.3.1   Application Translation

Users provide a set of application requirements and policies for the preferred application while different policies may govern a specific domain. The Application Translation mechanisms map these requirements to service logic requirements and combine them with the user-requested as well as the local policies, if present. In turn, a set of request parameters is extracted and forwarded to the Situation Acquisition mechanisms.

2.3.2   Situation Acquisition

The Situation Acquisition mechanisms receive a set of request parameters from the application translation mechanisms. These mechanisms enable the cognitive management framework to be able to aggregate and infer relevant situational dimensions (e.g. time, place, VO states), in order to describe the current situation and anticipate changes to it. The output result of the situation acquisition mechanisms is a set of request and situation parameters that are provided to the Situation and Request Matching mechanism in order to be processed.

3   A Smart Home Use Case

This section presents an indicative scenario for the operation of the proposed framework. The scenario comprises two different (business) domains; (a) a smart home, where an elderly woman (Sarah) who has opted for an assisted living service lives in, and (b) a medical center, where doctors monitor Sarah's environmental conditions and health status remotely, using the smart objects that exist in smart home.

Firstly, a doctor through an appropriate user interface provides a set of application requirements. From the Application Translation and Situation Acquisition entities, a set of request and situation parameters are extracted to be forwarded to the Request and Situation Matching mechanisms, which, in turn, search in the CVO registry for a previously created CVO that could fulfil the requested application. If an appropriate CVO is not found, the provided parameters are sent to the Decision Making entity, which will select the most appropriate VOs to satisfy the requirements and policies in the best possible way, and will trigger the creation of a new CVO. The newly created CVO is registered in the CVO registry together with the situation parameters under which it was requested for future reference by the Request and Situation Matching entity. Finally, the doctor, or member of the medical staff, can use the dynamically created CVO to monitor the medical status of Sarah, Feedback regarding the operation of the CVO can be provided.

4   Framework Implementation

This section describes a first implementation of the proposed Cognitive Management Framework.

4.1   Real World Objects

The RWOs that have been used in the framework are a set of sensors and actuators. More specifically, the Waspmote platform by Libelium [15] is exploited that hosts three different sensors (temperature, humidity and luminosity sensors) for sensing of the environmental conditions in the Sarah's Smart Home. Three different actuators are used (a fan, a colour lamp and a LED) that are connected with the Arduino platform [16]. The sensors and actuators are connected to the Cosm (former Pachube) IoT platform [17]. Sensing and actuation streams have been created on Cosm to save sensing values and commands for the actuators. The sensors are connected to Waspmote which sends the sensors' measurements to Cosm's databases through a gateway. The instantiated CVO communicates with Cosm, gets the measurements from the sensing stream, generates commands for the actuators, according to the service logic corresponding to the requirements provided at the user/stakeholder level, and sends them to Cosm's actuation stream. The Arduino platform automatically polls the actuation stream. As soon as it receives the corresponding command(s) it (de)activates the respective actuator(s). The RWOs represented as VOs and the information that describing these is stored in the VO Registry.

4.2   VO and CVO Registry

The VOs/CVOs registries have been implemented as Resource Description Framework (RDF) [18] graph databases with the use of Sesame, an extensible Java framework for the management of RDF data. A Sesame repository can host RDF graph databases and supports the use of the SPARQL query language [19]. The use of SPARQL queries allows the storing, querying and inferencing for RDF data that exist in the system registries. Access to the VO/CVO registry is provided via RESTful Web Services [20].

4.3   Request and Situation Matching

Application requests are issued through the graphical user interface (Figure 2) and then translated to machine-readable format and forwarded to the request and situation matching component via RESTful WS.

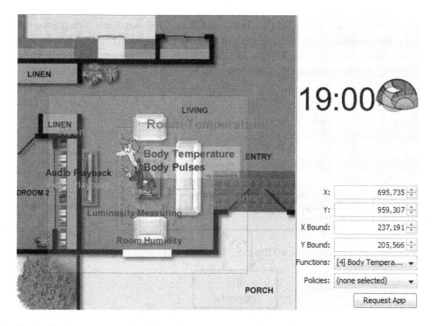

Fig. 2. Application request Graphical User Interface; VOs and the functions they can provide are shown

At this point the application request can be compared with past ones in the search for an adequate match. Past request records that contain CVO components (VOs) with functions that are unavailable in the current situation (either them or approximate ones) are filtered out, as they definitely cannot fulfil the application goals. The remaining records are ranked based on a satisfaction-rate similarity metric and the highest ranked one is tested against the similarity threshold. The satisfaction-rate depends on the amount of total requested functions being available as well as their correlations and it is implemented as a score (i.e. sum) of these correlations between the set of the requested and the required CVO functions. Besides the functions, the overall similarity metric considers also the rest of the situation and request parameters.

4.4   Decision Making

Decision Making (DM) is the process that is responsible for the creation of CVOs in our framework. These CVOs will deliver appropriate services according to the requested functionality, policies and the VOs that are available in the area of interest. Knowledge of these factors is necessary for the operation of the DM. Additionally, it comprises both optimization and cognition aspects and the DM itself is a main component of our framework's cognition loop. ILOG CPLEX is used in the implementation of the DM process.

As depicted in Figure 3, the DM is triggered by the request and situation matching mechanisms (step 1), interacts with the VO registry (step 2) and its objective is to find the optimal composition of VOs that fulfils the requested functions and policies (step 3). It receives as input a set of available VOs, a set of functions for each VO, a set of utility and cost values for these VOs and finally weights for these utilities and costs. A correlation matrix provides the suitability level of an offered function of a VO with the requested ones. The result of the DM process is the creation (step 4) and activation of a new CVO (step 5). The description of the newly instantiated CVO is recorded in the CVO registry in order to be available for future requests.

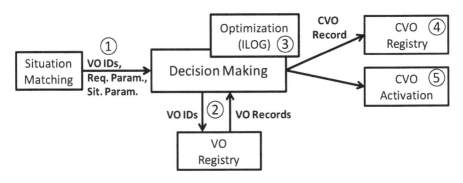

Fig. 3. Decision Making Process

4.5   Instantiated CVO – Smart Object

The CVO is the result of the elaboration of application requirements. It is created as a Smart Object that is comprised of different VOs and delivers a set of services in an efficient cognitive way. The CVO communicates with the RWOs that are available in Sarah's Smart Home, through the Cosm's data feeds. More specifically, the CVO gets the real-time sensor measurements through a sensing feed and elaborates these values in order to draw conclusions about Sarah's home environmental conditions and her health. After the measurements elaboration, the CVO makes a set of decisions regarding the manipulation of available actuators, based on the service logic created as a result of requirements provided at the user/stakeholder level.

5   Conclusions and Future Work

This paper has introduced the concepts of Virtual Object (VO) and Composite Virtual Object (CVO) as means for abstracting the heterogeneity and complexity of the IoT infrastructure and for enabling the dynamical creation of smart objects exploiting various devices, not bound to specific application domains. The main contribution of this paper within the framework is, however, the cognitive functionality of VO and CVO which ensures their self-management (configuration, healing, optimization, and protection) and learning. The proposed concepts and framework were implemented and tested in the context of an assisted living use case. The preliminary results demonstrate high potential of the proposed framework. Future work will involve the implementation of functional entities that are designed but not yet implemented. Cognitive mechanisms such as the "application translation" and "learning" mechanisms as well as mechanisms for the "user profile" information management will be further developed in order to enhance the system's functionality.

Acknowledgement. This article describes work undertaken in the context of the iCore project, 'Internet Connected Objects for Reconfigurable Ecosystems' (http://www.iot-icore.eu/). iCore is an EU Integrated Project funded within the European 7th Framework Programme, contract number: 287708. The contents of this publication are the sole responsibility of iCore project and can in no way be taken to reflect the views of the European Union.

References

1. Uusitalo, M.: Global Vision for the Future Wireless World from the WWRF. IEEE Vehicular Technology Magazine 1(2), 4–8 (2006)
2. Weinstein, R.: RFID: A Technical Overview and its Application to the Enterprise. J. IT Professional 7(3), 27–33 (2005)
3. Chong, C.-Y., Kumar, S.P.: Sensor Networks: Evolution, Opportunities, and Challenges. Proceedings of the IEEE 91(8), 1247–1256 (2003)
4. Romer, K., Schoch, T., Mattern, F., Dubendorfer, T.: Smart Identification Frameworks for Ubiquitous Computing Applications. J. Wireless Networks 10(6), 689–700 (2004)
5. Aberer, K., Hauswirth, M., Salehi, A.: Infrastructure for Data Processing in Large-Scale Interconnected Sensor Networks. In: Proceedings of the International Conference on Mobile Data Management (MDM 2007), pp. 198–205 (2007)
6. Beigl, M., Gellersen, H.-W., Schmidt, A.: MediaCups: Experience with Design and Use of Computer-Augmented Everyday Objects. J. Computer Networks 35(4), 401–409 (2001)
7. Mattern, F.: From Smart Devices to Smart Everyday Objects. In: Proceedings of the Smart Objects Conference (SOC 2003), pp. 15–16 (2003)

8. Streitz, N.A., Rocker, C., Prante, T., Van Alphen, D., Stenzel, R., Magerkurth, C.: Designing Smart Artifacts for Smart Environments. J. Computer 38(3), 41–49 (2005)
9. Cook, D.J.: Multi-agent Smart Environments. J. Ambient Intelligence and Smart Environments 1(1), 47–51 (2009)
10. FP7 project CASAGRAS, http://www.iot-casagras.org/
11. SOFIA project Website, http://www.sofia-project.eu/
12. Niezen, G., Van Der Vlist, B.J.J., Hu, J., Feijs, L.M.G.: From Events to Goals: Supporting Semantic Interaction in Smart Environments. In: Proceedings of the IEEE symposium on Computers and Communications (ISCC 2010), pp. 1029–1034 (2010)
13. Van Der Vlist, B.J.J., Niezen, G., Hu, J., Feijs, L.M.G.: Design Semantics of Connections in a Smart Home Environment. In: Proceedings of Design and Semantics of Form and Movement (DeSForM 2010), pp. 48–56 (2010)
14. EU/FP7 project SENSEI (Integrating the Physical with the Digital World of the Network of the Future, 215923), January 2008 - December 2010, The SENSEI Real World Internet Architecture, Version 1.1 (March 2010)
15. Libelium, WaspMote sensor platform, http://www.libelium.com/products/waspmote
16. Arduino platform, http://arduino.cc/
17. Cosm Connect to your world, https://cosm.com/
18. Resource Description Framework (RDF): Concepts and Abstract Syntax, W3C Recommendation (February 10, 2004), http://www.w3.org/TR/rdf-concepts/ (accessed June 2012)
19. SPARQL Query Language for RDF, http://www.w3.org/TR/rdf-sparql-query/
20. RESTful Web Services: The basics, Alex Rodriguez IBM Developer works page REST (November 2008), http://www.ibm.com/developerworks/webservices/library/ws-restful/

Implementation of Context-Aware Network Architecture for Smart Objects Based on Functional Composition*,**

Jose Luis Ferrer, Xavier Sanchez-Loro, Anna Calveras, and Josep Paradells

Escola Tècnica Superior d'Enginyeria de Telecomunicació de Barcelona (ETSETB)
JordiGirona 1-3, 08034 Barcelona, Spain
i2CAT Foundation, Gran Capità 2-4 (Nexus Building), 08034 Barcelona, Spain
{jlferrer,xsanchez,acalveras,josep.paradells}@entel.upc.edu

Abstract. Lack of flexibility of current Internet architecture led researchers to come up with new paradigms for a novel Internet architecture, which would be able to reduce complexity and increase flexibility compared to current Internet architecture. Functional composition is a promising approach to flexible and evolvable architecture design. The idea is composing complex protocol suites by dynamically bind and arrange different functions to obtain certain behavior. Herein, we present the implementation of a context-aware network architecture based on functional composition for smart objects. A sub-set of those basic functional blocks has been implemented and validated on an experimental testbed using different network topologies.

Keywords: Future Internet, functional blocks, context-awareness, smart objects, constrained devices, semantic routing.

1 Introduction

Nowadays, several different proposals of Future Internet (FI) architectures exist in Europe and worldwide that are taking the "clean-slate" path, redefining the architectonical principles of Future Networks (FNs) from scratch. Hence, lack of flexibility of current Internet architecture leaded researchers to come up with new paradigms for a novel Internet architecture, which would be able to reduce complexity and increase flexibility compared to current Internet architecture. But, at this moment, it is not clear which of these architectures neither which architectural paradigm will succeed or prevail as the new Internet architecture.

Functional composition is a promising approach to flexible and evolvable architecture design [1][2]. The idea is composing complex protocol suites by dynamically bind and arrange different functions to obtain certain behavior. The key aspect here is granularity and scope of functions. On one hand, the idea of

---

* This work is supported by the Spanish Government through the MICINN and FEDER project TEC2009-11453.
** The authors are grateful to the reviewers' valuable comments that improved the current paper.

A. Timm-Giel et al. (Eds.): MONAMI 2012, LNICST 58, pp. 207–216, 2013.

modularizing the stack is catching the great attention in the research community. The idea is to extract the functionalities out of the current network stack and place them as needed, by using this approach it will ease the introduction, reuse, change and placement of functionalities (e.g. application level, network level, etc.) and flexibility in terms of inclusion and exclusion of function with respect to application demands. Another similar idea that is catching up is using a flexible model of layers with dynamic bindings, opposed to the static binding between stacked modules/layers being used today. The idea here is to optimize the architecture for flexibility, designing it to support any protocol stack by using inheritance schemes (class-based), polymorphism and dynamic binding between modules/layers. This approach also aims to make a flexible functional composition, but with coarse-grained granularity of layers instead of small networking functions.

The paper is organized as follows: in section 2 we discuss the possibilities of functional composition to implement FI architectures suited for smart objects. Section 3 gives a brief overview design of our architecture proposal (see [3] for more details on the design of the architecture). Section 4 details the implementation of the architecture for constrained devices.

2   Functional Composition in Smart Objects

Functional composition architectures for FI have the potential to be able to cover the whole networking spectrum in its wider sense if they are provided with extensible, adaptable, customizable and personalized roles, vocabularies and control mechanisms. They have the potential to converge the different "Internet of" visions into a single architectonical paradigm; thus paving the way for convergence of heterogeneous networks and integration of smart objects and other constrained devices in the general framework of the Internet.

Hence, solutions should be designed and standardized with extensibility, flexible and loose-coupling as main design premises. Therefore, software-derived mechanisms for data abstraction, modularity, inheritance/delegation, dynamic bindings (opposed to static ones) and polymorphism should be applied in order to allow the evolution and change of the different aspects of the solution (roles, vocabularies and control mechanisms). By providing tools for changing the dynamics and behavior of networks and protocols FI architectures will have realistic means to evolve without requiring major breakthroughs, costly transition plans or architectural reformulations.

In accordance with this idea, we should design solutions for worst-case scenarios, such as constrained environments with capacity and power restrictions and hostile mediums (e.g. smart objects, actuators, sensors), and then extend them to work in more favorable environments without capacity restrictions. Therefore, if we can design flexible architectures that are adaptable to context variations and that work with minimalistic devices in constrained networks, it should be easier to extrapolate those architectures to work in more unconstrained environments, without capacity restrictions, such as wired computer networks. Furthermore, restricted devices like sensors/actuators and objects are becoming increasingly predominant in the Network (and will continue to grow in numbers); we cannot therefore ignore their impact on networking applications and should design a model capable of accommodating them.

3   Architecture Overview

In [3] we propose a clean-slate Role-Based Architecture [4] that advocates breaking current protocols in its fundamental pieces: those individual functions commonly used in networking protocols (i.e. acknowledgments, sequence numbers, flow control, etc.).The idea is creating new protocols using these atomic functions or services as basic building blocks. This way, the proposal uses ensembles of basic services to provide advanced communication services. We define those basic building blocks as Atomic Services (AS).

This shift of paradigm requires extensive research on feasible techniques for building up optimized protocols from scratch according to different criteria, ranging from energy efficiency to context-awareness. This reasoning should take into consideration the characteristics of the surrounding context (device capabilities, available network and computation resources, location and environment, etc.) solving the following issues [5]: which behaviour and outcome is desired; which functions are most suitable to achieve expected outcome; where they should be allocated; which mechanism (protocol, language/ontology) will be used to allocate and configure functions along communication path.

Other issues approached by the architecture are: discovery of desired services according to their semantic description; mechanisms for context interchange; resource reservation and ontologies for describing context characteristics (node, link, service, etc.), QoS agreements, service/resource description, locator/identifier schemes, etc. [6].The service discovery and AS allocation is performed by means of negotiation protocol based on reactive ad-hoc routing protocols suitable for smart objects which creates communications on demand.

For ontology and vocabulary support, we define a set of basic vocabularies for describing node capabilities, service and resource characteristics and QoS requirements. In order to support different environments and visions, this set of services/roles should be extended. Likewise, these vocabularies are designed with restricted devices in mind and, as such, are quite limited in their scope.

4   Implementation Design

The design of the architecture is divided in modules that run on event based operative system for constrained devices [3]. We have extended the architecture to be platform independent using an event based scheduler and a Medium Access Control (MAC) module able to inject and receive datagrams from different physical network interfaces. Furthermore, the architecture provides a framework to create functional blocks, i.e. ASs, and provide information about its characteristics to be utilized by allocation algorithms when establishing a new communication.

This section is divided as follows. First of all, we discuss the main patterns required to implement the functional blocks. Secondly, we detail the structures utilized to register and select those blocks in the architecture. Then, we describe the available interfaces to interchange information between the different functional blocks in an active communication. Finally, we describe a preliminary validation of the framework using several nodes with a basic set-up of functional blocks.

4.1   Atomic Services Patterns

In addition on creating taxonomy of types of basic network functionalities for services (e.g., cyphering, error control, etc.), we have identified the following patterns as the basic operations that are usually executed when implementing any networking protocol. These patterns should be available when executing an AS in order to provide flexibility and extensibility:

- *Payload data modification.* Services like coding, transcoding or ciphering mostly modify the payload from application data included in the datagrams. Therefore, the architecture must provide interfaces to the AS in order to access to packet payload independently on other AS executions.
- *Overhead data manipulation.* Network protocols require interchange and access to additional control data included as overhead in packets. Hence, the architecture must provide standard interfaces to access to packet metadata information.
- *Execution of periodic tasks.* Timers are required in order to evaluate certain conditions that could trigger events like retransmissions or QoS computations. Hence, the AS executions must be able to create timers to trigger those events.
- *Generation and processing of control data.* In addition to overhead control information added to data payloads, some services must be able to generate control data interchange, like the negotiating phase of security protocols.

4.2   Atomic Services

Atomic Services (AS) constitute the functional modules of the architecture utilized to set up communication paths. Once a communication has been established, the allocated AS are executed sequentially. We define the procedure of creating this list is as AS linkage (see Fig. 1). For each path created, each node maintains a linked list of the AS to be executed locally. Each network function is created using two AS blocks that represent the two endpoints of the network functionality. Each AS block can be configured as input, if processes receiving packets; output, if processes outgoing packets; or both in case that the AS is executed only in an intermediate node (e.g., a transcoding functionality).

We have classified AS in different groups or types, according to its main functionality. Examples of AS groups are error detection, transcoding, retransmission or acknowledgement [6]. For each of the AS groups, there exist different implementations for the same functionality, defined in the architecture as AS configurations. For instance, Stop-and-wait Automatic Repeat Request (ARQ) and Go-back-N ARQ are two different configurations of the retransmission functionality.

Therefore, each AS block is uniquely identified by its type and configuration. Currently, each AS type and configurations in the architecture are identified using 1 byte, enough to run a basic set on constrained devices but can be extended to allow a greater set of implementations. As a result, organizations and developers can provide a wide range of AS, where basic and simpler AS implementations can be applied in constrained devices and complex ones in carrier-grade networking equipment.

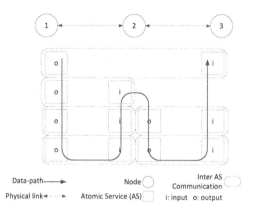

Fig. 1. Example of 2-hop AS linkage

4.2.1   AS Selection Rules

The selection of appropriate AS configurations become crucial to obtain the desired communication behavior based on applications requirements. Different approaches exist in the literature, authors in [7] propose and out-band signaling infrastructure to apply data-path services based on defined QoS policies and services conditions to be executed through nodes in the path. While in [8] is defined a framework to create offline functional composition of building blocks based on the weighted combination of multiple QoS attributes provided by each building block implementation.

We have defined the selection of the suitable AS configurations based on processing the context information available to nodes. In the case of smart object or infrastructure-less networks, context information is obtained via the negotiating protocol. That information is expressed by means of the context attributes, including node characteristics (available memory, battery level,...), link characteristics (bandwidth, delay, jitter, quality metrics, load,...) and network characteristics (e.g, domain). The selection rules consist on a combination of comparison operations using the values of context attributes as inputs.

The computation of the rules is performed as follows: first, each AS configuration that offers the QoS required for the application is evaluated using a cost function in order to determine its suitability to be allocated in a new communication path. Defining $AS_{i,j}$ as the configuration j for AS of type i, the equation (1) defines the cost function, $C_{AS_{i,j}}$, computed for all the applicable $AS_{i,j}$ in a communications. This cost function is the sum of a set of N weighted comparison operations for a set of context attributes $(a_{i,j,k})$ which represent the logical function, denoted as $logicf(a_{i,j,k}, A_{i,j,k}, CR)$ with weight $\omega_{i,j,k}, A_{i,j,k}$ as the constant value to compareand CR as the comparison relation to compute ($=, \neq, \geq, \leq, >$ or $<$) (see equation (2)).

$$C_{AS_{i,j}} = \sum_{k=0}^{N-1} \omega_{i,j,k} * logicf(a_{i,j,k}, A_{i,j,k}, CR) \tag{1}$$

$$logicf(a_{i,j,k}, A_{i,j,k}, CR) = \begin{cases} 0 & ; \ if \ a_{i,j,k}(CR)A_{i,j,k} = FALSE \\ 1 & ; \ if \ a_{i,j,k}(CR)A_{i,j,k} = TRUE \end{cases} \tag{2}$$

Finally, an AS configuration $AS_{i,j}$ is applicable for a communication path if the $C_{AS_{i,j}}$ is greater than a defined threshold ($Th_{AS_{i,j}}$). Note that the selection of weight and threshold values requires a previous learning or experimental phase in order to tune the allocation rules. For instance, the configuration CRC-16 for the Error Detection (ED) functionality $AS_{ED,CRC-16}$ can be utilized in a wireless link if the context attribute SNR ($a_{ED,CRC-16,SNR}$) is lower than a specified value.

4.2.2   AS Register (ASR)

The architecture provides a memory space where all the implementations of $AS_{i,j}$ are registered using a linked list of structures that include the function callbacks executed by the. $AS_{i,j}$ during run-time. That list is loaded with all available AS configurations when the architecture is initiated. Each $AS_{i,j}$ implementation must include in the register the following callbacks functions:

- *as_init()*. Called when the AS is allocated in a node during the negotiation phase. It is utilized to initiate AS memory structures or communication attributes.
- *exec_in()*. Executed for an AS configured as input after receiving a new data packet.
- *exec_out()*. Called by AS which are configured as output, i.e. data is transmitted to the network.
- *exec_inout()*. This function callback is utilized by AS that act as input and output at the same time (i.e., executed in the same node).
- *exec_timer()*. When a timer has expired for a specific AS block, this callback is utilized to run periodic tasks.
- *exec_control()*. Control packets receptions are processed via this callback.
- *as_destroy()*. Executed when closing the communication to free any memory allocated at AS initiation.

After selecting the AS configurations to be allocated in the data path, the node originator of the communication requests distributes the configuration information of the AS to the rest of the nodes of the data-path. Then, each node creates the sequential list of callbacks for the selected AS blocks in the new allocated communication. Afterwards, the data is transmitted from source to destination nodes.

4.2.3   Data-Path Processing

Once established the data path for the communication, the AS linkage provides a list of AS callbacks to be executed in each of the nodes among the data path. The execution of the AS processes the communication data and control information included in two types of packets: control and data packets, respectively(see Fig. 2).Each time a packet traverses a node, the AS Execution Manager in the responsible to execute sequentially the callbacks for each AS in the data path accordingly to its configuration and direction (input, output or both).Control packets include control data transmitted to an AS addressed using the 1 byte address, which is generated after AS allocation; while data packets include a header overhead with the following fields:

- *num* (1 byte). Indicates the number of parameters.
- *len* (1 byte). Total length of the overhead.
- *Type Value (TV) Parameters.* Parameters with fixed length (1, 2, 4 and 8 bytes) defined by its type, adding 1 extra byte of overhead indicating the parameter type.
- *Type Length Value (TLV) Parameters.* Parameters with variable length, adding 2 overhead bytes (TL).

Fig. 2. Description of packets defined in the architecture with AS metadata

The main interface utilized by the AS callbacks implementations is a common memory structure which is passed as argument to the callbacks implementations. This structure is allocated for each AS at AS linkage, requiring a total of46 bytes (using 32 bits architecture. The structure includes flags (4 bytes) and memory address pointers to structures that allow the AS to perform its patterns (10 pointers in total). The main structures required by the AS are the packet payloads, packet metadata (i.e., packet attributes), control data and global connection control data (i.e., connection attributes). The data path processing in a node takes the following stages (see Fig. 3):

- *Data packet reception at the MAC Layer Bundle.* A new packet is received from the MAC layer, encapsulating the data packet. The MAC bundle extracts the MAC Header and sends the packet to the Network Module of the architecture.
- *Processing of data packet at Network Module (NM).* The NM looks for the registered communication in the node that matches the data header. On positive matching, it sends the data payload to the AS Execution Manager.
- *Execution of AS linkage in the node.* First of all, the de-serializer extracts the AS metadata included as overhead in the data packets. Secondly, the AS list is executed sequentially. After each execution, the AS Execution Manager checks whether it is new control data generated to be transmitted to the network. Moreover, during any AS execution, the AS callback can add a timer to execute future tasks. Finally, the serializer adds the metadata (i.e. packet attributes after AS list execution) in the data packet to be transmitted in the network.

After data packet processing, the AS block can mark the packets status to be deleted or queued (in case that future actions are required). If AS do not set packet status to queued, the AS execution Manager removes the packet from queue after it has been processed.

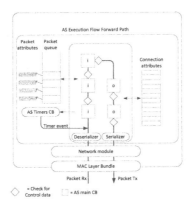

Fig. 3. Example of a communication data-path in a node

4.2.4   AS Communications

There are two possible methods to interchange data between AS blocks in a communication: inter AS communication, when AS blocks are allocated in different nodes; and intra AS communications, among AS blocks executed in the same node.

4.2.4.1 Inter AS Communications. The AS Execution Manager checks whether new control data has been generated after each AS block execution. When required, the AS Execution Manager creates the control packet and sends it to the network. Control packets transmissions are bi-directional in the AS linkage and can only be processed with two AS that share the same AS address, i.e., AS blocks that implement the same functionality but configured with the inverse behavior (input instead of output and vice versa).Fig. 4 shows and example of how control data is traversed through nodes using the reverse path until it reaches its destination AS block.

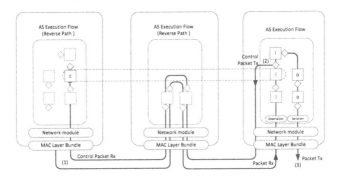

Fig. 4. Control packet processing through 2-hop communication

4.2.4.2 Intra AS Communications. The intra AS communication is generated via a shared memory space of connection metadata data using two different structures: packet attributes and connection attributes. Packet attributes include the metadata of current processed packet which is extracted by the de-serializer. After processing the AS linkage list, the serializer adds the packet attributes as data payload overhead (see Fig. 2). Connection attributes include global control attributes for each communication, creating a standard way to perform cross-layer operations between the different functions. Both packet and connection attributes schema can be extended to allow the architecture evolution.

4.3   Preliminary Validation of the Architecture

The architecture has been implemented in C language in Linux and OSX based distributions using an Ethernet MAC Layer Bundle with raw sockets and Berkeley Packet Filter (BPF), respectively. The interface network driver has been emulated in the MAC Layer Bundle running two separate threads to receive and send packets by the network module. The identifier for each node has been set to a fixed value and included in the MAC header of the MAC Layer bundle. We have implemented a total of 9 AS configurations grouped in 5 AS main functionalities as a basic sub-set in order to build reliable communications:

1. *Acknowledgement*: sequenced ACK, not-sequenced ACK.
2. *Data encoding*: base64 encoding.
3. *Error detection*: CRC-CCITT, CRC-16, CRC-32, RS-FEC.
4. *Retransmission*: Basic per packet retransmission.
5. *Sequencing*: Basic packet sequencing.

To validate the negotiation protocol, the AS Execution Manager and AS Selection rules, we have emulated different network topologies with up to 30 nodes by means of applying network address filters in the Network Module. The context information for each link has been emulated setting different link quality metric utilized to select the most suitable AS configuration. To be more precise, a link metric value of 1 indicates a very good link quality, while 0 indicates poor quality. For instance, we defined rules based on the link metric values to allocate the Acknowledgement and Retransmission AS configurations, resulting in allocation of AS blocks for these functionalities on the links where the link quality was below the 0.7 value.

   A simplified version of the described architecture has been coded and compiled for the CC2430 platform [3], based on 8-bit architecture System on Chip (SoC). This exercise demonstrates by one side the feasibility of the approach and by the other the need of more powerful platforms to benefic of the capabilities of the platform.

5   Conclusions and Future Work

Functional composition paradigm stands as one of the most promising paradigm for FI architectures. Constrained devices like smart objects will be predominant in the future; accordingly, we consider that FI architectures should be supported in smart objects. In this paper, we have presented an implementation of context-aware functional composition architecture suitable to run on constrained devices. The context semantic description (QoS, service, node and network) provides extensibility as it supports the easy adoption of future services provided by smart objects.

The Atomic Services (AS) are the basic building blocks of the architecture, each modular functionality is implemented as an AS configuration and registered in the architecture. Those AS are able to access dynamically to other AS data via the generic packet data headers and the global connection attributes, allowing a flexible cooperative and cross-layer access not supported in current architectures. A sub-set of those basic atomic services has been implemented and validated on experimental testbed with several machines and network topologies.

Currently, we are working in the implementation of additional AS configurations; in the extension of the AS interfaces and improving the previous 8-bit architecture to the MC1332x[1] platform (based on 32-bit ARM). Further research is required in order to analyze AS dependences and evaluate the performance of the AS configurations using different context attributes. Based on those attributes, we will design and implement different AS Linkage algorithms to be validated emulating different context attributes. Furthermore, final performance in testbed with constrained hardware platforms should be analyzed in order to validate the emulated network conditions. Finally, we plan to extend the architecture to be infrastructure based, using multi-interface elements that lead to a global connectivity.

References

1. Henke, C., Siddiqui, A., Khondoker, R.: Network functional composition: State of the art. In: Telecommunication Networks and Applications Conference (ATNAC), pp. 43–48. Australasian (2010)
2. Schinnenburg, M., Debus, F., Pabst, R.: Application of Functional Unit Networks to Next Generation Radio Networks. In: IEEE 63rd Vehicular Technology Conference (VTC) Spring, May 7-10, vol. 1, pp. 147–151 (2006)
3. Sanchez-Loro, X., Ferrer, J.L., Gomez, C., Casademont, J., Paradells, J.: Can Future Internet be based on constrained networks design principles? Computer Networks 55(4), 893–909 (2011)
4. Braden, R., Faber, T., Handley, M.: From protocol stack to protocol heap: role-based architecture. SIGCOMM Computer Communication. Rev. 33, 17–22 (2003)
5. Sanchez-Loro, X., Gonzalez, A.J., Martin-de-Pozuelo, R.: A Semantic Context-Aware Network Architecture. In: Future Network and Mobile Summit 2010, Florence, Italy (2010)
6. Sanchez-Loro, X., Ferrer, J.L., Casademont, J., Paradells, J., Vidal, A.: Proposal of a Clean Slate Network Architecture for Ubiquitous Services Provisioning. In: IEEE ICFIN 2009, Beijing, China (2009)
7. Shanbhag, S., Wolf, T.: Automated composition of data-path functionality in the future internet. IEEE Network 25(6), 8–14 (2011)
8. Völker, L., Martin, D., Rohrberg, T., Backhaus, H., Baumung, P., Wippel, H., Zitterbart, M.: Design Process and Development Tools for Concurrent Future Networks. In: 3rd GI/ITG KuVS Workshop on The Future Internet, GI/ITG Kommunikation und VerteilteSysteme, Munich, Germany (2009)

---

[1] FreescaleMC13224V: MC1322x Platform in a Package (PiP).
`http://www.freescale.com/webapp/sps/site/`
`prod_summary.jsp?code=MC13224V`

QoS Impact of Hierarchical Routing in Multi-channel Sensor Networks

Luis Torres and Ulrich Killat

Institute of Communication Networks
Hamburg University of Technology
Hamburg, Germany
{luis.torres,killat}@tuhh.de

Abstract. Enabling integration of Wireless Sensor Networks (WSN) and smart objects with the Internet is an important milestone towards the so called Internet of Things. Providing these networks with QoS capabilities is crucial for emerging applications that have end-to-end requirements on the border wireless network domain. Impairments such as delays and losses are heavily influenced by the quality of the communication channels, the routing, the MAC protocol and the interactions of these influential factors. In this work we report on a hierarchical routing scheme for sensor networks with multi-channel radios aiming at improving QoS. The scheme decouples the aforementioned influences: The MAC-protocol is responsible for a scheduling in a set of nodes called a cluster. Neighboring clusters use different frequencies. The routing is done at the level of clusters. The (distributed) algorithms executed by the network nodes to support this architecture are evaluated against optimal solutions for clustering, frequency allocation and routing derived from Integer Linear Programming.

Keywords: wireless sensor networks, end-to-end delays, optimization, heuristics, clustering, routing.

1   Introduction

The use of the Internet Protocol (IP) in resource constrained devices such as smart objects and Wireless Sensor Networks (WSN) has changed the Internet landscape drastically. The integration of such networks to the Internet in the form of Internet of Things (IoT) enables vast and exciting possibilities for application domains, such as building and home automation, smart metering, industrial manufacturing and e-health logistics [1]. These new horizon also brings some technical challenges. Integrating WSN into Internet with applications such as monitoring, control, and interactivity, requires these networks to explore QoS improvement possibilities. In this work, we focus on WSN and the impact of hierarchical routing based on clustering and channeling to meet this goal in terms of delays and reliabilities.

Delays in WSN are influenced by the traffic arrival process at all of its nodes, by the reliability and losses of the communication channels, the MAC protocol and the

A. Timm-Giel et al. (Eds.): MONAMI 2012, LNICST 58, pp. 217–230, 2013.

routing. MAC protocols [2]–[5], and routing [6]–[8] have attracted a lot of interest over the last years. If the routing metric is traffic dependent then the influencing factors on the delay are consequently of stochastic nature and it seems to be hard, if not impossible, to devise a system with a predictable delay performance. This contribution proposes a layered architecture for sensor nodes which – like the MEMSIC® IRIS motes [9] – have the capability of supporting several radio frequency (RF) channels but use only one half-duplex transceiver. The idea behind this architecture is as follows: The network is decomposed into clusters. Each node is member of at least one cluster. Communication within a cluster can take place with a high reliability, i.e. sufficiently high signal-to-noise ratio and is based on a MAC protocol, e.g. IEEE 802.15.4. Neighboring clusters use different frequencies thereby to a large degree avoiding the problem of interference. Neighboring clusters overlap and a node being member of two clusters is elected as a "bridge" and has to connect these two clusters by alternating between the two RF channels at each cluster. The benefits expected from such architecture are:

- high reliability because the influence of interference is drastically reduced and losses will occur only as excessive delays – if at all,
- routing has to be organized only for the sequence of clusters to be visited and thus is of reduced complexity.

To this end this contribution tries to approach the objective of a predictable delay performance by deriving all system parameters from an optimization problem which has the objective to minimize average delay. This approach is divided into two steps, each of which involves an optimization problem:

- Clustering and frequency allocation
- Multi-commodity flow routing with a (cluster) load dependent metric

The rest of this paper is organized as follows: In Section 2 we present the related work on study and harnessing end-to-end delay in WSN. Section 3 explains the network and channel model used throughout this work. Sections 4 and 5 present the global optimization models and corresponding distributed heuristic algorithms, respectively. Section 6 shows delay measurements in selected traffic scenarios, for which we compare the aforementioned approaches of Section 4 and 5. Finally in Section 7 we wrap up our findings and suggest future work.

2   Related Work

The sizes and traffic patterns of WSN make them suitable to establish hierarchies among the nodes, mostly grouping the nodes into clusters [10]–[11]. In this way, crucial tasks such as routing, information composition, channel access coordination, etc., are performed by a few nodes thereby simplifying the overall network behavior. In this work, we present the joint problem of clustering and channelization which ensures reliability for communications with the respective cluster coordinators. Moreover, the clustering not only groups nodes in the network, but also has to fulfill connectivity constraints to enable an inter-cluster multi-hop communication. The communication among clusters must go via bridge nodes, which due to having half-duplex single transceiver radios must alternate between clusters. The problem to assign channels is known as NP-Hard and is similar to the one in cellular networks [12]. Work towards time channelization has been addressed by [13] and [14], where the channel access is TDMA-based and a global synchronization is assumed. We do not assume such synchronization and favor RF-channelization to decouple the channel interference [15] across the network by imposing a limitation on the spatial reuse. Kaabi [16] discusses frequency channelization on the basis of multi-transceiver nodes. We assume common communication devices compliant with the IEEE 802.15.4 with only one transceiver. To address the problem of routing, we take the load-dependent metric of the expected waiting times of packets along queues in the clusters, following the classical approach and assumptions presented in [17], [18].

3   Network Model

The wireless sensor network is modeled as a graph with the set N of vertices representing the sensor nodes and where the edges represent bidirectional links. The existence of an edge in the graph will be determined by the channel model used, the transmission power and by the radiation pattern of the transceivers at the sensors. In our model, the nodes are assumed to be static and the links to have predictable expected behavior. This can be the case of industrial (manufacturing) applications where nodes are attached to machinery or to the walls forming a multi-hop network. Moreover, the sensors are equipped with transceivers that can be set to one out of several RF channel (IEEE 802.15.4 compliant devices).

3.1   Channel Model and Network Graph

We assume all nodes use the same transmission power P_t, and have omni-directional antennas. The channel is modeled as Log-distance Pathloss plus Log-normal Shadowing as presented in [19]. The model computes the received power as $P_r[dBm] = P_t - P_L$, where the loss is given by (1).

$$P_L(d) = 20 \log_{10}\left(\frac{4\pi}{\lambda}\right) + 10n \log_{10}(d) + X_\sigma[dB] \tag{1}$$

The pathloss exponent is $n = 3$ and the shadowing component is characterized by zero mean and standard deviation $\sigma = 5dB$. The wavelength λ and the distance d are in meters. If the average received power is above a threshold that ensures reliable successful packet decoding, then the link is considered as part of the network.

The information of the existing links in the graph is stored in the neighborhood lists N_i, which contain all the nodes j that are connected to node i in the graph. These neighborhood lists are created by every node during an initialization phase via exchange of control messages. This information serves as the basis of the later organization of the network into clusters.

3.2   End-to-End Demand Requests

Nodes in the network have to satisfy demands, that is, send a series of packets, towards other nodes in the network. A demand is characterized by the source and destination nodes, as well as by the nature of the packet arrival process to take place. In this work we assume that a set D of end-to-end demand requests is given, described by their mean traffic intensity $\rho_d^{dem}, d \in D$, and their source and destination nodes. The traffic generated follows an ON/OFF model with Poisson distributed ON and OFF times, and constant bit rate (CBR) during the ON phase. A source selects a destination randomly for the ON period based on the information of the demand traffic intensity, from which a weighted selection can be made. The information of the demand intensities will be used at the second step of our solution approach, the routing problem, as will be explained later. The clustering and channelization problems are independent of the requested end-to-end demands, decoupling, and thus simplifying, the architecture definition from the usage-dependent routing task.

4   Optimization

We present in this section optimization models for the two steps in our proposed solution. In the next section we will consider distributed algorithms that will, up to some extent, follow the optimization framework.

A route in the proposed network consists of a sequence of clusters visited. At each cluster hosting neither the source nor the destination two transmissions take place:

- from entrance bridge (node) to a node named cluster head (in the center of the cluster)
- from the cluster head to the exit bridge (node).

These transmissions are scheduled by the MAC protocol IEEE 802.15.4 and are highly reliable due to a sufficiently high threshold for the signal-to-noise ratio enforced by the clustering algorithm.

4.1   Clustering and Frequency Allocation

Minimizing the number of clusters will also reduce the number of hops to the destination. Defining a clustering that minimizes the distances among nodes in the new clustered topology (aggregated over all node pairs in the network) is taken as an optimization objective. The purpose of the clustering is to divide the network into groups characterized by the 1-hop connectivity of every node in the group to a coordinator node (cluster head). The clusters themselves must build a connected covering on the network, and have specific frequency channels assigned for operations. The frequency allocation problem is similar to the well known frequency allocation problem in cellular networks, presented by [12], and is solved here jointly with the network clustering using an Integer Linear Programming (ILP) formulation.

The optimization problem is subject to the following constraints:

- the roles of member, bridge and cluster head are assigned,
- each node associates with a cluster,
- within a cluster the communications between members and cluster head are highly reliable, based on the link selection criterion as explained in Section 3.1,
- clusters using the same frequency channel should be sufficiently separated to mitigate the interference among them and ensure reliable communications between member nodes and their cluster head.

We now present the ILP model for the clustering and channelization. First, we introduce the parameters and variables used in the model.

Parameters

N	set of nodes in the network
N_i	1-hop neighbor set of node i
I_i	set of nodes that cannot use the same channel as i (interference set)
L	number of channels available for the frequency assignment
P	set of node pairs $P = N \times N$
p^{src}, p^{dst}	source and destination nodes of node pair p, respectively

Variables

$f_{ij}^p \in \{0,1\}$	flow from i to j
$h_i \in \{0,1\}$	$h_i = 1 \leftrightarrow$ node i is cluster head
$m_{ij} \in \{0,1\}$	$m_{ij} = 1 \leftrightarrow$ node i is member of cluster (head) j
$b_{ij}^k \in \{0,1\}$	$b_{ij}^k = 1 \leftrightarrow$ node k is bridge between cluster heads i and j
$x_i^l \in \{0,1\}$	head node i uses channel l
$y_{ij}^l \in \{0,1\}$	head nodes i and j use simultaneously channel l

Objective

$$Minimize \quad \sum_{i \in N} \sum_{j \in N_i, p \in P} f_{ij}^p \tag{2}$$

Constraints

Connectivity Constraints

$$\forall i \in N, \ \forall p \in P: \sum_{j \in N_i} f_{ij}^p - \sum_{j \in N_i} f_{ji}^p = \begin{cases} 1, & i = p^{src} \\ -1, & i = p^{dst} \\ 0, & otherwise \end{cases} \tag{3}$$

From now on, we simplify the notations $\forall i \in N, \forall p \in P$ to $\forall i, \forall p$, respectively.

$$\forall i, j \in N_i, \forall p: \ f_{ij}^p \leq m_{ji} + m_{ij} \tag{4}$$

$$\forall i, j \in N_i, \forall p: \quad f_{ij}^p \leq 2 - h_i + h_j \tag{5}$$

$$\forall i, j \in N_i, \forall p: \quad f_{ij}^p \leq h_i + h_j \tag{6}$$

Membership Constraints

$$\forall i, j \in N_i: \quad h_i + h_j \leq 1 \tag{7}$$

$$\forall i, j \in N_i: \quad m_{ji} \leq h_i \tag{8}$$

$$\forall i: \quad 1 - h_i \leq \sum_{j \in N_i} m_{ij} \leq 2 \cdot (1 - h_i) \tag{9}$$

Bridging Constraints

$$\forall i, j < i: \quad b_{ij}^k = m_{ki} \cdot m_{kj} \tag{10}$$

$$\forall i, j < i: \quad \sum_{\substack{k \in N_i \\ k \in N_j}} b_{ij}^k \leq 1 \tag{11}$$

Channelization Constraints

$$\forall i: \quad h_i \leq \sum_l x_i^l \leq h_i \tag{12}$$

$$\forall i, j, l: \quad y_{ij}^k = x_i^l \cdot x_j^l \tag{13}$$

$$\forall i, j \in I_i, l: \quad y_{ij}^l = 0 \tag{14}$$

The objective function (2) represents the sum of all hop distances among all nodes in the network. This objective will try to form clusters that are close and well connected to other clusters via bridges. The rich connectivity via bridges shortens end-to-end path lengths in the network. This is a desirable property which chooses a convenient clustering independently from the demand information. The multi-commodity constraint, which also ensures a full multi-hop connectivity, is expressed by (3). Constraints (4)–(6) ensure that the path that a commodity flow follows on the network, goes through links connecting a head and a member and not two members or two heads. It is clear that members (and heads) in different clusters will use different RF channels, thus will be disconnected. However, in the model presented here, the intra-cluster communication is restricted to member or bridge node to the head. The membership is given by constraints (7)–(9). Two immediate neighbors should not be heads. Only a head can have members and a node can be a member of up to two clusters. When a node becomes member of two neighboring clusters, it becomes a bridge. Two clusters can share up to one bridge, as shown by (10) and (11). Constraints (12)–(14) deal with the channelization. Only heads are assigned a channel. Two heads that are within the interference set of each other cannot have the same channel. This set is defined as the 4-hop neighborhood, which ensures that two clusters using the same channel are separated more than 2 hops. The result of the clustering and channelization are the node roles, which determine the clustering in the network, and the channels on each cluster. As a final remark, constraints (10) and (13) are expressed as the product of two binary variables. Although a product is not a linear constraint, a straightforward linearization can be done (see [17]).

4.2   Routing

For the clustering a simple hop-count metric for the distance among node pairs was considered to be sufficient to produce a sensible clustering. For the routing, we take as input the result of the clustering and channelization step, and consider now the set D of end-to-end demands. An optimization problem formulation which tries to minimize the sum of the mean delays in all clusters i is proposed. This approach models a cluster as a (distributed) queuing system and relies on the Kleinrock's independence approximation [21] that arrivals at each cluster are all independent of each other.

We introduce the ILP model with its input parameters and variables.

Parameters

H	set of clusters i in the network
D	set of end to end demands d
R_d	set of routes r that connect the source and destination nodes of demand d
$\theta_{id} \in \{1,2\}$	intra-cluster traversed hops; it indicates the number of hops that demand d would require in cluster i. $\theta_{id} = 1$ only in case the cluster head is the source or destination of demand d
$\rho_d^{dem} \geq 0$	load introduced in the network by demand d

Variables

$w_i \geq 0$	mean waiting time for a packet to be transmitted at cluster i
$\rho_i^{clus} \geq 0$	traffic intensity at cluster i
$\delta_{id}^r \in \{0,1\}$	Kronecker symbol for which $\delta_{id}^r = 1$ indicates that route r of demand d transits via cluster i (link-path formulation [17]); otherwise $\delta_{id}^r = 0$

Objective

$$\text{Minimize} \sum_{i \in H} w_i \tag{15}$$

Constraints

$$\forall i \in H: \quad w_i = \frac{1}{c_{clus}} \cdot \frac{\rho_i^{clus}}{1 - \rho_i^{clus}} \tag{16}$$

$$\forall i \in H: \quad \rho_i^{clus} = \sum_{d \in D} \sum_{r \in R_d} \rho_d^{dem} \theta_{id} \delta_{id}^r \leq 1 \tag{17}$$

The traffic intensities for demands and clusters are normalized with respect to the cluster capacity c_{clus}. This capacity is derived from a sequence of experiments with increasing load in a single cluster environment running just the IEEE 802.15.4 protocol. The onset of substantial losses was taken as the criterion to identify the capacity in the cluster.

The objective function (15) expresses the minimization of the mean waiting times at all clusters, which are seen as a distributed queuing systems. Constraint (16) equates the waiting times to the known formula of the average waiting time in an M/M/1 queue [18]. Note that although this constraint is not linear, the expression is convex on ρ_i^{clus}, and a piece-wise linear approximation can be used instead (see Fortz and Thorup's method [17]). Finally, constraint (17) expresses that the total traffic in a cluster is made up of the traffic of those demands whose routes are traversing the cluster, and that this traffic is bounded to the cluster capacity. The solution of this step is the set of routes that minimize the end-to-end delays according to the information of the demand intensities on an already clustered and channelized network. The traffic is not split into several routes.

5   Distributed Algorithms

The ideal migration path from a global optimization approach to a distributed algorithm would be a formal decomposition method of the global optimization problem to a set of smaller local ones to be solved at each node, with the assertion that the latter will converge to the former one. Unfortunately, the necessary conditions to make this feasible (like convexity of the problems involved) are not met here. We therefore introduce heuristics for the clustering and channelization step as well as for the routing, and will evaluate in Section 6 how close they get to the desired optimum.

5.1   Clustering and Frequency Allocation

This algorithm is solved by the network at the initialization phase. And its results are used as inputs for the routing step. As output of the algorithm each node should be either: head, member or bridge, and heads will have a channel assigned in a greedy fashion taking into account the channel assignment in the neighborhood. In extensive experiments with different randomly generated networks and different number of nodes we found that the number of clusters exceeded the results from the global optimization by at most 15-20%.

In the following we explain the principles behind the heuristic which basically aims at a feasible solution of the problem rather than an optimal one, i.e., the algorithm fulfills the constraints of the presented optimization model, such as global inter-cluster connectivity and interference avoidance, but do not explicitly address a global hop-distance minimization in the clustered and channelized topology.

Every node exchanges control messages only with its 1-hop neighbors until the whole network enters a steady state in which neither roles nor channels are assigned or updated. The possible roles a node can take and their allowed update transitions are depicted in Fig. 1. Head, member and bridge are regarded as stable roles, whereas head candidate and orphan as transient roles. If a node uses a transient role, it will try to update to any other stable role allowed by the transition diagram. The transitions occur at each update round of the heuristic computation.

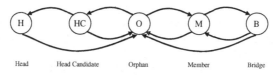

Fig. 1. Node roles and allowed transitions

Each node evaluates a set of rules periodically until it either reaches a stable role or a watchdog timer indicates that the clustering failed. In this work we accept networks where all nodes acquire stable roles and allow enough time for this.

The process assumes the selection of an initiator node, referred to as the "anchor". This node is distributedly selected in a similar manner as the root node in spanning tree bridges [22], where the node with the highest ID is chosen as root. To achieve this, each node broadcast locally its own address ID or the highest one it has heard. After a while, all nodes know the ID of the anchor, which starts the heuristic being a head himself. All the other nodes start as orphans and update their roles according to the following rules:

- The anchor is a cluster head using the first channel. It starts the clustering by broadcasting its information and remains in that state for the rest of the process.
- An orphan node will primarily try to become member of any cluster head in its immediate vicinity. If there is no head around but only member nodes, then it decides to become a head candidate to extend the clustered architecture, provided the clustered neighborhood allows the allocation of a non-conflicting channel.
- A member node checks for head candidates around and tries to become a bridge to that head candidate. If its own head gave up its role, the member becomes orphan.
- A bridge checks its two heads and depending on whether one or both have ceased of being cluster heads, the bridge will become a member or orphan. Otherwise, it remains committed as bridge between the clusters.
- A head candidate that realizes that a node is bridging it to the current clustered architecture becomes cluster head. Otherwise, it becomes orphan.
- A head checks if it connected to the anchor via its bridges. This ensures proper cluster connectivity. Otherwise, it becomes orphan.

The idea is that nodes around the anchor form the first cluster. Then nodes in the 1-hop neighborhood of this first cluster organize the second group of clusters and channel assignment. Once the nodes in this second tier reach stable roles, they greedily commit to their roles. The process goes on with the subsequent external tier. The global cluster connectivity is guaranteed by keeping (at least) the connectivity to the anchor node via multiple clusters.

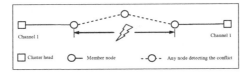

Fig. 2. Interference situation

Two clusters are considered to interfere when they (i.e., any of their members) are within 2-hops distance. This means that cluster heads should be more than 4-hops away. The situation is illustrated in Fig. 2. When the complete network achieves a valid and stable clustering and channelization the process enters into the next phase: routing of demands.

5.2   Routing

To obtain a load-aware routing, cluster heads periodically measure the traffic intensity ρ_d^{clus} of their cluster and disseminate this information to all other cluster heads in a broadcast manner. Although the traffic is generated by the nodes according to the mean intensity of the demands, it follows an ON/OFF model that matches the mean values but that makes the routing a dynamic process. On the adaptation, load is balanced to follow less congested (less costly) routes. The clusters are now be seen as "edges" in a logical graph and have a corresponding expected delay to traverse through them. The bridge nodes now look for the shortest route using Dijkstra's algorithm that traverses the least loaded clusters, i.e., via the shortest edges in the new simplified logical graph. The metric announced by the cluster heads is proportional to the mean delay as given in (18). Thus the modeling approach is the same as the one leading to the optimal problem (15–17) and the results are expected to closely follow those of the proposed ILP model.

$$m_i = \frac{1}{c_{clus}} \cdot \frac{\rho_d^{clus}}{1 - \rho_d^{clus}} \tag{18}$$

6   System Simulation

Simulations are carried out on the Network Simulation System OMNeT++ version 4.1 [23]. The chosen wireless simulation framework is MiXiM [24]. MiXiM is a set of libraries that provide the basis for physical modeling of wireless transmissions and operations up to MAC layer. Further, the module for IEEE 802.15.4 developed by Rousselot et al [25] was extended and used in the solution approach presented. In the following experiments the topology is generated randomly [20], transmission power is set to 1 mW and the packet size is assumed to be constant (40 Byte), which makes a packet transmission time to be around 1.3 ms.

In a first set of experiments we wish to observe the performance of the distributed algorithm for clustering and channelization with respect to the optimal solution based on the ILP model of Section 4.1. Fig. 3 shows the number of clusters found by the ILP model and by the distributed algorithm averaged over 10 experiments per point. The 90% confidence interval for a Student's t–Distribution is likewise shown.

It can be seen that the distributed algorithm follows closely the results of the optimal solution for the number of clusters formed in the network. We turn our attention to the hop distances among all nodes in the elicited architecture for both approaches. These values are captured by the objective values of the ILP model for clustering and channelization. We take the resulting architecture from the distributed algorithm and determine the aggregated hop distance among all possible node pairs. The normalization of such metric with respect to the optimal values is shown in Fig. 3 (See right-most vertical axis).

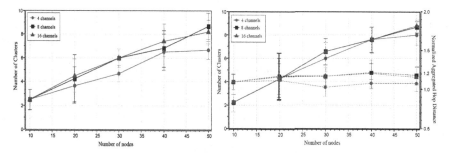

Fig. 3. (Left) Optimal number of clusters found by the ILP model for clustering and channelization for different numbers of channels available and nodes in the network. (Right) Results for the distributed algorithm. Dashed lines show the normalized objective value of the distributed solution with respect to the optimum value.

These results show that for the observed networks sizes from 10 to 50 nodes, the distributed algorithm keeps the aggregated end-to-end hop distances in the network up to 20% above the optimum. Although the hop distance cannot fully describe the end-to-end delays that packet incur during its advance towards their destination, this is a sensible metric directly associated to the total number of clusters that the shortest path between two nodes should traverse, and the fact that it is load-independent makes it possible to decouple it from the routing phase.

We now show the results for a 100-node network which meets the constraint of being connected in the sense of full (multi-hop) reachability using reliable wireless links. Packet transmission requests are generated in a Poisson process in each node following the ON/OFF model, the intensity of which corresponding to the values laid down in the demand intensity vector ρ_d^{dem}. In our experiments we consider that every node generates an aggregated normalized demand $\rho_{Node}^{dem} = \sum_d \rho_d^{dem}$ and distinguish between low load and high load scenarios:

- *Scenario 1:*   Each node generates $\rho_{Node}^{dem} = 0.001$ (low load).
- *Scenario 2:*   Each node generates $\rho_{Node}^{dem} = 0.0125$ (high load).

For both scenarios we have measured packet delays and have averaged their values over all flows of the scenario. The experiments were conducted for four cases:

DSDV Flat:	Destination Sequenced Distance Vector (DSDV) [6] routing in a flat single-channel network
Hier. Optimal:	clustering and hierarchical routing according to the results obtained from the global optimization
Hier. Distributed:	clustering and hierarchical routing according to the results obtained from the distributed algorithms
Dist. Rout/Opt. Clus.:	distributed hierarchical routing over optimal clustering

DSDV routing is a simple non-hierarchical routing using single channel which tries to minimize hop distance. We wish to compare the impact of the hierarchization against such a routing to establish the value of the QoS gain against no hierarchy at all. As seen in Fig. 4, the tendency to avoid high amount of losses which are observed with a flat routing is maintained in the scenarios for the optimal and distributed cases, thereby supporting the basic idea leading to our approach. However, it is also obvious, that the latter suffers from a poorer performance for lower delay values. The reason for this lies in the suboptimal clustering found by the distributed algorithm. When the distributed algorithm for the routing runs over the optimal clustering, the results become close to the expected performance.

On the other hand, even for the optimal case for clustering and routing, we observe significant delays compared to DSDV flat routing. The reason for this behavior is twofold: First, the routing via the cluster heads sometimes generates "unnecessary" hops which increase delays. Secondly, the scheduling within a cluster, in particular the communication between cluster head and bridges, which due to their dual homing in two clusters sometimes are unavailable, creates quite a control overhead, the mechanisms of which have to be tuned to optimal parameter settings of the MAC layer. Although opportunistic receptions within the clusters help to reduce the unnecessary hops, the results improve marginally.

The gap between optimal and distributed curves (approx. factor of 2-3) indicates that the clustering algorithm in the distributed approach has room for improvements. The positive impact of the proposed solution is evident for the high load scenario. When the flat routing DSDV has very high (30%) losses, the hierarchical routing reduce them to 5% (even in the optimal case), and avoid large delays for the 25% recovered traffic.

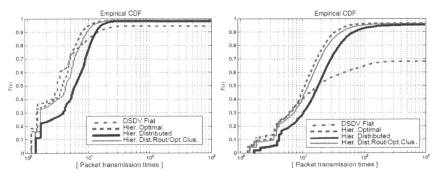

Fig. 4. (Left) Scenario 1: Cumulative distribution functions of the average delay for low load and for the 4 cases. (Right) Scenario 2: Distribution of the average delay with high load.

7   Conclusions and Future Work

We have shown that hierarchical routing in a sensor network with multi-channel capability will lead to a reduction of large delays and losses in WSN, which extends the QoS support for emerging services as these networks become more integrated to the incoming Internet of Things. We have presented results for an optimal cluster-based routing as well as for distributed algorithms of clustering, frequency allocation and routing. As practical wireless sensor networks are not suited for approaches based on centralized optimal solutions, we have tried to derive a heuristic using the optimization model as base. It comes not as a surprise that the global optimization algorithms perform better than the distributed ones. However, also the global optimization algorithms do not meet the low delay values found with the non-hierarchical routing for scenarios of low load. With high loads, the hierarchy shows better results in terms of end-to-end delays and losses, which indicates the applicability of the solution for the proposed scope, such as distributed manufacturing monitoring. A gap in the results between the distributed algorithms and the optimum was observed. The reason – and therefore also the topic for future work – lies in the scheduling overhead, the interaction between the scheduling at cluster level and the MAC layer, and the MAC parameter optimization, to speed up the two-hop forwarding within a cluster. Finally, to further improve the hierarchy against flat networks, a clustering algorithm which pursues the optimization of the objective function in a more formal context is expected to deliver better results.

Acknowledgments. The authors gratefully acknowledge the support of this work by the German Research Foundation (DFG).

References

[1] Atzori, L., Iera, A., Morabito, G.: The Internet of Things: A survey. Computer Networks, 2787–2805 (2010)

[2] IEEE 802.11 Wireless LAN Medium Access Control (MAC) and Physical Layer (PH4) Specifications (2009)

[3] IEEE 802.15.4 Low-Rate Wireless Personal Area Networks (LR_WPANs) (2011)

[4] Ye, W., Heidemann, J., Strin, D.: Medium Access Control With Coordinated Adaptive Sleeping for Wireless Sensor Networks. IEEE/ACM Tr. Netw. 12, 493–506 (2004)

[5] Richa, A., Scheideler, C., Schmid, S., Zhang, J.: A Jamming-Resistant MAC Protocol for Multi-Hop Wireless Networks. In: Lynch, N.A., Shvartsman, A.A. (eds.) DISC 2010. LNCS, vol. 6343, pp. 179–193. Springer, Heidelberg (2010)

[6] Perkins, C., Bhagwat, P.: Highly Dynamic Destination-Sequenced Distance-Vector Routing (DSDV) for Mobile Computers. In: Proc. ACM SIGCOMM, pp. 234–244 (1994)

[7] Perkins, C., Belding-Royer, E., Das, S.: Ad-hoc On-Demand Distance Vector (AODV) Routing. IETF RFC 3561 (2003)

[8] Murray, D., Dixon, M., Kozimèc, T.: An Experimental Comparison of Routing Protocols in Multi Hop AdHoc Networks. In: Proc. ANTAC: Australasian Telecommunication Networks and Applications Conference (2010)

[9] IRIS Mote Datasheet 6020-0124-02 Rev A: MEMSIC Inc., San Jose,

[10] http://www.memsic.com/products/wireless-sensor-networks (accessed November 2011)

[11] He, Y., Yoon, W., Kim, J.: Multi-level Clustering Architecture for Wireless Sensor Networks. J. Inf. Tech. 5, 188–191 (2006)

[12] Xing, L., Shrestha, A.: QoS reliability of hierarchical clustered wireless sensor networks. In: Proc. of 25th IEEE Performance, Computing and Communications Conference, IPCCC, pp. 641–646 (2006)

[13] Beckmann, D., Killat, U.: A New Strategy for the Application of Genetic Algorithms to the Channel-Assignment Problem. IEEE Tr. on Vehicular Tech. 48, 1261–1269 (1999)

[14] Li, S., Qian, D., Liu, Y., Tong, J.: Adaptive Distributed Randomized TDMA Scheduling For clustered Wireless Sensor Netwoks. In: Proc. Wireless Communications, Networking and Mobile Computing Conference, pp. 2688–2691 (2007)

[15] Ergen, S., Varaiya, P.: TDMA Scheduling Algorithms for Wireless Sensor Networks. J. Wireless Netw. 16(4), 985–997 (2010)

[16] Jain, J., Padhye, J., Padmanabhan, V., Qiu, L.: Impact of Interference on Multi-hop Wireless Network Performance. In: Proc. IEEE MOBICOM, pp. 66–80 (2003)

[17] Kaabi, F., Ghannay, S., Filali, F.: Channel Allocation and Routing in Wireless Mesh Networks: A survey and qualitative comparison between schemes. Int. J. Wireless and Mobile Netw., 132–150 (2010)

[18] Pioro, M., Mehdi, D.: Routing, Flow and Capacity Design in Communication and Computer Networks. Morgan Kaufmann Series in Networking (2004)

[19] Gross, D., Harris, C.: Fundamentals of Queueing Theory, 3rd edn. John Wiley & Sons (1998)

[20] Rappaport, T.S.: Wireless Communications: Principles and Practice, 2nd edn. Prentice Hall (2002)

[21] Kim, T., Tipper, D., Krishnamurthy, P.: Improving the Connectivity of Heterogeneous Multi-Hop Wireless Networks. In: IEEE Int. Comm. Conference, pp. 1–6 (2011)

[22] Bertsekas, D., Gallager, R.: Data Networks, 2nd edn. Prentice Hall (1992)

[23] Tanenbaum, A.S.: Computer Networks, 4th edn. Prentice Hall (2002)

[24] Varga, A.: Network Simulation Framework OMNeT++. Discrete Event Simulation System, http://www.omnetpp.org

[25] Koepke, A., Swigulski, M., Wessel, K., et al.: Simulating Wireless and Mobile Networks in OMNeT++ - The MiXiM Vision. In: Proc. 1st Int. Workshop on OMNeT++ (2008)

[26] Rousselot, J., Decotignie, J., Aoun, M., Van der Stok, P., Serva Oliver, R., Fohler, G.: Accurate Timeliness Simulations for Real-Time Wireless Sensor Networks. In: Proc. 3rd UKSim European Symposium on Computer Modelling and Simulation, EMS 2009, pp. 476–481 (2009)

Security Requirements for Managing Smart Objects in Home Automation

Stefanie Gerdes and Olaf Bergmann

Universität Bremen, Bremen, Germany
{gerdes,bergmann}@tzi.org

Abstract. Enabling technologies for the Internet of Things are well understood, and open standards exist that define how to use the Internet Protocol, Version 6, (IPv6) to interconnect smart objects with each other and to the public Internet. As these devices typically are quite limited in their hardware resources, security is often considered too expensive and is sacrificed for a marginal extension of battery lifetime. Missing security not only exposes the application logic to evildoers but also affects management functions. In this paper, we discuss potential threats to machine-to-machine communication and provide a detailed example how protection requirements can be inferred from a given application scenario.

Keywords: wireless sensor networks, 6LoWPAN, constrained devices, light-weight security, protection requirements, impact analysis.

1 Introduction

The Internet of Things (IoT) today is regarded as an integral part of the future Internet [1]. With IEEE 802.15.4 and 6LoWPAN [2] as enabling technologies, hardware manufacturers as well as software developers envision the Internet Protocol, Version 6, (IPv6, [3]) to become the standard communication protocol for interconnecting smart objects. This trend also has leveraged the replacement of proprietary protocol stacks for machine-to-machine (M2M) communication by standardized and open architectures that use IPv6 for data transport [4].

Exposing smart objects to the Internet also makes them vulnerable to various threats that do not exist or are at least ignored for isolated networks. While proven security protocols exist to defeat many of these attacks in the "old" Internet, the IoT has many inhabitants that have only limited capabilities in terms of processing power, available memory, and means for user interaction. Moreover, these devices often are battery-powered and thus are designed to consume very low energy during operation. Strong cryptography then would possibly render too expensive for most applications.

To provide a reasonable amount of security while still allowing device lifetimes of several years, light-weight security profiles for embedded devices are discussed in academia and standardization organizations (cf. Section 1.1). To trade the cost off against the achieved security level, it is required to examine

A. Timm-Giel et al. (Eds.): MONAMI 2012, LNICST 58, pp. 231–243, 2013.

the actual application thoroughly. In this paper, we show how this can be done by conducting a protection requirement analysis for a simple home automation scenario.

The paper is structured as follows: The remainder of this section gives some more background on security architectures for wireless sensor networks and the Internet of Things, followed by a short introduction of the application scenario that is used throughout the rest of this paper. Section 2 explains the categories of information that have been identified within the system. Section 3 then introduces the protection requirement categories and applies them to the individual types of information. The results of our analysis and their applicability for smart object design are discussed in Section 4. Section 5 then concludes this paper with a brief summary and a critical acclaim of our results.

1.1 Background

IoT-applications usually involve not only devices with limited resources but also challenging network capabilities such as small frame sizes, low bandwidth, and high variations of packet loss and transmission latency [5]. While some protocols such as the Simple Network Management Protocol (SNMP, [6]) can be used in these environments without any change, most protocols have initially been designed for a wired Internet with static hosts and less frequent route changes. Thus, new protocols have been developed to better deal with these deficiencies. One example is the Constrained Application Protocol (CoAP, [7]) that is intended to facilitate development of applications for the IoT.

Communication protocols for home automation systems have been discussed in [8]. The authors state that IPv6 and 6LoWPAN are well-suited for M2M-communication in home automation systems, with good solutions for security still missing. Both, CoAP and SNMPv3 rely on the underlying transport layer to provide a secure communication channel [7,9]. Datagram Layer Security (DTLS, [10]) currently is being regarded as the most viable solution to provide security for these two protocols.

Security threats on wireless sensor networks have been extensively discussed recently [11], and a concise classification of attacks is given in [12]. Overviews of light-weight security technologies for use with limited resources are presented in [13] and [14]. These publications focus either on attacks or on the solution space. We consider another approach useful for constrained devices: If detailed knowledge about the protection requirements of the various kinds of data in the system can be gained, it is possible to adapt the security concept accordingly. Security mechanisms can be explicitly chosen to meet the protection requirements and only mechanisms which are really needed in the scenario can be used. Thus the usage of resources like storage space, computing power and bandwidth can be reduced.

1.2 Scenario

In this paper, we discuss the protection requirements for automated light control in a "smart home". For simplicity, the scenario spans only two rooms, each of which is equipped with a group of lights. Each group has multiple lights controlled by a microcontroller to modify the illumination level. Light sensors are used to regulate the (electric) lights in a room according to the current daylight level. A main switch for the entire appliance provides three modes: "off", "on", and "automatic". In automatic mode, the available sensors can be used to achieve a certain illumination level. The more the daylight diminishes in the room, the more the brightness of the electric lights will increase.

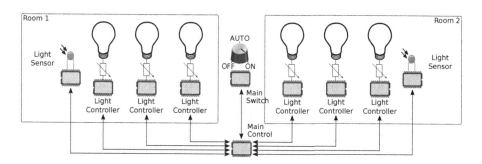

Fig. 1. System architecture with centralized main switch and separate rooms

The lights in a group are synchronized, i. e. they always have the same brightness value. All groups can be switched on or off at once using the main switch. Each group can have additional logic controls that maintain global state information for that particular group. State information is distributed in the network using multicast. Devices register at the main controller to get multicast messages for their group.

The scenario is based on an average private household. One or more occupants are living in the house who sometimes have visitors. Illumination in one or more rooms of the house is controlled by a constrained network using the architecture described above.

2 Data Categories

Communication within this network requires various types of information that can be divided in three main categories: State information of resources, configuration data and keying information for the cryptographic mechanisms.

Resources in this scenario are light bulbs, switches and sensors. The relevant state information of the switch is its position, whereas the light sensors' state information contains their measurements. Switch position and sensor values determine the state of the light bulbs, i. e. their illumination level. The main controller calculates the desired light bulb state and then sets this state using a control message. The state information can be retrieved from a light bulb as well to update e.g. a user interface.

The following list summarizes the data in the system:

- State information of resources
    - Switch position (on, off, auto)
    - Sensor data values (in lux)
    - Light bulb state (in percent)
- Type of resource (switch, sensor, light bulb, controller)
- Configuration data
    - Transport address of group
    - Transport address of main controller
    - Physical location of resource (optional)
- Cryptographic keying material

The configuration data is necessary for proper operation of the node and for communicating within the network, including gateway addresses, multicast groups to listen on and human readable node identifiers. Nodes (sensors as well as light bulbs) are assigned to groups in order to control several nodes at once as shown in the initial scenario description (see Section 1.2).

Each group has its own transport address to enable communication within a group, e.g. to distribute state updates of a light sensor that belongs to that specific group. Additionally, all groups are controlled by a main controller which coordinates the nodes. It gathers the information from the sensors and calculates the values the light bulbs have to apply. The controlling node has to be replaceable in order to circumvent the breakdown of the whole group if the controller stops operating. Therefore, another node can take over operation. The current controller is identified by the controller's transport address recorded in the configuration data. As additional information for the user, the configuration data can optionally contain the physical location of the resource.

Finally, cryptographic keying material is needed to protect the communication within the network. This data is part of the protection mechanism which has to be applied to the system and as such has to be considered within the analysis of the protection requirements.

3   Classification of Protection Requirements

The Bundesamt für Sicherheit in der Informationstechnik (BSI) defines three protection requirement categories which range from *normal* and *high* to *very high* [15]. These values indicate the severity of damage that might be caused by security breaches. A similar approach is used by the National Institute of Standards and Technology (NIST) [16]. They define the three categories *low*, *medium* and *high* to evaluate the magnitude of impact.

Both standards propose to classify the impact of compromising the main security objectives confidentiality, integrity and availability based upon these categories. The separation between the categories is facilitated by the definition of damage scenarios which include law violations, impairment of the right to informational self-determination, physical injury, impaired abilities to perform tasks, negative internal or external effects and financial consequences.

For our home automation scenario, we define the protection requirement categories (PRCs) as follows: Breaches with no or only minor effects are assigned to the category *normal*. The category *high* includes more severe vulnerabilities, which can cause, e. g., physical injuries or heightened financial losses or violate significantly someone's privacy. Only vulnerabilites which might have very serious consequences belong to the category *very high*, e. g. where danger for life and limb is possible or where financial losses are so severe that they can ruin the affected person or organization.

These protection requirement categories are used below to classify the impact of security breaches for each of the identified data types (see Section 2). To provide more details, the main security objectives confidentiality, integrity and availability are analyzed separately.

3.1   State Information

To allow for light control at all, the states of the resources have to be transmitted. For example, the main controller has to be informed about the switch position and the sensor values.

Generally, state information makes it possible to detect when devices are activated. This knowledge might be used to create a behavioural profile, e. g. of the times an occupant is at home or how often she uses one of her rooms. This can seriously affect her privacy. Thus the confidentiality of the state information is considered to belong to the PRC high.

The integrity of state information is also very important. If the data is manipulated, a light bulb can be turned off although it is supposed to be on. At worst, a person in the house might be injured when trying to find a switch or a flashlight in the dark. For example, she might trip over some object and fall down. Security breaches which might cause an unauthorized deactivation of the light bulbs are always high because they might lead to physical injuries. Accordingly, the integrity of the state information data has PRC high.

If no state information is available within the system, the lights keep their current state. This behaviour can lead to physical injury if the lights cannot be turned on. As already mentioned, this is correlated to the PRC high. If the lights cannot be turned off, this leads to financial losings for the owner. As we only consider light control in our analysis, the losings will likely remain minor and belong to PRC normal. The sum of these two aspects result in the state information's availability to fall into the PRC high.

Switch Position. The switch position is the most important state information, because it can directly control the lights and override the data of the light sensors. The confidentiality of the switch position is considered to be PRC high, because the occupant will likely turn off the lights when she is not at home. Thus her privacy is endangered by confidentiality breaches which leads to PRC high.

The light bulbs are directly controlled by the switch position. If it can be manipulated, the light bulbs can be turned off without permission. Thus, the integrity of switch state is also PRC high.

For similar reasons, the availability of the switch position has to be categorized as high as well. If it is impossible to control the light with the switch, the user has no direct control over the lights and therefore cannot turn it on or off. This might cause her to have to move around in the dark which endangers her physical integrity.

Light Sensor Values. The values of the light sensors seem less important, but still have serious impact. As the light sensors are applied to the room in order to measure the illumination level, they can be used to determine whether the light in a room is turned on or off. Like the switch position this information might endanger the privacy of the occupant. Thus, the light sensor values' confidentiality also belongs to the PRC high.

The integrity of this data is very important as well. The light bulbs can be directly regulated by them, at least as long as the switch is not used to control the light. If the light is turned off while no switch is within reach of the occupant, she might get hurt while trying to get there. Accordingly, the PRC of the integrity is high.

Availability is no issue in this case. If the light sensors fail, the light can still be operated with the switch. The PRC of the light sensor values' availability is therefore normal.

Light Bulb State. The importance of the light bulb state depends on the devices which are influenced thereof. As already mentioned, the main controller calculates the illumination level and sends it to the light bulbs. Therefore, the controller's light bulb state to-be is more important than the state of the single light bulbs.

Like the switch position, the state of the light bulbs might reveal details about the habits of the occupant. It therefore also has the PRC high. The modification of the light bulb state might cause one or, if the light bulb state sent by the controller is concerned, several lamps to be set to a certain state. They might be turned off or stay off although they should not. The integrity of the light bulb state therefore belongs to the PRC high. The availability of the light bulb state is only important for the light controller, because it tells the other lamps their status. Thus, the availability of the light bulb state is PRC normal while the availability of the controller's light bulb state is PRC high.

The classification of protection requirements for the state information is summarized in Table 1.

3.2   Resource Type

Confidentiality breaches in home scenarios can disclose personal information about the occupants. The type of the device reveals which devices are used

Table 1. Protection requirement classification: state information

Information	Confidentiality	Integrity	Availablity
State information	high	high	high
– Switch position	high	high	high
– Sensor data	normal	high	normal
– Light bulb state	high	high	normal
– Light bulb state of controller	high	high	high

within the house. This might be dangerous if thereby the existence of valuable items can be derived. For our home automation scenario only light control is considered. The according devices are assumed to be not particularly valuable. Thus, the confidentiality of the resource type is correlated to the protection requirement category normal.

Manipulating the integrity of the resource type might have a more serious impact. A node which wants to use the node's services might be mislead by a wrong or unreadable resource type. Thus, the sensor data might not be interpretable at all which results in the unavailability of the sensor data. The PRC of the resource type's integrity therefore is high, because it is at least as high as the category of the sensor data's availability. Additionally, if a device can be deluded to believe that a resource has a different type it might misinterpret the resource values. This might e. g. result in turning the lights off although they should be on, potentially leading to physical injuries. The classification therefore is high.

The availability of the resource type has the same protection requirement category as the integrity. If the resource type is not available the data might as well not be interpretable and hence cause failures. This means, the PRC of the resource type's availability is high as shown in Table 2.

Table 2. Protection requirement classification: resource type

Information	Confidentiality	Integrity	Availablity
Type of resource	normal	high	high

3.3   Configuration Data

The configuration data consists of information needed for the proper operation of the node and the communication within the network (see also Section 2).

Transport Address of Group. The disclosure of the transport address is not assumed to cause significant damage. No personal information can be derived from this information. The confidentiality of the transport address therefore has PRC normal.

A change of the transport address may cause the nodes to listen and send on a non-existing address and thereby lead to a failure of one or more nodes.

This might lead to unavailable state information and thus has at least the same PRC, which is high. Moreover, nodes may listen or send on the transport address of the wrong group. The results of this behaviour are difficult to predict. Although the consequences will in most cases be less severe it might still be possible that an occupant suddenly finds herself surrounded by darkness. All in all, the PRC of the group's transport address is high.

If the transport address of the group is not available to a single or several nodes, this might cause these nodes to fail. They can not send or receive messages any more and thus will keep their last state. Therefore the availability of this data belongs to the category high.

Transport Address of Controller. The confidentiality of the controller's transport address is not significant and therefore has PRC normal.

The Manipulation of the transport address would cause the light bulbs in the group to send their subscriptions to the wrong address which leads to wrong or missing state information. This equals the effects of integrity breaches of the group's transport address and has the same PRC (high). Additionally, the controlling node may be lead to believe another device to be the controller in which case he is not responsible for the distribution of state information to the light bulbs. This will cause all the light bulbs in the group to keep their last state. This is considered to be potentially harmful because the occupants might not be able to turn on the lights. The PRC is high in this case. According to these problems, the integrity of the controller's transport address is categorized as high.

Without the controller's transport address the nodes cannot register or refresh their registration. Eventually, they will not get any more status updates from the main controller and thus keep their last state. The availability is therefore PRC high.

Physical Location of the Node. The physical location of the node is very important for the user, because it helps him identifying the devices. Analyzing this data might reveal additional information about the occupants' living conditions. However, confidentiality breaches do not have a significant effect on the social or financial well-being of a person and thus fall into the protection requirement category normal.

Breaching the integrity by e. g. altering the node's location can mislead the user and delude him to assign the node to a wrong group. Thus a single, or in case of the light controller, all nodes of a group can fail. Therefore the protection requirement category for integrity has to be high.

As the physical location of the node is an optional item, the availability of this information is not important.

The protection requirement classification for configuration data is summarized in Table 3.

Table 3. Protection requirement classification: configuration data

Information	Confidentiality	Integrity	Availablity
Configuration data	normal	high	high
– Transport address of group	normal	high	normal
– Transport address of controller	normal	high	high
– Physical location of node	normal	high	normal

3.4 Cryptographic Keying Material

To determine the importance of the security objectives for the keying material it is necessary to understand the purpose of the keys, which is to enforce confidentiality and integrity for the system. Thus, the keys protect all information in the system. The confidentiality of the keys derives from the sum of all confidentiality and integrity classifications. If all data can be disclosed, the privacy of the occupants is endangered. This corresponds to the PRC high. The possibility of manipulating all data within the system might lead to financial losings because of heightened power consumption or to physical injuries. Finally, by breaking the confidentiality of the key, the keying material itself can be changed. Thus the protection requirement category of the key's integrity also has to be included. The resulting protection requirement category for the confidentiality of the keying material is therefore high (see Table 4). Manipulating the keys might result in communication problems. If one or more nodes believe the key to be different, they can no longer take part in the communication. Therefore the protection requirement category has to be derived from the overall availability category. Additionally, this might enable the attacker to infiltrate her own keys and thus break the confidentiality of the systems data. The protection requirement category is therefore high.

The loss of the keys has the same effect as either a confidentiality breach of the keying material, if the communication is continued without the protection of the keys or the unavailability of state information if no communication occurs without the keys. For both cases the PRC for the keying material is high.

Table 4. Protection requirement classification: encryption keys

Information	Confidentiality	Integrity	Availablity
Encryption keys	high	high	high

4   Discussion

Identifying the protection requirements of an information system is an essential part of each security analysis. It helps understanding the application domain, threats, and defining possible countermeasures. The application domains building control and home automation are well understood for wired networks that use mesh-under routing, i.e., addressing and forwarding happens "under the hood" of IP (if IP is involved at all).

Security concerns are very low in this scenario as the network is isolated, hence rising the costs for an attack. As long as the invest in breaking into this network exceeds the potential gain, there is little incentive to do so. Even if the damage that a security breach might cause was high, the low probability of occurrence still can justify from an economic perspective not to use better security measures.

The risk is increased substantially when the network is not isolated any more: Wireless communication can facilitate intrusion where attackers manage to get into the coverage area of the radio signal. And even worse, interconnecting the building network with the global Internet opens the door for all sorts of remote attacks seen in the Internet today.

Well-known countermeasures exist and are in frequent use not only for secured company networks but also for today's low-budget networking devices at home. For feature-rich devices and broadband connections, the overhead introduced by strong cryptography is not a major concern. Notwithstanding the actual protection requirements, application designers can follow traditional security guidelines and select the most powerful security technology that is available.

For the Internet of Things, where devices can be very limited in their capabilities, this approach is not feasible any more (cf. [17]). Bergstrom et al. [18] propose an architecture that imposes a gateway that shields the home network from the public Internet. Access to the Web-based remote interface is protected by strong cryptography while the dedicated point-to-point link to the home appliance uses a more light-weight protocol for exclusive communication with the access gateway.

One disadvantage of this intermediary-based approach is that it abandons end-to-end security and potentially leads to a vendor lock-in and constricts the evolution of M2M-applications—the foundation of the Internet of Things.

Where end-to-end security is required and light-weight cryptography is inevitable because of the devices' limitations, it is crucial to identify the actual protection requirements to avoid unnecessary cost on one hand, and too weak protection of resources on the other.

In our paper, we have presented an analysis of protection requirements for light control in a typical home environment. Using the classification from [15] only the classes "normal" and "high" were used. Conditions that would call for "very high" protection are hardly imaginable. As a result, key length and initialization vectors might be shorter in this scenario compared to applications where danger for life and limb is expected. Although the same security functions are applied, these provisions mean less overhead in transmission and processing, and hence lead to less power consumption.

The main effects of security breaches we have identified are: Disclosure of personal information, altering the state of the light bulbs so that the lights can be switched off and forcing the light bulbs to keep their last state, which means they do not react to pressing the switch. All of these consequences correlate to PRC high.

Our analysis shows that the impact of security breaches differs significantly for the distinct security objectives. Confidentiality breaches only have PRC high where state information is concerned, because these might reveal details about the habits of the occupants. Apart from that, only the encryption keys are confidential. This is not surprising as the secret keys are confidential by definition.

The integrity of the various data in the system is always PRC high. Every manipulation of data in the system might lead to the light bulbs to be switched off although they are supposed to be on. Therefore, it is essential to protect data integrity in the system.

In general, availability violations are less severe than integrity breaches. If the unavailability of data has consequences at all, these are almost always that the light bulbs keep their current state. Although this is correlated to PRC high, this does not pose a danger as severe as a sudden switch-off of the lights. In the former case, the occupant is used to the current conditions of his environment. In the latter, the environment of the user suddenly changes, which comes more unexpected and might startle the occupant. Therefore, the protection of data availability is important, but not as important as the protection of integrity.

In summary, integrity is the most important security objective in our scenario. Availability breaches are less severe, but might still have high impact. Confidentiality violations are only significant where state information is concerned. For other building control tasks such as HVAC, we anticipate similar results. That means, certain sensor values and configuration data have lower protection requirements than, e. g. control messages and the exchange of keying material.

This has consequences when selecting cipher suites for smart object communication: Where confidentiality is optional (e. g. for distribution of configuration data), cipher suites or modes that provide only data integrity could be used. For cipher suites that can provide both, data integrity and confidentiality, at the same time (such as Authenticated Encryption with Associated Data, AEAD, [19]), this knowledge is less important. Still, it helps selecting reasonable key and nonce lengths which is important to save bandwidth. memory and processing time.

5   Conclusions

In this paper we have demonstrated how protection requirements can be inferred for a given M2M communication scenario, with a specific interest on constrained devices.

Our paper gives a detailed overview of the damages security breaches might cause in a home automation scenario. This is the prerequisite for choosing the appropriate countermeasures to protect the data in the system. A subsequent risk assessment will help identifying where strong security is required. In constrained networks, devices are not able to manage security protocols with a considerable overhead, hence it is preferable to use light-weight security where this gives reasonable protection.

In the application scenario we have investigated, only normal and high protection is required. We argue that in general, these protection requirements classes allow for weaker cryptographic functions as if very high protection was necessary. Many applications in building control and home automation share this property.

When designing a secure system, the classification of protection requirements also helps selecting proper cryptographic functions that have as little overhead as possible. As an example, where confidentiality is less important than data integrity, the data may be only signed but not encrypted before transmission where this is more resource-conserving.

In summary, our approach helps designing effective security for constrained node networks. We anticipate that light-weight security mechanisms can be used safely in most M2M application scenarios, including resource management tasks and monitoring resource usage in the Internet of Things.

References

1. Atzori, L., Iera, A., Morabito, G.: The Internet of Things: A survey. Computer Networks 54(15), 2787–2805 (2010)
2. Mulligan, G.: The 6LoWPAN architecture. In: 4th Workshop on Embedded Networked Sensors (EmNets 2007), pp. 78–82. ACM, New York (2007)
3. Deering, S., Hinden, R.: Internet Protocol, Version 6 (IPv6) Specification. RFC 2460 (1998)
4. Pandey, S., Kim, M.-S., Choi, M.-J., Hong, J.W.: Towards management of machine to machine networks. In: 13th Network Operations and Management Symposium (APNOMS), pp. 1–7 (2011)
5. Bormann, C., Castellani, A.P., Shelby, Z.: CoAP: An Application Protocol for Billions of Tiny Internet Nodes. IEEE Internet Computing 16(2), 62–67 (2012)
6. Stallings, W.: SNMP and SNMPv2: the infrastructure for network management. IEEE Communications Magazine 36(3), 37–43 (1998)
7. Shelby, Z., Hartke, K., Bormann, C., Frank, B.: Constrained Application Protocol (CoAP). Internet-draft (2012),
   `http://tools.ietf.org/html/draft-ietf-core-coap` (work in progress)
8. Kovatsch, M., Weiss, M., Guinard, D.: Embedding Internet Technology for Home Automation. In: 15th IEEE International Conference on Emerging Technologies and Factory Automation (ETFA 2010), Bilbao, Spain (2012)
9. Harrington, D., Schoenwaelder, J.: Transport Subsystem for the Simple Network Management Protocol (SNMP). RFC 5590 (2009)
10. Rescorla, E., Modadugu, N.: Datagram Transport Layer Security Version 1.2. RFC 6347 (2012)
11. Garcia-Morchon, O., Keoh, S., Hummen, R., Struik, R.: Security Considerations in the IP-based Internet of Things.
    `http://tools.ietf.org/html/draft-garcia-core-security`.
    Internet-Draft (2012) (work in progress)
12. Padmavathi, G., Shanmugapriya, D.: A Survey of Attacks, Security Mechanisms and Challenges in Wireless Sensor Networks. International Journal of Computer Science and Information Security (IJCSIS) 4(1 & 2) (2009)
13. Arkko, J., Keranen, A.: CoAP Security Architecture.
    `http://tools.ietf.org/html/draft-arkko-core-security-arch`.
    Internet-Draft (2011) (work in progress)

14. Perrig, A., Stankovic, J., Wagner, D.: Security in wireless sensor networks. Communications of the ACM 47, 53–57 (2004)
15. Bundesamt für Sicherheit in der Informationstechnik: BSI-Standard 100-2. Version 2.0. IT-Grundschutz Methodology (2008), https://www.bsi.bund.de/cae/servlet/contentblob/471430/publicationFile/28223/standard_100-2_e_pdf.pdf
16. Stoneburner, G., Goguen, A., Feringa, A.: Risk Management Guide for Information Technology Systems. NIST Special Publication 800-30 (2012)
17. Potlapally, N.R., Ravi, S., Raghunathan, A., Jha, N.K.: Analyzing the energy consumption of security protocols. In: 2003 International Symposium on Low Power Electronics and Design (ISLPED 2003), Seoul, Korea, pp. 30–35 (2003)
18. Bergstrom, P., Driscoll, K., Kimball, J.: Making home automation communications secure. Computer 34(10), 50–56 (2001)
19. Rogaway, P.: Authenticated encryption with Associated-Data. In: Ninth ACM Conference on Computer and Communication Security (CCS-9), pp. 98–107 (2002)

Statistical Analysis of Contact Patterns between Human-Carried Mobile Devices

Tong Hu[1,2], Bernd-Ludwig Wenning[1], Carmelita Görg[1], Umar Toseef[1], and Zhongwen Guo[2]

[1] Communications Networks, TZI, University of Bremen, Germany
{tong,wenn,cg,umr}@comnets.uni-bremen.de
[2] Department of Computer Science & Engineering, Ocean University of China, China
guozhw@ouc.edu.cn

Abstract. In this paper, we focus on analyzing the impact of human-to-human contact patterns on opportunistic communication in Pocket Switched Networks (PSNs). We take advantage of statistical methods to consider the distributions of two different types of inter-contact time as well as the number of contacts between human-carried mobile devices. Different from the results from recent studies, we present empirical evidence that power law with exponential cutoff characterizes all three distributions of interest better than other possible long-tail distributions. We further show that each of the investigated distributions has a finite mean value. Having a finite mean value is of importance for each distribution, as it facilitates the design of distributed community detection algorithms as well as social-based forwarding algorithms. Finally, we make the recommendation to exploit the average number of contacts as a threshold for each device to determine their friend-set, which is a precondition for some distributed community detection algorithms.

Keywords: Statistical Analysis, Contact Pattern, Pocket Switched Networks.

1 Introduction

With the rapid deployment of portable devices (e.g., smart phone, PDA) that are equipped with increasing processing, storage and communication capacities, the requirement of content sharing among mobile users is becoming more pervasive, which makes device-to-device Opportunistic Communication a suitable addition to traditional infrastructure-based networks. On one side, for the Internet Service Providers (ISPs), Opportunistic Communication could improve system capacity and reduce cost from building expensive infrastructure. On the other side, from the users' perspective, device-to-device transfers could not only considerably reduce their expenses of data plans, but also provide infrastructure-independent services especially when or where infrastructure-based services are unavailable (e.g., in non-coverage areas). It is also worth noting that infrastructure is vulnerable to natural disasters or other failures. Thus in case of exceptional situations, Opportunistic Communication could be a necessity and thus an important field of study.

A. Timm-Giel et al. (Eds.): MONAMI 2012, LNICST 58, pp. 244–257, 2013.

Pocket Switched Networks (PSNs) are a typical application scenario [1] of Opportunistic Communication. The concept of PSNs evolved from Mobile Ad hoc Networks (MANETs) and Delay Tolerant Networks (DTNs). As a functional supplement of traditional infrastructure-based networks, PSNs focus on taking advantage of human mobility and local forwarding to exchange messages among mobile devices in a distributed manner. Based on proximity-based connectivity such as Bluetooth, store-carry-forward mechanisms are employed in PSNs to address those situations such as intermittent connectivity which is mainly due to geographical separation or mobility. As devices are carried by their users from location to location, contact opportunities occur when devices enter the mutual transmission range. Then messages are forwarded from device to device according to certain strategies with the intention that the messages are brought closer to their destinations spatially or temporally.

The mobility of the participants (usually people) of the PSNs is difficult to predict. Compared to the continuously changing topology of the network, people's social relationships vary much more slowly, especially in certain environments (e.g., campus, workplace). Recently, social-based forwarding algorithms in such dynamic environments have attracted additional interest. People's contact patterns such as contact frequency and duration could be used as means of inference to judge people's relationships locally, which means whether people are close to each other in space or time. Those people who contact each other frequently will present an intensive clustered structure, i.e., a community in a graph of relationships. Social-based forwarding in PSNs exploits such community information from community detection algorithms to make forwarding decisions when communication opportunities are available. Therefore, investigation of contact patterns between mobile devices is of high practical importance for both community detection and social-based forwarding algorithms, as well as realistic mobility models for protocol performance evaluation.

Recent studies have provided evidence suggesting that diverse aspects of contact patterns, such as inter-contact time and duration, between each pair of human-carried mobile devices could be characterized by power law distributions [1, 2]. However in this paper, based on connectivity trace data, we take advantage of statistical methods and present empirical evidence that the distributions of two different types of inter-contact time and the number of contacts all follow a power law with an exponential cutoff distribution, which fits better to the empirical data than either a pure power law distribution or alternative long-tail distribution. We further show that these distributions have different finite mean values. Having finite mean values is of different physical meaning for each of the distributions of interest, which would as well facilitate and provide guidance for the design of distributed community detection and social-based forwarding algorithms. For example, the finite mean value of inter-contact time indicates the average per-packet delay, which further determines whether a single-copy or multi-copy strategy is preferable for a certain application scenario in terms of delivery delay and cost. The friend-set of each node in PSNs is the basis of some distributed community detection algorithms, in this paper we also recommend to exploit the average number of contacts for each device as a threshold to determine their friend-sets.

The rest of this paper is structured as follows. We briefly describe the background and related work in Section 2. Further background discussion can be found in the corresponding sections. In Section 3, we introduce the experimental trace data and relevant definitions used in this paper. Section 4 describes the method and results of statistical contact pattern analysis between human-carried mobile devices. Finally, in Section 5, we conclude the paper with a brief discussion and suggested future work.

2   Background and Related Work

In order to study the mobility model and assist the design of forwarding algorithms in the context of opportunistic communication environments such as PSNs, several experiments have been conducted to acquire mobility data of contact frequency and duration between human-carried devices in the past years, for example in the Haggle Project [3], the MIT Reality Mining Project [4] and a recent Bluetooth-based intensive human trace acquisition experiment [5].

Analysis of contact patterns from the connectivity trace data is of high practical importance especially for community detection algorithms, social-based forwarding algorithms, and realistic mobility models research.

Community detection is an applicable method to understand the social relationships of people. Different from centralized offline algorithms, in PSN scenarios, distributed community detection algorithms exploit each device to detect its own local community structure in a peer-to-peer manner. In [6], Clauset defines a measure of local community structure and an algorithm that infers the hierarchy of communities. In [7], Hui et al. propose and evaluate several novel distributed community detection approaches with great potential to detect both static and temporary communities. Contact pattern analysis could help setting parameters or thresholds reasonably in community detection algorithms.

Social-based forwarding algorithms attempt to take advantage of community memberships among devices and/or centrality of each node in the network to assist making forwarding decisions. SimBet Routing [8] uses ego-centric centrality and social similarity to forward messages towards the device with which the possibility of finding a potential carrier to the destination is increased. Hui et al. proposed the BUBBLE algorithm [9] which combines the knowledge of the community structure with the knowledge of centrality of each node to forward messages. Bulut et al. defined social based metrics for relay node selection and presented a friendship based routing protocol for mobile social networks [10]. Mei et al. designed a social-aware, stateless forwarding mechanism, SANE [11], based on the intuition that people with similar interests tend to meet more often.

The mobility model which is used in a specified application scenario has strong impact on the performance of the forwarding algorithm. Recent studies have provided evidence suggesting that inter-contact time and contact duration could be characterized by power law behavior [2], while a common property of the most common mobility models is that the tail of the inter-contact time distribution decays exponentially. In [12], the author observed that the power law decay of the inter-contact time distribution holds up to a characteristic time, and is then followed by an exponential decay.

The most relevant papers for this work are [2] and [12]. In [2], the author studied data transfer opportunities between wireless devices carried by humans and observed that the distribution of the inter-contact time may be well approximated by a power law for inter-contact times between 10 minutes and 1 day. In [12], the author demonstrated that beyond a characteristic time of the order of half a day, the CCDF of inter-contact time exhibits an exponential decay. The dichotomy has important implications on the performance of opportunistic forwarding algorithms and implies that recent statements on performance of such algorithms may be over-pessimistic. In this paper, we take advantage of statistical methods to consider the distributions of two different types of inter-contact time as well as the number of contacts between human-carried mobile devices, and present empirical evidence that power law with an exponential cutoff distribution better characterizes the three distributions of interest.

3   Experimental Dataset and Definitions

3.1   Experimental Datasets

To study the properties of contact patterns in terms of inter-contact time and the number of contacts between human-carried mobile devices, we analyzed the commonly used MIT Reality Mining dataset [4] and the fine-grained PMTR dataset [13].

The MIT Reality Mining Project was conducted over a period of 9 months. In this experiment, one hundred subjects carried mobile phones with running software in order to record data about call logs, neighboring Bluetooth devices, cell tower IDs, application usage, and phone status. Among one hundred subjects, seventy-five users were either students or faculty in the MIT Media Laboratory, while the remaining twenty-five were incoming students at the MIT Sloan business school. In this paper we only focus on analyzing the logged Bluetooth proximity data in the context of the PSN scenario. Due to human mobility, each Bluetooth-enabled mobile phone was taken from location to location meanwhile logging contacts with other Bluetooth-enabled devices within 5-10 meters by doing device discovery every five minutes. Thus proximity information could be projected into social relationships between users of these devices.

The PMTR dataset includes connectivity traces from 44 mobile devices. In this experiment, 49 Pocket Mobile Trace Recorders (PMTRs) were distributed to faculty members, PhD students, and technical staffs who work in offices and laboratories located in a three-floor building and take lunches or coffee breaks in a nearby cafeteria. The contacts between these people were recorded by both devices approximately at the same time. At the end of the experiment, 5 PMTRs had not registered any contacts due to hardware failure. The experiment lasted for 19 days and used 1 second as maximum sampling rate in order to collect a rich dataset for analysis.

3.2   Definitions

In this paper, we adopt the consistent terminology of inter-contact time defined as the length of time interval elapsed between two successive contact periods as used in former studies. However, in the following section we will investigate distributions of two different types of inter-contact time, denoted as Distribution I and II. As both distributions are directly related to the time delay experienced by messages transferred in PSNs, the nature of the distributions will affect the choice of the suitable message forwarding algorithm to maximize successful transmissions in a bounded time delay. Besides, the statistics of such distributions may also affect appropriate parameter settings of certain distributed community detection algorithms.

Distribution I is the aggregated distribution of inter-contact time between each pair of nodes in the network. The inter-contact time of this type is the time interval elapsed between two consecutive contacts of each pair of nodes. Therefore, in a network-level perspective, the mean value of such a distribution indicates the mean packet delay in the network, as messages are forwarded through multiple node pairs.

Other than the aggregated distribution among all nodes in the network, Distribution II is about the distribution of each single node. Distribution II is the distribution of inter-contact time between each single node and any other encountered nodes. Thus the inter-contact time of this type is the time interval elapsed between two successive contacts, even though the encountered nodes in each contact may be different. In other words, to a certain node, the inter-contact time of this type means the shortest waiting time before another contact opportunity comes.

Moreover, in the next section, we will also investigate the distribution of the number of contacts in a certain time interval, denoted as Distribution III, which characterizes the nodes' encounter frequency. The number of contacts also quantifies the closeness of social relationships of each node in a local sighting. Therefore, in the PSN scenario, the statistics of the number of contacts would provide assistance to devise distributed community detection algorithms.

Finally, what should also be noted is that we only focus on analyzing distributions of inter-contact time and number of contacts, but not on contact duration. Without loss of generality, we make the same assumption as in former studies that the content data to be shared among mobile devices could be divided into multiple smaller messages, and each message could be transferred successfully during each contact opportunity. The suitable size of each message for successful transmission is beyond the scope of this paper.

4   Contact Patterns Analysis

In this section, we take advantage of statistical methods to investigate the empirical distributions of both types of inter-contact time introduced in the previous section as well as number of contacts between human-carried mobile devices. From the connectivity traces, we observed that power law with exponential cutoff characterizes all three distributions of interest better than either pure power law distribution or alternative long-tail distributions.

In the following, we will first introduce the statistical methods used in this paper, and then show the details of analyzing the distributions of interest. Finally, we will also present the finite mean values of the distributions together with the impact on distributed community detection algorithms.

4.1   Methodology

The power law distribution has attracted particular attention over recent years for its mathematical properties and its appearance in a diverse range of natural and man-made phenomena [14]. To the best of our knowledge, paper [2] might be the first work presenting empirical evidence to suggest that the distribution of inter-contact time between human-carried devices can be well approximated by power law over a range from ten minutes up to one day, as the CCDF of the inter-contact time is lower bounded by the CCDF of power law. Nevertheless values of inter-contact time above one day were not sufficiently considered in the distribution. In [12], the author examined the empirical distributions of inter-contact time between mobile devices on different datasets. On the basis that the CCDF plot of the inter-contact time follows a straight line in logarithm-logarithm scale over a range of values, the author confirmed the hypothesis that in many cases the aggregate distribution of inter-contact time follows a power law distribution up to a certain characteristic time. Above that characteristic time, the CCDF of the inter-contact time can be closely upper-bounded by a straight line in linear-logarithm scale, which indicates following exponential decay in the distribution. The author also provided analytical results showing that existing simple mobility models can exhibit the same qualitative dichotomy.

However, power law is not the only distribution presenting approximately straight-line behavior in a CCDF plot with logarithm-logarithm scale. In addition, the methods commonly used such as least-squares fitting may produce inaccurate estimates of parameters for the power law distribution. Therefore we make use of statistical methods from [15] to consider the empirical distributions of interest.

Mathematically, a quantity follows a power law distribution if the probability distribution function is defined as a form of

$$p(x) \propto x^{-\alpha} . \tag{1}$$

Whereas in practice, the power law distribution may only be applied for values greater than a certain minimum threshold denoted as x_{min}, rather than the complete range of all values for x. The normalized form of power law with x_{min} is

$$p(x) = \frac{\alpha-1}{x_{min}} \left(\frac{x}{x_{min}}\right)^{-\alpha} . \tag{2}$$

Generally, the proposed statistical framework in [15] to discern and quantify power law behavior works as follows. The parameters x_{min} and α in Eq. (2) are estimated first by means of the Kolmogorov-Smirnov statistic and maximum likelihood estimation for each. Then a goodness-of-fit test is calculated to verify if the power law distribution is a plausible hypothesis for the empirical data. Even if the empirical data is well fitted by the power law distribution, it is still possible that other alternative distributions (e.g., log-normal) might also fit well. Therefore, potential long-tail distributions will also be compared by means of a log-likelihood ratio test [16] to find which model is the better fit.

In this paper, we concentrate on finding out the best-fitting distribution. The definitions of potential long-tail distributions compared in this paper are summarized in Table 1.

Table 1. Definitions of potential long-tail distributions fitted and compared in this paper

Distribution	Probability distribution function
Power law with exponential cutoff	$p(x) = \dfrac{\lambda^{1-\alpha}}{\Gamma(1-\alpha,\lambda x_{min})} \cdot x^{-\alpha} e^{-\lambda x}$
Log-normal	$p(x) = \sqrt{\dfrac{2}{\pi\sigma^2}} \left[erfc\left(\dfrac{\ln x_{min}}{\sqrt{2}\sigma}\right) \right]^{-1} \cdot \dfrac{1}{x} exp\left[-\dfrac{(\ln x-\mu)^2}{2\sigma^2} \right]$
Stretched exponential	$p(x) = \beta\lambda e^{\lambda x_{min}^{\beta}} \cdot x^{\beta-1} e^{-\lambda x^{\beta}}$

4.2   Analysis of Distribution I

To investigate the expected per-packet delay, we first analyze the Distribution I, i.e., the empirical distribution of inter-contact time between each pair of nodes in the network. In order to compare with former results, here we set the minimum threshold x_{min} to the same fixed value for both datasets, 10 minutes, instead of estimating x_{min} by means of the Kolmogorov-Smirnov statistic.

In MIT Reality Mining dataset, we select the connectivity traces starting from September 2004. However, for different reasons, some interruptions could be found in the middle of the trace, some of which are longer than one month. We believe that such a long period should not be considered within the scope, because the contact pattern of the user in such a period cannot be reflected properly. Therefore we adopt a pre-process to avoid interference from those interruptions. We divide the complete connectivity trace by month and select the continuous connectivity trace of each node, on the condition that the longest interruption is less than 30 days.

Fig. 1(a) presents the CCDF plot of the aggregated distribution from MIT Reality Mining dataset and other fitted long-tail distributions in log-log scale. The tail in the CCDF plot indicates that long inter-contact times existed and should not be neglected, as they would induce unacceptable packet delay. Among four fitted long-tail distributions, the power law distribution deviates obviously further than another three candidates. From Fig. 1(b), similar result can be found in PMTR dataset, which indicates that power law with exponential cutoff fits the empirical distribution better than any other possible long-tail candidates.

Different from former studies, in Section 4.5, we will present the mean value of the power law with exponential cutoff distribution. Here the expected inter-contact time of each pair of nodes is 3.6 days in MIT Reality Mining dataset, and 16.32 hours in PMTR dataset. On the contrary, the exponent of the fitted power law distribution is 1.26 in MIT Reality Mining dataset and 1.37 in PMTR dataset, both of which are lower than 2, which means that the expected per-packet delay will be infinite according to that fitting.

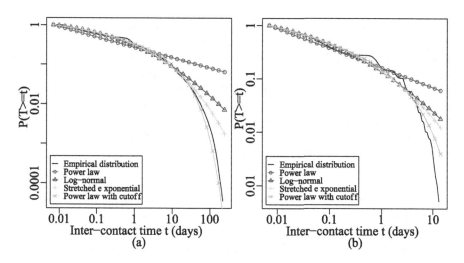

Fig. 1. Empirical and fitted long-tail distributions: (a) MIT Reality Mining, (b) PMTR

4.3   Analysis of Distribution II

After investigation on the expected per-packet delay in the complete network, now we focus on the contact pattern of each single node. The Distribution II is the distribution of inter-contact time between each single node and any other encountered nodes. Such expected inter-contact time contributes to quantifying the packet delay, which is the time elapsed before the packet is forwarded to the next node.

In the connectivity trace of each single node from both datasets, the contacting periods may overlap with each other, because each single node could encounter with multiple nodes at the same time. Thus for both datasets, we merge all those overlapped contacts in order to get the inter-contact time between each merged contact durations. The inter-contact time of this type indicates the shortest waiting time before the next contact opportunity comes.

Power law and power law with exponential cutoff are nested distributions, and the former one is a subset of the later one. In addition, the larger family of distributions will always provide a fit at least as good as the smaller. Thus we only adopt the log likelihood ratio test between: (1) power law and log-normal, (2) power law with exponential cutoff and log-normal, as well as (3) power law with exponential cutoff and stretched exponential. The minimum threshold x_{min} is also set to 10 minutes for both datasets.

According to the method of the log-likelihood ratio (LLR) test, the sign of LLR depends on which distribution is better, while a p-value indicates whether the observed sign of LLR is statistically significant. If p is small ($p<0.1$), then the sign of LLR is reliable. Otherwise the LLR test does not favor either model over the other, which means the result is only a possible case.

The results are summarized in Table 2. From MIT Reality Mining dataset, we only consider 82 out of 88 nodes, each of which has more than 100 observations, in order to ensure the accuracy of the statistical method. For 48 nodes among those nodes, the power law with exponential cutoff fits better than other alternative distributions, which we denoted as powerexp case. For only 7 nodes, the log-normal and/or stretched exponential fit better, which we denoted as non-powerexp case. The rest 27 nodes cannot be definitely categorized due to a large p-value ($p \geq 0.1$), which we denote as possible cases. However, from PMTR dataset, the number of observations per node is much less after merging overlapped contacts (only 3 nodes have more than 100 observations). Besides, as the number of the nodes participated in the experiment is also less than 100, we only use the MIT Reality Mining dataset to analyze Distribution II and III in this paper.

Table 2. Analysis results of Distribution II and Distribution III

Distribution	Powerexp	Possible	Non-powerexp
II (Reality)	48	27	7
III (Reality)	38	26	1

Based on the MIT Reality Mining dataset, we conclude that the inter-contact time between each single node and other encountered nodes follows power law with exponential cutoff. The expected value of the fitted distribution of each node in MIT Reality Mining dataset varies from 53 minutes to 28 hours. Fig. 2 presents the examples of powerexp and non-powerexp cases from the MIT Reality Mining dataset.

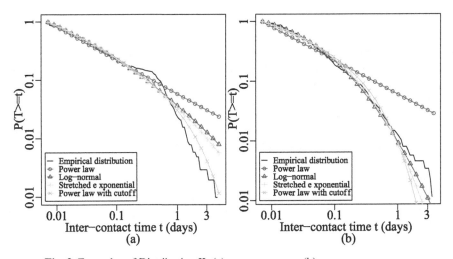

Fig. 2. Examples of Distribution II: (a) powerexp case, (b) non-powerexp case

4.4   Analysis of Distribution III

Distribution III characterizes the nodes' encounter frequency, i.e., the number of contacts between each single node to other encountered nodes within a certain time interval. We believe that the contact frequency could quantify the closeness of social relationships locally from the viewpoint of each node.

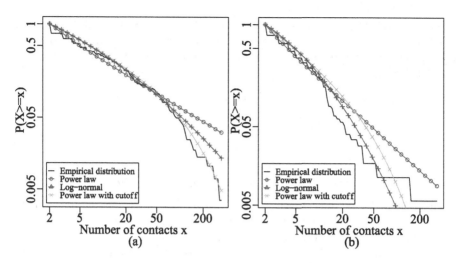

Fig. 3. Examples of Distribution III: (a) powerexp case, (b) non-powerexp case

To investigate the Distribution III, we select a fixed time interval for each node from September to December 2004 from the MIT Reality Mining dataset, because the majority of connectivity records took place during that period for most of the nodes. We get 87 nodes with non-empty traces during that period. Then we adopt the same method to fit possible long-tail distributions to the empirical data and take LLR tests between: (1) power law and log-normal and (2) power law with exponential cutoff and log-normal. The minimum threshold of number of contacts, x_{min}, is set to 2.

We only consider 65 out of 87 nodes which have more than 100 observations to ensure the accuracy. In other words, each of those nodes encountered with more than 100 other nodes during that period. The results are given in Table 2. The power law with exponential cutoff fits better for 38 nodes, compared to the log-normal which fits better for only 1 node. While another 26 nodes which have large p-values ($p{\geq}0.1$) cannot be definitely categorized.

Therefore, we consider that the number of contacts between each single node and other encountered nodes also follows a power law with exponential cutoff. Fig. 3 presents examples of powerexp case and non-powerexp case.

4.5   Impact of Finite Mean Value

So far, we have studied the aggregated distribution of inter-contact time for each pair of node in the network, in addition with the individual distributions of inter-contact time and number of contacts between each single node and other encountered nodes. Our conclusion is all three distributions of interest follow a power law with exponential cutoff. Former studies suggest that the inter-contact time of each pair of nodes has a CCDF with a power law tail. If the exponent of power-law is not larger than 2, there will not be a finite mean value, which implies that the expected per-packet delay in the network will be infinite. However in [2], the author observed that the exponents of Pareto distributions are smaller than 1 (i.e., the exponents of power law are smaller than 2) across diverse empirical datasets. In the following, we are going to investigate the mean value of each distribution of interest based on our conclusion. The probability distribution function of power law with exponential cutoff is defined as:

$$p(x) = C \cdot x^{-\alpha} e^{-\lambda x} . \tag{3}$$

with

$$C = \frac{\lambda^{1-\alpha}}{\Gamma(1-\alpha, \lambda x_{min})} . \tag{4}$$

where C is the normalization constant such that $\int_{x_{min}}^{\infty} p(x) \, dx = 1$, it could be obtained numerically, the Γ function in Eq. 4 is an incomplete gamma function. The x_{min} is the lower bound which we set to fixed values in this paper. The parameters α and λ can be obtained by means of *maximum likelihood estimation*.

Then the mean value of the power law with exponential cutoff could be deduced as follows:

$$\begin{aligned}
E(x) &= \int_{x_{min}}^{\infty} xp(x)dx \\
&= C \int_{x_{min}}^{\infty} x^{1-\alpha} e^{-\lambda x} dx \\
&= \frac{C}{\lambda} \left(x_{min}^{1-\alpha} e^{-\lambda x_{min}} + \frac{1-\alpha}{C} \right) \\
&= \frac{C x_{min}^{1-\alpha} e^{-\lambda x_{min} + 1 - \alpha}}{\lambda} .
\end{aligned} \tag{5}$$

We calculate the theoretical mean value for the individual distributions of inter-contact time and the number of contacts of each single node, i.e., Distribution II and Distribution III, with the value of x_{min} is set to 10 minutes and 2 times for each of them. Then we compare the average value from the observations with the theoretical mean value.

Fig. 4 illustrates that the theoretical mean value of the fitted power law with exponential cutoff is highly consistent with the average value from the observation. In the following, we use the average value from the observations to approximate the theoretical mean value.

Now we make an assumption that the contact pattern between human-carried devices remains similar from month to month, which means the nodes which contacted each other frequently in the past will also keep relatively frequent encountering compared to other nodes in the future. From a community-evolution perspective, the hypothesis behind it is that the main community structure in the same environment will not be changed suddenly. Before validation of this assumption, we define a concept of friend-set at first. The friend-set of each node is the collection including all those nodes which were encountered at least twice and the number of contacts is higher than the average value from the observations. Then we calculate both the ratio of friends to all nodes encountered and the ratio of contacts with friends to contacts with all nodes encountered from month to month.

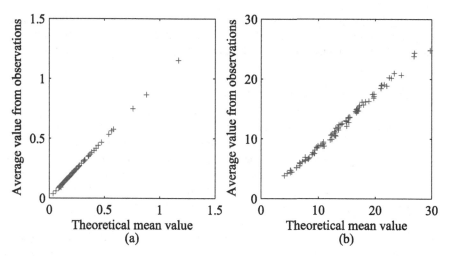

Fig. 4. Theoretical mean values and the average values from observations: (a) Inter-contact time, (b) The number of contacts

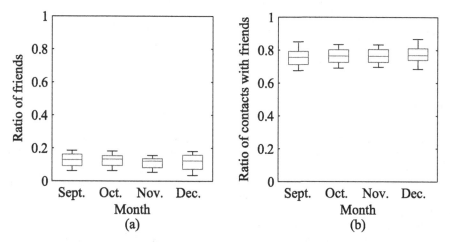

Fig. 5. The stability of contact patterns among close friends for four months in MIT Reality Mining dataset: (a) Ratio of friends to all nodes encountered, (b) Ratio of contacts with friends

Fig. 5 presents the result of the ratios calculated from the MIT Reality Mining dataset. In Fig. 5, the central line in each box is the median of the calculated values in that month. The top and bottom edges of each box are the 75th and 25th percentiles, which indicate the region that includes 50% of the calculated values, and the whiskers extend to the region where 90% of the calculated values are included.

Even though the number of friends accounts for only a tiny part of the nodes encountered, the number of contacts from those friends dominates from month to month, which indicates that the average value from the observations could be used as threshold to find out the friend-set of each node. As finding out the friend-set of each node is the first step for some distributed community detection algorithms [7], we believe our finding can also provide an adaptive manner to set the threshold for friend-sets in different environments and improve the accuracy of the algorithm.

5   Conclusion and Future Work

Based on the MIT Reality Mining and PMTR datasets, we have analyzed the contact pattern between human-carried devices in terms of inter-contact time and the number of contacts. Our conclusion is that the aggregated distribution of inter-contact time between each pair of nodes follows power law distribution with exponential cutoff. In addition, compared with other possible long-tail distributions, power law with exponential cutoff also characterizes the inter-contact time and the number of contacts of each single node better than other possible long-tail distributions.

We have shown that there will be finite mean values for the distributions of interest, and the theoretic mean values of fitted power law with exponential cutoff distributions can be approximated by the average value of observations. Moreover, we have also presented that the average number of contacts can be used as the threshold of friend-sets for distributed community detection algorithms.

In the future, we would like to validate our conclusions on more mobility traces around the PSN scenarios. Besides that, devising and evaluating distributed community detection algorithms taking advantage of setting the average number of contacts as the threshold of friend-sets will be another aspect of our future work.

References

1. Hui, P., Chaintreau, A., Gass, R., Scott, J., Crowcroft, J., Diot, C.: Pocket switched networks and human mobility in conference environments. In: 2005 ACM SIGCOMM Workshop on Delay-Tolerant Networking, pp. 244–251 (2005)
2. Chaintreau, A., Hui, P., Crowcroft, J., Diot, C., Gass, R., Scott, J.: Impact of Human Mobility on Opportunistic Forwarding Algorithms. IEEE Transactions on Mobile Computing 6(6), 606–620 (2007)
3. Haggle project, http://www.haggleproject.org
4. Eagle, N., Pentland, A.: Reality mining: sensing complex social systems. Personal and Ubiquitous Computing 10(4), 255–268 (2006)
5. Cabero, J.M., Molina, V., Urteaga, I., Liberal, F., Martín, J.L.: Acquisition of human traces with Bluetooth technology: Challenges and proposals. Ad Hoc Networks (published online June 6, 2012), doi:10.1016/j.adhoc.2012.05.007
6. Clauset, A.: Finding local community structure in networks. Physical Review E 72, 026132 (2005)
7. Hui, P., Yoneki, E., Chan, S.Y., Crowcroft, J.: Distributed community detection in delay tolerant networks. In: 2nd ACM/IEEE International Workshop on Mobility in the Evolving Internet Architecture, pp. 1–8 (2007)
8. Daly, E.M., Haahr, M.: Social network analysis for routing in disconnected delay-tolerant MANETs. In: 8th ACM International Symposium on Mobile Ad Hoc Networking and Computing, pp. 32–40 (2007)

9. Hui, P., Crowcroft, J., Yoneki, E.: Bubble rap: social-based forwarding in delay tolerant networks. In: 9th ACM International Symposium on Mobile Ad Hoc Networking and Computing, pp. 241–250 (2008)

10. Bulut, E., Szymanski, B.K.: Friendship Based Routing in Delay Tolerant Mobile Social Networks. In: IEEE Global Telecommunications Conference (GLOBECOM 2010), pp. 1–5 (2010)

11. Mei, A., Morabito, G., Santi, P., Stefa, J.: Social-aware stateless forwarding in pocket switched networks. In: 30th IEEE International Conference on Computer Communications (INFOCOM 2011), pp. 251–255 (2011)

12. Karagiannis, T., Boudec, J.-Y.L., Vojnovi, M.: Power law and exponential decay of inter contact times between mobile devices. In: 13th Annual ACM International Conference on Mobile Computing and Networking, pp. 183–194 (2007)

13. Gaito, S., Pagani, E., Rossi, G.P.: Fine-Grained Tracking of Human Mobility in Dense Scenarios. In: 6th Annual IEEE Communications Society Conference on Sensor, Mesh and Ad Hoc Communications and Networks (SECON), pp. 40–42 (2009)

14. Albert, R., Barabási, A.-L.: Statistical mechanics of complex networks. Reviews of Modern Physics 74(1), 47–97 (2002)

15. Clauset, A., Shalizi, C.R., Newman, M.E.J.: Power-Law Distributions in Empirical Data. SIAM Review 51(4), 661–703 (2009)

16. Vuong, Q.H.: Likelihood Ratio Tests for Model Selection and Non-Nested Hypotheses. Econometrica 57(2), 307–333 (1989)

Switching of Routing Algorithms in Wireless Networks for Fire Fighting

Chunlei An, Yunqi Luo, and Andreas Timm-Giel

Institute of Communication Networks, Hamburg University of Technology,
Schwarzenbergstr. 95E, 21071 Hamburg, Germany
{chunlei.an,yunqi.luo,timm-giel}@tuhh.de

Abstract. Fire fighters often work in dangerous and dynamic environments, which results in frequent change of network topologies and routing requirements. While the existing routing protocols are not able to cope with such a changeable environment, this paper proposes a self adaptive hybrid routing algorithm. This routing algorithm can switch between the proactive routing algorithm and reactive routing algorithm for each node pair automatically. An analytical model is created to describe the routing switch decision making algorithm. This model is based on a set of the cost functions. A numerical example shows the necessity of switching routing algorithms to reduce the overall control message overhead.

Keywords: Sensor Networks, Adaptive Routing, Hybrid Routing, Fire Fighting.

1   Introduction

Wireless sensor networks play an increasingly relevant role in various emergency and rescue scenarios, one of which is fire fighting. Nowadays fire fighters use different equipment for different functionalities. Each fire fighter needs one communication unit to keep contact with each other. This type of communication can be disturbed in noisy environments. Furthermore, each fire fighter also needs to carry a "dead man" alarm, which generates acoustic alarms when the fire fighter becomes incapacitated. One severe shortcoming of such a device is the limited alarming range. This means that only fire fighters who are close enough to hear the alarm can be informed about it. And it is also not reliable in noisy environments. In some cases the fire fighters have to risk their own safety for checking certain surroundings. This can happen when a fire fighter wants to open the door of a closed room. Due to the fact that the fire fighting gloves are designed with thermal insulation, currently the fire fighters need to take off one of the protective gloves, and put the back of the hand close to the door for estimating the inner room temperature. This may be dangerous if the outside temperature is already high, or the fire fighter touches the door accidentally.

The GloveNet project [1] was funded by the German Federal Ministry of Education and Research (BMBF), and was targeting to solve the aforementioned problems. The main concept of this project was to explore the possibility of

A. Timm-Giel et al. (Eds.): MONAMI 2012, LNICST 58, pp. 258–270, 2013.

building a WSN using intelligent gloves, which have compact sensor modules integrated. This module should provide alternatives to the functionalities mentioned before, so that the fire fighters can be better protected [3].

2   Problem Statement

In the fire fighting scenario depicted in Fig. 1, there are a group of fire fighters in a rescue mission. The red car at the lower left corner represents the command post, which is responsible to coordinating the fire fighting team. This requires it to be aware of the current situation of the scene, as well as of all the fire fighters. Therefore all the information has to be transferred to the command post, which is actually behaving as the sink node in the fire fighting network. The fire fighters are divided into two sub-groups. Both groups can operate shifts if it is needed, and in an emergency the group stays outside can back up the team inside. Complicated indoor environments, such as walls and other obstacles, can lead to severe changes to the radio strength, hence a volatile network topology. Therefore they are considered as mobile nodes in Fig. 2. In contrast, the fire fighters waiting outside are in a less complicated environment, and their movement won't result in frequent connectivity changes. They hereby are seen as static nodes (the middle cloud in Fig. 2).

Different routing schemes may fit different environments. For instance in Fig. 2, due to the frequent change of network topology, a reactive routing algorithm is preferred for the mobile nodes. While a proactive routing scheme may be suitable for the static nodes and the sink node. Thereby a hybrid routing algorithm is expected to show higher performance. Moreover, tasks of the fire fighters can

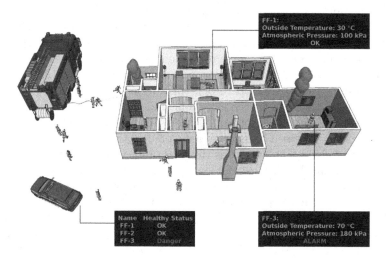

Fig. 1. Fire fighting scenario

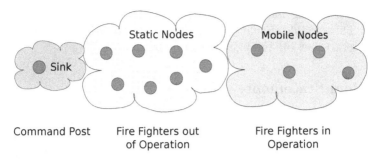

Fig. 2. Abstract network structure of the fire fighting scenario

change, so when some of the static nodes become part of the mobile nodes, their routing scheme should also change accordingly. This requires the adaptability from the routing algorithm.

3   State of the Art

Research towards adaptive and hybrid routing algorithms has been carried out in the recent years.

Figueiredo et al. present a hybrid and adaptive algorithm for routing in WSNs, called Multi-MAF, that adapts its behavior autonomously in response to the variation of network conditions [5]. In particular, the proposed algorithm applies both reactive and proactive strategies for routing infrastructure creation, and uses an event-detection estimation model to change between the strategies to save energy.

In [6] the authors propose a Programmable Routing Framework (PRF) that promotes the adaptability in routing services for WSNs. This framework includes a universal routing service and an automatic deployment service making use of different tunable parameters and programmable components. To change from one routing method to another, the proposed programmable routing framework must be reconfigured (by an operator), this means, it is not able to adjust its routing strategy according to the environmental change automatically.

The ChaMeLeon routing protocol [8] is a hybrid and adaptive routing protocol operating within a defined disaster area denoted as the Critical Area (CA). The main concept behind ChaMeLeon is the adaptability of its routing mechanisms towards changes in the physical and logical state of a MANET, e.g., the rescuers joining or leaving the network. ChaMeLeon adapts its routing behavior according to changes in the network size within a pre-defined CA. For small networks, ChaMeLeon routes data proactively using the Optimized Link State Routing (OLSR) protocol whereas for larger networks it utilizes the reactive Ad Hoc On Demand Distance Vector (AODV) Routing protocol so that overall routing performance is improved.

Another hybrid routing protocol called Adaptive Hybrid Domain Routing (AHDR) is proposed in [9]. AHDR organizes nodes within a 2-hop neighborhood into logical groups called Domains. Each domain has a Domain Lead. The proactive routing scheme disseminates Domain topology information through the network with the help of Bridge Nodes – a subset of nodes that have links to nearby Domain Leads. The reactive routing scheme is used when a source AHDR node does not have a known route to a required destination. This scheme uses only a small subset of the network nodes carry the network routing messages through the network which reduces the AHDR overhead.

In [7] a hybrid routing protocol called Adaptive Periodic Threshold-sensitive Energy Efficient Sensor Network Protocol (APTEEN) is proposed, which allows comprehensive information retrieval. This protocol divides the nodes insides the network into different clusters. Different CDMA schemes are applied to avoid inter-cluster interference, and inside each cluster the access to medium is controlled by TDMA schedules. Furthermore, APTEEN combines the best features of proactive and reactive networks by creating a Hybrid network with that sends data periodically, as well as responds to sudden changes in attribute values. Performance evaluation shows that APTEEN outperforms existing protocols in terms of energy consumption and longevity of the network.

Protocols like PRF, ChaMeLeon, and AHDR are capable to adapt to different network communication situations, but require a thorough switch a routing algorithm in the whole network. Moreover, ChaMeLeon and AHDR are not designed for working on resource constraint devices. The routing protocol APTEEN is designed for resource constraint WSNs. Although it has the keyword adaptive included in its name, no support to adaptability has been explicitly described in the protocol. Due to this reason, it is not considered as an adaptive routing protocol here. Moreover, none of these routing protocols have been optimized for energy efficiency. Taking the project requirements and the literature study into account, a new routing protocol needs to be developed, which then can be combined with positioning for further improvement of the energy efficiency.

4 Self Adaptive Routing Algorithm

The new routing protocol in design should be more flexible to change of the network topology, as well as to the data traffic characteristics. Considering the fact the different nodes, located at different part of the network, may have totally different environments, hence have different requirements to routing algorithms (as discussed in section 2), routing algorithms can be chosen on node pair base. Each individual inside the network is allowed to execute more than one routing algorithm. For instance, node A can communicate with node B in a proactive manner, if they both agree that the link in between is stable. Meanwhile node A may set up a connection with node C using a reactive routing algorithm.

Two important techniques: dynamic neighbor update and mobility detection are investigated, in order to obtain to date link status. The proposed self adaptive hybrid routing algorithm is then explained with an example afterwards.

4.1   Dynamic Neighbor Update

Dynamic neighbor update means that each node is aware of its immediate one-hop-neighbors at all the time. To achieve this, all nodes are periodically sending out beacons. Based on the reception of these beacons, each node maintainsbg a list of its direct neighbors.

Once a node detects a beacon from a previously unknown node, the receiving node will add the sending node to its own neighbor list. An entry in this dynamically created list contains the neighbor's address, the Received Signal Strength Indication (RSSI) of the last received beacon, and a Time To Live (TTL) integer. The RSSI value is used for the mobility detection and the TTL value determines the lifetime of the connection as follows.

A periodical timer has been implemented to detect the loss of a connection. Every time the timer expires, all entries of the neighbor list are processed once. First the TTL value of each entry is decreased by one. If the newly computed TTL value of a certain entry is now equal to zero, the corresponding neighboring node of this entry is considered lost, and therefore is deleted from the neighbor list.

Every time a node receives the beacon of an already known neighbor, it searches the according entry in the neighbor list and resets the TTL value to the default value. This will prevent this neighbor from timing out. Based on the above described method of maintaining a neighbor list, three parameters are considered critical for the live time of a connection: the TTL value, the TTL timer period and the beacon sending frequency. These values have to be tuned so that a lost connection is detected as fast as possible, meanwhile a few lost beacons should not result in a dropped connection.

4.2   Mobility Detection

Mobility Detection means that one node can detect if itself is moving or that other nodes are moving relatively to it. In this paper a method based on RSSI is implemented and tested. This method tracks the RSSI value of the nodes in the immediate neighborhood. This information is used to decide which nodes are moving relatively to the currently tracking node.

RSSI Based Mobility Detection. To detect if a neighbor is moving either towards or away from a node, the node uses the information from the neighbor list. It works in conjunction with the above described procedure. On reception of a packet the receiving node will check its neighbor list for the entry of the sender. If the sender is known, the RSSI value of the new packet will be compared to the previously saved value. Otherwise, it will be added to the list.

In the case that the RSSI value has decreased more than the specified threshold value, the neighbor will be assumed to be moving away. The TTL value for this neighbor will then be reduced, which effectively implies that the connection times out faster. In the current implementation it has been chosen to halve the

TTL value. This is done for testing the concept, and the value can be further optimized.

Two parameters, namely the beacon frequency and the RSSI threshold, mainly impact the speed of detecting a node's movement.

If the beacon frequency is set too high, it can theoretically happen that the difference between any two consecutively measured RSSI values is always lower than the threshold, even if the node is moving. However, this has not been observed in the simulations.

This RSSI based mobility detection has been proven to work quite nicely in TOSSIM [2]. It has been observed that in simulation scenarios with mobility, the reduction of connection timeout further reduces the packet loss by about 10%.

4.3   Self Adaptive Hybrid Routing

An example scenario (Figure 3) illustrates the situation where a self adaptive hybrid routing protocol can be applied. This network includes a proactive sub-network, which is composed of six nodes (n1-n6). With the help of the techniques described in section 4.1 and 4.2, each individual within this sub-network identi-fies its direct adjacent neighbors as in a static status. Hereby proactive routing protocol, e.g., OLSR, is utilized for inter node communication. Other nodes are supposed to be moving arbitrarily, so they use a reactive routing algorithm to exchange information, say AODV.

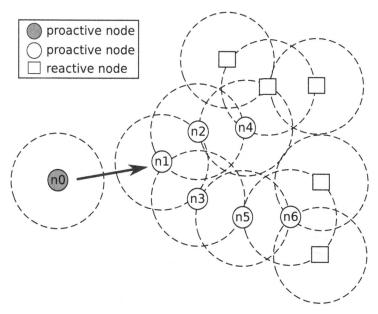

Fig. 3. Example Network Contains Nodes Using Both Proactive and Reactive Routing

Now the node n0 is approaching n1, and is getting stabilized. Thus according to the aforementioned techniques, n0 and n1 can take each other as a stable neighbor, and set up a proactive connection. The creation of this new connection cause topology change to the proactive sub-network (n1-n6), and triggers link states update through this sub-network. Similarly, if a node is leaving a proactive sub-network, the members of the corresponding proactive sub-network must update their link states again. It can thus be concluded, that the change of routing algorithms only affects nodes belonging to the proactive sub-network. Here arises the question: does the decision of switching routing algorithms make sense?

The primary idea of switching between different routing algorithms is to improve the overall routing performance. In the fire fighting scenario, this means to improve the transmission efficiency, i.e., to reduce the amount of control overheads. A decision of switching routing algorithms should be made only if this criteria is satisfied.

5   Analytical Model

Section 4 shows the necessity of making a reasonable routing algorithm switching decision. In the following subsections a preliminary analytical model is created with the aim to describe the decision making logic.

5.1   Routing Algorithm Switch Decision Making

A set of cost functions Equation 1-5 are defined to represent the basis of routing algorithm switch decision. The objective is to minimize the overall cost. The cost consists of two parts: the extra cost for switching to another routing scheme $Cost_{Switch}$ and the cost of using a routing scheme $Cost_{Algorithm}$ (Equation 2). Different from $Cost_{Switch}$, which is a once only expense, $Cost_{Algorithm}$ is time dependent. Equation 3 gives the definition of $Cost_{Switch}$. This cost is solely dependent on the number of overhead message, whose output is scaled to the range $0 \leq Cost_{Switch} \leq 1$ by the correspondent scaling function f_s^{Switch}. The result is further weighted by a weighting factor α, which lies in the range $0 \leq \alpha \leq 1$. $Cost_{Algorithm}$ is defined in Equation 4. This cost depends on the current routing scheme over time period t. $f_s^{Algorithm}$ and β are the scaling function and the weighting factor, accordingly. The sum of α and β should be 1. Depending on different routing scheme, the value of α and β could be different.

As discussed in [11], different scaling functions can be chosen depending on different criterion value range. In this work it is assumed that the values of all the parameters are limited by their respective minimums and maximums. Therefore the general form of scaling functions f_s^{Switch} and $f_s^{Algorithm}$ are represented by linear functions given in Equation 5, where m and n are constants that are determined by the respective minimum and maximum.

$$Objective : min(Cost) \tag{1}$$

$$Cost = \alpha Cost_{Switch} + \beta \int_t Cost_{Algorithm}(t)dt \tag{2}$$

$$Cost_{Switch} = f_s^{Switch}(Overhead_{Switch}^{CtrMsg}) \tag{3}$$

$$Cost_{Algorithm} = f_s^{Algorithm}(Overhead_{Algorithm}^{CtrMsg}) \tag{4}$$

$$f_s(x) = mx + n; \qquad x_{min} < x < x_{max} \tag{5}$$

The observation time period t is predefined and fixed. This set of cost functions are periodically applied with the time interval t. In the case that there are two routing algorithms available in a given network, say AODV and OLSR. Every time when t amount of time elapsed, the cost functions are called and the cost of using each algorithm is computed accordingly. If the current routing algorithm (say AODV) is about to cause a higher cost than the other one (OLSR) in the next t amount of time, a routing algorithm switching could be triggered. However, the final decision of whether to replace the current routing algorithm with the other candidate routing algorithm also depends on the switching expense, namely $Overhead_{Switch}^{CtrMsg}$. If the overall cost (Equation 2) of using the candidate routing algorithm (here OLSR) is higher than that of the current one, then it makes no sense to perform a routing algorithm switching in the next t amount of time (Equation 1).

Another thing to note is that the computation of $Overhead_{Algorithm}^{CtrMsg}$ may require knowledge from the past, such as the mean of initialized application traffics, and the mean of link breakages, which is usually a result of mobility. This information is updated after every observation time period t, and is used to estimate the cost of different routing algorithms in the next t.

From Equation 1-5 it can be seen that the most important thing to decide the decision making cost is to determine $Overhead_{Switch}^{CtrMsg}$ and $Overhead_{Algorithm}^{CtrMsg}$. They will be explained in more detail in the following sections.

5.2   Control Traffic Overhead by Routing Algorithms

In [10] control traffic overhead of different MANET routing protocols are studied. Routing protocols are classified as proactive and reactive routing protocols. The study shows that the control message overhead of different routing protocols is influenced by both network topology and the data traffic. A model is created (Equation 6-9) to show the computation of the number of control messages under different circumstances.

$$Reactive\ Fixed : \qquad N_{rf} = \lambda_{route}O_r N^2 + h_r N \tag{6}$$

$$Reactive\ with\ Mobility: \qquad N_{rm} = O_r \mu a L N^2 \qquad (7)$$

$$Proactive\ Fixed: \qquad N_{pf} = h_p N + O_p t_p N^2 \qquad (8)$$

$$Proactive\ with\ Mobility: \qquad N_{pm} = O_p \mu A N_p N^2 \qquad (9)$$

Equation 6 shows the amount of control messages N_{rf} when using a reactive routing algorithm. These messages include the periodic hello message, which are used to detect broken links. They are needed to maintain the basic functional features of the routing protocol, irrespective of nodes' mobility. They are supposed to be constant once the network, as well as the application, is configured. While Equation 7 describes how to calculate the amount of control messages caused by mobility. It is not difficult to find out the linear relationship between N_{rm} and μa (given $O_r L N^2$ is constant). This linear relationship can be further extended to $N_{rf} + N_{rm}$ and μa. Similarly, Equations 8-9 are for proactive routing protocols, and there exists the linear relationship between $N_{pf} + N_{pm}$ and μ.

The meaning of the parameters is given in Tables 1-2.

Table 1. Network and Traffic Parameters

(a) Network parameters

Network parameters	
N	number of nodes
μ	link breakage rate (mobility)
L	average length of a route

(b) Data traffic parameters

Traffic parameters	
λ_{route}	route creation rate per node
a	number of active routes per node (activity)

Table 2. Routing Protocol Parameters

(a) Proactive routing parameters

Proactive protocol parameters	
h_p	hello rate
t_p	topology broadcast rate
O_p	broadcast optimization factor
AN_p	active next hops ratio

(b) Reactive routing parameters

Reactive protocol parameters	
h_r	hello rate (0 when possible)
O_r	route request optimization factor

$Overhead_{Algorithm}^{CtrMsg}$ refers to the overall control message overhead, which consists of the control messages generated both when the node is static and mobile. Therefore, it can be expressed as in Equation 10.

$$Overhead_{Algorithm}^{CtrMsg} = N_{pf} + N_{pm}$$
$$or \qquad\qquad\qquad\qquad (10)$$
$$Overhead_{Algorithm}^{CtrMsg} = N_{rf} + N_{rm}$$

Based on the simulation results (50 nodes), [10] gives Fig. 4 and 5 to prove the existence of the linear relationship between routing overhead $N_{rf} + N_{rm}$ and μa in AODV, and between $N_{pf} + N_{pm}$ and μ in OLSR.

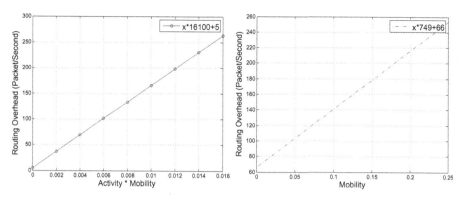

Fig. 4. Routing overhead AODV [10]   **Fig. 5.** Routing overhead OLSR [10]

One numerical example can help to have a better understanding of these two curves. In Fig. 5 is mobility μ equals to 0.1, the routing overhead of OLSR is around 140 packet per second. While using AODV, the amount of control overhead also depends on the traffic activity a. Taking $\mu = 0.1$ into account, if a is very low, say 0.02, μa will have the value of 0.002. In this case AODV's routing overhead is about 43 packets per second, which is significantly lower than that of OLSR. Therefore AODV should be used. However, if a increases to 0.12, the amount of AODV routing overhead jumps to around 200 packets per second. So OLSR is preferred.

Fig. 6 shows the routing overhead versus the nodes mobility and activity of the given network. The inclined plane represents the OLSR routing protocol, and the cambered surface represents the AODV routing protocol. It can be observed that OLSR causes higher routing overhead when the network activity is very low, irrespective of the node mobility. Therefore the reactive routing protocol AODV is preferred. OLSR outperforms AODV when the network activity increases. This is due to the fact that AODV needs to perform the route discovery process for each new data delivery request.

5.3   Control Traffic Overhead by Switching of Routing Algorithms

As it is discussed in Section 4, a routing algorithm switch only affects the proactive sub-network. Therefore, $Overhead_{Switch}^{CtrMsg}$ solely depends on the characteristics of the proactive routing protocol. For instance, in OLSR only a node's MultiPoint Relays (MPRs) are responsible to rebroadcast the according TC messages, i.e., the number of control messages is equal to the number of this node's MPR N_{MPR} (see Equation 11).

$$Overhead_{Switch}^{CtrMsg} = N_{MPR} \qquad (11)$$

In [10] the average number of MPRs is deduced from a set of simulation results, therefore it is difficult to judge the reliability of this value. In [4] an analytical model of the MPR selection algorithm is given under the assumption that all

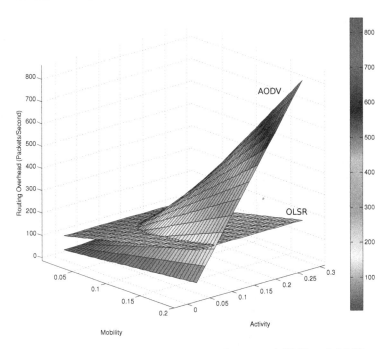

Fig. 6. Routing overhead comparison between AODV and OLSR

nodes are uniformly distributed. This model can be used for estimating the number of MPRs for a given node (Equations 12-14).

$$P(u \in MPR_1) \geq \frac{2}{R^2} P(d_0^+(u) > 0) \int_0^R \int_R^{R+r} f(x, r, R) e^{-\lambda(2\pi R^2 - A_1(R, x, R))} r \, dx \, dr \tag{12}$$

$$f(x, r, R) = -\frac{\lambda}{1 - e^{-\lambda(A_1(R, r, R) - \pi R^2)}} \left(\frac{\partial}{\partial x} A_1(x, r, R) - 2\pi x\right) e^{-\lambda(A_1(x, r, R) - \pi x^2)} \tag{13}$$

$$E[|MPR_1|] = \lambda \pi R^2 P(u \in MPR_1) \tag{14}$$

MPR_1 denotes the number of MPRs, which are selected in the first step of the Greedy MPR Heuristic. If node 0 is the current node, and u is one of 0's neighbors. From node 0's point of view, Equation 12 describes the lower bound of the probability that u belongs to MPR_1. $d_0^+(u)$ denotes the number of 0's two-hop neighbors, that are reachable via u. R is the radio transmission range. $A_1(R, x, R)$ refers to the union area of two discs of radius R, and x is the distance between the two disc centers. λ refers to the mean number of points by surface unit.

$f(x, r, R)$ is the probabilistic distribution function of nodes distribution, and is detailed in Equation 13. $\lambda \pi R^2$ is actually the expected number of neighbors of a given node, therefore the expectation of MPR_1 can be calculated using Equation 14.

Through running simulations, authors of [10] further proves that about 75% of the MPRs are included in MPR_1.

5.4 Routing Algorithm Co-existence

The numerical example in 5.2 can be further used to explain necessity of routing algorithm co-existence.

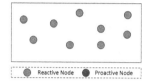   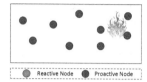   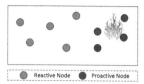

Fig. 7. Reactive Routing   **Fig. 8.** Proactive Routing   **Fig. 9.** Hybrid Routing

Imagine that all the 50 nodes are fire fighters, and they always have the same mobility characteristics, i.e., μ remains unchanged (equals to 0.1).

1. There are not many new events in the whole network ($a=0.02$), and all nodes use AODV for routing (Fig. 7). This results in the routing overhead of 43 packets per second.
2. In part of the network frequent new events, such as fire, are detected (Fig. 8). This means the increase of a (from 0.02 to 0.12, for instance). Keeping using AODV leads to a significant increase of the routing overhead - 200 packets per second. Due to the fact that OLSR generates less control message overhead (140 packets per second), all nodes should change to use OLSR.
3. If routing algorithm co-existence is possible, the overall routing overhead can be further reduced by using such a hybrid routing protocol. Assume that only half of the fire fighters are in the area where new events happen, then it turns out that only they need more intensive data exchange. Therefore only these half of the fire fighters change to use OLSR, and the rest remain using AODV (Fig. 9). This results in $\frac{43}{2} + \frac{140}{2} \approx 92$ routing control messages.

Table 3 summarizes the results discussed above. Note that there is no need of using the hybrid routing protocol when a equals 0.02 in this example, because all nodes are in the same situation.

Table 3. Routing overhead of AODV, OLSR and Hybrid Routing

	AODV	OLSR	Hybrid
$a=0.02$	43	140	-
$a=0.12$	200	140	92

6   Conclusion and Future Work

It is shown in the previous sections, for some real WSN application scenarios, a routing scheme which supports both proactive and reactive routing is needed. This paper proposes a self adaptive hybrid routing algorithm, which can automatically switch between the proactive routing and reactive routing based on the current situation or that of the near future. An analytical model, which is based on a set of cost functions, is established to describe the decision making algorithm. The total cost consists of two parts, one part is the cost for switching routing algorithm, and another part is the cost for using a routing scheme. An algorithm switch won't be performed, unless the overall cost after switching is going to be reduced.

For the future work, the proposed routing algorithm is to be evaluated in simulations.

References

1. Glovenet project, http://www.mrc-bremen.de/glovenet
2. Tinyos tutorial: Tossim, http://docs.tinyos.net/index.php/TOSSIM
3. An, C., Timm-Giel, A.: Applying wireless sensor networks in fire fighting. In: Pentikousis, K., Aguiar, R., Sargento, S., Agüero, R. (eds.) MONAMI 2011. LNICST, vol. 97, pp. 386–395. Springer, Heidelberg (2012)
4. Busson, A., Mitton, N., Fleury, E.: Analysis of the multi-point relay selection in OLSR and implications. Challenges in Ad Hoc Networking (2006)
5. Figueiredo, C.M.S., Nakamura, E.F., Loureiro, A.A.F.: A hybrid adaptive routing algorithm for Event-Driven wireless sensor networks. Sensors 9, 7287–7307 (2009)
6. He, Y., Raghavendra, C.S., Berson, S., Braden, B.: A programmable routing framework for autonomic sensor networks. In: Proc. Autonomic Computing Workshop, 5th Annual International Workshop on Active Middleware Services (AMS 2003), pp. 60–68 (2003)
7. Manjeshwar, A., Agrawal, D.: APTEEN: a hybrid protocol for efficient routing and comprehensive information retrieval in wireless sensor networks. In: Proceedings of the International Parallel and Distributed Processing Symposium, IPDPS, pp. 195–202 (2002)
8. Ramrekha, T., Panaousis, E., Millar, G., Politis, C.: A hybrid and adaptive routing protocol for Emergency Situations. Request for Comments, Internet Engineering Task Force, IETF (February 2010)
9. Ghanadan, R.: Adaptive hybrid domain routing, AHDR (2010), http://tools.ietf.org/html/draft-ghanadan-manet-ahdr-00
10. Viennot, L., Jacquet, P., Clausen, T.H.: Analyzing control traffic overhead versus mobility and data traffic activity in mobile Ad-Hoc network protocols. Wirel. Netw. 10(4), 447–455 (2004), http://dx.doi.org/10.1023/B:WINE.0000028548.44719.fe
11. Wenning, B.: Context-Based Routing in Dynamic Networks, 2010th edn. Vieweg and Teubner (August 2010)

A Re-optimization Approach for Virtual Network Embedding

Márcio Melo[1,2], Jorge Carapinha[1], Susana Sargento[2], Ulrich Killat[3], and Andreas Timm-Giel[3]

[1] Portugal Telecom Inovação, Aveiro, Portugal
{marcio-d-melo,jorgec}@ptinovacao.pt
[2] Instituto de Telecomunicações, University of Aveiro, Aveiro, Portugal
susana@ua.pt
[3] Institute of Communication Networks, Hamburg University of Technology, Hamburg, Germany
{killat,timm-giel}@tuhh.de

Abstract. Network Virtualization is claimed to be a key component of the Future Internet by enabling the coexistence of heterogeneous (virtual) networks in the same physical infrastructure, providing the dynamic creation and support of different networks with different paradigms and mechanisms in the same physical network. A major challenge in the dynamic provision of virtual networks resides in the optimal embedding solution of virtual resources into physical ones.

Since this problem is known to be $\mathcal{NP}$-hard, previous research focused on designing heuristic-based algorithms; most of them do not consider either a simultaneous optimization of the node and the link mapping or the re-optimization of VNs, leading to non-optimal solutions.

This paper proposes an extension of Virtual Network Embedding - Node-Link Formulation to support the re-optimization of existing VNs and to provide the optimal bound. It also presents an evaluation of the proposed approach when applied to a previous heuristic in the literature. Simulation experiments show significant improvements when using the VN re-optimization process: not only the bandwidth consumption have been reduced by 17.5%, but the same is true for the maximum utilization levels on the CPU and on the memory.

Keywords: Assignment, Embedding, ILP, Mapping, NP-Hard, Network Virtualization, Optimization, Re-Optimization, Virtual Network.

1 Introduction

Network Virtualization has gained an increasing prominence in the last few years. Initially, the interest in network virtualization was mainly pushed by Future Internet research initiatives [1,2,3,4], mainly with the objective to find a platform on which novel Internet architectures could be experimented and evaluated without limitations or constraints, namely those associated with the traditional IP model.

A. Timm-Giel et al. (Eds.): MONAMI 2012, LNICST 58, pp. 271–283, 2013.

Later on, it became clear that virtualization could constitute a key component of next-generation Internet architecture itself [5], and not just as a mere platform for experimentation. Perhaps more importantly for network operators, it also became clear that network virtualization could provide a number of short/medium term business advantages, with potential reduction of costs and increase of revenues, as an interesting tool from an operational point of view [6,7].

Although there is a large interest on virtualized networks both from the research community and network operators, several challenges still prevent them from being deployed in real environments [8]. One of the major obstacles lies in providing the exact embedding[1] solution of a Virtual Network (VN) into a physical network. Some solutions to this problem were already proposed [9,10,11], mostly based on heuristic approaches; however, they have failed to provide the optimal solution for each VN mapping. An earlier publication [12] proposed a mathematical formulation, Virtual Network Embedding - Node-Link Formulation (VNE-NLF), that uses Integer Linear Programming (ILP) to provide the optimal bound. However, the optimal re-assignment of VNs previously embedded was not considered.

This paper focuses on the VN re-optimization process: it proposes an extension to VNE-NLF to support the re-optimization of VNs previously assigned, providing an optimal bound. First, the performance of VNE-NLF is analyzed, where it is compared with a heuristic, the Virtual Network Embedding - Enhanced Shortest-Path Heuristic (VNE-ESPH) [12]. Second, the re-optimization approach is proposed and compared to VNE-NLF. Simulation experiments show significant improvements when using the VN re-optimization process. Not only the bandwidth consumption has been reduced by 17.5%, but it has also reduced the maximum utilization levels on either the CPU and the memory, where it achieves maximum levels of utilization 20% and 16% lower, respectively.

The rest of the paper is organized as follows. After summarizing the related work in section 2, section 3 describes the virtual network embedding problem, and explains the mathematical formulation proposed to support the VN re-optimization on the assignment process. Section 4 analyzes the performance of both the VNE-NLF and of the VNE-ESPH, and also evaluates the performance of the re-optimization process when compared to VNE-NLF. Section 5 concludes the paper and describes the future work.

2   Related Work

The simultaneous node and link mapping optimization can be formulated as an un-splittable flow problem [9], known to be $\mathcal{NP}$-hard, and therefore, it is only tractable for a small amount of nodes and links. In order to solve this problem, several approaches have been suggested, mostly considering the *off-line* version of the problem where the VN requests are fully known in advance.

---

[1] The terms embedding, mapping and assignment are used interchangeably in this paper.

In [13] a backtracking method based on sub-graph isomorphism was proposed; it considers the on-line version of the mapping problem, where the VN requests are not known in advance, and proposes a single stage approach where nodes and links are mapped simultaneously, taking constraints into consideration at each step of the mapping. When a bad mapping decision is detected, a backtrack to the previous valid mapping decision is made, avoiding a costly re-map.

The work in [14] defines a set of premises about the virtual topology, i.e. the backbone nodes are star-connected and the access-nodes connect to a single backbone node. Based on these premises, an iterative algorithm is run, with different steps for core and access mapping. However, the algorithm can only work for specific topologies.

A distributed algorithm was studied in [15]. It considers that the virtual topologies can be decomposed in hub-and-spoke clusters, and that each cluster can be mapped independently, therefore reducing the complexity of the full VN mapping. This proposal has lower performance and scalability when compared with centralized approaches.

Zhu et al. [9] proposed a heuristic, centralized, algorithm to deal with VN embedding. The goal of the algorithm is to maintain a low and balanced load of both nodes and links of the substrate network. However, the load of nodes and links does not consider heterogeneity on their characteristics.

Yu et al. [10] proposed an embedding algorithm which considers finite resources on the physical network, and enables path splitting (i.e. virtual link composed by different paths) and link migration (i.e. to change the underlying mapping) during the embedding process. However, this level of freedom can lead to a level of fragmentation that is infeasible to work on large scale networks. In [11], a formal approach was taken to solve the on-line VN embedding problem using a mixed integer programming formulation in a two-step approach. This approach, despite providing a better coordinated node and link mapping, does not solve the VN assignment problem, and does not support heterogeneity of nodes.

Butt et al. [16] proposed a topology-aware heuristic for VN embedding and also suggested a set of algorithms to avoid bottlenecks on the physical infrastructure, where they consider virtual node reallocation and link reassignment for this purpose. Nogueira et al. [17] proposed a heuristic that takes into account the heterogeneity of the VNs and also of the physical infrastructure. The algorithm is evaluated by means of simulation and also on a small scale testbed, where it achieves mapping times of the order of tens of milliseconds.

Botero et al. [18] proposed an algorithm to solve the VN embedding problem considering also the CPU demand by the hidden hops. Lu et al. [19] proposed an adaptive algorithm based on multi-commodity flows to solve the VN embedding. Chowdhury et al. [20] extended his preliminary results [11] and included a generalized window-based VN embedding to evaluate the effect of look ahead on the mapping of VNs. Melo et al. proposed in [12] a mathematical formulation to solve the VN mapping using ILP, and compared it with the heuristic in [17].

Although all these algorithms provide a solution for the VN mapping problem, the optimal re-assignment of existing VNs is not considered. This is the purpose of this paper, which evaluates both VNE-NLF ILP embedding approach and its heuristic (the VNE-ESPH), and proposes the optimal re-assignment of VNs currently embedded through VNE-NLF.

3   Problem Description and Mathematical Formulation Extension

In this section, we start with the description of the VN assignment problem. The mathematical model extension for VN re-optimization is then presented.

3.1   Network Description

We consider a physical network with a given number of nodes, N, and with a given topology, as depicted in figure 1a. Each node is described by the number of Central Processing Units (CPUs), which corresponds to letter C in the figure, the clock CPU frequency, F, and by the Random Access Memory (RAM) amount it possesses, M. With respect to the links, we consider the bandwidth capacity, B, and we assume that each link is a unidirectional link. Virtual networks are described the same way as physical networks, as shown in figure 1b. We use superscript to distinguish virtual from physical resources, where the letter P is used for the physical resources, e.g. C^P, and the letter V is used for virtual resources, e.g. C^V. The convention used for the index notation is: i, j for nodes and links in the physical network, and m, n for nodes and links in the VN.

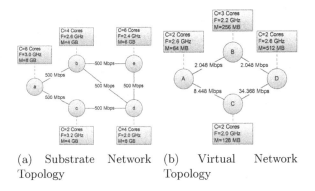

(a)   Substrate   Network   (b)   Virtual   Network
Topology   Topology

Fig. 1. Network Topology Description

3.2 Mathematical Formulation Extension - Re-optimization Support

An extension to VNE-NLF [12] is proposed in order to support the embedding problem of VNs using re-optimization. The proposed formulation only uses two assignment variables for the VN mapping problem: one for the assignment of the virtual nodes to physical nodes, and another to express the assignment of virtual links into physical links. The binary variable x is used for the virtual nodes and is expressed in equation (1), where $x_i^m \to W^V \times N^P$ matrix (and $W^V = \sum_k N^{V_k}$ which is the sum of all virtual network size's currently embedded on the physical network). For the virtual links, the binary variable y is used and it is represented in equation (2), where $y_{ij}^{mn} \to (W^V)^2 \times (N^P)^2$ matrix.

The objective function is represented in equation (3) and achieves two goals: the primary goal is to minimize the maximum load per physical resource and, in the case of having different mapping solutions with the same maximum utilization, the second part of the objective function is activated which will opt for the solution which consumes the lowest bandwidth, where ϵ represents a small constant.

Assignment Variables

$$x_i^m = \begin{cases} 1, \text{virtual node } m \text{ is allocated at physical node } i \\ 0, else \end{cases} \quad (1)$$

$$y_{ij}^{mn} = \begin{cases} 1, \text{virtual link } mn \text{ uses physical link } ij \\ 0, else \end{cases} \quad (2)$$

Optimization Function

$$minimize\ \mathcal{C}_{max}^{load} + \mathcal{M}_{max}^{load} + \mathcal{B}_{max}^{load} + \epsilon \times \sum_{m,n \in N^V(m), n<m} y_{ij}^{mn} \times B_{mn}^V \quad (3)$$

Constraints

(Maximum) Resource Utilization of the CPU

$$\forall i : F_i^P \times \frac{C_i^P + \sum_m x_i^m \times C_m^V}{C_i^P(0)} \leq \mathcal{C}_{max}^{load} \quad (4)$$

(Maximum) Resource Utilization of the Memory

$$\forall i : F_i^P \times \frac{M_i^P + \sum_m x_i^m \times M_m^V}{M_i^P(0)} \leq \mathcal{M}_{max}^{load} \quad (5)$$

(Maximum) Resource Utilization of the Bandwidth

$$\forall i,j \in N^P(i), i < j : \frac{B_{ij}^P + \sum_{m,n \in N^V(m)} y_{ij}^{mn} \times B_{mn}^V}{B_{ij}^P(0)} \leq \mathcal{B}_{max}^{load} \quad (6)$$

Assignment of virtual nodes to physical nodes

$$\forall m : \sum_i x_i^m = 1 \tag{7}$$

One virtual node per physical node

$$\forall k, \forall i : \sum_{m \in VN_k} x_i^m \le 1 \tag{8}$$

Multi-commodity flow conservation with $node-link$ formulation

$$\forall m, n \in N^V(m), m < n, \forall i : \sum_{j \in N^P(i)} (y_{ij}^{mn} - y_{ji}^{mn}) = x_i^m - x_i^n \tag{9}$$

CPU conservation

$$\forall i : \sum_m x_i^m \times C_m^V \le C^{P_i} \tag{10}$$

Memory conservation

$$\forall i : \sum_m x_i^m \times M_m^V \le M^{P_i} \tag{11}$$

Bandwidth conservation

$$\forall i, j \in N^P(i), i < j : \sum_{m,n \in N^V(m), m<n} B_{mn}^V \times (y_{ij}^{mn} + y_{ji}^{mn}) \le B_{ij}^P \tag{12}$$

CPU frequency requisite

$$\forall i : \sum_m x_i^m \times F_m^V \le F_i^P \tag{13}$$

Remarks
The (maximum) utilization per resource type, i.e. memory RAM ($\mathcal{M}_{max}^{load}$), CPU ($\mathcal{C}_{max}^{load}$), and bandwidth ($\mathcal{B}_{max}^{load}$), is represented in equations (4),(5),(6), respectively, where C_i^P represents the currently available capacity and $C_i^P(0)$ represents the total capacity. The resource utilization on the CPU and on the memory is also multiplied by the CPU frequency, in order to firstly use physical nodes with lower CPU frequency and to preserve the remaining for virtual nodes with higher CPU frequency demand. Therefore, the second term of (4) and (5) is not only the maximum resource utilization, but it is the CPU frequency multiplied by the resource utilization either on the CPU or on the memory.

Equation (7) ensures that each virtual node is assigned and it is to just one physical node.

In order to support the re-optimization process, equation (8) is proposed and differs from the initial formulation [12] once it takes into consideration all the VNs that are currently assigned, and not only one VN request. Equation (8), is also used to guarantee that each physical node accommodates, in maximum, one virtual node per VN[2], where k is used to represent all VNs running on that specific physical node. However, each physical node can accommodate, in principle, more virtual nodes from other VNs (i.e. VN_k).

In order to optimize the mapping of the virtual links and at the same time to cope with the optimization of the virtual nodes, the multi-commodity flow constraint [21] is applied with a $node - link$ formulation [22], and the notion of direct flows on the virtual links is also used, which is represented in equation (9). To ensure that the available capacity at the CPU, memory and bandwidth is not exceeded, equations (10), (11) and (12) are used, respectively. Finally, equation (13) is used to guarantee that we do not violate that requirement on the CPU frequency.

4   Evaluation Results

In this section we depict our main results. Our evaluation is primarily focused, on the impact due the VN size and due to the physical network size, on VN acceptance ratio according to the VN size, i.e. the number of virtual nodes, and also on the number of VNs that can be accommodated on the physical network using the proposed model. We compare the VNE-NLF with the VNE-ESPH [12] embedding approach, and we then evaluate the performance, in terms of resource utilization, of the re-optimization proposal when compared to VNE-NLF.

4.1   Simulation Parameters - VNE-NLF and VNE-ESPH

In order to evaluate the VNE-NLF and the VNE-ESPH, we have implemented a discrete event simulator in Matlab®. The physical network topology was created using the Waxman random topology generation method [23], and the number of physical nodes was set to 30, 40 and 50, according to the evaluated scenario.

The recommended parameters for link probability, $\alpha = 0.4$ and $\beta = 0.1$, were used although some topologies did not have full connectivity, i.e. one physical node with no viable path to all the remaining nodes (e.g. a node with no links or non-connected clusters). In order to circumvent this, after generating the topology, additional links were added to the nodes with fewer interfaces, until total connectivity was reached.

For each substrate node, a set of parameters was attributed using an uniform distribution, such as RAM amount, number of CPUs and CPU frequency. The physical link's bandwidth was set to a fixed bitrate.

The VNs requests were created using the same topology generation model, and the number of virtual nodes was fixed from 2 to 10 virtual nodes with intervals of 2 nodes, where the size of the VN was changed according to the evaluated scenario. After generating the virtual topology, the same set of specifications was assigned, with a uniform distribution. Either the physical network or the virtual network specifications can be observed on table 1.

---

[2] This assumption is also taken by other authors, i.e., [9,10,11].

We assume that each VN request arrives according to a Poisson process, and that each VN has an associated lifetime with an average of $1/\mu = 75$ time units, following an exponential distribution. Regarding the average number of VN requests per time unit, they are set to 1.8 VN requests per time unit. For each considered size of VN, 10 trials were performed. For each trial, a new set of VN requests and new physical network topology were generated. All simulations were set to run until 1000 time units. A confidence interval of 95% is used for every result presented below. The CPLEX [24] version 12 was used to solve the linear programming problem, and a time limit of 600 seconds was defined for each VN mapping, although most VNs were embedded in hundreds of milliseconds.

4.2   Simulation Results - VNE-NLF and VNE-ESPH

This section compares VNE-NLF with VNE-ESPH methods through several metrics: VN request acceptance ratio, number of VNs that were running after the simulation experiment was finished, average resource utilization, e.g. memory RAM and CPU, on the nodes, and average bandwidth utilization on the links.

The VN request acceptance ratio is depicted in Fig. 2a. It decays linearly with the VN size for both embedding methods, which is due to the fact that both try to accommodate more virtual resources with the same amount of physical resources available; the slope is sharper for the case of the VNE-ESPH. Therefore, we can infer that the performance of the heuristic is influenced by the size of the virtual network. We can also infer that the size of the physical network influences significantly the VN request acceptance ratio, where smaller physical networks are more prone to reject VN requests. Another important aspect to retain is the fact that the VNE-NLF method applied on a physical network with 40 physical nodes is able to have the same VN request acceptance ratio as the VNE-ESPH method applied on a physical network with 50 nodes, which is 20% larger.

The average number of accommodated VNs is presented in Fig. 2b. The number of VNs running on the substrate decays linearly with the VN request size for both embedding methods, and the slope is sharper in the case of the heuristic. This kind of behavior is expected once we are trying to embed larger VNs with the same amount of physical resources, although the total number of virtual nodes is almost the same. If we consider the case of a physical network with 50 physical nodes and running the VNE-NLF as a embedding method, we have the

Table 1. Physical Network and Virtual Network Parameters

Parameters	Physical Network	Virtual Network
N. CPUs	{2; 4; 6}	{1; 2; 3; 4 }
CPU Frequency (GHz)	{2.0 to 3.2 in 0.2 steps }	{2.0 to 2.6 in 0.1 steps }
RAM Memory (GB)	{2; 4; 6; 8}	{64; 128; 256; 512 }
Link Bandwidth (Mbps)	{500}	{2.048; 8.448; 34.368}

same number of virtual nodes running on the substrate either with VN requests of 8 nodes or with VN requests of 10 nodes, i.e. $8 \times 100 = 10 \times 80$.

The average CPU utilization is shown in Fig. 2c. The same levels of average CPU utilization, i.e. 75%, are reached in the VNE-NLF, independent either on the physical network size or on the virtual network size. Regarding the VNE-ESPH, the average CPU utilization does depend on the virtual network size, and for VNs larger or equal to 4 virtual nodes, the average CPU utilization starts to decay linearly with the VN size. This is strongly related with the VN acceptance ratio which is lower for VNs with the same network size; this embedding method performs worse with larger VNs.

The average memory utilization as a function of the VN size is depicted in Fig. 2d. The same behavior is perceived for the average memory utilization as for the average CPU utilization for both embedding methods. The average memory utilization reaches values of 80% for both embedding methods, although the average memory utilization using the VNE-ESPH starts to decay with VNs larger than 4 nodes.

The average bandwidth utilization is depicted in Fig. 2e. The same behavior is perceived for both the average bandwidth utilization and the average memory or CPU utilization, where the average bandwidth utilization reaches values of 80%. The average memory utilization reaches values of 80% for both embedding methods, although the average bandwidth utilization using the VNE-ESPH starts to decay with VNs larger than 4 nodes.

4.3 Re-optimization

This section, presents the simulation results obtained using the optimization method VNE-NLF, and its extension for re-optimization of virtual network embedding. Our evaluation is primary focused on the minimum and maximum resource utilization on the CPU and on the memory, and on the average bandwidth utilization.

The simulation parameters applied here are the same as in 4.1, except for the physical and the VN size. VN requests ranging from 0.8 VN per time unit to 1.8 VN per time unit were considered. Regarding the re-optimization process, the results were obtained using a virtual machine configured with 4 cores (Intel Xeon X5650@2.67GHz) and the CPLEX was set to use up to 4 threads, the relative gap tolerance was set to 0.05 (i.e. feasible integer solution proved to be within percent of optimal), and a time limit of 24 hours was used in order to avoid long time simulations. However, most of the re-optimizations were performed within the 24 hours' time frame.

The maximum and minimum CPU utilization are depicted in Fig. 3a. We can observe that the re-optimization process clearly reduces the maximum CPU utilization. The gain is higher when the physical network is not loaded and lowers when the network is almost fully loaded. The re-optimization achieves values 20% lower for a maximum CPU utilization of 0.8 VN request per time unit, and 5% lower for 1.8 VN request per time unit. We can observe also that the re-optimization process increases the minimum CPU utilization, where it

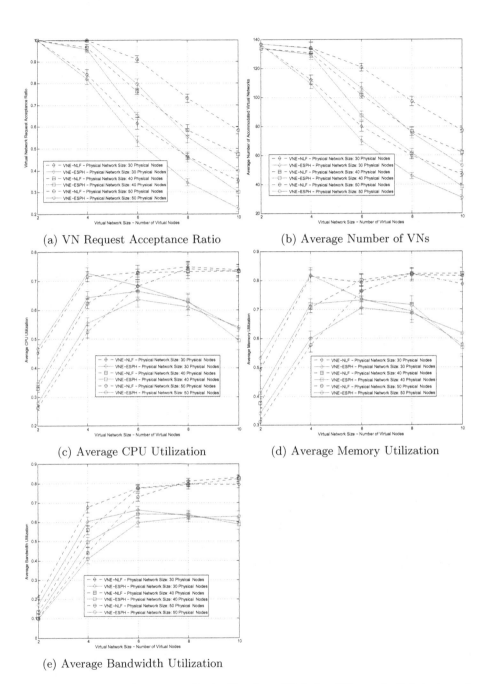

(a) VN Request Acceptance Ratio

(b) Average Number of VNs

(c) Average CPU Utilization

(d) Average Memory Utilization

(e) Average Bandwidth Utilization

Fig. 2. VN Request Acceptance Ratio, Number of Existing VNs on the Substrate and Resource Utilization as a function of the VN Size

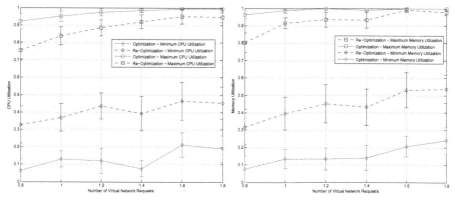

(a) Maximum and Minimum CPU Utiliza-   (b) Maximum and Minimum Memory Uti-
tion   lization

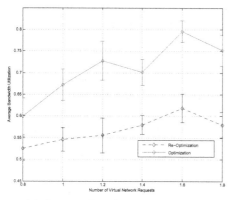

(c) Average Bandwidth Utilization

Fig. 3. Resource Utilization as a function of the Number of VN requests

achieves values 25% larger for minimum CPU utilization. The variation on the
number of VN requests does not seem to affect substantially the gap between
the two embedding processes.

The maximum and minimum memory utilization is shown in Fig. 3b. The
same behavior, as for the maximum CPU utilization or minimum CPU utilization
can be observed, where the re-optimization process reduces significantly the
maximum memory utilization. The re-optimization achieves values 16% lower
for maximum memory utilization of 0.8 VN request per time unit, and 3% lower
for 1.8 VN request per time unit. We can also observe that the minimum memory
utilization with the re-optimization process increases, where it achieves values
25% higher for memory utilization.

Figure 3c shows the average bandwidth utilization as a function of the number
of virtual network requests. We can observe that applying the re-optimization
reduces significantly the average bandwidth utilization on the physical links. This
gain is even higher with the increase on the number of VN requests, reaching
values 17.5% lower for 1.8 VN requests per time unit.

5 Conclusion

This paper proposed a re-optimization mechanism to enhance the performance of the virtual network embedding process. The proposed re-optimization approach proved to be a very efficient approach. It was not only able to reduce significantly the overall bandwidth consumption, where the average bandwidth utilization decreased 10%, but it also decreased clearly the maximum CPU and memory utilization levels. This is not only important from a load balancing perspective, where the load of nodes that are already at critical levels is being moved to nodes less loaded, but it is also important from a revenue perspective, where bandwidth that was previously provisioned is being released and that could be leased to new VNs.

Future work will endorse the utilization of the re-optimization as a way to improve the VN request acceptance ratio. The evaluation of the VNE-NLF with different cost functions and with other heuristics available in the literature will also be performed, as well as its evaluation using other metrics, e.g. revenue or provisioning cost.

Acknowledgement. The author was partially supported by the Portuguese Foundation for Science and Technology (FCT) with a scholarship No. SFRH/BDE/33751/2009. The research leading to these results has also received funding from the European Union Seventh Framework Programme (FP7) under grant agreement number 257448.

References

1. Peterson, L., Anderson, T., et al.: A blueprint for introducing disruptive technology into the internet. SIGCOMM Comput. Commun. Rev. 33(1), 59–64 (2003)
2. Anderson, T., Peterson, L., et al.: Overcoming the Internet Impasse through Virtualization. Computer 38, 34–41 (2005)
3. Feamster, N., Gao, L., Rexford, J.: How to lease the internet in your spare time. SIGCOMM Comput. Commun. Rev. 37(1), 61–64 (2007)
4. Zhu, Y., Zhang-Shen, R., et al.: Cabernet: connectivity architecture for better network services. In: Proceedings of the 2008 ACM CoNEXT Conference, CoNEXT 2008, pp. 64:1–64:6. ACM, New York (2008); ACM ID: 1544076
5. Touch, J., Wang, Y.S., et al.: A virtual internet architecture. ISI Technical Report ISI-TR-2003-570 (2003)
6. Carapinha, J., Jiménez, J.: Network virtualization: a view from the bottom. In: Proceedings of the 1st ACM Workshop on Virtualized Infrastructure Systems and Architectures, pp. 73–80. ACM, Barcelona (2009)
7. Melo, M., Sargento, S., Carapinha, J.: Network Virtualisation from an Operator Perspective. In: Proc Conf. Sobre Redes de Computadores, CRC (2009)
8. Chowdhury, N.M.K., Boutaba, R.: Network virtualization: State of the art and research challenges. IEEE Communications Magazine 47(7), 20–26 (2009)
9. Zhu, Y., Ammar, M.: Algorithms for assigning substrate network resources to virtual network components. In: Proceedings of the 25th IEEE International Conference on Computer Communications, INFOCOM 2006, pp. 1–12 (2006)

10. Yu, M., Yi, Y., et al.: Rethinking virtual network embedding: Substrate support for path splitting and migration. ACM SIGCOMM Computer Communication Review 38(2), 17–29 (2008)
11. Chowdhury, N., Rahman, M., Boutaba, R.: Virtual network embedding with coordinated node and link mapping. In: INFOCOM 2009, pp. 783–791. IEEE (2009)
12. Melo, M., Carapinha, J., Sargento, S., Torres, L., Tran, P.N., Killat, U., Timm-Giel, A.: Virtual network mapping – an optimization problem. In: Pentikousis, K., Aguiar, R., Sargento, S., Agüero, R. (eds.) MONAMI 2011. LNICST, vol. 97, pp. 187–200. Springer, Heidelberg (2012)
13. Lischka, J., Karl, H.: A virtual network mapping algorithm based on subgraph isomorphism detection. In: VISA 2009: Proceedings of the 1st ACM Workshop on Virtualized Infrastructure Systems and Architectures, pp. 81–88. ACM, New York (2009)
14. Lu, J., Turner, J.: Efficient mapping of virtual networks onto a shared substrate. Tech. rep., Washington University in St. Louis (2006)
15. Houidi, I., Louati, W., Zeghlache, D.: A distributed virtual network mapping algorithm. In: IEEE International Conference on Communications, ICC 2008, pp. 5634–5640 (2008)
16. Farooq Butt, N., Chowdhury, M., Boutaba, R.: Topology-awareness and reoptimization mechanism for virtual network embedding. In: Crovella, M., Feeney, L.M., Rubenstein, D., Raghavan, S.V. (eds.) NETWORKING 2010. LNCS, vol. 6091, pp. 27–39. Springer, Heidelberg (2010)
17. Nogueira, J., Melo, M., et al.: Virtual network mapping into heterogeneous substrate networks. In: IEEE Symposium on Computers and Communications, ISCC 2011 (2011)
18. Botero, J., Hesselbach, X., et al.: Optimal mapping of virtual networks with hidden hops. Telecommunication Systems, 1–10, doi:10.1007/s11235-011-9437-0
19. Lü, B., Huang, T., et al.: Adaptive scheme based on status feedback for virtual network mapping. The Journal of China Universities of Posts and Telecommunications 18(5), 87–94 (2011)
20. Chowdhury, M., Rahman, M.R., Boutaba, R.: Vineyard: Virtual network embedding algorithms with coordinated node and link mapping. IEEE/ACM Transactions on Networking 20(1), 206–219 (2012)
21. Even, S., Itai, A., Shamir, A.: On the complexity of time table and multicommodity flow problems. In: 16th Annual Symposium on Foundations of Computer Science, pp. 184–193 (1975)
22. Pióro, M., Medhi, D.: Routing, Flow, and Capacity Design in Communication and Computer Networks. Elsevier/Morgan Kaufmann (2004)
23. Waxman, B.: Routing of multipoint connections. IEEE Journal on Selected Areas in Communications 6(9), 1617–1622 (1988)
24. IBM ILOG Optimization Products,
    www-01.ibm.com/software/websphere/products/optimization

OConS Supported on Demand Radio Resource Allocation for Virtual Connectivity

Luisa Caeiro[1,2], Filipe D. Cardoso[1,2], and Luis M. Correia[2]

[1] CESET/ESTSetúbal
Polytechnic Institute of Setúbal, Setúbal, Portugal
[2] Instituto de Telecomunicações/Instituto Superior Técnico
Technical University of Lisbon, Lisbon, Portugal
{luisa.caeiro,filipe.cardoso}@estsetubal.ips.pt,
luis.correia@lx.it.pt

Abstract. With the increase of mobile network utilisation, the virtualisation of wireless resources becomes an important issue in the overall Virtual Networks (VNets) process. In this paper, the On Demand Virtual Network Radio Resource Allocation (OnDemand VRRA) mechanism is proposed to take advantage of the set of shared resources available within a cluster of wireless resources from different Radio Access Technologies (RATs) for wireless virtualisation. Optimising resource utilisation satisfying the VNet contracted capacity is its main objective. Furthermore, the mechanism is modelled according to the Open Connectivity Services (OConS) architecture, in order to demonstrate the advantages of its use within the OConS framework. Simulation results show that the introduction of OnDemand VRRA allows supporting the minimum bandwidth requirement in a wireless cluster, composed of several physical base stations from different RATs. The percentage of operation out of contract (i.e., below the virtual operator's contracted capacity) for a VNet with guaranteed minimum service is zero for a number of end users in the VNet up to 80% of the total, which is higher than in other circumstances. One also observes that VNets providing guaranteed services can achieve the contracted data rate independently of the number of end users in other VNets.

Keywords: Virtual Networks, Open Connectivity Services, Radio Resource Management, Heterogeneous Networks, Resource Allocation.

1   Introduction

Nowadays, networks have to support a lot of services, e.g., voice, web browsing, file transfer, and video streaming, with totally different requirements. The main drawback is that it is not always feasible to integrate all of them into a single protocol. Network virtualisation makes it possible to offer multiple optimised transport services, allowing clean-slate and legacy protocols to be deployed on separate Virtual Networks (VNets) [1]. The concept of network virtualisation provides the basis for an architecture that enables the deployment of multiple network solutions on top of a common network infrastructure, being considered the approach to be adopted for the

A. Timm-Giel et al. (Eds.): MONAMI 2012, LNICST 58, pp. 284–297, 2013.

Future Internet. Several proposals for the virtualisation of networks have emerged in recent years, some being related to testbeds, e.g., PlanetLab [2] or Orbit [3], and others being designed for the Future Internet, e.g., [4] and [5].

It has been predicted that in the near future, mobile Internet usage will increasingly surpass the fixed one. In 2016, wired devices will account for 39% of IP traffic, while Wi-Fi and mobile devices will take the remaining 61% [6]. Hence, the fixed networks virtualisation has to include wireless and mobile networks, transporting the main features of virtualisation to those environments.

The virtualisation of the wireless access as a component of virtual networks is a challenging problem if, in addition to sharing the infrastructure resources, the infrastructure provider wants to provide some level of guarantees to the virtual network operator, e.g., minimum data rate or delay. Currently, the wireless resources at the Base Station (BS) are fixed, but limited and variable in capacity, due to channel conditions, interference, and End Users (EUsers) mobility. Therefore, resources to be shared and allocated to different Virtual Network (VNet) operators with diverse requirements should be monitored and reallocated to satisfy the established settings.

Several Radio Resource Management (RRM) strategies have been proposed in the scope of Mobile Virtual Network Operators (MVNOs) for 3G (Third Generation) systems. The allocation of radio resources to sharing operators based on RRM with non-preemptive [7] and preemptive priority queuing in the admission control [8], the adaptive partitioning with borrowing [9], and the cooperative resource allocation game in shared networks based on the concept of preference functions [10]. Concerning VNet environments, a Virtual Radio framework for efficient radio resource sharing without interference among different virtual radio networks is presented in [11]. However, in MVNOs' mechanisms, operators are forced to use similar network functions, as defined by 3G specifications, and in Virtual Radio, the scope of the proposed framework is the provision of shared radio resources to EUsers within one physical network resource, e.g., a BS.

Considering the existence of various BSs from different Radio Access Technologies (RATs) covering a given area, one can use cooperative RRM [12] on the wireless access virtualisation, taking advantage from trunking gains among the heterogeneous wireless networks. This allows one to keep the Always Best Connected concept, ensure VNet Quality of Service (QoS) requirements, and optimise radio resource utilisation.

The novelty of this paper is to address wireless virtualisation by sharing a set of physical resources from different RATs through the adaptive allocation of radio resources to VNets on demand, i.e., only when EUsers are requesting service. The mechanism proposed, designated as OnDemand VNet Radio Resource Allocation (VRRA), ensures the amount of capacity (data rate) requested for guaranteed virtual access to networking services. OnDemand VRRA is modelled according to the Open Connectivity Services (OConS) architecture defined within the ICT SAIL project [13], allowing its activation and configuration through a service access point only if a request for virtual access is received. The mechanism is evaluated for different percentages of EUsers in VNets. The main objective is to investigate the kind of support that can be given to provide guaranteed virtual connectivity in a given geographic area.

This paper is structured as follows. In Section 2, the network architecture is presented. In Sections 3 and 4, the proposed OnDemand VRRA algorithm is introduced and explained, and mapped onto the OConS architecture. Scenarios and results are presented in Sections 5 and 6, respectively. Finally, conclusions are drawn in Section 7.

2   Network Architecture

The considered network environment envisages the existence of multiple VNets created by a Virtual Network Enabler. Service Providers will use these VNets, formed on demand to satisfy their service requirements, to deliver services to their customers. In this way, the physical infrastructure is shared among several VNets, providing services with different requirements, and to multiple Service Providers. Fig. 1 depicts the physical view of the network architecture. For simplicity, Service Providers' requests are illustrated as being just a capacity demand, although their requirements cannot be limited to that.

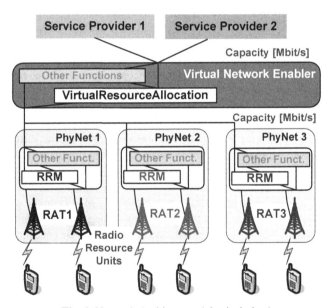

Fig. 1. Network Architecture (physical view)

Based on the request for capacity and infrastructure availability, the Virtual Network Enabler defines a VNet adequate to service delivery, performing the Virtual Resource Allocation. Virtual resources composing the VNet are then created on top of the network infrastructure, by sharing the available physical network capacity.

Within the scope of this work, only the VNet resources deployed over wireless infrastructures are considered, from now on designated as Virtual Base Stations (VBSs). The virtual resources are then assumed to be implemented on top of a set of heterogeneous wireless networks serving the geographic area over which the capacity demand is issued. The requested virtual capacity might be split over one or several VBSs by the virtualisation process. In case several VBSs co-exist, a partial capacity requirement is established for each one. The VBSs' capacity is provided by the allocation of Radio resource Units (RUs) over the several BSs constituting the cluster. The RU is the minimum radio unit that can be allocated to an EUser in a physical BS, being dependent on the RAT, e.g., a time slot in TDMA or a code in CDMA.

Fig. 2 depicts the Virtual Network Operators' (VNO) view of the network, the logical view. VNOs are the players that manage and operate the VNets, including their virtual resources, to satisfy Service Providers' requests. They know only the virtual resources that are part of the VNet with their associated capacity, the set of physical resources being hidden from them.

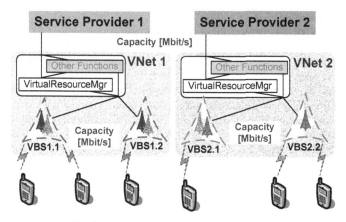

Fig. 2. Network Architecture (logical view)

To make use of a service, the EUser connects physically to the BSs, Fig. 1, but the connection to the VNet providing the service is made logically via a VBS, through a virtual link, as illustrated in Fig. 2. The physical link is the group of RUs allocated to the EUser, whereas the virtual link is the capacity, in bit/s, allocated from the VBS. The mapping between the physical and virtual links is essential to compute the VBS aggregated capacity, a contract satisfaction measurement being required, and consequently keeping the trustiness between the VNO and the Infrastructure Provider.

3   OnDemand VRRA

3.1   Strategies and Algorithms

The OnDemand VRRA, as the previous VRRA algorithm presented in [14], is developed to perform the mapping between virtual and physical links, dynamically adapting the allocation of radio resources to the wireless networks conditions and VBS usage. These functionalities are distributed between the virtual resource allocation and the RRM. Since one is dealing with heterogeneous networks, it will be implemented at the cooperative RRM level, managing all the heterogeneous wireless networks in the area, and at the actual network RRM level, being locally implemented at the BSs. At the cooperative RRM level, it manages the aggregated capacity provided to the virtual resource, by sharing the set of available radio resources, from all RATs. At the actual network RRM level, it maps the requested capacity to a particular RAT onto RUs allocated to EUsers, and applies data rate reduction strategies.

VNets are created with a certain level of guarantees for their requirements, according to the contract being established. This is also applied to the VBSs composing the VNet in the several geographical locations. In this work, two different possibilities are considered: Guaranteed (GRT), and Best-Effort (BE). The former ensures that the requested constraints will not be violated at any time, under normal network operating conditions, while the latter provides a best-effort service, i.e., no guarantees are given when data will be delivered.

OnDemand VRRA is responsible for dynamically (re)allocating RUs to reflect the network operation condition, satisfying the VNet minimum capacity. This is supported by a *VNet priority scheme* and a *data rate reduction strategy*, besides the *access selection mechanism*.

Concerning the *access selection*, EUsers are connected to the different virtual resources according to the requested service and their contract with the operator(s). The physical connection is established over one of the existing RATs in the coverage area, according to a list of preferences related to the requested service, the available capacity, and the strategy defined for resource evaluation. This strategy, e.g., minimum load, minimum cost, and/or minimum energy state, is based on a cost function derived from [15], where several Key Performance Indicators are weighted.

The *VNet priority scheme* runs in a Cluster Manager (CM), allowing the differentiation in handling EUsers according to the type of VNet and the VBS serving data rate. VNets are initialised to be handled with priority, all the BSs in the cluster being informed of this, to activate the data rate reduction process. When the minimum contracted data rate is reached, the priority to be given to EUsers who wish to connect to this virtual resource is deactivated. This priority scheme based on the VBS serving data rate, allows one to implement a data rate reduction strategy whenever the GRT VNets have priority, preventing starvation on BE VNets if the contracted data rate in GRT VNets is reached.

The *data rate reduction strategy* is as follows. Whenever the VNet priority is activated for a GRT VNet, and the EUser tries to connect to a BS in which there are not enough radio units to assign to the EUser, BE EUsers connected to the BS are reduced according to:

1. the QoS priority class of the performed service [16], EUsers performing services with lower priority being the first to be reduced;
2. their Signal-to-Interference-plus-Noise-Ratio (SINR), EUsers with lower SINR being reduced first to allow optimising radio resource utilization;
3. if still there are not enough RUs to reach the requested data rate, the CM is requested to do the evaluation of co-located BSs, in order to select the one with enough RUs available and the minimum cost for handover of EUsers.

It is worthwhile to note the difference between this mechanism and the radio resource allocation and adaptation mechanisms at the Medium Access Control level, which deal with the EUser performance instead of the global VBS one.

3.2   Metrics and Parameters

OnDemand VRRA works on a time frame basis, greater than all time frames associated to the RATs under consideration. This time frame is of the same order of magnitude of the time scale defined for common/joint RRM algorithms. Two sets of parameters have been identified: one related to EUsers and another to VBSs.

The parameters related to EUsers are:

- *Typical service data rate*, R_{typ}^{EU} – typical data rate of the service the EUser is performing, being fixed for each service.
- *Minimum service data rate*, R_{min}^{EU} – minimum data rate of the service the EUser is performing, being fixed for each service.
- *Served data rate*, R_{serv}^{EU} – data rate with which the EUser is being served, depending on the number of RUs assigned to the EUser and the data rate the RU is achieving, being obtained by:

$$R_{serv[\text{bit/s}]}^{EU} = N_{RU}^{EU} \cdot R_{MCS_n}[\text{bit/s}].$$ (1)

where:

- N_{RU}^{EU} - number of RUs assigned to the EUser;
- R_{MCS_n} - data rate achieved by each RU assigned to the EUser, according to the applied modulation and coding scheme, MCS_n.

The parameters related to VBSs are:

- *Minimum contracted data rate*, R_{min}^{VBS} – data rate contracted by the VNet Operator as the minimum value the Infrastructure Provider should provide when requested.
- *Requested data rate*, R_{req}^{VBS} – data rate requested by EUsers to the VBS, being the aggregation of the typical data rates of all EUsers services in the VBS:

$$R_{req[\text{bit/s}]}^{VBS} = \sum_{n=1}^{N_{EU}} R_{typ_n[\text{bit/s}]}^{EU}.$$ (2)

where:

- $R_{typ_n}^{EU}$ - typical service data rate for EUser n.
- N_{EU} - Number of EUsers requesting service in the VBS.

- *VBS Serving data rate*, R_{serv}^{VBS} – data rate served to all EUsers in the VBS:

$$R_{serv[\text{bit/s}]}^{VBS} = \sum_{n=1}^{N_{EU}} R_{serv_n[\text{bit/s}]}^{EU}.$$ (3)

The following network performance indicators have been defined to assess the OnDemand VRRA algorithm in different scenarios and network conditions.

- *VBS Average Serving Data Rate* – average of the VBS serving data rate over the observation time interval:

$$\overline{R_{serv}^{VBS}}_{[bit/s]} = \frac{\sum_{n=1}^{N_{TF}} R_{serv\,n}^{VBS}[bit/s]}{N_{TF}}. \tag{4}$$

where:

- $R_{serv\,n}^{VBS}$ - VBS serving data rate in time frame n.

- N_{TF} - number of time frames during the observation time interval.

- *Out of contract* – total number of time frames the VBS is out of contract (i.e., capacity is below the minimum contracted one) over the observation time interval:

$$r_{TF}^{out} = \frac{N_{TF}^{out}}{N_{TF}}. \tag{5}$$

where:

- N_{TF}^{out} - number of time frames out of contract, i.e., the number of time frames in which $R_{serv}^{VBS} < R_{min}^{VBS} < R_{req}^{VBS}$.

4   Mapping OnDemand VRRA on OConS Architecture

The OConS architecture [17] is an open architecture for connectivity services that provides a flexible framework, supporting both legacy and enhanced connectivity mechanisms. It is able to dynamically adapt the operation of the involved mechanisms according to the particular requirements of the services and applications. This open architecture is based on three main entities: information, decision and enforcement; they replicate the basic functionalities of any connectivity mechanism, respectively, information gathering, decision taking, and decision enforcement. By having a common way of representing current and future mechanisms, the OConS operation eases the instantiation, launch, and composition of mechanisms by specified orchestration procedures, to provide enhanced connectivity services.

OnDemand VRRA was modelled according to the OConS architecture, to take advantage of its flexible approach, e.g., concerning the activation and configuration during network operation. A Decision Element (DE) has been identified in the Cluster Manager (CM) that is responsible to manage a given set of BSs, and local resource management is performed by other DEs per BS. The former is responsible to apply the priority scheme described in Section 3.1, and to reallocate RUs in co-located BSs for vertical handovers; the latter, based on the VNet priority scheme, implements the data rate reduction strategy. An additional DE is taken at the User Equipment (UE), to deal with the access selection mechanism; although it can be external to the OnDemand VRRA algorithm, it has been also considered within this work. Fig. 3 illustrates the mechanism mapping, the numbers in the boxes being a possible sequence of steps produced.

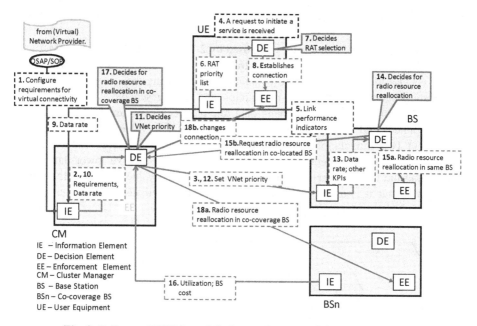

Fig. 3. OnDemand VRRA modelled according to the OConS Architecture

When an OConS user connectivity request is received, via the Orchestration Service Access Point, the Service Orchestration Process handles and instantiates or (re)configures the OnDemand VRRA mechanism for the new connectivity requirements (**1**), e.g., QoS type for the virtual resource, minimum data rate contracted or delay. Connectivity requirements are passed onto the cluster manager DE (**2**), which activates the priority of all VNets in the cluster by sending this information to the several DEs in the BSs (**3**). An EUser requests to initiate a service/application (**4**), activates the access selection mechanism on the UE, which according to link performance indicators (**5**) and the RAT priority list (**6**), information gathered from the Information Element (IE), decides the initial RAT selection (**7**) and establishes the connection (**8**) enforcing the decision in the corresponding Enforcement Element (EE). The CM receives data rates requests from all EUsers in the VNets (**9**), compares the VNet serving data rate and the contracted one, with the information in the IE (**10**), and decides the VNet priority (**11**). The result of this decision is then sent to all BSs to set the VNet priority (**12**), accordingly. The BS DEs use the Key Performance Indicators from the IEs (**13**), e.g., wireless rate and usage, to run the data rate reduction mechanism, and decide the reallocation of RUs to EUsers connected to the BS (**14**). The decision can be to keep EUser in the same BS (**15a**), or to request the CM to try the radio resource allocation in a co-located BS (**15b**). To support the decision for reallocation of RUs in co-located BSs (**17**), the CM requests information from the co-located BSs (**16**), in order to evaluate the best one to reallocate the RUs (**18a**), informing the UE to change the connection to the new BS (**18b**).

5   Scenario for Simulation

A reference scenario of one cluster composed by 2 TDMA, 1 CDMA, 4 OFDMA and 8 OFDM BSs is considered, Fig. 4 (central area). A maximum cluster serving data rate of 6 171.4 Mbit/s was obtained by summing the serving data rates of each BS in the cluster, when the higher rate modulation and coding scheme is applied. Two intermediate values for cluster serving data rate has been considered, 3 774.5 Mbit/s (MCS_1 applied) and 2 163.1 Mbit/s (MCS_2 applied). These values correspond to the subsequent two modulation and coding schemes, which are more robust in the compensation for SINR degradation, but only possible to achieve lower data rates. Concerning the total data rate contracted by the VNets, a value of 2 750 Mbit/s was used; given that it is a value in-between the two intermediate cluster serving data rates. Each VNet is composed of one VBS within the cluster.

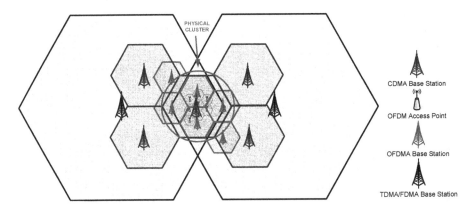

Fig. 4. Physical cluster of heterogeneous BSs

There are two types of VNets: one provides guaranteed services (GRT), VoIP and video streaming, while the other provides Best-Effort services (BE), e.g., FTP, P2P, web browsing, and email. GRT services have an expected served and typical data rates, and a minimum one under which EUsers cannot be served, being delayed. BE services have also an expected served data rate, nevertheless they can be served with any one, down to zero, since they can be reduced in order that GRT EUsers maintain the VBS contracted data rate.

EUsers are uniformly distributed within the cluster, potentially being served by one set of BSs covering the area. The behaviour of EUsers in the network is determined by the profile of the service they are performing. For the sake of simplicity, one considers only one service profile per session level, being the service defined by the session inter-arrival time distribution, and the session data volume or duration distributions, according to the type of service.

In order to reduce the complexity of simulations, one assumes that an equal transmit power is allocated to each RU, and that all transmitted packets are received correctly. Moreover, users are static and experience the same SINR values for all RUs. Network conditions that can cause reduction in the capacity of virtual resources have been forced, by setting a high percentage of active EUsers and dynamically changing their SINR in order to reflect wireless medium variation. In particular, SINR changes according to a uniform distribution, every time frame in which the EUser performs service.

BSs are modelled by the coverage area, the number of RUs, the SINR thresholds, and the related data rates per RU, specific for each RAT under consideration.

Three use cases were considered for the scenario with two VNets deployed in the cluster, Fig. 5. For each, the distribution of EUsers in VNets changes, Table 1. By increasing the total number of EUsers in the cluster, the satisfaction of data rate contracted for GRT VNets and the isolation from the traffic in BE VNets was investigated.

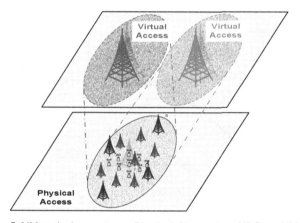

Fig. 5. VNets deployment on a Physical Cluster (one VBS per VNet)

Table 1. Use cases for simulation

Use Case ID	VNet Type	Contracted Data Rate [Mbit/s]	EUsers per VBS [%]	Services Provided
20/80	GRT	1 250	20	VoIP, Video
	BE	1 500	80	File Download, Web, Email
50/50	GRT	1 250	50	VoIP, Video
	BE	1 500	50	File Download, Web, Email
80/20	GRT	1 250	80	VoIP, Video
	BE	1 500	20	File Download, Web, Email

6   Analysis of Results

A simulator, developed in C++, was used to evaluate the performance of the OnDemand VRRA algorithm. Simulation time was 1 hour minutes of network operation, after discarding the first 10 minutes of simulations, for initial convergence; the sampling period for network monitoring was 1 s. In what follows, one presents results for the VBS average serving data rate, and the out of contract.

6.1   VBS Average Serving Data Rate

The VBS average serving data rate, $\overline{R_{serv}^{VBS}}$, computed from (4), can be observed in Fig. 6. When the number of EUsers is unbalanced between the two VBSs (use cases 20/80 and 80/20), the serving data rate increases in the VBS with more EUsers, exceeding the contracted data rate ($\overline{R_{serv}^{VBS}} \approx 1\ 840$ Mbit/s) for approximately 4 000 and 5 000 EUsers, respectively. This behaviour is similar in this initial phase whatever the type of VNet with the greatest number of EUsers, the maximum serving data rate being only bounded by the cluster total capacity.

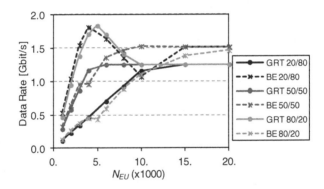

Fig. 6. VBS average serving data rate for different percentages of EUsers

After that, when the number of EUsers increases, both VBSs decrease their serving data rate, tending to reach the contracted value, being in accordance to the cluster capacity. However, due to the VNet priority mechanism, the serving data rate of BE VBS for the use case 20/80, decreases below its minimum contracted value (for 10 000 EUsers, $R_{serv}^{VBS} \approx 0.75\ R_{min}^{VBS}$) to allow the GRT VBS to achieve its R_{min}^{VBS}. When the number of EUsers in both VBSs is similar (use case 50/50), the serving data rates increases with the number of EUsers, having the trend to reach the contracted minimum of each VBS more or less linearly.

6.2   VBS Out of Contract

VBS Out of contract, r_{TF}^{out} , computed from (5), Fig. 7, shows that it is always zero for the GRT VBS, meaning that it is served at least with the minimum contracted data rate, whenever the requested data rate is greater than the contracted one. The BE VBS on the other hand, presents a peak in out of contract (r_{TF}^{out} =1), corresponding to the situation in which the data rate requested for one VBS is above the minimum data rate contracted and the other is reaching this value. In this situation, the VNet priority scheme and reduction strategy enforce the BE EUsers to reduce their data rate in order to allow the GRT VBS to be served with its contracted data rate. This occurs sooner for the use case 50/50, r_{TF}^{out} =1 for 4 000 EUsers, and latter for use cases 80/20 and 20/80, r_{TF}^{out} =1 for 10 000 EUsers. For use case 20/80, the BE VBS presents an earlier region out of contract (r_{TF}^{out} =0.28), though transient, reflecting the situation when the requested data rate is near the contracted one, but it is not enough to compensate the data rate reduction imposed by the GRT VBS. For use case 80/20, the out of contract starts increasing for 5 000 EUsers (r_{TF}^{out} = 0.67), because the requested data rate in the BE VBS is near the contracted minimum, increasing slowly, which produces the effect referred also for use case 20/80. Is worthwhile to note that when both VBSs are serving the contracted data rate, the network comes to a state in which the BE VBS out of contract is roughly maintained, $r_{TF}^{out} \approx 0.45$. This is due to the dynamic of the network, which allows in some time frames to achieve the contracted data rate due to the adaptation to the network state.

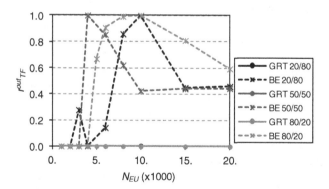

Fig. 7. VBS out of contract for different percentages of EUsers

7   Conclusions

An OnDemand Virtual Network Radio Resource Allocation (VRRA) mechanism is proposed, aiming at minimising the effect of QoS degradation inherent to radio interface, by globally evaluating the impact of heterogeneous network environment into the virtualisation approach. This mechanism is an evolution of a VRRA mechanism presented in [14], though the approach is slightly more flexible, since it considers only the allocation of radio resources to the VNets when EUsers request a service. The dynamic allocation of radio resources to reflect the network operation condition is supported by a VNet priority scheme, and a data rate reduction strategy in order to satisfy the VNet minimum capacity requirement. OnDemand VRRA was modelled in the OConS architecture, to enable its flexible utilisation supported by the service orchestration process.

The simulation results for the use cases considered in this paper shows that even when the number of EUsers in the network is in the order of 20 000, meaning that the requesting data rate is much greater than the VBSs' contracted data rate, the GRT VBS serving data rate can achieve the contracted data rate. Although this is independent of the EUsers distribution per VBS, the BE VBS serving data rate is dependent on the operation of GRT VBS. This is more evident in the use case where the number of EUsers in BE VBS is 80% of the total, in which the BE VBS reduces from 1 840 Mbit/s to 1 105 Mbit/s (less than the contracted data rate) when the GRT VBS requesting data rate is near or exceeds the contracted one.

The GRT VBS is maintained within contract at the expenses of the BE VBS, which may operate out of the contract whenever the physical network conditions require so. In fact, the out of contract value, for the three use cases analysed, are always zero for the GRT VBS and increase for the BE VBS, depending on the mixing of traffic in both VBSs.

Results show that the OnDemand VRRA allows achieving isolation among the virtual resources, since the requested data rate of one VBS does not prevent the other to achieve the contracted data rate, if they are guaranteed. As an example, for 80% of EUsers in the BE VBS, the GRT VBS reaches the contracted data rate as soon as the requested data rate is greater or equal to it.

According to simulation results, the introduction of OnDemand VRRA allows supporting the minimum bandwidth requirement for virtual access in a wireless cluster, composed of several physical BSs from different RATs, providing service over a given coverage area. This is valid for the use cases considered in the paper, in which the total data rate contracted is below the maximum physical data rate the cluster can provide. Further evaluations will be made to assess different use cases.

In conclusion, the virtualisation of radio resources looks promising, enabling an efficient use of radio channels and good quality of the service provided to end-users.

Acknowledgments. The support of the European Commission by partially funding this work via the FP7-ICT-2009-5-SAIL project, Grant Agreement Number 257448, is acknowledged.

References

1. Raychaudhuri, D.: Future Internet Research at WINLAB,
   http://www.winlab.rutgers.edu/events/iab/2010-011/
   documents/RAY_Future_Internet_IAB_Spring2010_DR.pdf

2. Peterson, L., Muir, S., Roscoe, T., Klingaman, A.: PlanetLab Architecture: An Overview. Technical Report PDN–06–031, PlanetLab Consortium (2006)
3. Raychaudhuri, D., Ott, M., Seskar, I.: Orbit radio grid tested for evaluation of next-generation wireless network protocols. In: IEEE TRIDENTCOM, Washington, DC, USA (2005)
4. Schaffrath, G., Werle, C., Papadimitriou, P., Feldmann, A., Bless, R., Greenhalgh, A., Wundsam, A., Kind, M., Maennel, O., Mathy, L.: Network Virtualisation Architecture: Proposal and Initial Prototype. In: 1st ACM SIGCOMM Workshop on Virtualized Infrastructure Systems and Architectures, Barcelona, Spain (2009)
5. Zhu, Y., Zhang-Shen, R., Rangarajan, S., Rexford, J.: Cabernet: Connectivity Architecture for Better Network Services. In: ACM Workshop on Re-Architecting the Internet, Madrid, Spain (2008)
6. Cisco Systems: The Zettabyte Era (May 2012),
   http://www.cisco.com/en/US/solutions/collateral/ns341/
   ns525/ns537/ns705/ns827/VNI_Hyperconnectivity_WP.pdf
7. Johansson, M.K.: Radio Resource Management in Roaming Based Multi-Operator WCDMA Networks. In: 59th IEEE Vehicular Technology Conference, Milan, Italy (2004)
8. Al-Jarbou, Y., Baroudi, U.: Performance of Heterogeneous Traffic in Roaming Based Sharing Multi-Operator WCDMA Networks. In: 2nd International Symposium on Wireless Communication Systems, Siena, Italy (2005)
9. AlQahtani, S.A., Mahmoud, A.S., Sheltami, T.R., El-Tarhuni, M.: Adaptive Radio Resource Management for Multi-Operator WCDMA Based Cellular Wireless Networks with Heterogeneous Traffic. In: 17th IEEE International Symposium on Personal, Indoor and Mobile Radio Communications, Helsinki, Finland (2006)
10. Hew, S., White, L.B.: Fair Resource Bargaining Solutions for Cooperative Multi-Operator Networks. In: International Zurich Seminar on Communications, Zurich, Switzerland (2006)
11. Sachs, J., Baucke, S.: Virtual radio: a framework for configurable radio networks. In: 4th Annual International Conference on Wireless Internet, Maui, HI, USA (2008)
12. Sachs, J., Wiemann, H., Lundsjo, J., Magnusson, P.: Integration of multi-radio access in a beyond 3G network. In: 15th IEEE International Symposium on Personal, Indoor and Mobile Radio Communications, Barcelona, Spain (2004)
13. Suciu, L., et al.: Architectural concepts of connectivity services. Deliverable D4.1, EU-FP7 SAIL project (2011)
14. Caeiro, L., Cardoso, F.D., Correia, L.M.: Adaptive Allocation of Virtual Radio Resources over Hetrogeneous Wireless Networks. In: European Wireless 2012, Poznan, Poland (2012)
15. Serrador, A., Correia, L.M.: Policies for a Cost Function for Heterogeneous Networks Performance Evaluation. In: 18th IEEE International Symposium on Personal, Indoor and Mobile Radio Communications, Athens, Greece (2007)
16. IEEE Std. 802.1Q-2005: Virtual Bridged Local Area Networks (December 2005),
    http://standards.ieee.org/getieee802/download/
    802.1Q-2005.pdf
17. Ferreira, L., Aguero, R., Caeiro, L., Miron, A., Soellner, M., Schoo, P., Suciu, L., Timm-Giel, A., Udugama, A.: Open Connectivity Services for the Future Internet. Submitted to Guest Editors of the Springer Telecommunication Systems (March 2012)
18. Klemm, A., Lindemann, C., Lohmann, M.: Traffic Modelling and Characterization for UMTS Networks. In: Globecom, Internet Performance Symposium, San Antonio, TX, USA (2001)

On the Addition of a Network Coding Layer within an Open Connectivity Services Framework

David Gómez[1], Sofiane Hassayoun[2], Arnaldo Herrero[1], Ramón Agüero[1], David Ros[2], and Marta García-Arranz[1]

[1] Universidad de Cantabria, Santander, Spain
[2] Institut Mines-Télécom / Télécom Bretagne, Cesson Sévigné cedex, France
{dgomez,ramon,marta}@tlmat.unican.es,
{sofien.hassayoun,david.ros}@telecom-bretagne.eu

Abstract. In this work we propose a tailored Network Coding (NC) solution to be fitted within the scope of a novel communication architecture designed to address the requirements of the *Future Internet*, thus taking advantage of the subjacent flexibility and openness that this concrete framework is able to provide. Besides, we evaluate the behavior of TCP over a wireless mesh network in order to assert the benefits that such NC solution might bring about, compared to a legacy store-and-forward routing scheme, thus filling the gap encountered over the tuple *NC-Wireless Mesh Networks-TCP*.

Keywords: Future Internet, Wireless Mesh Networks, OConS architecture, Network Coding, TCP.

1 Introduction

The ever-increasing evolution regarding communication technologies has left behind the classical network infrastructure model, whose obsolete concepts and overwhelming limitations showcase the need of a revolutionary change, thus giving rise to a brand new way of thinking and acting in order to fulfill the the goals imposed by the new paradigm known as "Internet of the Future", where the flexibility and the openness are settled to be the cornerstones of any system.

Considering the relevance of the consequent new challenges, the *Open Connectivity Services (OConS)* architecture[1] aims at finding a way to smartly insert a fully-featured Network Coding scheme, thus augmenting the range of functionalities that *OConS* will perform once the whole infrastructure is finished.

The aforementioned framework deals with some of the most relevant challenges which are posed by the new communication paradigms created from the necessities of both network and end-users. One of the most highlighting issues

---

[1] Currently under development in the Scalable and Adaptive Internet Solutions (SAIL) project, which belongs to the 7th IST Framework Programme.

A. Timm-Giel et al. (Eds.): MONAMI 2012, LNICST 58, pp. 298–312, 2013.

pursued by this new current of thoughts focuses on the flexibility and open-ness, in order to ease a future incorporation of new i.e. functionalities, protocols, technologies, etc. The cornerstone of this work addresses the last point, since it studies, by means of simulation, the impact that Network Coding might bring about over TCP performance when applied over wireless mesh topologies.

Although wireless communications based on the IEEE 802.11 standard date back more than ten years, the relationship between this concrete medium and upper layer transport protocols, mainly the ones which focus on a connection oriented behavior (whose most representative example is TCP), is far from being ideal. The error and congestion control inherent to the latter ones directly clash with i.e. the retransmission scheme supported by an IEEE 802.11 transmission, thus yielding a harmful effect over the global system performance. In the latest years, the scientific community has proposed the use of Network Coding tech-niques in order to overcome theselimitations, in particular over *Wireless Mesh Networks (WMNs)*. In this paper we illustrate how the *OConS* framework can act as an enabler to apply these techniques.

The paper is structured as follows: Section 2 briefly depicts the most relevant activities carried out by the research community on the topics introduced above. Section 3 discusses how a fully functional Network Coding framework could be fitted within the aforementioned architecture, introducing as well its main features. In Section 4 we depict the scenarios which were carried out so as to evaluate the performance of *NC* over a *WMN*. Section 5 presents the most relevant results achieved over the simulation campaign we carried out. Finally, Section 6 concludes the document and presents ideas and open issues to be tackled in the future.

2   Related Work

This section is clearly divided into two main realms: the first one focuses on the design and implementation of novel architectures able to deal with the challenges and goals posed from the unstoppable advances in communication technologies and the insatiable demand of resources by the end-users; on the other hand, we review the most relevant works which have addressed the analysis of the joint performance of *NC* and TCP over wireless mesh networks.

Starting with the former branch, the EU Ambient Networks project (see e.g. [10] and the references therein), proposed a novel architecture which fo-cused on the selection of an optimum access in heterogeneous scenarios, thus implementing a whole framework which allowed the cooperation between differ-ent networks, encompassing topics as mobility, context-awareness, security and other control mechanisms.

Taking a step forward, the *OConS* framework [1,11] aims at tackling some of the most relevant challenges which were posed by the new communication paradigms, brought about by the so-called Internet of the Future. Such frame-work addresses the fulfillment of two key aspects which will define the behavior of this sort of architectures: *flexibility* and *openness*, thus identifying a common denominator for most of connectivity operations: (1) the harvesting of information; (2) the decision taking on the basis of such information; (3) the enforcement of taking care of such decision by the appropriate network elements. *OConS* allows this cycle to be executed both reflexively and recursively and it fosters the cooperation between peer entities for any of the corresponding connectivity services (for instance, to implement a distributed decision mechanism).

Regarding Network Coding, since its inception in the year 2000 by Ahlswede *et al.* [2], it has been foreseen as a promising technique called to complement (even substitute) the legacy and traditional store-and-forward routing scheme. There are various benefits that this novel mechanism shall bring about, such as performance enhancement (i.e. higher throughput, improved robustness or lower power consumption); besides, it could provide as well many other advantages, such as the capability to allow different receivers to efficiently recover lost packet simultaneously [4] or the addition of a new security layer that protects the wireless communication against potential eavesdropping attacks [13] (thus taking advantage of the intrinsic properties of *NC*), among many others. However, the relationship between *NC* and connection-oriented protocols, such as TCP, though addressed in several works, has not yielded clear conclusions yet, since there are still open discussions which pose the actual improvement performed by TCP when used over an *NC* scheme.

For instance, one of the most popular contributions which helped NC to gain its current relevance, carried out by Katti et al [8], was the first research paper which introduced the analysis of TCP performance over *WMNs* when *NC* is enabled, through a coding algorithm called COPE. They found out that *NC* does not show a relevant improvement over TCP, yielding a throughput gain of just 2-3%. Authors attributed this poor performance to a high loss rate and the appearance of such unexpected behaviors (i.e. the hidden terminal problem).

In [7], Huang *et al.* presented a testbed implementation of a proprietary *NC* protocol, in order to study the performance of TCP over a *WMN*. This protocol is similar to COPE, in the sense that it looks for coding opportunities and uses XOR operations to code packets. However, there is no opportunistic listening; each node coding based only on what it has already sent or received, and not on what neighbors have received from other nodes. The implementation carried out in mesh routers uses an *"NC timer"*, associated with each outgoing packet. This timer is used to delay sending the packet to wait for a coding opportunity. They showed that the performance of TCP is sensitive to the value of the timer. A high value increases coding opportunities, leading to a lower loss rate (since coding packets decreases contention for the wireless medium) but it also increases the *Round Trip Time* (*RTT*) experienced by TCP flows. A small value of the timer leads to few coding opportunities but also to a lower RTT. They found that, with an appropriate empirical choice of the *NC* timer, the throughput gain offered by *NC* may vary from 20% to 70%, depending on experimental conditions.

In [6], Hassayoun *et al.* studied the impact of random losses and packet loss synchronization on TCP performance in *WMNs*. They found that the opportunistic listening used by *NC* algorithms can decrease the *NC* gain and that, in some situations, TCP performance could be better without *NC*. They also found that a high loss synchronization level between TCP flows, caused by the loss of coded packets, contributes to the degradation of TCP performance.

This work aims at going a step forward, merging a novel architecture that is called to face the challenge requirements by an *Internet of the Future* compliant framework (as *OConS* does), demonstrating one of its main virtues (the openness) and easily fitting a whole *NC* scheme, thus increasing the range of functionalities performed by such architecture.

3   NC Integration within the Scope of OConS Framework

In order to face the challenges arisen from this work, we addressed the development of a brand new *NC* scheme, starting from the following list of issues:

- First of all, we need to design a tailored *NC* framework which perfectly fits with the *OConS* architecture principles; for that purpose, we had to split the *NC* behavior into three main entities (thus respecting the *OConS* topology specifications), keeping a clear separation between their functionality.
- It is well-known that the key process of Network Coding aims at mixing the content of different packets; for that reason, it is deemed necessary to include a new header into the coded packets, thus providing enough information to decode and retrieve the original information. For this purpose, we have inserted an *NC* layer at the top of the network level, since we will need to handle the information held by i.e. the TCP header.
- Regarding the tuple composed by both *WMNs* and TCP, it is well known that the performance of this protocol is heavily damaged as the error presence grows within wireless channels (due to their intrinsic nature). The main reason is attributed to the congestion and error control inherent to this concrete transport protocol, since it is not able to differentiate between a packet loss triggered by the congestion of the medium or, on the other hand, is due to the intrinsic properties of a wireless link (i.e. propagation, interference with other transmissions...). Furthermore, every time a packet gets lost, the TCP protection mechanisms will drastically decrease the traffic flow, thus reducing the sending rate of the involved source nodes.

As depicted above, one of the most challenging issues to be tackled throughout this work focuses on the design and implementation of a brand new Network Coding scheme within the scope of the *OConS* framework [1], taking into account the rules, elements, entities, interfaces and communication mechanisms that define the overall *OConS* environment. This architecture addresses the orchestration (at various levels) of different instances into three main entities, each of which is responsible of one of the following functions: information harvesting, decision taking and execution enforcement. We show below how the proposed solution is tailored to fit within such framework:

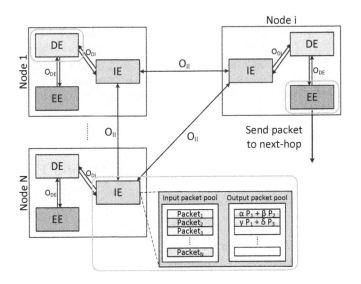

Fig. 1. NC functionality mapping within the OConS architecture

- *Information Element (IE).* This entity will be in charge of the storage of all the overheard packets that a node is able to capture within its coverage area; for that purpose, an *IE* will handle two different buffers: the first one (we will name it *input packet pool*) will keep track of all the overheard original (uncoded) packets, whilst the second buffer (*output packet pool*), will hold the packets (coded or not) before being forwarded to the lower layer. All the information gathered by both buffers will be asynchronously delivered to the *OConS* intelligence, located at the *Decision Element*, where will be parsed and consequently handled by means of the corresponding decision engines.
- *Decision Element (DE).* It can be seen as the cornerstone of the architecture; it is in charge of taking the coding/decoding decisions, according to the information received from the local *IEs* as well as from remote neighboring reports. In the same way, this entity shall also decide the next neighboring node that an encoded packet should be forwarded to. Finally, once the whole decision process is finished, the *DE* will instruct the *EE* to act accordingly.
- *Execution Element (EE).* As a last step, the *EE* will be the responsible of the following list of tasks according to the information gathered from the other entities:
  - Serialize/deserialize the *NC* headers.
  - Encode/decode packets (through a linear XOR operation).
  - Request the retransmission of the appropriate original (uncoded) packets.
  - Forward the resulting packet (coded or not) to the lower (coding) or the upper (decoding) layer.

Figure 1 illustrates the composition of a simplified generic *WMN* consisting of N "*OConS* nodes". It is worth highlighting the definition of an interface for each pair of entities (excepting the one which links the *IE* with the *EE*: O_{IE}), leaving the door opened for a future node cooperation[2] which will increment the complexity of the solution (i.e. joint adaptive Network Coding, neighbor packet guessing, probabilistic forwarding) and improve the overall performance at the same time.

Finding a Optimal Configuration of the NC Parameters

The cornerstone of an *NC* scheme focuses on its ability to find the best coding/decoding equilibrium, that is to say, the coding nodes shall always choose the best packet combination so as to be successfully decoded at the corresponding destinations (i.e. encode as many packets together with as possible; nonetheless, these coded packets shall be decoded as soon as possible, without leading to a massive uncoded packet retransmission request from the involved neighbors). For that purpose, several *NC* schemes rely on an additional complexity level, such as sharing information between the neighboring nodes (such technique is introduced as *learning neighbor state* in [8]), implementing a brand new *NC* Acknowledgement scheme [12] or even by means of the estimation of the packets received by the surrounding neighbors of a concrete node through a guessing algorithm [3].

In this work we evaluate the effect of the configuration of some *NC* buffering parameters (as we will analyze through a thorough simulation campaign in Sections 4 and 5, where we tweaked the size and the packet sojourn time inside these aforementioned buffers) over one of the most widespread topologies that can be found in the literature: the Butterfly (it will be explained in more detail in Section 4 and in Figure 3).

For the sake of simplicity, we will make the next assumptions so as to theoretically model the coding rate probability analysis:

1. As will be inferred from the topology description, there are only deployed two flows over the scenario.
2. The sole coding criteria consists in parsing the destination address of a received packet, extracted from the IP layer: if different, triggers a coding opportunity and the corresponding packets will proceed to be coded together with and stored into the output packet pool.
3. The Coding Buffer Timeout (T_C) will not join in the analysis, hence we will assume it is infinite.
4. Only TCP data packets are candidates to be coded; therefore, any other ones (i.e. TCP ACKs, ARP...) will pass through the *NC* layer without processing.
5. If the input packet pool is empty, any overheard packet will be directly stored into the input packet pool.
6. Extracted from the first point, the input packet pool (or coding buffer) will only get filled with packets of the same flow; otherwise, if arrives a packet with a different destination, it will be coded with the oldest one stored in the buffer.

---

[2] The current implementation does not support any cooperation among nodes, leaving all the NC-related decision to be resolved locally.

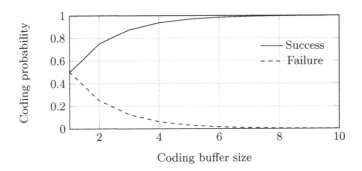

Fig. 2. Coding success/failure probability model output

7. A coding opportunity failure will be triggered if and only if the buffer is full (remark again that it will only contain packets from a same flow at the same time) and a new packet is overheard.

Once listed the constraints we have imposed over the environment, we will proceed to calculate the probability of having a coding opportunity as a function of the input packet pool size (let us name N as the maximum number of packets that this buffer is able to store). Since we have two flows over the scenario, we will use p as the probability of receiving a packet from the first flow and $1 - p$ from the second one.

A coding success is accomplished when we have the buffer in a non-empty state and we receive a packet from a different flow, as resumed in Eq. 1:

$$P_{success} = (1 - p) \cdot \sum_{i=1}^{N} p^i + p \cdot \sum_{i=1}^{N}(1 - p)^i \tag{1}$$

On the other hand, in order to lose a coding opportunity, the coding node must receive consecutively a frame of $N + 1$ packets from the same flow (easily extracted from Eq. 2), hence triggering a buffer overflow on the input packet pool. In this case, the oldest packet in the buffer will be forwarded to the next level (the output packet pool).

$$P_{failure} = p^{N+1} + (1 - p)^{N+1} \tag{2}$$

Therefore, we can see in Figure 2 the shape of the curves calculated above, being easily appreciated the complementary nature of such functions; however, the most highlighting issue consists in the fact that there a moment from which the growing tendency smoothly flattens, showing that we have reached an optimum buffer size from that the performance will barely improve (remark again that this simple model is only valid for this concrete two-flowed topology).

4   Test Scenario

Once depicted the main features that the *OConS* architecture shall settle in order to redefine the concept of a new future Internet framework and established the bindings with a brand new *NC* scheme, in this section we will introduce a basic test scenario, whose main goal aims at evaluating the performance of TCP over *WMNs*.

For this reason, we have opted for a concrete scenario which has been carried out by a number of previous research studies [2,4,5,6] along *NC*'s history: the *Butterfly* topology, shown in Figure 3. The main advantage of this scenario is that, despite its simplicity, it can easily illustrate the benefits of transmitting several packets coded together with instead of using the traditional mechanisms carried out by the mainstream store-and-forward routing mechanisms. Furthermore, this topology will stress the synchronization effect between the two TCP flows, due to the location of the middle link ($R_1 - R_2$) that will be in charge of delivering all the coded packets flow.

In particular, in this concrete topology, there will be established two long-lived TCP flows: the first one between S_1 and D_2 and the second one follows the opposite subscript notation ($S_2 - D_1$). As can be inferred from the figure, source nodes (S_1 and S_2) will not make use of the *OConS* functionalities, because they will not need to exchange any type of information at the *NC* layer. The distance between the nodes is chosen so that D_j is out of the range of S_i but within the scope of S_j, with $i, j \in [1, 2]$ and $i \neq j$. This configuration allows D_i to overhear the packets sent from S_i to D_j for decoding purposes. Since the destination nodes are not able to capture the packets directly sent from R_1, R_2 will play the role as a relay node (it will not be in charge of encoding nor decoding and hence, as well as S_1 and S_2, will not use the set of functionalities performed by the *OConS* framework). Furthermore, R_1 (and consequently S_1 and S_2) must now go through R_2 to reach D_1 and D_2. The key elements involved into the *NC* process (R_1 for coding and D_1/D_2 for decoding issues) will carry out a strong utilization of the features supported by the *OConS* framework.

Besides, in order to evaluate the behavior of the *NC* scheme under different channel conditions, we have carried out the simulations according to the following configurations:

1. **Normal links.** This configuration belongs to the most realistic scenario, in which every link is prone to bring about transmission losses.
2. **Side links.** This concrete error distribution addresses the analysis of the packet losses over the links $S_1 - D_1$ and $S_2 - D_2$, thus only having influence on decoding issues (the destination nodes will overheard these packets; however, they are not headed to them and in a default transmission they would be immediately dropped).
3. **Middle links.** This latter model aims at showcasing the effect of the synchronization between two TCP flows. In this case, only the link $R_1 - R_2$ is prone to lose a frame.

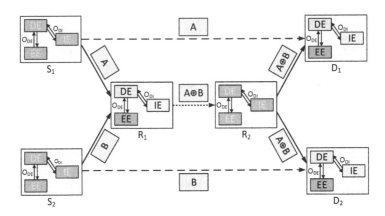

Fig. 3. X topology with the built-in OConS nodes

Simulation Description

In order to evaluate the performance of TCP over wireless mesh networks, we have modeled the aforementioned scenario by means of the well-known network simulator ns-2 [9]. The list below describes the main simulation parameters which we have followed:

- The nodes were configured by means of the IEEE 802.11b standard at its maximum legacy capacity: 11 Mbps.
- The sending rate of the source nodes (at application level) was set according to the maximum IEEE 802.11b bearable bit rate: 11 Mbps
- The maximum number of IEEE 802.11 retransmissions was set to a value of 3.
- The traffic pattern consisted in two TCP flows: $S_1 \rightarrow D_2$ and $S_2 \rightarrow D_1$.
- Each of the flows had a duration of 60 seconds.
- All the TCP data segments had a fixed size of 1460 bytes.
- All the non-TCP data were not prone to be corrupted during its transmission.

In addition to the parameters mentioned above, we tweaked as well the following elements so as to study the behavior of the TCP flows by means of the variation of some *NC* buffer parameters and the link quality (*Frame Error Rate - FER*):

1. **NC Coding Buffer Timeout** (T_C). Amount of time during which a coding node will hold a packet; after that time, if it does not appear a coding opportunity, the corresponding packet will be forwarded to the IE's output packet pool. Namely, we have started with a $T_C = 0$ msec until reaching a value of 80 msec.
2. **NC Coding Buffer Size.** Size, in packets, that the input packet pool is able to store into a node's *IE*. In this case, we have tested this buffer from an empty value to a size of ten packets.

3. **FER.** Ratio between the erroneous 802.11 frames and the overall transmission attempts over the scenario. The range covered from a $FER = 0$ to 0.4. For the sake of simplicity, this value is set for each link individually (in this work this value will be the same for all of them, though).

5   Results

After a brief description of the scenario, the channel configuration and the simulation workout, in this section we will evaluate the main results achieved during the campaign carried out. Namely, we aim at characterizing the impact of NC over simultaneous TCP transmissions through $WMNs$, comparing the outputs obtained with a legacy store-and-forward routing scheme.

For that purpose, we will focus on the following metrics:

- **Throughput.** Key statistic that measures the (TCP) performance. We define it as the total amount of information (payload) *correctly* received by the corresponding destination nodes (i.e. D_1 and D_2) divided by the TCP transmission elapsed time. Namely, we will show the average throughput observed by each node.
- **Coding rate.** This value relies exclusively on the coding node R_1, showing the ratio between the encoded and the total number of packets sent.
- **TCP Congestion Window Size.** This parameter illustrates in an eye-catching way the effect that synchronization brings about between different flows over a TCP transmission.

It is worth highlighting that we have carried out up to 75 independent runs per channel configuration (FER, Coding Buffer Size and Coding Buffer Timeout). Figures 4 and 5 represent the average values of the overall simulations as well as the 95% confidence intervals for each analyzed point. On the other hand, Figure 6 shows the results for a particular measurement.

First, in order to evaluate the improvement that NC shall bring about over a legacy TCP transmission, we have carried out a first batch of simulations over error-free wireless links ($FER = 0$), comparing the results obtained with the NC scheme and through a traditional store-and-forward mechanism. Figure 4 illustrates both *Coding Rate* (Figure 4a) and *throughput* (Figure 4b) as functions of the NC parameters (Coding Buffer Size and T_C). In the former case we can observe an increment over the coding opportunities as the NC parameters grows up (following a rather similar shape to the one we modeled and drew in Figure 2, yet in this case we have introduced the influence of T_C), covering a range of values from 0.5 to approximately 0.9, depending on the values of the NC parameters. The figure showcases as well that there is a point from which the coding rate stops growing, albeit the NC parameters keep their ascending behavior, thus demonstrating that in this concrete case (of two flows), this increment does not necessarily lead to a higher percentage of coding opportunities. On the other hand, we can see a performance increment (in terms of throughput) of approximately 33% between the utilization of NC and the legacy operation.

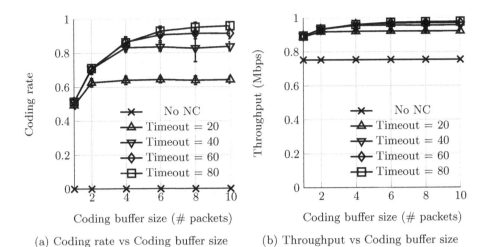

(a) Coding rate vs Coding buffer size   (b) Throughput vs Coding buffer size

Fig. 4. Performance output over a lossless scenario

Anew, although this means a significative improvement, the curve keeps close to its maximum value (the growth is rather negligible), thus illustrating again that the system has already reached its maximum performance, albeit the *NC* parameters keep going up.

After analyzing the response of *NC* over a lossless scenario we have studied the performance by introducing transmission losses, according to the error configurations described in Section 4. Figure 5a shows the relationship between the coding rate and the FER for each channel setup. We do observe a decreasing pattern as the error rate grows in both *Normal* and *Side* configurations, undoubtedly due to the harmful effect that frame losses bring about over the system performance. Nevertheless, we can see a different behavior on the *Middle* configuration, where the coding rate holds 90% - 95% for all the FER range of values. Even, with a $FER \leq 0.3$, the curve follows an increasing trend[3]. In order to find an explanation, we rely on the synchronization between the two flows, getting higher as the error rate rises (as we will see in the next batch of figures).

Regarding the average throughput per flow shown in Figure 5b, we compare the performance achieved through both with and without *NC* for each channel error pattern configuration. In the *Normal* case, when an error can arise everywhere, we can see as the *NC* shows a better performance until reaching a $FER \approx 0.08$; from that point, the legacy operation yields a higher throughput. On the other hand, when errors are only prone over the *Middle* link, the *NC* scheme outperforms the legacy one for all the range of values. This effect is due to the synchronization between the two flows, which leads to a greater number

---

[3] Although the average value with FER=0.4 is lower than the previous ones, we can observe through the 95% confidence interval that there an enormous variance that does not allow us to establish a strong conclusion.

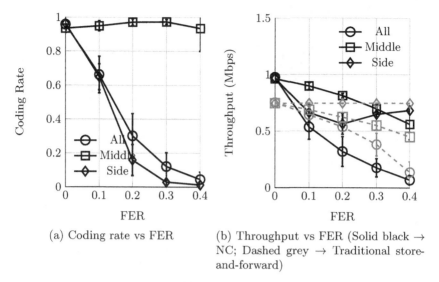

(a) Coding rate vs FER

(b) Throughput vs FER (Solid black → NC; Dashed grey → Traditional store-and-forward)

Fig. 5. Simulation results over an error-prone channel (Buffer size = 10 packets, T_C = 80 msec)

of coding opportunities. Finally, we can see an unexpected behavior over the last configuration (losses on *Side* links), where the *NC* performance shows a decreasing trend until $FER = 0.2$, but start growing from this point. This "strange" effect is explained by the fact that a receiver cannot decode an encoded packet because it had not overheard any original packet so as to retrieve enough information to recover the original messages. Nevertheless, when the error rate shows high values ($FER = 0.3$ and $FER = 0.4$) the number of coding opportunities are practically null, thus recovering the performance lost and converging towards the legacy operation.

Finally, we have chosen a representative measurement of each channel configuration in order to showcase the effect that common losses (in other words, error that affects both flows simultaneously) bring about over a legacy TCP transmission. Figure 6 shows the TCP congestion window size (represented in number of packets) along the simulation time for each flow[4]; on the first hand, we can see that in the first two cases (with errors over all the links or only over the side ones) the distribution of the bandwidth performs a random shape, thus any flow could capture the channel and "dominate" over the other one, showing a lack of synchronization between both flows; on the other hand, where the errors are only present over the middle link $R_1 - R_2$, it is easily appreciated how synced the flows are. The main reason of this behavior is that the majority of the errors affect to coded packets, thus damaging both flows at the same time. Therefore, both nodes trigger simultaneously their respective mechanisms

---

[4] In order to have a good visibility, we have zoomed the first half of the simulation time.

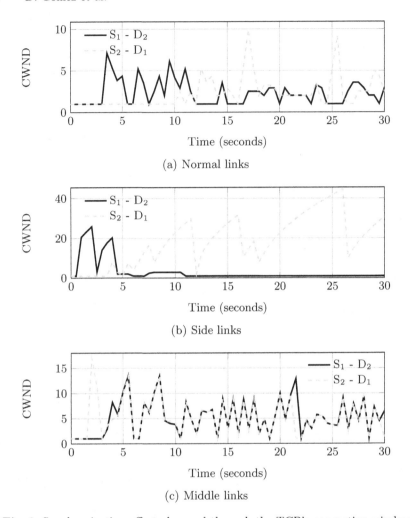

Fig. 6. Synchronization effect observed through the TCP's congestion window

against the channel congestion, yielding the overlapping contention windows as
observed in Figure 6c.

6   Conclusions and Future Work

In this work we have addressed the integration of a whole new Network Coding
fully-functional scheme within the scope of a flexible and open architecture,
which was designed to fulfill the new challenges arisen from the new current of
thoughts that have given the name of *Internet of the Future*. Hence, we had to
adapt the performance of an *NC* scheme to the requirements imposed by such
framework, whose global operation is shared between three types of entities,
each of one covering a specific area: information gathering, decision making and
execution enforcement.

We carried out a thorough analysis through an extensive simulation campaign (by means of the `ns-2` network simulator) so as to evaluate the impact of Network Coding (namely, the configuration of the buffers used for coding/decoding issues) over *WMNs*; in particular, we aim at studying how TCP interacts with *NC* over such networks. We have observed that *NC* do actually improve the TCP performance in scenarios with a low error presence ($FER \leq 0.1$). Notwithstanding, from this value, all the benefits that *NC* is supposed to bring about disappear and even induce negative effects over the communication, in comparison with the traditional store-and-forward scheme. Besides, we have analyzed as well the influence that a correct configuration of some parameters within the *NC* solution (both by means of a simple mathematical model and the `ns-2`), namely, the size of an input packet pool and the time during which it will hold the packets waiting for a coding opportunity, might induce over the global performance. At last, it is worth remarking the effect we have observed when losses affect simultaneously to different TCP flows, leading to a situation where the two transmissions lead to a synchronized behavior, increasing the number of coding opportunities.

For the future, we plan to branch our work in order to encompass a number of open issues:

- The most immediate step to be done aims at including the control/management information (i.e. TCP ACKs, etc.) within the scope of the *NC* decision engine, thus becoming prone to be coded together with other packets (yet they can lead the opposite direction).
- Another interesting issue to be tackled is the use of "random" generated *WMNs*, thus getting closer to a more realistic scenario (i.e. a flash crowd scenario) considered in the scope of the SAIL project itself. Under this new environments, there will rise new challenges to be dealt with: i.e. interferences, hard coding decision (with several packets involved)...
- Besides, it could be insightful the analysis of the combination of *NC* with a more advanced transport protocol, based on splitting the subjacent flows of a concrete connection into *multiple paths*, leading to a substantial increment over the global throughput, still without jeopardizing the concurrent legacy flows.
- Finally, we envisage to increase the complexity of the proposed *NC* solution, thus augmenting the number of encoding patterns of the decision engine, adding a fully featured signalling messages that allow the cooperation among the neighboring nodes, i.e. allowing the harvest of new pieces of information, such as a proprietary ACK scheme or the explicit neighbor's overheard buffers content. All this new stuff will be consequently mapped in order to fulfill the *OConS* architecture requirements.

Acknowledgements. This work has been supported by the EU FP7 project SAIL, Scalable and Adaptive Internet Solutions (FP7-ICT-2009-5-257448) as well as the Spanish government for its funding through the project C3SEM,

"Cognitive, Cooperative Communications and autonomous SErvice Management" (TEC2009-14598-C02-01).

References

1. Agüero, R., Caeiro, L., Correia, L.M., Ferreira, L.S., García-Arranz, M., Suciu, L., Timm-Giel, A.: OConS: Towards open connectivity services in the future internet. In: Pentikousis, K., Aguiar, R., Sargento, S., Agüero, R. (eds.) MONAMI 2011. LNICST, vol. 97, pp. 90–104. Springer, Heidelberg (2012)
2. Ahlswede, R., Cai, N., Li, S.Y., Yeung, R.: Network information flow. IEEE Trans. on Information Theory 46(4), 1204–1216 (2000)
3. Chi, K., Jiang, X., Horiguchi, S.: A more efficient cope architecture for network coding in multihop wireless networks. IEICE Transactions 92-B(3), 766–775 (2009), http://dblp.uni-trier.de/db/journals/ieicet/ieicet92b.html#ChiJH09
4. Fragouli, C., Katabi, D., Markopoulou, A., Médard, M., Rahul, H.: Wireless network coding: Opportunities and challenges. In: Proc. of IEEE MILCOM, pp. 1–8 (October 2007)
5. Gkelias, A., Leung, K., Ling, C.: The effect of wireless channel on network coding opportunities. In: Proc. of IEEE PIMRC, pp. 637–641 (September 2009)
6. Hassayoun, S., Maille, P., Ros, D.: On the impact of random losses on TCP performance in coded wireless mesh networks. In: Proc. of IEEE INFOCOM, pp. 1–9 (2010)
7. Huang, Y., Ghaderi, M., Towsley, D., Gong, W.: TCP performance in coded wireless mesh networks. In: Proc. of IEEE SECON, pp. 179–187 (2008)
8. Katti, S., Rahul, H., Hu, W., Katabi, D., Médard, M., Crowcroft, J.: XORs in the air: practical wireless network coding. ACM SIGCOMM Computer Communications Review 36(4), 243–254 (2006)
9. McCanne, S., Floyd, S.: ns Network Simulator, http://www.isi.edu/nsnam/ns/
10. Niebert, N., Schieder, A., Zander, J., Hancock, R.: Ambient Networks: Co-operative Mobile Networking for the Wireless World. Wiley Publishing (2007)
11. Suciu, L., Agüero, R., Miron, A., Aranda, P., Pérez, S., Bertin, P.: Architectural concepts of connectivity devices. Deliverable D4.1, EU-FP7 SAIL Project (July 2011)
12. Sundararajan, J., Shah, D., Meddard, M., Jakubczak, S., Mitzenmacher, M., Barros, J.: Network coding meets TCP: Theory and implementation. Proceedings of the IEEE 99(3), 490–512 (2011)
13. Tan, J., Medard, M.: Secure network coding with a cost criterion. In: 2006 4th International Symposium on Modeling and Optimization in Mobile, Ad Hoc and Wireless Networks, pp. 1–6 (April 2006)

Threat Model Based Security Evaluation
of Open Connectivity Services

Peter Schoo[1] and Ronald Marx[2]

[1] Fraunhofer AISEC Research Institution for Applied and Integrated Security
Parkring 4, 85748 Garching (near Munich), Germany
`peter.schoo@aisec.fraunhofer.de`
[2] Fraunhofer Institute for Secure Information Technology SIT
Rheinstrasse 75, 64287 Darmstadt, Germany
`ronald.marx@sit.fraunhofer.de`

Abstract. Open Connectivity Services (OConS) is a new approach for
an improved control of connectivity and services on the level of physical
or data link, routing and transport, flow and session control. The approach builds on the principles of open networking and access to open
control interfaces. One characteristics of the OConS approach is that the
control implementation are foreseen as distributable components that
can be spread and deployed over computing nodes. To enable the necessary and suitable security and privacy protection addressing misuse,
availability obstacles and to identify potential privacy issues, this paper
contributes a threat analysis on OConS.

1 Introduction

Future networks need to adapt to the changes in traffic patterns in a timely
manner. The driving forces behind those changes are the increased number and
diversity of mobile devices connecting to the Internet, the variety of application
requirements, the increasing number of communication technologies and networks, the dynamicity of social networks, and the flexibility at which new services
and content are made available. To meet this demand better than today, the concept of OConS has been started and is currently developed. Specifically, OConS
addresses a new paradigm to combine existing connectivity services deployed in
the current Internet and mobile systems. It addresses efficiently orchestration of
several connectivity services spanning multiple protocols, layers and interfaces.
OConS orchestration is an additional layer of control on top of existing service
control of physical/data link, routing and transport, and flow/session control.

The work on OConS and the design and specification that have been produced and presented [1, 2] are a challenging attempt to improve service delivery
based on innovative concepts for the service control. On the other hand, also the
targeted deployment environment forms some challenges in itself, when open
and elastic systems will be enablers. Both trends are motivated by a freedom
of control and for the purpose to lower costs, since less specialized computing
infrastructure is required.

A. Timm-Giel et al. (Eds.): MONAMI 2012, LNICST 58, pp. 313–322, 2013.

In many such cases when new ideas are elaborated, the core functionality goes first and security is only a second thought. It reflects the significance why to first concentrate on the effects of the *raison d'être* – the reason the new concept exists for. Only if this reason is justifiable any further steps can be taken. One aspect to consider in such an evaluation is in fact security, namely questions like: is the proposed solution secure and can the envisaged new solution be developed and operated without additional security risks that may in the end negatively affect its operation in a communication infrastructure? Such developments are typically iterative processes, i.e. the development may undergo several cycles through different e.g. so-called Technology Readiness Levels (TRLs) [3]. From the level where technology and its application is formulated (TRL2) to the level where a system prototype that is operated in a high fidelity environment (TRL7) different properties are improved of which security is one. One way for starting to encompass also security aspects is an initial threat analysis, which later on in the development will turn into security requirements and eventually design decisions that formulate qualified security properties or functions of the systems under consideration.

The contribution of this paper is a threat analysis of OConS and it is considered to contribute to the development and technical improvements of the OConS concept.

The paper is structured as follows: Section 2 describes the OConS concept, i.e. the way OConS Nodes (OConS Nodes) are build, how they interact and how the mechanisms should work to orchestrate existing connectivity services; next the threat modeling is introduced in Section 3 and in Section 4 applied. We discuss approach and findings and conclude in Section 5.

2   The OConS Concept

OConS, the Open Connectivity Services, is an approach to combine existing and deployed connectivity services of the current Internet and mobile systems [1, 2]. The main idea behind is that it builds on existing services and their situational resource management situation. This approach some logic that allows to reasons and make decisions according to an orchestrations strategy defined by a designer, and carries decisions taken in the orchestration forward to be enforced. It raises some situational awareness beyond the scope of an individual connectivity services and allows to take decisions for *multi-p*, namely multi-point, multi-path and multi-protocols services.

The following sections will present UML information models that describe the OConS concept as it has been elaborated. In different perspectives the focus will be on the services that can be provided by an implementation of OConS for the user of OConS-based services, the way OConS entities, the implementation components that structure the implementation of OConS functionality and, last not least, the basic process that achieves the situational awareness, decision taking and enforcement. Computational aspects of OConS entities and the basic engineering that makes OConS entities interacting are mentioned where appropriate with references to further details.

2.1   Services in OConS

The way that OConS services create an added value based on existing services is outlined in Figure 1. For any such OConS service there will be a mechanisms that builds on the controls of e.g. existing Flow Connectivity Services, Network Connectivity Services or Link Connectivity Services. Where a service is considered here the (hopefully useful) effect caused on invoking some functionality (typically via an interface to hide the implementation details behind that interface). It should be obvious that session type of flows use Network Connectivity Services, which in turn make use of Link Connectivity Services. Examples of each such services are given in Figure 1.

The challenging part is the actual mechanism that senses and measures the actual resource situation, may take decision concerning the use of services OConS orchestrates and eventually enforces decision that have been taken.

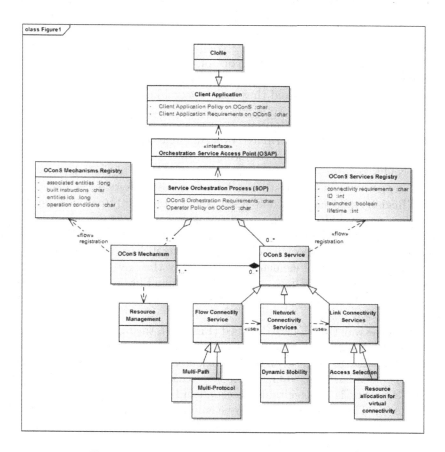

Fig. 1. OConS Service building on existing services

The orchestration is made available via a Service Access Point (SAP) to client applications that are interested in using connectivity services that have flexible OConS capabilities. It is this orchestration that is responsible to consistently convey and match the requirements and policies that are given by the using client application and the service providing operator. The OConS Services that orchestrate the OConS Mechanisms are responsible registries, allow to convey information about the resources and capabilities.

2.2   Entities of OConS

The underlying design of OConS Entities is presented in Figure 2 and centered around the concept of OConS Functional Entities (FEs) and OConS Nodes. FEs encompass

Information Management Entities (IEs) – component type for resource monitoring and sensing to derive basic information about the current state and situation to which the control shall become re-active in its decisions,

Decision Making Entities (DEs) – component type responsible for the decision taking and performing the control, and

Execution and Enforcement Entities (EEs) – component   type   that enforces taken decisions and thus make control happen.

The FEs classes enable to instantiate its entities as processes on OConS Nodes and they may basically be distributed over different OConS Nodes. FEs register at an OConS Registry (OConS Registry) so that they can be found; likewise OConS Nodes register to be known in the environment of each domain. Each domain represents the administrative boundaries of a system has exactly one OConS Registry and each OConS Node belongs to exactly one domain. This model does not exclude that FEs are deployed over different domains.

An OConS Node is an abstract network element that can host FEs and this network element can be specialized e.g. to the control element of an open router. Examples of such control elements are the hosts that run the processes that control the management of flows, as opposed to Open Flow routers that manages such flows. An OConS Node is such an abstraction of the environment controls for flow control is hosted.

Apart of the way the FEs are designed (Figure 2), their operational semantics is of some importance. There is a basic scheme according to which the components act together to perform an orchestration on existing services. The process of this scheme is basically to first sense the situation and monitor available resources. Once this is done suitable decision can be taken according to some defined strategy. These decisions need to be enforced in the next step. Overall this strategy supports actually that the task-oriented semantics is also distributed able in individually separate processes of the IEs, DEs and EEs.

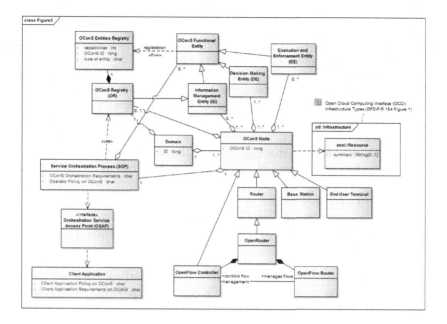

Fig. 2. Component design of OConS

3   Threat Modelling

Threat modelling is an appropriate instrument to assess the IT security of a system [4], allowing to discuss the security properties of a systems in relation to e.g. defined misuse or resource depletion cases, and can be used as dedicated instrument within development processes. These processes are typically iterative and often start when the system design is not focusing on security yet. However, threat modelling presents eventually analysis results that contribute to a development processes and helps designers early on to encompass or elaborate the adequate and required security properties in the next cycle of design [5]. The quality of such a threat model is determined by completeness and consistency and it is solely based on expert knowledge.

Threat models may take different forms. An *attacker-centric threat model* assumes the role of an attacker, describes her ambitions, motivations and capabilities and analyses what harm can be done to the analysed system, which is the Orchestration in our case. Alternatively, another form is the *protocol-centric* approach. In this case protocols from the underlying protocol stack are looked at, investigating to what extend their known vulnerabilities affect the security of the entire systems being analysed. We focus in this paper on the attacker perspective. A complementary protocol-centic approach would in principle be applicable too.

4   OConS Threat Model

In modelling the threats caused by an arbitrarily strong attacker the following aspects will be distinguished:

Orchestration misuse which basically attacks the integrity of the coordination of mechanisms that are subject of the Orchestration such that either the attacker will have an advantage or other users will perceive an unexpected behaviour or disadvantage.

Orchestrated mechanism misuse attacks the subjects of the orchestration for the attackers advantage, for example, to save money or receive a priority compared to other users of the system.

Disturbance of Orchestration is an attack that not necessarily results in an advantage for attackers. This attack is addressing resource depletion mainly.

Privacy violation that puts the data protection of end user or operator at risk.

When the attacks are detailed, it is assumed that the attacker has all the necessary technical means to achieve her goals and mission. This will be a helpful assumption to challenge the protection that is foreseen in the OConS design.

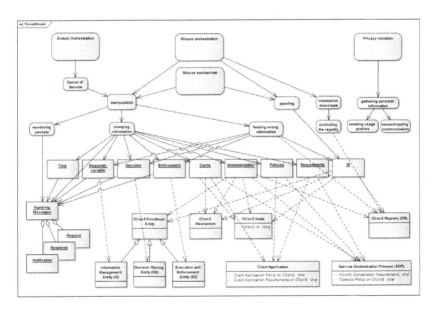

Fig. 3. Overview over identified threats to OConS orchestration

Orchestration Misuse

– by spoofing the id of a legitimate interface via the interface registry – OConS domains, nodes, services, mechanisms, and functional entities use unique IDs to identify. If an attacker can make another party believe that he is the rightful owner of this ID authenticity is not guaranteed. This attack can lead to further attacks like to illegitimate controlling the orchestration decision e.g. by injecting wrong information/decisions.

– by sinkholing the registry that maintains interface references – The registry holds a lot of valuable information for an attacker that can be used to place more extensive attacks against users and the orchestration. This threat endangers the confidentiality of network topology as well as the privacy of the users.

– by MitM attacking the content of signalling messages – Integrity of signalling messages are crucial for the correct execution of orchestration processes. Tampering with any kind of signalling message can negatively affect these processes resulting e.g. in denial-of-service or the use of hostile mechanisms in orchestration.

– by MitM attacking the order of signalling messages – One special form of packet manipulation is the change of the order of packets. This may cause problems if fragmented data is sent using multiple packets or if decisions are taken on a first-come, first-serve basis.

– by manipulating the cache of a node – OConS mechanisms and services run on OConS Nodes. Caches in OConS Nodes temporarily store value and variables that need to be protected as the correct execution can only be guaranteed if the underlying execution environment cannot be manipulated.

– by replacing/manipulating (parts of) the implementation on an OConS Node – If the implementation in OConS Nodes can be replaced or manipulated the attacker is able to control orchestration process as he likes, e.g. favouring certain (hostile) services.

– by manipulating the client application policy/requirements (somewhere also referred to as 'demand profile') – Policies and requirements specify the service the client application is about to receive. Changing these could effect that the client will not get what he expects, e.g. more expensive or less quality services.

– by manipulating network state input – OConS bases orchestration decisions on the current network state. Changing the state also affects the decision.

– by spoofing the OConS Registry – The OConS Registry maintains all information about FEs, OConS Mechanisms (OConS Mechanisms), and OConS Services (OConS Services), which is used by the SOP. An attacker that can spoof an OConS Registry can for instance shut out certain unfavoured FEs, OConS Mechanisms, or OConS Services. Thereby, he can rule the SOP.

– by tampering with OConS Registry notifications/registrations – The attack has similar effect as the spoofing of the OConS Registry.

– by manipulating cascaded orchestration – If an attacker has access to a rogue or manipulated OConS Mechanism he could use this to contact different other mechanisms than specified in the orchestration. The aim of an attacker might be to use similar but different and more expensive OConS Mechanism.

Orchestrated Mechanism Misuse

– by spoofing the value IEs are supplying to the orchestration – DEs base their decision on the values sent by IEs. Thus, in order to make correct decision values sent need to be correct and unmodified.

– by tampering with IE values by affecting measured variable – As an alternative to manipulating the value sent by an IE, an attacker might tamper with the value that is measured by the IE. If for example an attacker can make an IE believe a network segment is at full capacity, the IE will report this to the DE, who in turn may choose another mechanism on another OConS Node in a different network segment.

– by manipulating a decision taken by a DE – The orchestration process is heavily based on the decisions taken by DEs. Tampering with decisions can negatively affect orchestration processes resulting e.g. in denial-of-service or the use of hostile mechanisms in orchestration.

– by manipulating an enforcement carried out by an EE – Similar to manipulations of decisions mentioned above.

– by spoofing the id of a legitimate mechanisms – An attacker that can successfully spoof an ID of a legitimate mechanism would be able to send decisions or enforcements in the name of this mechanism and thereby influence the SOP.

– by manipulating or replacing the implementation or configuration of a legitimate mechanisms – If the implementation of an OConS Mechanisms is replaced or manipulated by an attacker he will be able to alter the mechanisms procedures as he likes, e.g. denying service for certain users or influencing the decision making of relying mechanisms and services.

– by high-jacking OConS service subscription – This attack would enable that mechanisms in a service can be exchanged by other (potentially hostile) mechanisms.

Disturbance of Orchestration

– by knowing how to address an interface, messages can be send such that resources are depleted – Depending on the used protocol or interface certain messages could be sent to exceed memory or processing capacity in a certain OConS Node, OConS Service, OConS Mechanism or process. The result is denial-of-service, at least temporarily.

– by manipulating mechanism definition – The SOP uses the service definition to select mechanisms for orchestration. If an attacker succeeds in manipulating this definition, he can stop the mechanism to be selected by the SOP.

– by preventing OConS Registry to update information – In order to keep the current configuration in the OConS Registry an attacker may intercept, drop, or replay signalling messages from the FEs, e.g. publish/notification/registration messages.

– by disturbing resource/mechanism allocation – Instead of exceeding memory or processing capacity from outside an orchestration process can also be disturbed by inhibiting an OConS Node to allocate the needed resources on a node e.g. by initiating many resource-consuming mechanisms.

– by intercepting/retaining/suppressing messages that are necessary for the SOP – If an attacker can suppress packets he can inhibit the SOP to execute correctly or at all.

– by tampering with time source – Most cryptographic processes need a reliable time source in order to function properly. If this time source is manipulated expired certificates could be accepted, erroneously. On the other hand, this can also result in a denial-of-service if all timestamps or certificates are rejected because the verifier think the timestamp is outdated.

Privacy Violation

– eavesdropping communication – Communication data can include personal data that can be eavesdropped by an attacker or a rogue OConS Node. If the eavesdropper has access to configuration or log files he can also use these to derive some personal information from the client.
– creating usage profiles – An attacker may be interested in all the different services a client is using. From these usage profiles he then could derive other information that can be used for tracking or identifying a person.

5   Conclusions and Future Work

The results of the treat analysis presented here describe potentially foreseeable attacks on OConS. In fact the OConS design that is the basis for this analysis and presented in Section 2 is concentrating on the new paradigm of distributing FEs that sense, decide and enforce to enable an orchestration of existing services. Aspects concerning the management of OConS have not been discussed and will require to enlarge the scope of the threat model. This threat model improves the awareness of the designer which aspects of the resulting solution can be misused and how this may happen. As such it prepares the ground for the next cycle of the development process when OConS is brought forward.

Part of the specification of OConS is that FEs that are distributed over node or reside on the same node make use of Intra/Inter-Node Communication (INC) to interact with each other [1]. Considering this part of the OConS design, a complementing protocol-centric threat analysis seems to be useful in some future work, because INC will be a concrete protocol implementation placed on the Internet layer its protocols.

In future OConS designs could improve by using e.g. solutions that handle authorised use of FEs in a way that helps to differentiate legitimate from non-legitimate users. It can be assumed that this will prevent most of the misuse of orchestrations and mechanisms depicted in Figure 3. As part of such a naming and addressing solution an interaction across different administrative domains should be considered to allow a spread of FEs e.g. also into the end user terminal or into other administrative domains.

Acknowledgements. The authors would like to express their gratitude to the European Commission for its funding through the "Scalable and Adaptive Internet Solutions", SAIL Project (FP7-ICT-2009-5-257448).

References

[1] Suciu, L., et al.: Architecture and Mechanisms for Connectivity Services. Deliverable D.C.2, EU-FP7 SAIL Project (July 2012)

[2] Ferreira, L.S., Agüero, R., Caeiro, L., Miron, A., Soellner, M., Schoo, P., Suciu, L., Timm-Giel, A., Udugama, A.: Open connectivity services for the future internet. In: Proceedings of MON-AMI 2012 (2012)

[3] Deputy Under Secretary of Defense for Science and Technology. Technology Readiness Assessment (TRA) Deskbook. Department of Defense (May 2005)

[4] Eckert, C.: IT-Sicherheit: Konzepte - Verfahren - Protokolle. Oldenbourg, 6th revised and extended issue. edn. (2009)

[5] Haley, C.B., Moffett, J.D., Laney, R., Nuseibeh, B.: A Framework for Security Requirements Engineering. In: SESS 2006: Proceedings of the 2006 International Workshop on Software Engineering for Secure Systems, pp. 35–42. ACM Press, New York (2006)

Prototype: OConS Multi-path Content Delivery with NetInf

Asanga Udugama[1], Carmelita Goerg[1], and Andreas Timm-Giel[2]

[1] University of Bremen, Bremen, Germany
{adu,cg}@comnets.uni-bremen.de
[2] Hamburg University of Technology, Hamburg, Germany
timm-giel@tuhh.de

Abstract. One of the primary activities of today's networks is the movement of content. This has made the point-to-point communication architecture of current networks unsuitable for today's needs. Information Centric Networking (ICN) changes this model with newer networking architectures such as the Network of Information (NetInf). The multi-path capabilities that are much admired in current networks, have also been integrated into these architectures. But, these architectures do not define formal mechanisms to utilise these multiple paths to avail their benefits. The prototype presented in this work demonstrates the use of multi-path content delivery in NetInf based ICN networks through the Open Connectivity Services mechanisms and framework.

Keywords: Information Centric Networking, Network of Information, Open Connectivity Services, Multi-path.

1 Overview

Multi-path connectivity to networks in modern computing devices is becoming the norm in todays computing. These multiple paths can be used in many ways to benefit the users of these devices as well as the different service providers involved. The Information Centric Networking (ICN) architectures that are currently being defined such as Network of Information (NetInf) [1] [2], have considered the use of multiple paths natively. Though these architectures provide the use of multiple paths simultaneously, no formal mechanisms have been defined to utilise them in the best possible manner. The framework and the mechanisms defined in the Open Connectivity Services (OConS) work package of SAIL project [3] identifies a number of multi-path strategies that utilise the multiple paths to request and receive content with NetInf in the best possible manner. The prototype developed and demonstrated in this work shows the operations of the OConS framework and the mechanisms [4].

NetInf [1] is an ICN architecture that is able to handle content requests and retrievals based on named information, instead of the named hosts of today's networking. The architectural components of NetInf and their functionalities have been identified through the work done in 4WARD [5] and SAIL projects. Following are the high level components of NetInf and the function they perform.

A. Timm-Giel et al. (Eds.): MONAMI 2012, LNICST 58, pp. 323–327, 2013.

- **Message Forwarding** - handles the routing aspects of requests for content and content themselves
- **Name Resolution** - performs the resolution of Network of Information (NI) names to names based on the different underlying networking technology names (protocols)
- **Convergence Layers** - handles the underlying networking technology used (such as IP/UDP)

NetInf has the built-in capability to perform retrieval of content over multiple attachments or paths. The OConS mechanism together with the components of its framework steers this built-in capability of NetInf in retrieving content. The Decision Elements (DE) of the OConS framework located in NetInf based devices makes decisions related to selecting the best multi-path strategy to use. There are 3 types of strategies:

- **Splitting** - This strategy relates to distributing the NetInf content request (GET) messages of a single content stream between the multiple paths
- **Replication** - This strategy replicates the GET messages to the multiple paths
- **Distribution** - This strategy distributes the GET messages of different content streams to the multiple paths

The identification of the multiple paths and the strategy to be adopted by the DEs are based on the information provided by the Information Elements (IEs) of OConS. The IEs located in the network as well as the user devices, have a number of information collection modules such as the module to collect information about currently active network attachments. A DE use this information to evaluate a set of rules held in the DE to obtain a set of actions. These actions specify the strategy to adopt. Once the decisions on the strategy and the multiple paths to be used are made, this information is given to an Enforcement Entity (EE) in a NetInf based device to implement the content retrieval strategy. This process is a continuous process where decisions are re-evaluated based on new information.

2   Prototype

The prototype is based on the NEC NetInf Router Platform (NNRP), a NetInf prototype developed in the SAIL project [6]. NNRP is a platform for developers to build and integrate modules to extend the functionality supported in NetInf. NNRP is a Linux based implementation. NNRP uses a module chaining mechanisms similar to iptables [7] in Linux with a clearly defined interface for the different NetInf modules to interact with each other. The OConS enabled NNRP prototype for supporting multi-path content delivery consists of a number of NNRP modules. These extensions have the following features.

- Segment based content retrieval where content is split into chunks and request pipelining is used to retrieve content

- Use of IP networks as the underlying networking technology to request for and retrieve content
- Network attachments of NetInf nodes are considered as individual paths
- Use of the GET and CHUNK messages of NNRP for content retrieval
- Implements the Splitting strategy

The prototype uses UDP as the underlying transport network (Figure 1-(1)). It supports a number of different NetInf enabled applications including the NetInf enabled Video LAN Client (VLC) video streaming tool [8]. The NNRP modules for multi-path content delivery are as follows:

- **vlc_input** - handles the requests for content from NetInf enabled VLC applications (VLC)
- **vlc_output** - handles the serving of content requests of NetInf enabled applications
- **strategy** - handles the Orchestration and DE functionality of the OConS framework to select the multi-path strategy
- **ocons** - handles the interactions with the IEs to obtain information
- **nrs** - handles the name resolution functionality
- **mpudp_cl** - handles the EE functionality of OConS where the selected strategy is implemented

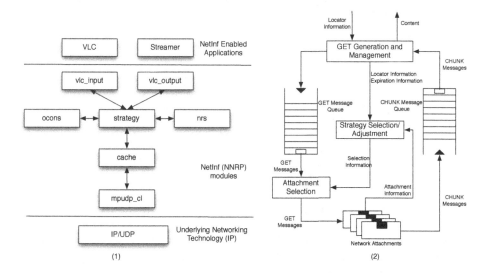

Fig. 1. (1) OConS Multi-path Enabled NetInf Node Architecture (2) Splitting Strategy Algorithm

The Splitting strategy implemented in the NetInf nodes of the prototype utilises the multiple paths by distributing the NetInf GET requests for content chunks into the multiple paths. This strategy uses the Additive Increase/ Multiplicative Decrease (AIMD) mechanism [9] to adjust the distribution of GET requests (Figure 1-(2)).

3   Demonstrated Scenario and Demonstration

The demonstration is based on the Event with Large Crowd scenario developed in the SAIL project [6]. The scenario consists of a flash crowd that requires downloading content based on spontaneous decisions that are related to the interests of the participants of the flash crowd. The participants use NetInf based computing devices and some of these devices are deployed with the OConS multi-path extensions of NNRP. These devices are equipped with multi-path support and the operation of the OConS extensions demonstrate the use of multiple paths to deliver the required content.

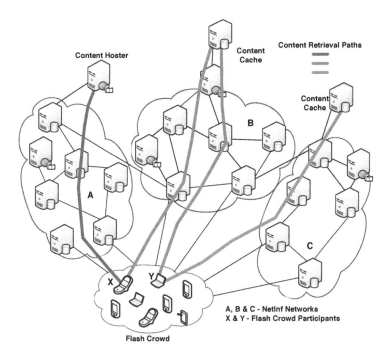

Fig. 2. Flash Crowd Scenario with OConS Multi-path for NetInf

The devices of the flash crowd devices connect to 3 NetInf base networks (Figure 2). These networks are currently loaded with content download traffic of the participants of the flash crowd. A new participant (X) commences downloading content using a NetInf based device and since this device is OConS multi-path capable, it immediately uses the multiple attachments it has. Based on the splitting strategy used, the GET requests are distributed and the content is received smoothly without interruptions. Another participant (Y) joins and attempts to download content. This results in participant X experiencing problems momentarily. But the operation of the Splitting strategy results in balancing the load through the control of GET requests to improve the user experiences of both of these flash crowd participants.

4   Conclusion

The work presented here is one of the results of the work done in the OConS work package of the SAIL project related to the mechanism of multi-path content delivery for NetInf. The prototype demonstrated included a subset of the functionality identified. The scenario used to show the demonstration was based on the project wide scenario but with the specific focus on the behaviour of a flash crowd. The prototype demonstrates the viability of implementing and using the mechanisms and the framework of OConS.

Acknowledgement. The authors would like to thank the partners of the WP-C and the WP-B work packages of the SAIL project for the valuable views provided during the preparation of this work.

References

1. Dannewitz, C.: NetInf: An Information-Centric Design for the Future Internet. In: Proc. 3rd GI/ITG KuVS Workshop on The Future (May 2009)
2. Dannewitz, C., Golic, J., Ohlman, B., Ahlgren, B.: Secure Naming for a Network of Information. In: INFOCOM IEEE Conference on Computer Communications Workshops (August 2010)
3. SAIL Project (FP7), http://www.4ward-project.eu (accessed on August 2012)
4. Zaki, Y., Udugama, A., Toseef, U., Goerg, C., Timm-Giel, A.: Open Connectivity Services for Future Networks. In: CEWIT 2011 (November 2011)
5. 4WARD Project (FP7), http://www.4ward-project.eu (accessed on August 2012)
6. Kutscher, D., et al.: NetInf Content Delivery and Operations, FP7-SAIL Project Deliverable (D.B.2) (May 2012)
7. Andreasson, O.: IPTables Tutorial 1.2.2 (2006),
   http://homes.di.unimi.it/sisop/qemu/iptables-tutorial.pdf
8. Video LAN Client (VLC), http://www.videolan.org (accessed on August 2012)
9. Chiu, D.-H., Jain, R.: Analysis of the increase and decrease algorithms for congestion avoidance in computer networks. Computer Networks and ISDN Systems 17 (1989)

Author Index